Steel Seizure:

~~26~~, ~~38~~, ~~40~~, ...
~~56-57~~, ~~64~~, ~~68~~, ~~74~~, 93,
99-100, 152-53, 170, 176,
179, 199, 201, 214, 245,
249-50, 269-71, 274, 288,
295, 306, 315-16, 319

Constitutional Diplomacy

Constitutional Diplomacy

Michael J. Glennon

with a foreword by
J. William Fulbright

PRINCETON UNIVERSITY PRESS
PRINCETON, NEW JERSEY

Published by Princeton University Press, 41 William Street,
Princeton, New Jersey 08540
In the United Kingdom: Princeton University Press, Oxford

Library of Congress Cataloging-in-Publication Data

Glennon, Michael J., 1947–
Constitutional diplomacy / Michael J. Glennon ; with a foreword by
J. William Fulbright.
p. cm.
ISBN 0-691-07842-4
1. United States—Foreign relations—Law and legislation.
2. Treaty-making power—United States. 3. War and emergency powers—
United States. 4. Separation of powers—United States. I. Title.
KF4651.G59 1990
342.73'0412—dc20
[347.302412] 89-39071
CIP

This book has been composed in Linotron Times Roman

Princeton University Press books are printed on acid-free paper,
and meet the guidelines for permanence and durability of the
Committee on Production Guidelines for Book Longevity of the
Council on Library Resources

Printed in the United States of America by Princeton University Press,
Princeton, New Jersey
1 3 5 7 9 10 8 6 4 2

To Mildred and Carl Marcy

Who will never know where their influence stops.

CONTENTS

FOREWORD

J. William Fulbright

The Allied victory of World War II brought the world suddenly into the phase of history that Tocqueville had predicted a century earlier—an era in which geopolitics would be dominated by the United States and Russia. Across the globe, an old order had been destroyed. With scant forethought and little preparation for world leadership, America emerged from the twentieth century's second great war with a relative strength that seemed to offer no alternative to the assumption of heavy responsibility for the shaping and management of a new order.

In the years that followed, the United States was to play its new global role with varying degrees of wisdom and success, about which much has been written. But American actions on the international stage were accompanied by a remarkable byplay at home that is less understood: the continuing struggle to reconcile an eighteenth-century Constitution with a heightened activism in the world arena. In a famous turn of phrase, the great scholar Edward Corwin wrote that the American Constitution—with its separation of powers, checks and balances, and often vague delineation of foreign-policy powers—presents to the President and Congress a permanent "invitation to struggle." In the shaping of postwar American foreign policy, this struggle was often to be intense, precipitating profound issues that remain unresolved today.

These issues—centering on the competitive partnership of the President and Congress but including such related constitutional questions as the role of the Judiciary, the relationship between United States law and international law, and the nature of American treaty commitments—represent a crucial domestic dimension of American foreign policy. In their considerable complexity and fundamental importance, they are the subject of Michael Glennon's excellent book. A former legal counsel of the Senate Foreign Relations Committee, Professor Glennon dissects these issues with an insight enhanced by experience. His underlying theme—both idealistic and profoundly practical—is the need to define and achieve a "constitutional diplomacy." His work is a masterful exposition of issues that inhere in the United States Constitution but have crystallized into conflict during America's postwar international experience.

In looking back to the origins of the postwar period, one sees in early American actions a remarkable breadth of vision and magnanimity of spirit, especially in view of the parochialism of America's prewar role and world outlook. At Yalta in February 1945, when the Allies agreed to establish an international peace organization to replace the failed League of Nations, President Roosevelt represented a citizenry whose attitudes toward global responsibility had been transformed by the war experience. In 1937, a national poll found only one-fourth of the American people favorable to such an organization. But by September 1943, the House of Representatives had voted more than 10 to 1 in favor, and by the spring of 1945, more than 80% of Americans supported creation of the United Nations.

The ensuing five years—seminal for American foreign policy and for the world as we know it today—began with idealism. Two months after Yalta and even before V-E or V-J day, fifty nations met in San Francisco to establish the UN—an act of faith in the internationalist spirit that soon blossomed, under United States leadership, into today's elaborate multilateral structure of political, economic, scientific, and cultural organizations. In 1946, America's best hopes were again manifest in two additional measures: the Baruch Plan to share and control nuclear technology multilaterally, which unfortunately did not bear fruit, and my proposal for an international exchange program, which fortunately did.

But American idealism was rapidly becoming immersed in realpolitik. On the day of the UN's founding in April 1945, American and Soviet forces linked up in Germany for a brief moment of common celebration. But the East-West split, which was to define world politics for the next half century, appeared quickly, and by 1947, the exigencies of the cold war were dominant in American foreign policy. In that year the Truman Doctrine launched a United States foreign-aid program aimed at forestalling Communist insurgencies, and with the Marshall Plan, the United States assumed a full and specific cold war burden—defending Western Europe from economic vulnerability to Communist subversion. In 1948, the Berlin airlift dramatized the American commitment to European defense, and the Vandenberg Resolution affirmed congressional support for a formal alliance. By 1949, the establishment of the North Atlantic Treaty Organization codified the leadership role of the United States in a global contest with communism.

The United States took such momentous steps—from founding the UN to founding NATO—with little hint of the constitutional struggles over foreign policy that were to follow. Vis-à-vis a Republican Congress after the 1946 election and the Democratic Congress returned by the election of 1948, the Truman Administration carefully courted legislative opinion to ensure support for America's emerging world role. Neither the President nor his representatives voiced any challenge to the constitutional premise that United States commitments abroad required an Executive-Legislative partnership and were impossible by executive fiat. Thus, what is now remembered as the golden age of bipartisanship in American foreign policy was a product not only of international statesmanship but also of Executive behavior that did not seek to test the limits of presidential prerogative constitutionally.

The Korean War changed this pattern abruptly. The Constitution's Framers had clearly vested in Congress the power to decide the question of war. And although the experience of a century and a half had seen American forces fight limited engagements without the formality of a declaration of war—sometimes, as during the Mexican War in the 1840s, occasioning constitutional questions—no president had ever asserted a right to commit the United States to war on his own authority. In June 1950, however, when North Korean forces crossed the thirty-eighth parallel, President Truman did precisely that. In dispatching American forces to the Korean peninsula without congressional authorization, the Truman Administration asserted—with the full trappings of elaborate legal argument—an inherent and seemingly unlimited presidential authority to protect any "interest of American foreign policy."

Although the full constitutional significance of this moment was not clear to me at the time, an extraordinary progression had in fact occurred in Executive-Legislative relations. With the famous bipartisanship of the late 1940s, the Senate and the House of Representatives had cooperated in a series of steps by which the United States assumed a role of world leadership. But having done so, Congress found itself facing an Executive increasingly disposed to point to its global responsibilities as justification for bypassing traditional requirements for congressional approval.

The irony, in time, would prove considerable. Congress, as partner, had approved an American role that would be used to justify presidential rejection of the partnership. Congress, having acted to support American leadership of a world order based on international law, now confronted an extended presidential challenge to its own role under constitutional law.

I must promptly confess that at the time of its first appearance, this evolution in Executive-Legislative relations did not strike me as unwarranted or dangerous. The Korean War, though frustrating in its failure to produce a clean American victory, seemed a necessary exercise in resistance to international aggression. And domestically it was difficult to take great institutional umbrage, even as a conscientious senator, on behalf of a Congress that had allowed itself to become a forum for the shameful anticommunist witchhunt of McCarthyism.

As the 1950s proceeded, and in a Congress where parochialism still reigned, it was not difficult to be persuaded that modern realities required greater latitude for the President and that proponents of congressional prerogative were agents of unenlightened reaction. Indeed, I concluded that American diplomacy in general, and particularly our need to achieve a measure of regularity in relations with the Soviet Union, would be better served if Congress generally deferred to the President. It was on such grounds, for example, that I opposed Senator Bricker, whose efforts to control the use of executive agreements seemed to me to represent a threat to enhanced cultural, educational, commercial—and military—links to friendly nations.

In 1959, I became Chairman of the Senate Foreign Relations Committee, still persuaded of this ''pragmatic'' argument for congressional deference in foreign policy. The election of President Kennedy a year later served only to confirm me in this view, and indeed I became its vocal advocate. I quote here, with due chagrin, from a law-review article I wrote in 1961:

> [T]he price of democratic survival in a world of aggressive totalitarianism is to give up some of the democratic luxuries of the past. We should do so with no illusions as to the reasons for its necessity. It is distasteful and dangerous to vest the executive with powers unchecked and unbalanced. My question is whether we have any choice but to do so.[1]

Thus it was that for my first two decades in the Senate—from the mid-1940s until the mid-1960s—I saw scant need for any substantial congressional ''checking'' of executive foreign-policy initiatives.

For me, the turning point, when it came, was not Vietnam but an event now scarcely recalled: the Johnson Administration's military intervention in the Dominican Republic in April 1965. The action was taken to ''save endangered American lives,'' a rationale that has become a perennial subterfuge. Here, the true aim was to prevent the Dominican Republic from becoming another Cuba. Yet the evidence was never persuasive that Communists within the rebel movement had anything approaching control. The invasion violated international law, traduced the ''good neighbor'' policy we had honored for thirty years, maintained a reactionary military oligarchy in the Dominican Republic, and dashed the confidence and trust generated throughout Latin America by President Kennedy's Alliance for Progress. The United States appeared the enemy of social revolution, and therefore social justice, in Latin America.

The intervention was of course not authorized by Congress; this was an ''emergency.'' I tried to convince my old friend and former Senate colleague, President Lyndon Johnson, that the operation was a mistake. He seemed impervious to my efforts. With great reluctance, therefore, I took to the Senate floor and reviewed my reservations about the invsaion. Johnson took great offense. I had broken the great consensus, or at least his great consensus, and personal relations between us were never the same after that.

As I saw it, I had merely fulfilled my obligation as a senator. The United States Constitution, it seemed to me, gave members of Congress, and the Foreign Relations Committee in particular, a special responsibility for reviewing the President's foreign-policy initiatives, at least initiatives as questionable as this. I was still ambivalent, and I would have preferred to play a role of supporting the Executive. Nonetheless, as our involvement in Vietnam escalated and more questions arose, I concluded that the Committee on Foreign Rela-

[1] *American Foreign Policy in the 20th Century Under an 18th Century Constitution*, 47 Corn. L. Rev. 1 (1961).

tions might appropriately serve as a forum for the free and open discussion of these issues. We therefore held extensive hearings to which we invited distinguished professors, scholars, diplomats, and military men to talk with the Committee on a wide variety of matters, including the Vietnam War, American relations with its European allies and the Soviet Union, and, later, our vast web of foreign commitments.[2]

What we learned only intensified my growing belief that Congress had been lax in fulfilling its constitutional obligations. I had served as floor manager, for example, of the notorious Gulf of Tonkin Resolution. President Johnson had urged us to enact it immediately. He told us it was needed to respond to North Vietnamese aggression. He said that on August 2, 1964, the United States destroyer *Maddox* was attacked in the Gulf of Tonkin by North Vietnamese torpedo boats, and that on August 4, the *Maddox* and another destroyer, the *Turner Joy*, were attacked again. I believed President Johnson. We held perfunctory hearings, had a hurried floor debate, and adopted the Gulf of Tonkin Resolution two days after he had asked for it, with two dissenting votes in the Senate[3] and none in the House. Every time I later raised a question about the war, the blank check of the Tonkin Resolution was waved in my face.

A few years later, we held hearings on the Gulf of Tonkin incident, and it turned out that events apparently unfolded differently than we had been told. For one thing, the South Vietnamese were engaged in hit-and-run attacks against the North Vietnamese coast at roughly the same time and in the same area as the *Maddox* attack. For another, the *Maddox* was loaded with sophisticated electronic equipment directed at North Vietnam—and thus was possibly considered by the North Vietnamese to be a participant in the coastal attacks. Finally, it is highly doubtful that the second attack on the *Maddox* and *Turner Joy* ever occurred.[4]

Now, in contract law, a contract induced by fraud or mistake is voidable. Perhaps some analogous doctrine in constitutional law should apply when statutory authority is given a president on the basis of fraudulent or mistaken representations. The political realities of ''voiding'' a war when the troops are in the field, the flags flying, and the bands playing make that option impractical. But Congress can exercise its oversight responsibilities vigorously at the outset, and the courts can exercise their constitutional prerogative of judicial review vigilantly to prevent the usurpation of power by the Executive.

Largely as a result of my experience during the Vietnam War, then, I came

[2] *See* United States Security Agreements and Commitments Abroad: Hearings Before the Comm. on Foreign Relations, United States Senate, 91st. Cong. (1969–70).

[3] The opponents deserve to be remembered: Senators Wayne Morse of Oregon and Ernest Greuning of Alaska.

[4] *See* The Gulf of Tonkin, The 1964 Incidents: Hearing Before the Comm. on Foreign Relations, United States Senate, 90th Cong., 2d Sess. (1968).

to alter my view about the role of Congress and the courts in our constitutional scheme. Having experienced the frenetic *mobility* and oscillation of American policy in the years after the 1950s—having experienced nearly three decades of overheated activism, global messianism, and undue militarism—I came to see merit in occasional delay or inaction.

One learns or tries to learn from experience. Events of recent years tend to support certain premises implicit in the Constitution—that pluralism is preferred in policy-making, that hasty action is often unrewarding, that precipitous decisions tend to be unwise decisions, resulting in unwanted commitments from which it is difficult to extricate ourselves. Experience, I believe, points at least as much to the dangers of precipitous and excessive action as it does to the dangers of inaction.

I am in short convinced, as Michael Glennon cogently argues in this book, that the active involvement of all three branches is required if this nation's foreign policy is to be measured successfully against the requirements of the Constitution and if the balance intended for our constitutional structure is to be restored.

The cause of that constitutional imbalance has been crisis. I do not believe that the Executive has in most instances willfully usurped the constitutional authority of Congress; nor do I believe that Congress has knowingly given away its traditional authority, although some of its members have sometimes—as I once did—shown excessive regard for executive freedom of action. In the main, however, it has been circumstance rather than design that has given the Executive its great predominance in foreign policy. The circumstance has been crisis, an entire era of crisis in which urgent decisions have been required again and again, decisions of a kind that the Congress is ill equipped to make with what has been thought to be the requisite speed. The President has the means at his disposal for prompt action; the Congress does not. When the security of the country is endangered, or thought to be endangered, there is a powerful premium on prompt action, and that means executive action. I might add that I think there have been many occasions, such as the Gulf of Tonkin "crisis," when the need of immediate action has been exaggerated, resulting in mistakes that might have been avoided by greater deliberation.

The question addressed in this book is how the constitutional balance can be restored. It is improbable, whatever the success of *perestroika* or the START talks, that we will soon return to a kind of normalcy in the world. It is impossible, whatever our frustration with the UN or other international institutions, that the United States will return to its pre-1940 isolationism. How then can Congress and the courts do what the Constitution does not simply ask of them but positively requires of them, under precisely the conditions that have resulted in the erosion of their authority? It is not likely that the President, beset as he is with crisis and set upon by conflicting pressures and interests, will take the initiative in curtailing his freedom of action and restoring congressional and judicial prerogatives. It is up to Congress and the courts, acting on Napoleon's maxim that the tools belong to those who can use them, to reevaluate their roles and reexamine their proper responsibilities.

I have the feeling that constitutional change is again in the making. I have a sense that the mistakes, misjudgments, and deceptions of the last administration—the needless loss of 240 Marines in Lebanon, the "disinformation" campaign against Libya, the initial denials of governmental links to Eugene Hasenfus, the knowingly inaccurate charges concerning the Korean Airline shoot-down, the effort to put the "spin" of success on our national embarrassment at Reykjavík, the tragicomic effort to buy off the Ayatollah with a cake and an autographed Bible—have brought about a growing awareness of the loss of congressional power, a growing uneasiness over the extent of executive power, and a growing willingness to raise questions that a few years ago might have gone unasked, to challenge decisions that would have gone unchallenged, and to try to distinguish between real emergencies and situations that, for reasons of executive convenience, are only said to be emergencies.

Governmental deceit is saddening because it bespeaks a distrust of the insight and good sense of the people. When government ceases to trust the people, the people cease to trust government. Mistrust breeds mistrust. Truth is the lifeblood of democracy; a government that forgoes respect for truth forfeits the respect of the people and its legitimacy in governing. No significant foreign policy can succeed if the government lacks the support of the people. Yet as sad as it is to see government beget this cycle of suspicion, it would be sadder still to see citizens compound deceit with error by believing government when it should not be believed.

I am sad, too, in that I expressed many of these same thoughts over twenty years ago without much effect at a time when it appeared that Congress was on the verge of setting right the constitutional balance.[5] Congress began to take some major steps in that direction until it lost its nerve during the Reagan era. Congressional oversight largely collapsed. The illegal mining of the harbors of Nicaragua, the United States' unlawful denunciation of the compulsory jurisdiction of the International Court of Justice, the sale of arms to Iran, and the most massive Pentagon procurement scandal in the nation's history—all took place without a peep out of Congress until well afterward. In part this may be an aspect of the phenomenon of historical cycles described by Arthur Schlesinger,[6] although I would have thought, and preferred, that the period of congressional activism within the cycle would have been a bit more pro-

[5] Separation of Powers: Hearings Before the Subcom. on Separation of Powers of the Comm. on the Judiciary, U.S. Senate, 90th Cong., 1st Sess. 43 (1967).

[6] A. Schlesinger, The Cycles of History (1987).

tracted. In addition, the Democratic party during the Reagan years failed to play the role of an opposition party, just as the Republican party failed to do so during the Johnson Administration's prosecution of the war in Vietnam.

I share Professor Glennon's concern about tilted consultation. Arranged in haste, almost always under the spur of some real or imagined emergency, these meetings are not consultations but briefings that serve to hit Congress when it is down, getting it to sign on the dotted line at exactly the moment when, for reasons of politics and patriotism, it can hardly refuse. During the Cuban missile crisis in October 1962, many members of Congress were at home campaigning, and none of us was given any official information until after the Administration had made its policy decisions. President Kennedy called the congressional leadership back for a meeting from 5:00 P.M. to 6:00 P.M. on October 22; at 7:00 P.M., he went on national television to announce the decisions reached before we were called in. The meeting was not a consultation but a briefing, a kind of courtesy call or ceremonial occasion. We were called in with no background information on which informed counsel could be based, no staff to assist in our deliberation, and no real chance to think through alternatives. The process of "co-optation" that Professor Glennon refers to is one that almost every congressional leader has experienced firsthand. The wonder, as he suggests, is that consultation mechanisms continue to be proposed by members of Congress, with no real consideration given to the underlying structural problems that too often render consultation a charade.

Hearings that truly get to the bottom of things and consultation that represents a genuine exchange of informed views are thus two important means of carrying out the Congress's constitutional role in foreign-policy-making. The most important reform, however, must be not procedural but attitudinal: Members of Congress must develop a thoroughgoing intolerance of law violation by the Executive. It is inevitably shortsighted and self-defeating for a government like ours to disregard the law, international or domestic. For the law is by its very nature a buttress of the status quo. The United States, as a conservative power in the world, has a particular interest in stability and order. In 1966, in *The Arrogance of Power*, I wrote words that have had an unfortunate timeliness during recent years: "When we violate the law ourselves, whatever short-term advantage may be gained, we are obviously encouraging others to violate the law; we thus encourage disorder and instability and thereby do incalculable damage to our own long-term interests."[7]

This is a book about law, about the highest order of law by which our society governs itself: the United States Constitution. It suggests that we look to the Constitution in the making of foreign policy, and that in so doing we no longer cede to the Executive extensive and exclusive diplomatic power. It pro-

[7] The Arrogance of Power 96 (1966).

poses that we respect constitutional limits when they obstruct our personal wishes as much as when they advance them. As we begin a new administration in Washington, the first since the self-congratulatory and largely mindless celebrating that marked our constitutional bicentennial, it strikes me as fitting that we consider constitutionalism as an idea whose time has come for the making of American foreign policy.

PREFACE

DIPLOMACY CLASHES with constitutionalism. The policies undertaken by the United States in conducting its foreign relations could be formulated more efficiently and carried out more consistently without domestic legal constraints. In recent years, pressures for greater efficiency and consistency in foreign-policy-making have caused the interests of diplomacy to prevail over the interests of constitutionalism. In cases of perceived conflict, therefore, processes established by the Constitution to safeguard the integrity of democratic institutions have often been disregarded in favor of perceived foreign-policy needs.

This book proposes that the United States recognize and return to its constitutional moorings in the making of foreign policy. It argues that the interests of diplomacy cannot be pursued by discarding the interests of constitutionalism. Specifically, it contends that the Constitution gives Congress important responsibilities in foreign-policy decision making and that it gives the courts the responsibility of resolving disputes between Congress and the President concerning the power to make foreign policy. The courts must give effect to the will of Congress, the book suggests, except in those rare instances where the President possesses an independent constitutional power. It discusses how those powers are identified and what they are. In this connection, the book reviews the scope of the prime tools of diplomacy—the war power and the treaty power. It concludes with a commentary on national security, examining the implication of recent foreign-policy disputes for the constitutional structure of foreign-policy-making.

No book has taken on these issues in over fifteen years. Since then, much has happened. The War Powers Resolution has been enacted, tested, and challenged; amidst heated disagreement over the Senate's role, several major treaties have received its advice and consent; controversy over executive agreements has flared and abated; intelligence abuses have been revealed and remedial legislation debated; the Iran-Contra affair has highlighted anew the extent of disagreement on first principles; and the American Law Institute has published a new *Restatement of the Law (3d): The Foreign Relations Law of the United States* (referred to hereafter as the *Restatement*), vastly revising and expanding its previous summation of applicable American law.

Many commentators assume the propriety of executive supremacy and judicial passivity. This book argues the contrary. In doing so, it applies an amalgam of constitutional principles and international-law norms that are part of our domestic legal system. Our constitutional system has much to learn from the international legal system, in both the methodology of customary international law and the application of its substantive norms. The intricate weave of these two legal systems creates the fabric of this work.

The work's central thesis is that the supine roles often assigned our legislative and judicial branches in foreign-policy-making must be abandoned. Chapters 1 and 2 establish a framework of analysis. Chapter 1 discusses the "big" cases in this area of the law and reveals the inclination of the Supreme Court to give controlling effect to the intent of Congress. It discusses the comparative institutional attributes of the political branches as foreign-policymakers and suggests that from a public-policy perspective, executive hegemony over all foreign-relations matters is unjustified. Chapter 2 deals with sources of constitutional power, analyzing how the Court has identified the respective powers of Congress and the President. It proposes a methodology for discovering the proper limits of presidential foreign-relations powers—a methodology that accords high priority to customary law, familiar to international lawyers. These chapters, which might seem digressive, are critical in that they set forth premises concerning principles of constitutional interpretation that shape the conclusions of subsequent chapters. Chapter 3 applies this structure to the war-making powers of the federal government. It includes a discussion of the constitutionality and effectiveness of the War Powers Resolution. Chapter 4 deals with the making, interpretation, and termination of treaties. Chapter 5 discusses executive agreements and presidential policy pronouncements not rising to the level of treaties. Chapter 6 discusses a topic common to the previous two chapters: treaties that authorize or require the use of force. Chapter 7 discusses the incorporation of international law into federal common law and how that incorporation serves as a further check on executive action. Chapter 8 deals with the role of congressional oversight and judicial review in matters of national security, arguing that only the rarest cases should be regarded as not fit for judicial resolution. The chapter includes some reflections on the propriety of structural reform in the wake of the Iran-Contra affair, including a discussion of the scope of the power of the purse as a check on executive foreign-policy-making. Throughout this analysis, the book comments extensively on the new *Restatement*.

Rather than striving for a comprehensiveness that might derive from an extended treatment of hypothetical questions, I focus on actual recurring disputes. A measure of theoretical discussion is still unavoidable; so too is a thorough analysis of case law. This is, as Senator Fulbright points out, a book about *law*; it is not a book about how, from an historian's perspective, the foreign-affairs power came to be allocated as it is, or how, from a political scientist's perspective, that power ought to be allocated. (Few today, of course, would contend that these disciplines are entirely distinct; the analytic approach outlined in Chapter 2 attempts to include elements of history—I call it "constitutional custom"—and political science—discussed under "functionalism.") Because it is a book about constitutional law, though, it is in good part a book about Supreme Court cases. While these are not the only source of the Constitution's meaning, surely they are a major one. I try nonetheless to avoid jargon and undue abstraction, and to include concrete contemporary examples. The book should therefore have a particular utility to those in government, academia, and the law who deal regularly with these matters, although I believe that interested, informed laypersons will also find it accessible. The questions it addresses ought to be at the center of public discourse; they are monumental in the life of any constitutional democracy—even one two hundred years old.

ACKNOWLEDGMENTS

Several organizations and individuals helped prepare this book. Professors Larry Berman, Louis Fisher, Thomas Franck, and Seth Tillman provided insight and encouragement throughout. Alan Morrison, consummate constitutional litigator and cocounsel in *Lowry v. Reagan*, helped form my thoughts about the role of the courts. Professor Loch Johnson assisted in working through the issues of congressional oversight and consultation. John Ritch, deputy staff director of the Senate Foreign Relations Committee, was generous with documentary and editorial assistance. I am indebted to Ann Graham's typing and computer skills for sorting out the intricacies of ever-newer versions of the word-processing program used in the preparation of this manuscript. Beth Celani, of Meade Data General, generously made the NEXIS data base available for accurate, up-to-date citations to newspapers and other periodicals. The University of California, Davis, Law School provided support during the summers of 1987, 1988, and 1989. Special thanks is owed to the research assistants who aided in the preparation of the articles on which much of this book is based, and a personal note of appreciation must be expressed to James Wolf, University of California, Davis, Law School, class of '88; Amy Alpaugh, class of '90; and John McCaull, class of '91. Robert K. Burdette's copyediting was thorough, sensitive, and punctual.

Portions of this book appeared initially in various law journals and books. Gratitude is extended to the respective journals and publishers for permitting the excerpting of those articles (with modifications; a close read will reveal my "evolved" views): "Foreign Affairs and the Political Question Doctrine," 83 *American Journal of International Law* (1989) [reprinted with the permission of the American Society of International Law (ASIL)]; "Publish *and* Perish: Congress's Effort to Snip *Snepp*, Before and *AFSA*," 10 *Michigan Journal of International Law* 163 (1989); "Two Views of Presidential Foreign Affairs Power: *Little v. Barreme* or *United States v. Curtiss-Wright*?" 13 *Yale International Law Journal* 5 (1988); "Constitutional Issues in Terminating U.S. Acceptance," in *The International Court of Justice at a Crossroads* (L. Damrosch, ed.; Transnational Publishers, 1987) [reprinted with permission of ASIL]; "Interpreting 'Interpretation': The President, the Senate, and When Treaty Interpretation Becomes Treaty Making," 20 *University of California, Davis, Law Review* 912 (July 1987) [copyright © 1987 by The Regents of the University of California; reprinted with permission]; "Can the President Do No Wrong?" 80 *American Journal of International Law* 923 (Oct. 1986) [reprinted with the permission of ASIL]; "United States Mutual Security Treaties: The Commitment Myth," 24 *Columbia Journal of Transnational Law*

509 (Apr. 1986) [excerpts also appear as "The NATO Treaty: The Commitment Myth," in *First Use of Nuclear Weapons: Under the Constitution, Who Decides?* (P. Raven-Hansen, ed.; Greenwood Press) [copyright © 1985 Columbia Journal of Transnational Law Ass'n]; "Raising *The Paquete Habana*: Is Violation of Customary International Law by the Executive Unconstitutional?" 80 *Northwestern University Law Review* 321 (Nov. 1985); "Nicaragua v. United States of America: Constitutionality of U.S. Modification of ICJ Jurisdiction," 79 *American Journal of International Law* 571 (July 1985) [reprinted with permission of ASIL]; "The War Powers Resolution Ten Years Later: More Politics Than Law," 78 *American Journal of International Law* 571 (July 1984) [reprinted with permission of ASIL]; "The War Powers Resolution: Sad Record, Dismal Promise," 17 *Loyola of Los Angeles Law Journal* 657 (1984) [reprinted with the permission of the Loyola of Los Angeles Law Review; copyright © 1984 by Loyola of Los Angeles, all rights reserved]; "The Use of Custom in Resolving Separation of Powers Disputes," 64 *Boston University Law Review* 109 (1984); "Liaison and the Law: Foreign Intelligence Agencies' Activities in the United States," 25 *Harvard International Law Journal* 1 (Winter 1984) [copied with the permission of the Harvard International Law Journal; copyright © 1984 by the President and Fellows of Harvard College]; "Treaty Process Reform: Saving Constitutionalism Without Destroying Diplomacy," *University of Cincinnati Law Review* 84 (Apr. 1983); "The Senate Role in Treaty Ratification," 77 *American Journal of International Law* 257 (Apr. 1983) [reprinted with permission of ASIL]; "Investigating the Intelligence Community: The Process of Getting Information for Congress," in *The Tethered Presidency* 140 (T. Franck, ed.; NYU Press, 1981) [reprinted by permission of New York University Press; copyright © 1981 by New York University]; and "Strengthening the War Powers Resolution: The Case for Purse-strings Restrictions," 60 *Minnesota Law Review* 1 (Nov. 1975) [reprinted with permission].

Constitutional Diplomacy

Chapter One

CONGRESS VS. THE PRESIDENT

> Presidential powers are not fixed but fluctuate, depending upon their disjunction or conjunction with those of Congress.
> —Justice Robert Jackson[1]

LITTLE V. BARREME

Imagine, if you will, the following facts:

> During a period of congressionally authorized hostilities against a foreign nation, Captain South, a United States naval officer, receives a presidential order to seize certain vessels found trading with the enemy. The order is not authorized by Congress, but neither is it expressly prohibited; the law is silent concerning the President's authority to issue the order. Captain South carries out the President's order, and the owners of the seized vessel bring an action for damages against Captain South personally for the seizure. The theory of the suit: The President's order, not having been authorized by Congress, is illegal. The key issue: Should Captain South be held personally liable for damages?

For several reasons, one might be inclined to decide in the negative. Indeed, at first blush, many might regard this as an easy case. One might agree with Lewis A. Tambs, former United States Ambassador to Costa Rica, that subordinates must assume the legality of their orders. Tambs testified before the Iran-Contra committees that National Security Council aide Lieutenant Colonel Oliver North had ordered him to open a new military front in southern Nicaragua.[2] The order may well have violated the law—the so-called Boland Amendment[3]—which Tambs testified that he had never read.[4] The Ambassador said:

[1] The Steel Seizure Case, 343 U.S. 579, 635–38 (1952) (Jackson, J., concurring).

[2] N.Y. Times, May 30, 1987, at A8.

[3] The ''Boland Amendment'' is actually a series of several amendments to appropriations and authorization acts enacted by Congress between 1982 and 1986. The amendments restricted or barred the use of funds by the Departments of State and Defense, the CIA and other entities of the United States government involved in intelligence for direct or indirect support of the Nicaraguan Contras. For a chart of the unclassified ''Boland Amendments,'' *see* 133 Cong. Rec. H4982–H4987 (daily ed. June 15, 1987).

[4] N.Y. Times, May 30, 1987, at A8.

> The people in the field who are trying to do a job are going to assume that orders from Washington are legal and legitimate. I certainly do not want to see the United States government brought to paralysis while people are getting private legal counsel before they carry out orders from their legitimate superiors.[5]

One might further argue that it is hardly practicable to have a lawyer on every naval vessel, and that consequently naval officers may simply assume that their orders are legal. Captain South might do well to follow the immortal words of Fawn Hall: "It was a policy of mine not to ask questions and just to follow instructions."[6]

Second, one might claim that the order is not at all illegal—that indeed it did not contravene the will of Congress since Congress did not prohibit the order; Congress merely declined to authorize it.[7]

Third, one might think that this foreign-relations controversy is a dispute best left to the political branches to work out, not one for the courts to decide.[8]

Finally, one might respond that the President's independent, express power as commander-in-chief of the armed forces[9] permits him and him alone to make the decision whether these foreign ships should be seized. Under this view, to the extent that a congressional enactment precludes the President from ordering such a seizure, it can be regarded as unconstitutional.[10]

In fact, the dispute sketched out above is not at all hypothetical. It occurred—in 1799—and it was adjudicated. The case: *Little v. Barreme*.[11] The author of the opinion: Chief Justice John Marshall. The decision: Judgment against the ship captain, affirmed by a unanimous United States Supreme Court.[12]

[5] N.Y. Times, May 30, 1987, at 6. *See also* letter from George Bush, Director of Central Intelligence, to Edward Levi, Attorney General (May 5, 1976) *quoted in* Armstrong & Kornbluh, *On Trial: North and Our System*, N.Y. Times, Feb. 27, 1989, at A15 ("Many employees have difficulty understanding how their activities in performing assignments directed by higher authority can be subject to legal question").

[6] Testimony of Fawn Hall, 100-5 Iran-Contra Investigation: Joint Hearings Before the House Select Committee to Investigate Covert Arms Transactions with Iran and the Senate Select Committee on Secret Military Assistance to Iran and the Nicaraguan Opposition, 100th Cong., 1st Sess. 486 (1987). Her boss, Lt. Col. Oliver North, apparently followed a similar policy: "[I]f the Commander in Chief tells this lieutenant colonel to go stand in the corner and sit on his head, I will do so." Testimony of Oliver North, *id.* at 246.

[7] *See generally* Tribe, *Towards a Syntax of the Unsaid: Construing the Sounds of Congressional Silence*, 57 Ind. L.J. 515 (1982) (where constitutional text is vague, congressional inaction does not necessarily constitute a prohibition of executive action).

[8] *See* Baker v. Carr, 369 U.S. 186, 217 (1962).

[9] U.S. Const. art. II, § 2.

[10] *See, e.g.*, M. Glennon & T. Franck, United States Foreign Relations Law: Documents and Sources 125–28 (1981) (War Powers Resolution vetoed by President Nixon as unconstitutional infringement of his commander-in-chief power).

[11] 6 U.S. (2 Cranch) 170, 179 (1804).

[12] *Id.* at 179.

The facts were fairly simple. During the administration of President John Adams, the United States fought an undeclared naval war with France.[13] Although the war was not formally declared, Congress prohibited American vessels from sailing to French ports.[14] Congress also enacted the means to carry out this restriction; it authorized the President to order United States naval officers to (a) stop any American ship if they had reason to suspect the ship bound for a French port[15] and (b) seize the ship if, upon searching it, it appeared to be so bound.[16] Congress further provided that the captured ship be condemned—auctioned or sold—and, rather generously, that half the proceeds go to the United States, the other half to the person who initiated the capture and sale, presumably the ship's captain.[17]

When the Secretary of the Navy issued orders a month after the law was enacted, he included a copy of the law. One recipient of those orders was Captain George Little, commander of the United States frigate *Boston*. Unknown to Little, however, the orders departed from the law in two key respects. First, they directed the seizure not only of ships that were clearly American but also of ships that appeared to be foreign but *might* be American or merely carrying American cargo.[18] Second, they directed the seizure not only of ships bound *to* French ports but also of ships sailing *from* French ports.[19] The order therefore seemingly expanded Little's authority, and the United States' risk of hostilities, significantly beyond what Congress had contemplated.

Sure enough, the Navy seized the wrong ship—a vessel with Danish papers sailing *from* a French port. Captain Little captured this ship, the *Flying Fish*, and sought to have her condemned.[20] The central issue in the condemnation proceedings was not whether the *Flying Fish* should have been condemned; Chief Justice Marshall agreed with the courts below that the seizure of a neutral vessel was unlawful.[21] The case turned on whether the Danish owners of the *Flying Fish* should be awarded damages for the injuries they suffered.[22] Little's defense was that he had merely followed orders and that those orders

[13] *Id.* at 173, 177. *See* H. Blumenthal, France and the United States: Their Diplomatic Relationship 1789–1914, 13–17 (1970); D. Mckay, The United States and France, 81–83 (1951).

[14] Non-Intercourse Act, ch. 2, § 1, 3 Stat. 613 (1799) (expired 1800).

[15] *Id.* at § 5.

[16] *Id.*

[17] *Id.* at § 1.

[18] *Id.* at 171.

[19] *Id.*

[20] *Id.* at 176. Little had some reason to suspect the *Flying Fish*'s true nationality: "[D]uring the chase by the *American* frigates, the [*Flying Fish*'s] master threw overboard the logbook, and certain other papers." *Id.* at 173 (emphasis in original).

[21] *Id.* at 172, 175–76.

[22] *Id.*

excused him from liability.[23] Because the *Flying Fish* fell squarely within the class of ships that the President had ordered seized, the Supreme Court had to consider whether the President's instructions immunized his officer personally from an action for damages arising under the statute.[24]

The Supreme Court affirmed the circuit court's judgment awarding damages to the owners.[25] Marshall's first reaction, he confesses in the opinion, was that, given Little's orders, a judgment against him for damages would be improper. It is "indispensably necessary to every military system," he writes, that "military men usually pay implicit obedience . . . to the orders of their superiors."[26] Yet Marshall changed his mind when he considered the character of Captain Little's act: It directly contravened the will of Congress. "[T]he legislature seems to have prescribed the manner in which this law shall be carried into execution," and in so doing, "exclude[d] a seizure of any vessel not bound to a French port."[27] Under the law enacted by Congress, therefore, Captain Little "would not have been authorized to detain" the *Flying Fish*.[28] "[T]he instructions [from the Secretary of the Navy]," Marshall concludes, "cannot change the nature of the transaction, or legalize an act which, without those instructions, would have been a plain trespass."[29] Marshall thus forthrightly rejects the "good-soldier" defense: it is of no consequence that Little was merely following orders.[30]

Little v. Barreme is, in all, an extraordinary case—extraordinary not only for what the opinion says but also for what it does not say. A number of issues not addressed by the Court might have been resolved in a manner that would

[23] *Id.* at 178–79.

[24] *Id.*

[25] *Id.* at 179.

[26] *Id.* at 177.

[27] *Id.*

[28] *Id.*

[29] *Id.*

[30] It is most extraordinary that the "good soldier" defense should be addressed and disposed of by no less than John Marshall. The Chief Justice's finding that no executive immunity exists apparently had no statutory or common-law basis. In fact, in a later opinion, Marshall implied that a certain degree of executive immunity was *required* by the Constitution.

In Osborne v. Bank of the United States, 22 U.S. (9 Wheat.) 738, 865–66 (1824), Marshall acknowledged that executive-branch immunity from civil suits is not explicitly granted by the Constitution. However, because of the faithful-execution clause, immunity may by impliedly granted by Congress in statutes creating public agencies; *accord* Nixon v. Fitzgerald, 457 U.S. 731, 749–50 (1981) ("the President is absolutely immune from civil damages liability for his official acts in the absence of explicit affirmative action by Congress."). Modern Supreme Court opinions find executive immunity required by the "inherent" or "structural assumptions of our scheme of government," *Id.* at 748 n.26, or public policy; *see also* Butz v. Economou, 438 U.S. 478, 508–10 (1977). Congress has never expressly granted or limited presidential immunity, nor is it clear that it has the power to do so. *Nixon*, 457 U.S. at 748. *See generally* Glennon, *Two Views of Presidential Foreign Affairs Power*: Little v. Barreme *or* Curtiss-Wright*?* 13 Yale J. Int'l L. 5, 8 n.30 (1988).

have provided Captain Little with a plausible defense: nonjusticiability of political matters, ambiguity of congressional intent, and infringement of the President's "sole-organ" power.

Marshall does not even consider the possibility that the dispute might have constituted a political question, unsuitable for judicial resolution. The great Chief Justice well knew that such suits existed, having written less than a year before, in *Marbury v. Madison*,[31] that "the President is invested with certain important political powers" with respect to which "the decision of the executive is conclusive" and which therefore "can never be examined by the courts."[32]

Nor does Marshall address the argument that the President's orders might not have been contrary to the will of Congress. The problem of ascertaining congressional intent in the face of congressional silence was not foreign to Marshall. In the *Little* opinion, he considers whether the President would have had the authority to issue Captain Little's orders had Congress remained completely silent on the issue. The Chief Justice says he is not sure:

> It is by no means clear that the President of the United States, whose high duty it is to "take care that the laws be faithfully executed," and who is commander in chief of the armies and navies of the United States, might not, without any special authority for that purpose, . . . have empowered the officers commanding the armed vessels of the *United States*, to seize . . . *American* vessels . . . engaged in this illicit commerce.[33]

Thus, Marshall did not feel compelled in *Little* to define the limits of presidential power in the face of complete congressional silence. His decision seems to presuppose that congressional authorization of a specific scope of executive action is an implicit denial to the President of authority to order action outside that scope. Marshall's understanding of congressional intent thus sets a stage for direct confrontation between the executive and legislative branches over foreign affairs, and on that stage he unfolds the central meaning of his decision, a proposition that gives it abiding timeliness: *The will of Congress controls*.

Finally, nowhere in *Little* does Marshall consider the possibility that the President's order might have fallen within independent powers the Executive

[31] 1 U.S. (Cranch) 137 (1803).

[32] *Id.* at 167. Eighty-seven years later, the Supreme Court cited *Little* as authority for *declining* to find a political question. In *In re* Cooper, 143 U.S. 472 (1891), the Court said that "[t]he right of the executive to deal with persons and property can never, under the Constitution of the United States, be a political question. *Little v. Barreme*." *Id.* at 499–501.

[33] *Little*, 6 U.S. (2 Cranch) at 177 (emphasis in original). Corwin suggests, wrongly, that Marshall believed that the President would have had the power to order such seizures in the absence of a statutory prohibition. *See* E. Corwin, The Constitution and What It Means Today, 128 (14th ed. 1978).

enjoys as "sole organ" of the United States in its foreign relations. Yet it was John Marshall, speaking only two years earlier on the floor of the House of Representatives, who apparently coined the term. In the context of a debate on President Adams's power to extradite to Britain an individual charged with murder, Marshall declared: "The President is the sole organ of the nation in its external relations, and its sole representative with foreign nations."[34] Although we might imagine that such rhetoric, if taken seriously, would lead Marshall to declare the statute in *Little* an unconstitutional infringement of presidential power, such an interpretation could not have been further from Marshall's meaning. Far from arguing in his speech that President Adams had an "inherent" or "independent" power to extradite an individual charged with murder, Marshall in fact contended that it was Adams's *duty* faithfully to execute the Jay Treaty,[35] and that it was that Treaty, not the President's exclusive constitutional power, that authorized and indeed required the extradition in question.[36] Therefore, the truth is that it probably never occurred to John Marshall (or to any of his colleagues in 1804) that the President, acting within the Constitution that many of them had helped write, could disregard this congressional restriction. That is probably why *Little* is silent on the issue. The argument for a royal prerogative was not new to these Founding Fathers; while they had not encountered Oliver North, they had encountered his ideological if not genealogical ancestor, Lord North.[37]

The Steel Seizure Case

It was not until the Korean War, however, that Marshall's analysis again became timely. In 1952, *Youngstown Sheet & Tube Co. v. Sawyer*, the famed *Steel Seizure Case*, presented the Supreme Court with a stark choice. A nationwide strike had broken out in the steel industry. According to the *Youngstown* Court:

> The indispensability of steel as a component of substantially all weapons and other war materials led the President to believe that the proposed work stoppage would immediately jeopardize our national defense and that governmental seizure of the steel mills was necessary in order to assure the continued availability of steel.[38]

President Harry S. Truman consequently issued an executive order directing the Secretary of Commerce to take possession of most of the mills and keep

[34] 6 Annals of Cong. 613 (1800).

[35] Jay Treaty, Nov. 19, 1794, United States–United Kingdom, 8 Stat. 116, T.S. No. 105.

[36] *Id.*

[37] Lord Frederick North, Prime Minister to George III at the time of the War of Independence, was seen by many Englishmen and Americans alike as subverting the British constitution with the aim of achieving royal absolutism. S. Morrison, The Oxford History of the American People 198–99 (1965).

[38] The Steel Seizure Case, 343 U.S. 579, 583 (1952).

them running, arguing that the President had "inherent power" to do so. The companies objected, complaining that the seizure was not authorized by the Constitution or any statute.

Congress had not statutorily authorized the seizure, either before or after it occurred. Congress had, however, enacted three statutes providing for governmental seizure of the mills in certain specifically prescribed situations, but the Administration never claimed that any of those conditions had existed prior to its action. More important, Congress had in fact considered, and rejected, authorization for the sort of seizure Truman ordered.[39]

[39] Justice Frankfurter described the consideration of those amendments at some length:

Congress in 1947 was again called upon to consider whether governmental seizure should be used to avoid serious industrial shutdowns. Congress decided against conferring such power generally and in advance, without special congressional enactment to meet each particular need. Under the urgency of telephone and coal strikes in the winter of 1946, Congress addressed itself to the problems raised by "national emergency" strikes and lockouts. The termination of wartime seizure powers on December 31, 1946, brought these matters to the attention of Congress with vivid impact. A proposal that the President be given powers to seize plants to avert a shutdown where the 'health or safety' of the nation was endangered, was thoroughly canvassed by Congress and rejected. No room for doubt remains that the proponents as well as the opponents of the bill which became the Labor Management Relations Act of 1947 clearly understood that as a result of that legislation the only recourse for preventing a shutdown in any basic industry, after failure of mediation, was Congress. Authorization for seizure as an available remedy for potential dangers was unequivocally put aside. The Senate Labor Committee, through its Chairman, explicitly reported to the Senate that a general grant of seizure powers had been considered and rejected in favor of reliance on *ad hoc* legislation, as a particular emergency might call for it. An amendment presented in the House providing that where necessary "to preserve and protect the public health and security" the President might seize any industry in which there is an impending curtailment of production, was voted down after debate, by a vote of more than three to one.

. . . In any event, nothing can be plainer than that Congress made a conscious choice of policy in a field full of perplexity and peculiarly within legislative responsibility for choice. In formulating legislation for dealing with industrial conflicts, Congress could not more clearly and emphatically have withheld authority than it did in 1947. Perhaps as much so as is true of any piece of modern legislation, Congress acted with full consciousness of what it was doing and in the light of much recent history. Previous seizure legislation had subjected the powers granted to the President to restrictions of varying degrees of stringency. Instead of giving him even limited powers, Congress in 1947 deemed it wise to require the President, upon failure of attempts to reach a voluntary settlement, to report to Congress if he deemed the power of seizure a needed shot for his locker. The President could not ignore the specific limitations of prior seizure statutes. No more could he act in disregard of the limitation put upon seizure by the 1947 Act.

It cannot be contended that the President would have had power to issue this order had Congress explicitly negated such authority in formal legislation. Congress has expressed its will to withhold this power from the President as though it had said so in so many words. The authoritatively expressed purpose of Congress to disallow such power to the President and to require him, when in his mind the occasion arose for such a seizure, to put the matter to Congress and ask for specific authority from it, could not be more decisive if it had been written into §§ 206-210 of the Labor Management Relations Act of 1947.

Id. at 598–602.

Justice Hugo Black delivered the opinion of the Court. The President, Justice Black wrote, had engaged in lawmaking, a task assigned by the Constitution to Congress.[40] The seizure was therefore unlawful; the "President's power, if any, to issue the order must stem either from an act of Congress or from the Constitution itself."[41] Notwithstanding the elegant simplicity of Black's opinion, it has not withstood the test of time; as Corwin noted, this seems not to have been the first instance of a president's doing something that Congress might also have done.[42] *Youngstown* is remembered mostly for the concurring opinion of Justice Robert Jackson. In reasoning strikingly reminiscent of Marshall's in *Little*, Jackson wrote that "[p]residential powers are not fixed but fluctuate, depending upon their disjunction or conjunction with those of Congress."[43] Because of the importance of Jackson's opinion, key portions follow without paraphrase:

> The actual art of governing under our Constitution does not and cannot conform to judicial definitions of the power of any of its branches based on isolated clauses or even single Articles torn from context. While the Constitution diffuses power the better to secure liberty, it also contemplates that practice will integrate the dispersed powers into a workable government. It enjoins upon its branches separateness but interdependence, autonomy but reciprocity. Presidential powers are not fixed but fluctuate, depending upon their disjunction or conjunction with those of Congress. We may well begin by a somewhat over-simplified grouping of practical situations in which a President may doubt, or others may challenge, his powers, and by distinguishing roughly the legal consequences of this factor of relativity.
>
> 1. When the President acts pursuant to an express or implied authorization of Congress, his authority is at its maximum, for it includes all that he possesses in his own right plus all that Congress can delegate. In these circumstances, and in these only, may he be said (for what it may be worth), to personify the federal sovereignty. If his act is held unconstitutional under these circumstances, it usually means that the Federal Government as an undivided whole lacks power. A seizure executed by the President pursuant to an Act of Congress would be supported by the strongest of presumptions and the widest latitude of judicial interpretation, and the burden of persuasion would rest heavily upon any who might attack it.
> 2. When the President acts in absence of either a congressional grant or denial of authority, he can only rely upon his own independent powers, but there is a zone of twilight in which he and Congress may have concurrent authority, or in which its distribution is uncertain. Therefore, congressional iner-

[40] *Id.* at 587–89.

[41] *Id.* at 585.

[42] *See* E. Corwin, The Constitution and What It Means Today, 198 (1978).

[43] 343 U.S. at 635 (Jackson, J., concurring).

tia, indifference or quiescence may sometimes, at least as a practical matter, enable, if not invite, measures on independent presidential responsibility. In this area, any actual test of power is likely to depend on the imperatives of events and contemporary imponderables rather than on abstract theories of law.

3. When the President takes measures incompatible with the expressed or implied will of Congress, his power is at its lowest ebb, for then he can rely only upon his own constitutional powers minus any constitutional powers of Congress over the matter. Courts can sustain exclusive Presidential control in such a case only by disabling the Congress from acting upon the subject. Presidential claim to a power at once so conclusive and preclusive must be scrutinized with caution, for what is at stake is the equilibrium established by our constitutional system.

. . . I have no illusion that any decision by this Court can keep power in the hands of Congress if it is not wise and timely in meeting its problems. A crisis that challenges the President equally, or perhaps primarily, challenges Congress. If not good law, there was worldly wisdom in the maxim attributed to Napoleon that "The tools belong to the man who can use them." We may say that power to legislate for emergencies belongs in the hands of Congress, but only Congress itself can prevent power from slipping through its fingers.[44]

The opinion is thus notable for its unwillingness to decide the case by reference to "inherent" presidential power and the weight it accords congressional will. It remained for a former Jackson clerk, Justice William Rehnquist, to give Jackson's opinion the force of law. The Supreme Court formally adopted this mode of analysis in *Dames & Moore v. Regan*,[45] in which Justice William Rehnquist applied Jackson's approach to uphold President Jimmy Carter's Iranian-hostage settlement agreement as authorized by Congress.[46] In so doing, Rehnquist wrote that Jackson's opinion "brings together as much combination of analysis and common sense as there is in this area."[47] Rehn-

[44] The Steel Seizure Case, 343 U.S. 579, 635–38 (1952) (Jackson, J., concurring).

[45] 453 U.S. 654 (1981).

[46] *Id.* at 688.

[47] *Id.* at 661. Before *Dames & Moore*, it had occasionally been argued that the *Steel Seizure Case* did not pertain to the scope of the President's foreign-affairs powers because the seizure of the steel mills occurred within the territory of the United States or because the seizure violated the just compensation clause. It is difficult to believe that the outcome in *Steel Seizure* would have been different had the American-owned steel plants seized by the Executive been located in, say, Canada, rather than in the United States. Nor did Jackson decline to reach the commander-in-chief claim because individual rights were violated. Indeed, his opinion turned neither upon the locus of conduct or property affected by the executive act nor upon the putative violation of individual rights but upon the Truman Administration's argument that a continuing supply of steel was necessary to prosecute the war in Korea and that the power to seize and operate the steel mills flowed from the President's constitutional power as commander in chief. That claim provided Jackson the opportunity for an extended and highly illuminating discussion of the contours of that

quist then quoted from Jackson a passage that today is as significant as it is timely. He said: "The example of such unlimited executive power that must have most impressed the forefathers was the prerogative exercised by George III, and the description of its evils in the Declaration of Independence leads me to doubt that they were creating their new Executive in his image."[48]

However, Justice Rehnquist recognized in *Dames & Moore*—as had Jackson[49]—that the framework is somewhat simplistic.[50] A more extended look at the tripartite analysis reveals why that is so.

Congressional Disapproval

When the President acts in the face of congressional *disapproval*, that action falls into Jackson's third category, and the Court, if it is to decide the case, faces a difficult task: It must determine whether the President or Congress has exclusive power over the matter. If the Court finds that the President has such power (variously, *independent, plenary, inherent*, or *implied*), then Congress is by definition disabled from acting. Understandably, few cases have been decided in this category. Virtually all have been decided against the Execu-

"cryptic" constitutional provision. Similarly, in *Dames & Moore*, the dispute was again treated by the Court as implicating the President's power "in the field of international relations"—notwithstanding the domestic locus of the conduct and property affected by the Executive's nullification and suspension orders. Each case thus involved the validity of an executive act that had international effects, even though "domestic" private conduct and property were also affected by that act.

In short, the two cases in which Jackson's analysis has been applied, first by him and then by the entire Supreme Court, involved the conduct of the Korean War and settlement of the Iran hostage crisis. These were quintessential foreign-affairs cases.

[48] *Id.* at 662. *Compare* Heren, Chapter 8, and Alexander Hamilton (no admirer of legislatures):

> The history of human conduct does not warrant that exalted opinion of human virtue which would make it wise in a nation to commit interests of so delicate and momentous a kind as those which concern its intercourse with the rest of the world to the sole disposal of . . . a President of the United States.

The Federalist No. 75, at 505–6 (A. Hamilton) (J. Cooke ed. 1961).

An important recent reaffirmation of the *Dames & Moore* approach is found in Webster v. Doe, 108 S. Ct. 2047 (1988), discussed further below. Despite the protestations of the two dissenters, the Court, speaking again through Chief Justice Rehnquist, grounded on congressional will rather than constitutional principle its conclusion that a former CIA employee was not precluded from seeking judicial review of the decision by which he was dismissed. Justice Scalia, dissenting, worried that the majority's opinion

> will have ramifications far beyond creation of the world's only secret intelligence agency that must litigate the dismissal of its agents. If constitutional claims can be raised in this highly sensitive context, it is hard to imagine where they cannot. The assumption that there are any executive decisions that cannot be hauled into the courts may no longer be valid.

[49] Youngstown Sheet & Tube Co. v. Sawyer, 343 U.S. 579, 635 (1952) (Jackson, J., concurring).

[50] Dames & Moore v. Regan, 453 U.S. 654, 669 (1981).

tive. In *Little*,[51] as we have seen, an implied congressional prohibition against certain naval seizures prevailed over the President's constitutional power as commander-in-chief. Similarly, in the *Steel Seizure Case*,[52] the President was found to lack the power to seize the nation's steel mills in the face of an implied statutory prohibition. In *Ex parte Garland*,[53] on the other hand, the Court held that the President possessed a pardon power "not subject to legislative control."[54]

CONGRESS'S REMARKABLE SUCCESS RATE

In no case touching on foreign relations has the Supreme Court invalidated an act of Congress because it impinged upon the President's sole power under the Constitution. In two hundred years of dispute between the President and Congress over war and peace, commitment and neutrality, trade embargoes and arms sales, Congress has never lost before the High Court. Indeed, as discussed in Chapter 8, in only one case, *National Federation of Federal Employees v. United States*,[55] has *any* court invalidated an act of Congress on the ground that it violated general presidential foreign-affairs powers. This may not be saying much; the Supreme Court has not decided many cases dealing with these momentous issues, and efforts to get the courts to resolve such disputes are frequently dismissed as "nonjusticiable," as political questions not admitting of judicial review.[56]

Nonetheless, the record is a sobering one for anyone arguing that a subject falls within the President's exclusive constitutional domain. The only cases in which a presidential foreign-affairs power controlled the outcome pertained to policies promulgated by states. And these cases, only two, deal with the same transaction. President Franklin Roosevelt recognized the Soviet Union in 1933 and as part of the package, entered into an executive agreement with the Soviets in which the two nations settled outstanding claims against each other. The courts of New York refused to enforce the agreement, which effectively required them to enforce the confiscation orders of the Soviet government. In *United States v. Pink*[57] and *United States v. Belmont*,[58] the Supreme Court affirmed that New York's refusal interfered with the President's recognition power.[59]

[51] 6 U.S. (2 Cranch) 170 (1804).

[52] 343 U.S. 579 (1952).

[53] 71 U.S. (4 Wall.) 333 (1867).

[54] *Id.* at 380.

[55] 695 F. Supp. 1196 (D.D.C. 1988).

[56] The application of the political-question doctrine in foreign-affairs cases is discussed at length in Chapter 8.

[57] 315 U.S. 203 (1942).

[58] 301 U.S. 324 (1937).

[59] "Plainly," Justice Douglas wrote for the Court in *Belmont*, "the external powers of the United States are to be exercised without regard to state laws or policies." *Id.* at 331. It was, he

Because states have little claim to international power, and because the foreign-affairs powers of Congress are substantial, *Pink* and *Belmont* cannot readily be applied to find limits on congressional power. The dispute in these cases was between the President and a state—indeed, between the President and the *courts* of a state—not between the President and Congress. The powerful limitation of federal supremacy thus further reinforced the President's claim to power, an arrow absent from the executive quiver in disputes with Congress.

IMPLIED CONGRESSIONAL WILL

In Jackson's first and third categories of executive action, then, the Court must identify the will of Congress. Determining whether Congress has approved or disapproved of the presidential act is relatively easy if the legislative will is express; the Court need only look to the relevant statute. If congressional approval or disapproval is implied, however, the matter is made more complex by the possibility that congressional silence can signify consent. That seemed, at least to the dissenter, to be the way the Court construed congressional silence in *Webster v. Doe*.[60] The Court found that Congress had not precluded review of the constitutional validity of a dismissal decision by the Director of the Central Intelligence Agency. Justice Antonin Scalia, dissenting, saw the issue as "whether Congress could constitutionally *permit* the courts to review all such decisions. . . ."[61] This question arises repeatedly: When Congress knows that inaction will have certain foreseeable results, cannot Congress be regarded as having affirmatively *intended* those results?

Congressional will can be implied in a number of ways other than silence, including (1) the enactment of legislation on similar subjects; (2) the creation of a particular legislative history, which might include the remarks of a measure's sponsor upon its introduction, comments in the committee report, or the

---

opined, a matter of supremacy; treaties and other international agreements are supreme with respect to state laws. In United States v. Pink, 315 U.S. 203 (1942), Douglas wrote that the "[p]ower to remove . . . obstacles to full recognition . . . certainly is a modest implied power" of the President who is "the sole organ of the federal government in the field of international relations." 315 U.S. at 229. He continued:

> Effectiveness in handling the delicate problems of foreign relations requires no less. Unless such a power exists, the power of recognition might be thwarted or seriously diluted. No such obstacle can be placed in the way of rehabilitation of relations between this country and another nation, unless the historic conception of the powers and responsibilities of the President in the conduct of foreign affairs . . . is to be drastically revised. . . . Recognition and [the executive agreement] were interdependent. We would usurp the executive function if we held that a decision was not final and conclusive in the courts.

Id. at 229–30.

[60] Webster v. Doe, 108 S. Ct. 2047 (1988). *See also* Petterson v. McClean, 108 S. Ct. 1419 (1988) (ordering reargument whether Runyon v. McCrary, 427 U.S. 160 (1976) should be reconsidered).

[61] *Id*. (Scalia, J., dissenting).

rejection of other measures bearing upon the same subject; and (3) custom, which in certain circumstances can be a source of decisional authority. In *Dames & Moore v. Regan*,[62] for example, the Court found congressional approval implied in statutes on analogous topics. In *Little v. Barreme*,[63] Marshall found congressional disapproval; the statute in question authorized an act different from the act Adams had ordered. In *United States v. Midwest Oil*,[64] a long-standing executive custom, acquiesced in by Congress, supported an inference of congressional approval. And in the *Steel Seizure Case*,[65] Justice Jackson inferred congressional disapproval from a similar statutory scheme, whereas Justice Frankfurter inferred it from the rejection of an amendment that would have authorized the seizure of the steel mills.[66]

Jackson's ''Zone of Twilight''

Finding Congress's implied will is difficult in such circumstances because the sources from which it must be inferred are of indeterminate relative weight and because the logic of some of these inferences is dubious.[67] In some such cases, a more candid assessment of congressional will by the Court would seemingly have led it to conclude that *no* congressional intent existed. If no congressional intent exists, the President's action falls into Jackson's second category.

CONCURRENT POWER

The term *concurrent power* is often used to refer to Jackson's middle tier, the ''zone of twilight.''[68] But this usage is inaccurate, for properly speaking, the concept of concurrent power refers not to the congressional will or lack thereof but to the posture of the Constitution. The Constitution sometimes appears silent with respect to issues of decision-making authority. In such circumstances, concurrent power is said to exist in both political branches. Congress may act, and if it does, the President must comply with its will, since he *ex hypothesi* lacks plenary power. Congress may fail to act, and if it fails, the President may initiate action, subject to congressional countermand.

Thus, concurrent presidential power in a subject area connotes a presidential initiating power. If Congress has enacted no governing statute, the Presi-

[62] 453 U.S. 654 (1981).

[63] 6 U.S. (2 Cranch) 170 (1804).

[64] 236 U.S. 458 (1914).

[65] Youngstown Sheet & Tube Co. v. Sawyer, 343 U.S. 579 (1952).

[66] *See supra* note 39.

[67] In *Steel Seizure*, for example, Jackson seems to reason, ''A, B, or C; therefore not D''; Frankfurter, ''Not A; therefore, B.''

[68] Youngstown Sheet & Tube Co. v. Sawyer, 343 U.S. 579, 637 (1952) (Jackson, J., concurring).

dent can take the lead in implementing a policy, but that policy can later be restricted by Congress. (If Congress cannot restrict it, the President has a plenary power to act.) Acts within this realm of concurrent power can be performed constitutionally by the President, but only so long as Congress fails to act. The President's initiatives here are contingently constitutional; their validity depends upon congressional *inaction*. Dicta in *Little v. Barreme*[69] and the *Steel Seizure Case*[70] imply that presidential action might have been permissible had Congress remained silent. Implied congressional disapproval in those cases, however, placed the question in Justice Jackson's third tier, where the President's powers are weakest.[71] Treaty termination, discussed in Chapter 4, is probably a good example of a concurrent power.

PLENARY CONGRESSIONAL POWER

Some acts cannot be performed by the President constitutionally without prior statutory approval. The President may not initiate policy in such areas in the face of congressional silence. In this category, Congress has exclusive power to act; indeed it might be said that this is a realm of *plenary* congressional power. These cases too are few, the most prominent example perhaps being *Brown v. United States*,[72] in which Chief Justice Marshall found that the President lacked authority to seize enemy property located in the United States in time of war without prior statutory approval.[73]

In this realm of exclusive congressional power, the President confronts a constitutional roadblock. No solely presidential initiative is permitted. The reason, by definition, has nothing to do with the will of Congress; Congress is silent. The reason is that the *Constitution* prohibits the act.

The concept of prohibition is of course fundamental in American constitutionalism. The President is prohibited by the Constitution from doing many things; the Bill of Rights provides a ready list. These are flat *prohibitions*. The Constitution uses negative words to delimit the power of the President (and Congress).

Yet other provisions of the Constitution prohibit governmental action, even though they contain no words of limitation or proscription. In fact, these provisions contain only grants of power. An example is the commerce clause, which provides that "Congress shall have power . . . [t]o regulate commerce with foreign nations, and among the several states. . . ."[74] The commerce clause has been construed as empowering Congress to enact legislation regu-

[69] 6 U.S. (2 Cranch) 170, 177 (1804).

[70] 343 U.S. 579, 585–86 (1952).

[71] *Id*. at 637.

[72] 12 U.S. (8 Cranch) 110 (1814).

[73] *Id*. at 128. This case is discussed in Chapter 7, dealing with international law as part of our law.

[74] U.S. Const. art. I, § 8, cl. 3.

lating activities that affect interstate commerce. But it has also been construed as a limitation; the Court has relied on it repeatedly in striking down state legislation. The commerce clause, it has been said, is a double-edged sword; its very status as a source of authority for Congress makes it a source of *prohibition* for the states. In this latter sense, it is said, the commerce clause has "negative implications"; there is a "dormant" commerce clause.

So too with various foreign-affairs provisions. The declaration-of-war clause[75] and the treaty clause[76] both have "negative implications" and serve as constitutional prohibitions against certain presidential acts without congressional approval. The war clause empowers Congress to declare war. Yet it also serves as a limitation on executive war-making power, placing certain acts off limits for the President. The treaty clause empowers the President, with the advice and consent of the Senate, to make treaties. Yet it also serves as a limitation on the scope of presidential authority to use executive agreements.[77] Even in the "zone of twilight," therefore, the courts have struck down presidential acts as unconstitutional. In *Yoshida International, Inc. v. United States*,[78] for example, President Nixon's executive order imposing a 10 percent surcharge on imports was held invalid on the ground that the imposition of duties represented a tax and a regulation of foreign commerce; only statutory authorization, the district court held, could support such an act.[79]

One might first think that law is absent from this middle tier dominated by "the imperatives of events and contemporary imponderables."[80] That seemed to be Jackson's implication, eschewing as he did the application of "abstract theories of law" in this zone. As the chapters on the war power and treaty power demonstrate, however, the stuff of which the Constitution is made pervades the zone of twilight. There is simply too much material from traditional sources of constitutional authority to throw every issue to the winds of politics. The conclusions one reaches, when supported by constitutional sources, should thus be regarded as *constitutional* conclusions, with all that term implies.

Congressional Approval

The Court prefers to ground the validity of a presidential action upon congressional power rather than presidential power; such resolution avoids thorny and

[75] U.S. Const. art. I, § 8, cl. 11.

[76] *Id.*, art. II, § 2, cl. 2.

[77] *See* Chapter 5.

[78] 378 F. Supp. 1155 (Cust. Ct. 1974), *rev'd*, 526 F.2d 560 (C.C.P.A. 1975).

[79] On appeal, such authorization was found to exist in the Trading with the Enemy Act. *Id.*, 526 F.2d at 579–80.

[80] Youngstown Sheet & Tube Co. v. Sawyer, 343 U.S. 579, 637 (1952) (Jackson, J., concurring).

momentous constitutional questions since no judgment need be made about the distribution of powers between the other two branches. The Court has on occasion thus appeared disingenuous in "finding" congressional approval where none is apparent.[81] *Webster v. Doe*,[82] the *Prize Cases*,[83] *Korematsu v. United States*,[84] and *United States v. Curtiss-Wright Export Corp.*[85] were all decided on the basis of legislative will. Where Congress can be found to have approved, the pain is taken out of constitutional decision making, for the exercise then becomes statutory construction. The best-known foreign-affairs case falling within this category is *United States v. Curtiss-Wright*.[86]

United States v. Curtiss-Wright

That the Supreme Court should have taken this unfortunate case is perhaps attributable to its need to resolve the confusion it had created six months earlier in the two "delegation" cases, *Panama Refining Company v. Ryan*[87] and *United States v. Schecter Poultry Corp.*[88] In these cases the Court invalidated statutory centerpieces of the New Deal because these laws, in conferring standardless discretion on the President, unconstitutionally delegated legislative power to the Executive. As the menace of Hitler loomed, however, concern developed that this new doctrine might straitjacket the United States in dealing with the Nazi threat.

Hence the need to clarify. Absent that need, the facts of *Curtiss-Wright* surely did not cry out for a landmark decision on the President's foreign-affairs powers. Congress had enacted a very ordinary law making certain arms sales illegal upon a finding by the President that a ban on those sales would serve the cause of peace. President Roosevelt made the finding. Curtiss-Wright violated the law, was indicted and convicted, and on appeal challenged the constitutionality of the law on the ground that it violated the six-month-old delegation doctrine. It was no momentous international issue, for the case might easily have been resolved by holding simply that the law did not confer unlimited authority upon the President and then reviewing the real standards set forth in the statute. Nothing Sutherland says in *Curtiss-Wright* indicates that the law did *not* meet delegation standards. But the Court felt the need to clarify, and into its lap fell the perfect opportunity to say, "But we didn't mean that."

And that's what the Court said. The Court wasted no words in dispelling

[81] *See, e.g.*, Haig v. Agee, 453 U.S. 280 (1981) (discussed in Chapter 2).
[82] Webster v. Doe, 108 S. Ct. 2047 (1988).
[83] 67 U.S. (2 Black) 635 (1863).
[84] 323 U.S. 214 (1944).
[85] 299 U.S. 304 (1936).
[86] 299 U.S. 304 (1936).
[87] 293 U.S. 388 (1935).
[88] 295 U.S. 495 (1935).

any notion that its doctrinal creation would present a Frankenstein monster for American diplomacy; the delegation doctrine need be of concern only (or almost only) in the case of prodigal *domestic* authorizations. ''[A]ssuming that the challenged delegation, if it were confined to internal affairs, would be invalid, may it nevertheless be sustained on the ground that its exclusive aim is to afford a remedy for a hurtful condition within foreign territory?''[89] The answer, Sutherland said, is yes: The law was not ''vulnerable to attack under the rule that forbids a delegation of the lawmaking power.''[90] What would be invalid under the delegation doctrine if directed at internal affairs is not necessarily invalid if directed at external affairs.

Precisely *why* this should be so is not clear. It is not clear for policy reasons, Justice Rehnquist later explained;[91] as discussed in Chapter 6, policy reasons seem to militate for, not against, applying the delegation doctrine to foreign-affairs legislation.

''External Sovereignty'' as a Source of Power

Sutherland's central contention is that in foreign affairs, the President exercises powers not set forth in the Constitution. The source of those powers? ''[E]xternal sovereignty.'' ''When . . . the external sovereignty of Great Britain in respect of the colonies ceased, it immediately passed to the Union.''[92] ''As a member of the family of nations,'' Sutherland maintained, the United States assumed all the ''right and power of the other members of the international family. Otherwise, the United States is not completely sovereign.''[93] Thus ''the powers to declare and wage war, to conclude peace, to make treaties, to maintain diplomatic relations with other sovereignties, if they had never been mentioned in the Constitution, would have vested in the federal government as necessary concomitant of nationality.''[94] Winding up, Sutherland throws in the ''sole-organ'' quote from Marshall, with no reference to its limiting context, and follows up with a paragraph quoted from an 1816 Senate Foreign Relations Committee report, to the effect that the ''President is the constitutional representative of the United States with regard to foreign nations.''[95] He then reaches this climax:

> It is important to bear in mind that we are here dealing not alone with an authority vested in the President by an exertion of legislative power, but with such an authority plus the very delicate, plenary and exclusive power of the President

[89] United States v. Curtiss-Wright Export Corp., 299 U.S. 304, 315 (1936).

[90] *Id.*

[91] Industrial Union Dep't v. American Petroleum Ins't, 448 U.S. 607, 685 (1980) (Rehnquist, J., concurring).

[92] *Curtiss-Wright*, 299 U.S. at 317.

[93] *Id.* at 318.

[94] *Id.*

[95] *Id.* at 319.

> as the sole organ of the federal government in the field of international relations—a power which does not require as a basis for its exercise an act of Congress, but which, of course, like every other governmental power, must be exercised in subordination to the applicable provisions of the Constitution.[96]

WHAT "PLENARY" POWERS?

The first thing to be said of this breathtaking exegesis of "plenary powers" is that it is sheer dicta.[97] This is demonstrably not a plenary-powers case. A "plenary presidential power" is one that is not susceptible of congressional limitation. "Plenary power" refers to the power of the President to act *even if Congress prohibits that act*. I gather that this is what Sutherland means by the term.[98] Now, what plenary power did President Roosevelt exercise under the facts of *Curtiss-Wright*? Under no accepted principle of American constitutional jurisprudence could the President promulgate by executive fiat a criminal prohibition and without congressional concurrence, proceed to impose criminal penalties. It is emphatically the task of Congress to legislate[99]—most surely to enact statutes imposing criminal penalties. One wonders what Sutherland has in mind, therefore, when he announces that "we are dealing here" not with statutory power alone but with statutory power "plus the very delicate, plenary and exclusive power of the President"—"a power which does not require as a basis for its exercise an act of Congress. . . ."[100]

[96] *Id.* at 319–20.

[97] The minority report of the congressional committees investigating the Iran-Contra affair strains to establish that Sutherland's plenary-powers analysis is the *holding* of *Curtiss-Wright*:

> The need for legislation before *criminal* sanctions could be imposed for *domestic* activity in turn brought the delegation issue into play. In *Curtiss-Wright*, the court held that solely *because* the President is the sole organ of the country's foreign relations, Congress does not have to spell out the conditions under which a presidential proclamation may invoke criminal sanctions with the same precision as it must to meet constitutional standards in a case of domestic policy. The underlying premises about the President's foreign policy powers thus were essential to the holding in *Curtiss-Wright*. . . .

S. Rept. 100-216 & H. Rept. 100-433, 100th Cong., 1st Sess. 473 (1987) (Iran-Contra affair).

Aside from the elementary error in mistaking *ratio decidendi* for holding, *see* S. Mermin, Law and the Legal System: An Introduction (2d. ed. 1982) 283–91, this argument overlooks the constitutional requirement of a statutory predicate for criminal sanctions. It thus necessarily regards Sutherland's discussion of the *delegation doctrine* as dicta (contrary to Sutherland's own explicit statement, *Curtiss-Wright* at 315), for if the minority is correct in supposing that legislation is not needed before criminal sanctions can be imposed for nondomestic activity, then no discussion of the delegation doctrine is required, since the President could have imposed the sanctions himself. The minority makes no effort to support this startling assertion; as pointed out in the text, no basis exists in American law.

[98] He refers to these powers as "exclusive" and in the next sentence, contends that legislation "within the international field must often accord to the President a degree of discretion and freedom from statutory restriction which would not be admissible were domestic affairs alone involved." *Id.* at 320.

[99] The Steel Seizure Case, 393 U.S. 579, 587–88 (1952).

[100] United States v. Curtiss-Wright Export Corp., 299 U.S. 304, 320 (1936).

Does Sutherland seriously mean to suggest that the President could have imposed criminal penalties on Curtiss-Wright without any statutory "basis"? Can he truly mean that in the absence of any trace of congressional authorization, the Executive could somehow have fined or jailed Curtiss-Wright? Suppose under the facts that Congress had taken a contrary position, that instead of *prohibiting* the arms sales, it had affirmatively *permitted* those sales. If "we are dealing here" with a plenary power, then the conclusion must be that the President could criminalize the arms sales, even over Congress's statutory opposition—an absurd proposition that even Sutherland would presumably reject. Perhaps he meant for this impressionistic essay to be read less rigorously. Perhaps by "here" he does not mean "here in this case," but "here" in these generalized flights of fancy about the manifold delicacies of plenary power. Perhaps. A little precision would have gone a long way. In any event, one is compelled to conclude that the discussion of plenary power has no place in this case since the posture of Congress is support for the President, not opposition.[101] As Justice Jackson noted sixteen years later in the *Steel Seizure Case*, Sutherland's opinion means at most that "the President might act in external affairs without congressional authority, but not that he might act contrary to an Act of Congress."[102] The Sutherland opinion is a rewritten old essay, shoehorned with considerable pinch into the United States Reports.[103]

TWO PROBLEMS: HISTORY AND LOGIC

As to the merits of Sutherland's theory, the history and logic of constitutionalism reject his idea that external, international right is perforce a source of

[101] Oliver North, after introducing *Curtiss-Wright* into his congressional testimony, quickly backed off:

> MR. NORTH [I]n the 1930s in the *U.S. vs. Curtiss-Wright Export Corporation* . . . the Supreme Court again held that it was within the purview of the President of the United States to conduct secret activities and to conduct secret negotiations to further the foreign policy goals of the United States.
>
> MR. MITCHELL If I may just say, Colonel, the *Curtiss-Wright* case said no such thing. It involved public matters that were the subject of a law and a prosecution. . . .
>
> I just think the record should reflect that *Curtiss-Wright* was on a completely different factual situation and there is no such statement in the *Curtiss-Wright* case.
>
> MR. SULLIVAN I disagree with you. I think it is a little unfair . . . to have a debate with Colonel North. . . .

Testimony of Oliver North, 100-7 Iran-Contra Investigation: Joint Hearings Before the House Select Committee to Investigate Covert Arms Transactions with Iran and the Senate Select Committee on Secret Military Assistance to Iran and the Nicaraguan Opposition, 100th Cong., 1st Sess. [part II] 38 (1987).

[102] Youngstown Sheet & Tube Co. v. Sawyer, 343 U.S. 579, 636 n.2 (1952) (Jackson, J., concurring).

[103] G. Sutherland, Constitutional Power and World Affairs (1919); G. Sutherland, The Internal and External Powers of the National Government, Sen. Doc. No. 417, 61st Cong., 2d Sess. (1909).

internal, domestic power. That a nation exercises certain prerogatives under international law logically says nothing about whether under its domestic law the government of that nation is accorded the power to exercise such prerogatives. The history of constitutionalism is largely the history of the *rejection* of such sovereign prerogatives.[104] It is the history of governments' renouncing sovereign prerogatives—often the history of governments' being *forced* to renounce sovereign prerogatives. The United States surely has the right, as a sovereign member of the international community, to impose a steep tax on all tea entering Boston harbor—to impose taxation without representation. That international prerogative can hardly mean, however, that the federal government, let alone the President, has the constitutional authority to do so. It might—he or she might—but the answer depends not upon international law but upon the United States Constitution.

What of the limitations in the Constitution? Sutherland professes to believe that presidential powers deriving from "external sovereignty" must still be exercised "in subordination to the applicable provisions of the Constitution." But it is hard to see why that follows. Indeed, it seems fundamentally inconsistent with his theory. There is no logical reason why a power that flows from a source that transcends the Constitution should be subject to the prohibitions and limitations of the Constitution. Such a power should be immune from mere constitutional limits such as the first amendment, the fourth amendment—or the delegation doctrine.

The delegation doctrine, after all, derives from article I of the Constitution, which confers all legislative power on Congress. This provision is a significant restraint on executive power; the President cannot make laws, and Congress cannot make laws that permit the President to make laws. If the President's powers must be exercised in subordination to article I, the conclusion would seem to be the opposite of Sutherland's—the conclusion would seem to be that the statute in *Curtiss-Wright* must be judged not by a more lenient standard than the one applied to domestic legislation but by the same standard. Otherwise, how can one say that the power is "subordinate" to the applicable provision of the Constitution? Perhaps Sutherland means "subordinate" in a different sense; perhaps presidential power is "subordinate" to constitutional limitations such as article I that shrink in scope in the face of the awesome presidential power at issue. If this is what he meant, is presidential power "subordinate" to the first amendment, the fourth amendment, and all the other protections of civil and political rights set forth in the Constitution in the same contorted way? Some subordination!

Sutherland's sovereignty theory dangerously undermines freedoms safe-

[104] *See generally* C. McIlwain, Constitutionalism, Ancient and Modern 22 (1947) ("[T]he most ancient, the most persistent, and the most lasting of the essentials of true constitutionalism still remains what it has been almost from the beginning, the limitation of government by law").

guarded in the Bill of Rights. In Justice Jackson's memorable characterization of another such decision, *Korematsu v. United States*,[105] the precedent "lies about like a loaded weapon ready for the . . . claim of an urgent need."[106]

Yet, curiously, by extension, that theory might also be seen as applying limitations not set forth in the Constitution. For if *powers* common to all sovereign states under international law become powers of the federal government, should not the *limitations* imposed by sovereignty also apply domestically to the federal government? For example, if sovereign states are precluded by international law from waging aggressive war, imposing capital punishment on minors, or engaging in racial discrimination, should not such prohibitions also be seen as applicable domestically to the exercise of presidential power? If international law permits the United States, as Sutherland suggests, to "expel undesirable aliens,"[107] can it not be regarded as also prohibiting the United States from torturing undesirable aliens or detaining them indefinitely without trial?[108]

Sutherland's view that sovereignty passed from the Crown to the "Union" fails to note that the "Union" was the third governmental entity to appear on the American scene following Britain's departure. First came the colonies, which in many ways related to one another, at least immediately after Yorktown, as independent nations.[109] Then came the Articles of Confederation, our first unsuccessful try at a "Union," unsuccessful in good part because the former colonies refused to cede enough "sovereignty" (if that's the right word) to the central authorities. The most reasonable view would seem to be that even if one accepts the notion of external right as a source of internal power, that power filtered through, or trickled down from, two prior possessors.

What reason is there to believe that that power trickled down only to 1600 Pennsylvania Avenue? Even if the federal government is somehow the beneficiary in powers or rights bestowed by international law, should not Congress be seen as partaking in the exercise of at least *some* of those powers? As Sutherland himself notes, a number of those powers, such as the power to declare war, are expressly conferred by the Constitution not on the Executive but on Congress. Did not the Framers have the right to allocate powers as they wished?

It does not do to say that such powers devolved upon the Executive because

[105] 323 U.S. 214 (1944).

[106] *Id.* at 246.

[107] *Curtiss-Wright*, 299 U.S. at 318.

[108] In the earlier essay on which his *Curtiss-Wright* opinion is based, Sutherland implies that "fundamental principles of the law of nations" may place restraints upon the treaty power. G. Sutherland, Constitutional Powers and World Affairs 141 (1919).

[109] *See* Levitan, *The Foreign Relations Power: An Analysis of Mr. Sutherland's Theory*, 55 Yale L.J. 467 (1946).

the Executive is the United States' representative to the community of nations. Aside from blatantly begging the question, the argument mistakes policy *communication* with policy *formulation*. Few would now quarrel with Sutherland's assertion that ''the President alone has the power to speak or listen as a representative of the nation.'' But the power to speak *what*? The power to say that the United States will coin a new ten-dollar gold piece to relieve pressure on the dollar? The power to say that in the interest of hemispheric stability, the United States will reimburse the Bank of America for bad loans made to developing nations? The power to declare war against Nicaragua? Of course not: These powers, and many others, are allocated by the Constitution, and policies concerning such matters must be made as prescribed by the Constitution. Some of those policies may be made by the President alone; others require that he seek congressional authorization. But his power to act as the ''sole organ'' or ''representative of the United States'' in communicating those powers to foreign countries hardly implies that he alone may formulate those policies. That is what the Foreign Relations Committee was referring to in 1816—the President's sole power to *communicate*, not the power to do *its* job or that of the Senate or Congress. And that is why in 1981, the D.C. Circuit rejected a broad reading of *Curtiss-Wright*: ''To the extent that denominating the President as the 'sole organ' of the United States in international affairs constitutes a blanket endorsement of plenary Presidential power over any matter extending beyond the borders of our country, we reject that characterization.''[110] ''Clearly, what Marshall had foremost in mind was simply the President's role as instrument of communication with other governments,'' Corwin concluded.[111]

EXECUTIVE EMBARRASSMENT

Sutherland argues for broad foreign-affairs power for the President as a means of avoiding international embarrassment. ''[E]mbarrassment—perhaps serious embarrassment—is to be avoided'' in the maintenance of our international relations by according the President ''a degree of discretion and freedom from statutory restriction which would not be admissable were domestic affairs alone involved.''[112]

It is doubtless correct that law violation by the Executive might result in embarrassment. But again, it is useful to be more specific. Embarrassment might result in two situations. First, the President might begin an international initiative in accordance with the congressional will, only to have Congress change its mind after that policy had been undertaken, making illegal what

[110] American Intern. Group v. Islamic Republic of Iran, 657 F.2d 430, 438 n.6 (D.C. Cir. 1981).

[111] E. Corwin, The President: Office and Powers 1787–1957, at 178 (1957).

[112] United States v. Curtiss-Wright Export Corp., 299 U.S. 304, 320 (1936).

had earlier been legal. Second, the President might begin an initiative in the face of a statutory prohibition—acting illegally at the outset.

The two situations are alike in that in both the President would be "embarrassed" only if Congress or the courts were to call upon him to stop. But the situations are different in an important respect: In the first instance, a policy initiative is lawfully under way when Congress "pulls the rug;" in the latter, the President undertakes the policy, knowing at the outset that it violates the law Congress enacted.

The most recent example that comes to mind in thinking of the first situation, "rug pulling," is support for the Contras. Congress permitted lethal aid in 1982, prohibited it in 1984, and permitted it in 1986. Another recent example is the 1973 phased congressional termination of the Vietnam War, which Congress had initially authorized, at least in part, in the 1965 Gulf of Tonkin Resolution.

Now, as a matter of *policy*—not constitutional law, but *policy*—these congressional changes of mind may be unwise. It may appear to the world community that the United States is irresolute, divided, undependable. Precisely these concerns animated the Executive to continue to prosecute the war into the 1970s.[113] On the other hand, the statutory fluctuations may be seen as reasoned responses to changed circumstances—changes in our ability to win within reasonable cost expenditures, changes in the assessment of our clients or their opponents, changes in the willingness to negotiate on the part of either, changes in the posture of our allies, the World Court, or the American people, who may, on reflection, regard as a blunder what appeared an epiphany.

Whether the congressionally mandated policy changes are wise, however, says nothing about the constitutionality of those changes. Nothing in the Constitution prohibited Congress from deciding to support the Contras following nonsupport. Nothing in the Constitution prohibited Congress from deciding not to support the government of South Vietnam following support. Embarrassment is one factor to be taken into account in deciding whether to change the policy. At one point or another, virtually every policy is changed, and embarrassment is sometimes a cost of that change. But the benefits may outweigh the costs, and there is nothing in the Constitution that locks the United States into a given policy merely to avoid embarrassment.

Similarly, where the President undertakes a policy against the will of Congress, it may be embarrassing if the President is called to task for it. Such a situation apparently obtained regarding arms sales to Iran, a statutorily designated "terrorist" state. But embarrassing to whom? Embarrassing to Congress? Congress enacted the arms-sale ban knowing the political consequences of its violation. Embarrassing to the courts? Chief Justice Marshall didn't

[113] The Pentagon Papers 491–92 (N. Sheehan ed. 1971).

seem terribly embarrassed in *Little v. Barreme*,[114] which involved precisely this situation—a President undertook a policy at odds at the outset with an act of Congress. There was no handwringing, no knucklecracking[115] from John Marshall when he was called upon to enforce the law. The embarrassment is the President's, and it comes from being seen for what he is—a law violator.

Should the President escape embarrassment for violating the law? In international law, as well in these frequently nonjusticiable stretches of constitutional terrain, embarrassment is the principal and sometimes the only sanction that the law can impose. It is the central means of maintaining the integrity of the legal system. A President who violates the law *should* be embarrassed. If the embarrassment affects the ''maintenance of our international relations,'' the Constitution is operating as it should.

Some might complain that embarrassment will ''cripple'' the President. But as Arthur Schlesinger says, ''When an Administration's foreign policy is incoherent, duplicitous and dedicated to rash and mindless policies, what indeed is so awful about a crippled Presidency? Surely a crippled Presidency is far better for the nation and for the world than an unchastened and unrepentant one.''[116] Moreover, he points out,

> the crippling of a President who does foolish or criminal things [does not] mean a crippling of the Presidential office. The reaction against Watergate did not prevent Reagan from having a relatively successful first term, nor would it have handicapped Ford and Carter had they been more competent in the job.[117]

For these reasons, Sutherland's ''external sovereignty'' provides little to commend it as a source of power on which a president might rely. A more compelling source of authority for identifying presidential power in foreign affairs is the United States Constitution. This, presumably, is why Justice Black, in *Steel Seizure* only sixteen years after *Curtiss-Wright*, began his analysis with the observation that ''[t]he President's power, if any, to issue the order must stem either from an act of Congress or from the Constitution itself.''[118] No mention of ''external sovereignty,'' no discussion of ''delicate, plenary powers''—nothing else. It would be hard to imagine a more purpose-

[114] 6 U.S. (2 Cranch) 170, 179 (1804).

[115] *Compare* the comments of the federal district court that dismissed the action of shipowners for damage to their vessel caused by the illegal mining of Nicaragua's harbors:

> As the news articles . . . point out, the White House, the CIA and the State Department all publicly denied that the Government was directly involved in the mining. An inquiry by this Court into these matters, which might result in proving that the prior declarations were erroneous, could indeed be embarrassing to the Government.

Chaser Shipping Corp. v. United States, 649 F. Supp. 736 (S.D.N.Y. 1986).

[116] A. Schlesinger, ''Why Not Question the Presidency?'' N.Y. Times, Jan. 2, 1987, at 25.

[117] Schlesinger, *The Constitution and Presidential Leadership*, 47 Md. L. Rev. 54, 69 (1987).

[118] The Steel Seizure Case, 393 U.S. 579, 585 (1952).

ful repudiation of Sutherland's theory of external sovereignty as a source of constitutional power.

A Tilting Functional Analysis

Sutherland considers the comparative institutional attributes of the presidency: "[H]e, not Congress, has the better opportunity of knowing the conditions which prevail in foreign countries. He has his confidential sources of information. He has his agents in the form of diplomatic, consular and other officials. Secrecy in respect of information gathered by them may be highly necessary, and the premature disclosure of it productive of harmful results."[119]

THE CASE FOR THE PRESIDENCY

The Presidency indeed holds advantages in navigating the shoals of diplomacy. Sutherland alludes to two—intelligence sources and secrecy. He might have added the remaining ones on Hamilton's famous list: unity, dispatch, and decision.[120] Foreign-policy practitioners and political scientists have identified other positive attributes: leadership, energy, and command of the bureaucracy.

No one can dispute that "confidential sources of information" pose a tremendous advantage in a wide gamut of diplomatic activities, ranging from treaty making and negotiations to covert action and war. But why are these "his" sources? Why are they "his" agents? The officers of the Central Intelligence Agency, the National Security Agency, the Defense Intelligence Agency, and other entities of the "community" are employees of the *government of the United States*, not the personal minions of the individual in the Oval Office. They are paid by the United States Treasury. Their "take" is the property of the United States government, not of the President. It begs the question to assert, as Sutherland does, that only the President has access to their work product. It would be peculiar indeed if Congress should be entrusted with the constitutional responsibility of *making* laws yet be constitutionally *denied* the information indispensable for determining the need for legislation.[121] Congressional committees normally have a claim to intelligence information at least as forceful as their policy-making counterparts in the Executive.

Sutherland's cursory discussion of the advantages of executive secrecy is similarly question begging. It assumes that the Executive, but not Congress, can be trusted with classified intelligence. To this day, no one has established

[119] United States v. Curtiss-Wright Export Corp., 299 U.S. 304, 320 (1936).

[120] The Federalist No. 75 (A. Hamilton).

[121] As Dean Landis put it, "To deny Congress power to acquaint itself with facts is equivalent to requiring it to prescribe remedies in darkness." Landis, *Constitutional Limitations on the Congressional Power of Investigation*, 40 Harv. L. Rev. 153, 209 (1926).

a greater likelihood of ''leaks'' by Congress than by the Executive. In some instances, the demands of secrecy may suggest the propriety of restricting the dissemination of certain information to senior executive officials, although it is hard to imagine why the leaders of the House and Senate are less to be trusted. But these instances are few[122] and hardly form sufficient bedrock for the major reallocation of constitutional powers that Sutherland desires.

A stronger case for presidential primacy, it would seem, can be made from institutional attributes that Sutherland overlooks. Only one individual need act for the Executive—the President. Obviously a majority of a quorum of the two houses of Congress—some 139 individuals—cannot form a consensus so quickly. In a crisis requiring prompt action, there is no gainsaying that the difference could be critical. Also, the internal organization of the Executive is hierarchical and centralized;[123] the Congress is collegial and sequential.[124] This form of organization allows the President to exercise power with unity and dispatch. It also can allow the incorporation of eclectic components of a ''chessboard'' view of the world or what President Nixon in 1970 called the ''interrelationship of international events.''[125] Where there is no time for Congress to act and the stakes are critical, the case for presidential power is compelling.

The President is expected to lead, especially in foreign affairs.[126] Although he can face the electorate only twice, he is the only person elected by and accountable to the entire nation.[127] James Madison favored infrequent presidential elections in order to foster veneration for the government as personified by the President.[128] Yet the President was intended to be responsive to more than the popular will.[129] The President is also listened to and held accountable by foreign chief executives. Thus he may sometimes be more circumspect about the repercussions of his statements.[130]

Energy is a special quality of the President.[131] A report of the National Academy of Public Administration states that ''[t]he prestige of the Presidency is a powerful magnet, constantly attracting proposals. . . .''[132] These

[122] *See* Chapter 2.

[123] *See* J. Sundquist, The Decline and Resurgence of Congress (1981).

[124] *See* Hammond, *Congress in Foreign Policy*, in E. Muskie, K. Rush & K. Thompson, eds., The President, the Congress and Foreign Policy, 75 (1986).

[125] *See* J. Sundquist, *supra* note 123, at 305.

[126] *See* L. Berman, The New American Presidency, 10–11 (1987).

[127] *See* Tulis, *The Two Constitutional Presidencies*, in The Presidency and the Political System. 78 (M. Nelson, 1984).

[128] *Id.* at 65.

[129] *Id.* at 67.

[130] *See* Newsom, *The Executive Branch in Foreign Policy*, in The President, the Congress and Foreign Policy, *supra* note 124, at 104–5 (1986). See also J. Sundquist, *supra* note 123, at 109.

[131] *See* Tulis, *supra* note 127, at 69.

[132] L. Berman, *supra* note 126, at 110–11.

and other factors have lead Professor Arthus Maass to conclude that the President is and should be the primary initiator of legislation.[133] Many presidents have maintained that the field of foreign relations ought be largely free of legislation.[134]

Finally, the President has a massive professional bureaucracy. This factor is key in explaining executive leadership in the legislative process.[135] The President has ready access to the bureaucracy's vast information banks and professional expertise. The bureaucracy also gives the President unequalled geographical reach. Its internal hierarchy and continuity are useful in foreign-policy formation and execution.[136]

Yet with all these institutional advantages, the President is still not immune to foreign-policy blunders. The attributes that benefit the Executive may also work to its detriment. The vaunted bureaucracy may well create more problems than solutions. Agency competition thwarts policy coordination.[137] An agency may have its own agenda, the President's popular mandate notwithstanding.[138] On the other hand, the President may assume too much power from an electoral majority. One of the greatest fears of the Framers was executive demagoguery.[139] These fears, happily, have not often been realized, though President Reagan's manipulation of popular prejudice and public emotion muted criticism of his Libyan bombing raid and invasion of Grenada. A president, as a native of the political culture, may feel pressure to act, even where delay may be propitious.[140] This pressure can be imperceptible, especially if the President's foreign-policy advisors take on the trappings of what Senator Edmund Muskie called, while arguing in favor of the War Powers Resolution, a "royal court."[141] The Bay of Pigs and Cambodia adventures make it clear that such a coterie is highly vulnerable to "group think."[142]

A president may ignore the bureaucracy's professional expertise.[143] In foreign policy particularly, presidents have become disillusioned with the performance of the Departments of State and Defense and the CIA. Unfortunately,

[133] A. Maass, Congress and the Common Good, 13 (1983).

[134] J. Sundquist, *supra* note 123, at 96. On signing a resolution imposing a mandatory arms embargo on both Italy and Ethiopia in 1935, Franklin D. Roosevelt warned, "History is filled with unforeseeable situations that call for some flexibility of action. It is conceivable that situations may arise in which the wholly inflexible provisions of [this resolution] might have exactly the opposite effect from that which was intended." *Id.* at 96–97.

[135] *Id.* at 10.

[136] Nelson & Tillman, *The Presidency, the Bureaucracy and Foreign Policy: Lessons from Cambodia*, in The Presidency and the Political System, *supra* note 127, at 496 (1984).

[137] Newsom, *supra* note 130, at 109.

[138] Nelson & Tillman, *supra* note 136, at 498.

[139] *See* Tulis, *supra* note 127, at 61, 79.

[140] *See* Newsom, *supra* note 130, at 95.

[141] J. Sundquist, *supra* note 123, at 255.

[142] Nelson & Tillman, *supra* note 136, at 498–516.

[143] Newsom, *supra* note 130, at 109.

presidents who do not try to sidestep the bureaucracy are vulnerable to cabinet secretaries co-opted by the bureaucracy's attitudes.[144] As a result, administrations since 1960 have generally increased the power and influence of the White House–based National Security Council (NSC) at the expense of cabinet bureaucracies.[145] This trend reached its apogee in the second term of the Reagan Administration, when the NSC moved into intelligence gathering and analysis as well as foreign-policy formulation and execution. It was possible for a National Security Advisor to plan and carry out major foreign-policy initiatives without the knowledge of members of the cabinet or even the President.

THE CASE FOR CONGRESS

Sutherland completely ignores the functional attributes that commend Congress as a foreign-policy decision maker. True, Congress, especially in foreign affairs, has been primarily a reactive institution.[146] As Professor James Sundquist has written, "Congress can act negatively, to disrupt the policy the President pursues, but it cannot act affirmatively to carry out a comprehensive substitute policy of its own, even if through structural reform it could develop the capacity to create it."[147] Institutional characteristics of Congress account for its reactive posture. Congressional committee debates are not always useful in creating foreign policy. Considerations of personality and turf may supplant issues of policy and diplomacy. While a professor, Woodrow Wilson said that committee debates "represent a joust between antagonistic interests, not competing principles."[148] Also, Congress has not fared well in dealing with complex foreign-relations matters, such as international trade or Soviet emigration.[149] And even if the institution could be perfectly reformed, constituents still expect the first priority of Congress to be local issues, not foreign policy.[150]

In Wilson's era and beyond, Congress was controlled tightly by various committee bosses. Reforms of the 1970s have broken centralized boss power,[151] but now Congress often appears to lack coordination and direction. Many committees have overlapping jurisdictions: at least twenty-five committees from both houses deal with foreign policy.[152] Because of the decline in the seniority system, the rise in open committees and voting, and increased

[144] *Id.* at 97.

[145] *Id.* at 106–7; *see also* Nelson & Tillman, *supra* note 136, at 498.

[146] Hammond, *supra* note 124, at 75, 90.

[147] J. Sundquist, *supra* note 123, at 306.

[148] Tulis, *supra* note 127, at 77.

[149] J. Sundquist, *supra* note 123, at 100, 280–81.

[150] Nelson & Tillman, *supra* note 136, at 496.

[151] Ornstein, *The Constitution and Sharing of Foreign Policy Responsibility*, in The President, the Congress and Foreign Policy, *supra* note 124, at 53–58.

[152] Hammond, *supra* note 124, at 77.

national-media presence on Capitol Hill, junior legislators have discovered that the way to get along often is not to go along but to buck the system.[153]

Or to jump on an interest-group bandwagon. Opening committee hearings, votes, and markups has brought a dramatic increase in foreign-affairs lobbying by ethnic groups, foreign governments, and commercial organizations.[154] Sundquist attributes the congressional cutoff of Turkish military aid more to the intense lobbying of Americans of Greek descent than any other factor.[155] Non-committee members can offer floor amendments and build ad hoc coalitions.[156] This makes majority-building efforts of the President increasingly difficult.[157]

Yet Congress also has vital functional attributes that commend it as a foreign-policy decision maker. Congress is particularly expert at consensus building. Congress is the focal point for the expression and organization of public opinion.[158] Thus could Vice President Hubert Humphrey state that legislation "reflects the collective judgment of a diverse people."[159] Congress's response to presidential initiatives can reflect public opinion through a variety of means—criticism, amendment, approval or rejection, and oversight.[160] Each legislator has a unique constituency, and Congress as a body seems to serve a different public than the President's.[161] As a result, Congress has a capacity for change, a capacity to reflect changing public values.[162] Deputy assistant secretaries of state do not fly back to Minneapolis, Little Rock, and San Francisco on Thursday afternoon to attend a beanfeed—and get an earful of complaints about United States policy toward the Philippines, Israel, or Nicaragua. Members of Congress do.

Some critics of congressional involvement see this as a drawback; apparently, foreign policy ought to reflect what is in the nation's long-term interest, not what is currently popular. There is some truth to the argument. Although most of the public at first supported the war in Vietnam, few today would

[153] Freshman Senators Zorinsky and DeConcini received tremendous national media—and presidential—attention for their opposition to the Panama Canal Treaty. Ornstein, *supra* note 151, at 58–59.

[154] *Id.* at 59.

[155] J. Sundquist, *supra* note 123, at 284–85. One congressman explained his vote for the embargo this way: "There are more Greek restaurants in my district than Turkish baths." *Id.* at 285 n.37.

[156] Hammond, *supra* note 124, at 75, 82.

[157] Before the Panama Canal Treaty was signed, executive officials consulted personally with at least seventy senators. In the end, Senate consent to ratification was achieved with a one-vote margin. J. Sundquist, *supra* note 123, at 301.

[158] A. Maass, *supra* note 133, at 11.

[159] *Id.*

[160] *Id.* Congress's first oversight investigation involved a failure of President Washington's military policy toward Indian nations. *See* Hammond, *supra* note 124, at 72.

[161] A. Maass, *supra* note 133, at 12.

[162] *Id.* at 12.

argue that it was in the nation's long-term interest to pursue that war. In general, a policy cannot be sustained for any significant period without broad public support; that surely is the larger moral of Vietnam. And if a policy can't be sold to Congress, the odds are that it can't be sold to the public.

The other advantage Congress brings to foreign-policy-making is diversity of views. Executive officials normally are chosen for their support of the administration's policies. "No" men are generally former administration officials. In Congress, the reverse is usually true. While on occasion significant pressure can be brought to bear on a legislator to toe the party line, often criticism rather than support brings more public attention—something to which most on Capitol Hill are not averse. But it would be unfair to suggest that headline hunting is the primary motive of congressional participants in the process. Many have strongly held views on a variety of foreign-policy issues, and anyone attending a typical hearing of the House Foreign Affairs Committee or the Senate Foreign Relations Committee would likely be struck by how much those views differ from member to member.

Diversity of viewpoint in foreign-policy decision making is useful for two reasons. First, as an end in itself, it gives the public a sense that its viewpoint has been heard and considered. Diversity is thus crucial for legitimacy. Congress was designed for deliberation. Deliberation lends legitimacy to governmental acts by building records of policy formation.[163] This policy process brings new ideas to government. Nongovernmental witnesses are regularly consulted to evaluate foreign-policy initiatives.[164] The process benefits if the process is seen as "regular," as producing decisions as a matter of right. When the spread of opinion voiced in the decision-making process is seen as overly narrow, its legitimacy suffers. That perhaps is why the Supreme Court has emphasized the importance of free and open debate to the proper operation of separated powers:

> That this system of division and separation of powers produces conflicts, confusion, and discordance at times is inherent, but it was deliberately so structured to assure full, vigorous and open debate on the great issues affecting the people and to provide avenues for the operation of checks on the exercise of governmental power.[165]

The Reagan Administration's diversion of funds from Iranian arms sales to support the Contras demonstrates the dangers of closing the doors and turning off the microphones. An executive decision-making process removed from the full panoply of public or at least congressional opinion easily falls prey to the

[163] *See* Hammond, *supra* note 124, at 84.
[164] A. Maass, *supra* note 133, at 40.
[165] Bowsher v. Synar, 106 S. Ct. 3181, 3187 (1986).

peculiar distortions of groupthink, to the pressures that cause the myopia of the quick fix to be mistaken for the insight of statesmanship.

Second, diversity of viewpoint is useful as a means—a means of avoiding error and a means of achieving consensus. The greater the number of viewpoints heard, the greater the likelihood that the resulting policy will reflect accurately the common interests of the whole. This is even truer as Congress has improved its ability to contribute to foreign-policy proposals. The quality of committee questioning and reporting seems generally to have improved with the growth of committee staff in size and expertise.[166] Overseas congressional travel has also increased. These trips can be an important factor in achieving Executive-Legislative cooperation in foreign policy.[167]

Conclusion

Curtiss-Wright presents questions that, in international law, fall under the topic "doctrine of sources," the body of law that tells us what we may properly rely upon to identify rules of law. To what extent is it permissible to refer to "external sovereignty" to answer questions of constitutional power? To what extent are the comparative advantages and disadvantages of the two political branches actually relevant to their foreign-policy-making authority?

In thinking about what the proper sources are and how they should be weighted, international law is instructive. For it has something that American constitutional jurisprudence lacks: an articulated "rule of recognition" that explicitly identifies sources of law.

The idea of a "rule of recognition" comes from H.L.A. Hart. It is a rule that allows us to recognize other rules; a rule that sets out criteria that tell us whether another rule is a valid, effective rule of the system; a rule to which other rules owe their status as "law."[168] No such rule is set forth in the text of the United States Constitution—which is why a vigorous debate could have occurred recently concerning the Framers' intent in constitutional interpretation; the Framers didn't tell us, at least not expressly.[169] In international law, on the other hand, such a rule is spelled out.[170] The Statute of the International Court of Justice,[171] which "forms an integral part of the [United Nations] Charter,"[172] specifies that in deciding disputes, the International Court of Justice shall apply "international conventions"; "international custom, as ev-

[166] In 1983 over 450 foreign-policy experts were employed by the Congress. *See* Hammond, *supra* note 124, at 78.

[167] *Id.* at 83.

[168] H. Hart, The Concept of Law 100 (1961).

[169] *See generally* Greenawalt, *The Rule of Recognition and the Constitution*, 85 Mich. L. Rev. 621 (1987).

[170] *See* Restatement, § 102.

[171] 59 Stat. 1055 (1945), TS No. 993.

[172] 59 Stat. 1031, TS No. 993 (1945).

idence of a general practice accepted as law''; ''the general principles of law recognized by civilized nations''; and ''judicial decisions and the teachings of the most highly qualified publicists,'' although this latter source is described as ''subsidiary.''[173] One might hypothesize analogues in United States constitutional interpretation. The text of the Constitution, for example, occupies roughly the place of conventional law in the international schemata (at least certain treaties, such as the United Nations Charter).[174] Although no official status has ever been accorded to the views of commentators, law-review articles by ''highly qualified publicists'' are in fact cited with increasing frequency by the Supreme Court.

American constitutional jurisprudence may in a sense lag behind international law in its failure to articulate a rule of recognition. But it does offer a rich platter of doctrines aimed at letting us know which candidates for rulehood qualify. In the realm of Legislative-Executive disputes about foreign relations and other matters, the salient doctrine is that pertinent to the separation of powers. It is to this doctrine that we now turn.

[173] Art. 38(1), Statute of the International Court of Justice, 59 Stat. 1055 (1945), TS No. 993.
[174] 59 Stat. 1031, TS No. 993 (1945).

Chapter Two

THE SEPARATION-OF-POWERS DOCTRINE IN FOREIGN-AFFAIRS DISPUTES

> [T]he provisions of the Constitution are not mathematical formulas having their essence in their form; they are organic, living institutions transplanted from English soil. Their significance is vital not formal; it is to be gathered not simply by taking the words and a dictionary, but by considering their origin and line of growth.
>
> —Justice Oliver Wendell Holmes[1]

THROUGHOUT A LONG AND HEATED HISTORY of resolving disputes between the political branches of our federal government, the Supreme Court has faced the most momentous of constitutional issues: war and peace, international commitment, recognition and derecognition of foreign governments, appointment and removal of federal officials, and legislative review of executive activities. When the Court has confronted these issues, it has often had to address a difficult threshold question: To what source of authority may it properly refer? What weight should be accorded to historical precedent? What difference does it make that United States presidents have introduced the armed forces into hostilities 125 times without congressional authorization,[2] or that they have entered into thousands of executive agreements?[3] Or (the problem can run in both directions) should it matter that Congress has enacted over two hundred "legislative vetoes,"[4] or that presidents have almost never, acting alone, introduced the United States armed forces into large-scale hostilities,[5] or that executive agreements have not been used for mutual-security undertakings?[6] Similarly, what weight should be accorded the Framers' intent? And what about the policy or "functional" considerations discussed in the last chapter?

Despite the frequency and import of separation cases, the Court has failed

[1] Gompers v. United States, 232 U.S. 604, 610 (1914).

[2] Office of the Legal Adviser, U.S. Dep't of State, *The Legality of the United States Participation in the Defense of Vietnam*, 75 Yale L.J. 1085, 1101 (1966).

[3] Rehm, *Making Foreign Policy Through International Agreement*, in The Constitution and the Conduct of Foreign Policy 127 (1976).

[4] Immigration and Naturalization Service v. Chadha, 462 U.S. 919 (1983).

[5] *See generally* F. Wormuth, The Vietnam War: The President Versus the Constitution (1968).

[6] *See generally* Chapter 5.

to articulate a consistent theoretical framework for determining the significance of these sources. In some cases, such as *Dames & Moore v. Regan*[7] and *Haig v. Agee*,[8] the Court has relied heavily upon custom, apparently viewing it as determinative. In other cases, such as *Nixon v. Administrator of General Services*[9] and *INS v. Chadha*,[10] custom has been virtually ignored. The Court's references in these cases to the separation-of-powers doctrine—a nebulous concept finding no express articulation in the constitutional text—seem to reduce it to a concept consisting of aggregated historical precedent more than articulated constitutional principle.

A separation-of-powers doctrine of independent vitality must apply a prescriptive norm different from the rule or rules that might be drawn from other jurisprudential approaches necessarily subsumed within it; it must direct an outcome that would not otherwise obtain. In this sense, separation of powers is not a distinct analytical doctrine.[11] The cases that the Supreme Court has purportedly resolved by relying on the doctrine have in fact been decided by referring to other traditional sources of decisional authority directly relevant to the specific matter in dispute: the constitutional text, constitutional custom, the intent of the Framers, and functional considerations. The essential task for the Court in separation-of-powers disputes has thus been to discover which of these sources will be determinative.

The Separation-of-Powers Doctrine: A Constitutional Oakland?

The separation-of-powers doctrine may be the constitutional analogue of Oakland, California: "There's no there there."[12] Professor Kurland has pointed out that the Framers declined to adopt the "strict" model of separation advanced by Montesquieu, opting instead for a less rigorous division incorporating notions of "checks and balances"—suggesting "the joinder, not separation, of two or more governmental agencies before action could be validated—or the oversight of one by another."[13] Justice Frankfurter put it well:

[7] 453 U.S. 654 (1981).

[8] 453 U.S. 280 (1981).

[9] 433 U.S. 425 (1977).

[10] 462 U.S. 919 (1983).

[11] As Professor Philip Kurland has noted, "At the beginning . . . it was clear that the doctrine of separation of powers was not a rule of decision. The inefficacy of resorting to a general notion of separation of power to resolve contests between the branches of government has long since been demonstrated by our history." *The Rise and Fall of the 'Doctrine' of Separation of Powers*, 85 Mich. L. Rev. 592, 603 (1986) (hereinafter "Kurland").

[12] N.Y. Times, May 9, 1983, at A10, col. 1 (attributed to Gertrude Stein).

[13] Kurland, *supra* note 11, at 593.

> On the whole, "separation of powers" has been treated by the Supreme Court not as a technical legal doctrine. Again barring some recent decisions, the Court has refused to draw abstract analytical lines of separation and has recognized necessary areas of interaction among the departments of government. Functions have been allowed to courts as to which Congress itself might have legislated; matters have been withdrawn from courts and vested in the executive; laws have been sustained which are contingent upon executive judgment on highly complicated facts. . . . Enforcement of a rigid conception of separation of powers would make modern government impossible.[14]

This haziness in the doctrine's application should come as no surprise; even at the outset, the doctrine was recognized as one that provided not three glaring beacons to guide wayward constitutionalists but something more in the nature of three flickering candles.[15] Madison had little hope that the truistic notion of separated powers would provide much practical guidance. "[N]o skill in the science of Government has yet been able to discriminate and define, with sufficient certainty, its three great provinces, the Legislative, Executive, and Judiciary. . . . [O]bscurity reigns in these subjects, and [they] puzzle the greatest adepts in political science."[16]

The Court has often referred to the doctrine as the juridical principle on which a decision is based.[17] And it has attempted to spell out a more precise test for determining whether a statute violates the doctrine. In *Nixon v. Administrator of General Services*, upholding legislation that controlled presidential papers after resignation, the Court focused on "the extent to which [a provision of law] prevents the Executive branch from accomplishing its constitutionally assigned functions."[18] The same standard was applied in *Morrison v. Olson*,[19] where the Court upheld the validity of the independent-counsel statute, and in *Mistretta v. United States*,[20] where the Court upheld the validity of the Sentencing Reform Act. However praiseworthy the Court's effort to sharpen separation inquiries, it takes little insight to realize that this test is of

[14] F. Frankfurter, The Public and Its Government 78 (1930).

[15] Reviewing the origins of the doctrine, Professor Philip Kurland has shown that those who first ran our government seemingly expected nothing more:

> When we turn from the framing and the attitudes of the Framers to the early execution of the Constitution by the first Congresses, the first President, and the first Supreme Courts, it quickly becomes evident that the doctrine of separation of powers as a practical guide to the division of power was not to be determined by reasoning from principle to application. Rather, like the common law, and constitutional law as a whole, the principle tends to be derived from the actions—sometimes contradictory—that are seen to have invoked this constitutional doctrine.

Kurland, *supra* note 11, at 601.

[16] The Federalist No. 37 (J. Madison).

[17] *See, e.g., Nixon*, 433 U.S. at 441.

[18] 433 U.S. 425, 443 (1977).

[19] 108 S. Ct. 2597, 2616 (1988).

[20] 109 S. Ct. 647 (1989).

little help. For whether a law "impermissibly interferes with the exercise of the President's constitutionally appointed functions"[21] is hardly self-evident; recourse to some further source is needed to identify *what* those functions are and whether the degree of interference is impermissible. The "test," such as it is, represents more a conclusional label than a normative standard. And an examination of its decisions indicates that the Court has relied ultimately not upon the application of any such test but upon the same jurisprudential sources ordinarily used to resolve other constitutional controversies. These are the constitutional text, custom, the intent of the Framers, and on rare occasions, functional considerations. Most often, the Court applies a combination of the four approaches.

A survey of separation cases reveals no discernible system for deciding which of these sources of authority should be regarded as controlling. Most of these cases do not involve claims of plenary power by the Executive, and few involve foreign relations; they do, however, shed light on the allocation of power generally between the political branches and thus inform any effort to devise a methodology for allocating power in foreign affairs.

Reliance upon the Constitutional Text

The Court on occasion disposes of a case simply by categorizing the challenged activity as legislative, executive, or judicial, and assigning the activity accordingly. Few cases lend themselves to this treatment, probably because a controversy will reach the Court only if there is room for reasonable dispute and because there can be no dispute if the Constitution has explicitly allocated the activity.[22] *Springer v. Philippine Islands*[23] is illustrative, involving a challenge to the validity of several acts of the Philippine legislature when the Philippines was a United States territory. The legislature had divested the Governor-General of his authority to appoint the directors and officers of several government-owned corporations and placed that function instead in the hands of the legislature.[24] The acts were challenged as conflicting with the Organic Act,[25] the fundamental law governing the Philippine Islands. The Court found that the Organic Act was the functional equivalent of a state constitution, containing the same if not stricter separation principles as those set forth in the United States Constitution.[26] The Court declared that the appointment of business managers or of any other agents charged with carrying out the law was an inherently executive function; it thus held that the assignment of that func-

[21] Morrison v. Olson, 108 S. Ct. 2597, 2616 (1988).

[22] An explicit allocation in the Constitution has the same degree of specificity as an express prohibition: No rational basis exists for any meaning but one.

[23] 277 U.S. 189 (1928).

[24] *Id.* at 198–200.

[25] Organic Act, ch. 416, 39 Stat. 545 (formerly codified at 48 U.S.C. §§ 1001 *et seq.*).

[26] 277 U.S. at 200–201.

tion to the legislative branch was invalid.[27] Similarly, as discussed in Chapter 1, the Court held in the *Steel Seizure Case*[28] that President Truman could not order the Secretary of Commerce to seize the nation's steel mills because the order had a predominantly legislative character.[29] The Court based its conclusion squarely on the text of the Constitution, which specifies that legislative powers shall vest in Congress;[30] except for a limited authority to recommend and veto legislation, the Court found that the Constitution restricts the President's power to the faithful execution of the law.[31]

Reliance upon the Framers' Intent

When the constitutional text is not dispositive, the Court frequently turns to other sources of authority, including the Framers' intent. In *Myers v. United States*,[32] for example, the issue was whether a president could remove a postmaster without the consent of the Senate when Senate concurrence was required by law. The Court found that no express provision in the constitutional text addressed the issue[33] but nonetheless held that the statute requiring Senate consent was invalid[34] based on the Framers' intent as inferred from the First Congress.[35]

Nine years later, when the Court limited the scope of the *Myers* opinion in *Humphrey's Executor v. United States*,[36] it again looked to the Framers' intent in restricting the President's power to remove commission members. Referring to the First Congress's grant of exclusive removal power to the President, the Court drew support from statements of the Framers that had construed the

[27] *Id.* at 202–3.

[28] Youngstown Sheet & Tube Co. v. Sawyer, 343 U.S. 579 (1952).

[29] *Id.* at 589.

[30] U.S. Const. art. I, § 1. Article I directs that "[a]ll legislative powers herein granted shall be vested in a Congress of the United States."

[31] 343 U.S. at 587–88.

[32] 272 U.S. 52 (1926).

[33] *Id.* at 109–10. The Court did note that article II, § 4 of the Constitution provided for the removal of executive officers by impeachment. *Id.* at 109. That provision was, however, irrelevant to the dispute in *Myers*.

[34] *Id.* at 176.

[35] The Court noted that as conceived in early drafts of the Constitution, the President would have had all the executive powers Congress had under the Confederation, presumably including the power of removal. *Id.* at 110. Although subsequent changes resulted in limitation of the President's appointment power by the requirement of Senate consent, the First Congress, in legislation providing for the creation of executive departments, expressly granted the President sole removal power over the officers staffing those departments. *Id.* at 110–51. The Court viewed this action as constitutionally significant because many members of that Congress had been among the Framers, *id.* at 114–15, 175, and it could thus be taken as representing the Framers' unexpressed intent because the First Congress had the greatest responsibility for effectuating the provisions of the Constitution. *Id.* at 174–75. The opinion was bolstered by repeated citations to Madison's view of the proper functioning of a constitutional government. *Id.* at 119–31.

[36] 295 U.S. 602 (1935).

grant as limited to officers whose functions are wholly executive.[37] In addition to legislation enacted when many Framers were members of Congress, the Court has relied upon the debates of the Philadelphia Convention to divine the Framers' intent. In *Powell v. McCormack*,[38] the Court held that the article I, section 5, grant of power to both houses of Congress to pass on the "qualifications" of their members was limited to applying the textual requirements for membership set forth in that clause.[39] And in *Morrison v. Olson*,[40] the Court canvassed debate at the Convention in concluding that the Framers did not intend to deny Congress the power to provide for interbranch appointments.

Reliance upon Custom

The Court has frequently relied upon custom as a source of decisional authority.[41] As early as 1803, the Court so relied in upholding the power of the Supreme Court justices to sit as circuit judges in *Stuart v. Laird*.[42] Noting that the practice was several years old—dating, in fact, from the inception of the federal judiciary—and that it enjoyed general acceptance, the Court held that the challenged practice itself provided "a contemporary interpretation . . . too strong and obstinate to be shaken or controlled."[43]

Stuart was cited with approval in what is perhaps the seminal custom case, *United States v. Midwest Oil Co.*[44] At issue was the President's power to withdraw specified public lands from private acquisition in the face of a congressional declaration that such lands be "free and open to occupation, exploration and purchase by a citizen of the United States."[45] The President's action was upheld on the basis of a long-standing executive practice. The Court was aware of the apparent circularity involved in relying on the challenged practice

[37] *Id.* at 624–27, 631 (citing acknowledgment by Madison that President's broad removal power might not be appropriate with respect to Comptroller of the Treasury, whose functions were quasi-judicial, and citing Chief Justice Marshall's statement that a District of Columbia justice of the peace would not be removable at the President's will because his functions were not related to any executive duties).

[38] 395 U.S. 486 (1969).

[39] *Id.* at 521–47.

[40] 108 S. Ct. 2597, 2610 (1988).

[41] *See, e.g.*, Ray v. Blair, 343 U.S. 214 (1952); Missouri Pac. Ry. v. Kansas, 248 U.S. 276 (1919); Cooley v. Board of Wardens, 53 U.S. (12 How.) 299 (1851); *but see Chadha*, 462 U.S. at appendix to opinion of White, J., dissenting (Court refused to consider fifty-year custom concerning use of legislative vetoes).

In some cases in which the Court has refused to recognize a custom, the decision has been justified by weaknesses in the custom itself. *See, e.g.*, Powell v. McCormack, 395 U.S. 486 (1969); *Steel Seizure Case*, 343 U.S. 579.

[42] 5 U.S. (1 Cranch) 299 (1803).

[43] *Id.* at 309.

[44] 236 U.S. 458, 473 (1914).

[45] *Id.* at 466.

to justify its holding but defended its conclusion by reasoning that unchallenged executive actions create a presumption of authority and that such a presumption serves the need for continuity and stability in the proper administration of laws.[46]

The Court again emphasized the probity of custom when in 1925 it found in *Ex parte Grossman*[47] that the practice of several United States attorneys general in pardoning contempts had established that criminal contempt of court was an "offense against the United States" within the meaning of article II, section 2, clause 1, and that that provision thus conferred power upon the President.[48] Specifically, the Court held that such a practice, when combined with legislative acquiescence, "strongly sustains the construction it is based on."[49] Four years later, custom again played a role in the *Pocket Veto Cases*.[50] At issue was the President's power to veto legislation presented to him within ten days of an adjournment of Congress without returning the bill to Congress for an "override" vote. Although the Court's holding was based on its interpretation of the Constitution, it also noted that its construction of the provision was "confirmed by the practical construction that has been given to it by the Presidents through a long course of years, in which Congress has acquiesced."[51] Most recently, in *Mistretta v. United States*,[52] the Court reviewed practices from Chief Justice (and treaty negotiator) John Jay to Chief Justice

[46] *Id.* at 473. The Court stated:

> [G]overnment is a practical affair, intended for practical men. Both [*sic*] officers, law-makers, and citizens naturally adjust themselves to any long-continued action of the Executive Department, on the assumption that unauthorized acts would not have been allowed to be so often repeated as to crystallize into a regular practice. That presumption is not reasoning in a circle, but the basis of a wise and quieting rule that, in determining the meaning of a statute or the existence of a power, weight shall be given to the usage itself, even when the validity of the practice is the subject of investigation.

[47] 267 U.S. 87 (1925).

[48] *Id.* at 118–19.

[49] *Id.* The Court also addressed the contention that its interpretation eviscerated the concept of an independent judiciary mandated by the separation-of-powers doctrine. *Id.* The Court stated that the independence of the three branches of government was not complete, but subject to qualification. It then gave examples drawn from the constitutional text of instances in which one branch could frustrate the actions of another. *Id.* at 119–20. Thus, despite the respondent's assertion of an independent separation-of-powers principle that mandated a different result than the one arrived at by the Court, resolution of this issue was made, not by reference to such a principle, but by analogy from the Constitution.

[50] Indian Tribes of Washington v. United States (The Pocket Veto Case), 279 U.S. 655, 690 (1929).

[51] *Id.* at 688–91. The precise scope of the President's pocket-veto power remains unclear. The *Pocket Veto Case* established the President's authority to veto legislation without returning it when Congress was in an intersession recess. *Id.* at 678–81. In later cases, however, courts refused to extend this authority to situations in which Congress was in briefer intrasession recesses, holding that such adjournments do not prevent the President from returning a bill. *See* Wright v. United States, 302 U.S. 583, 589–96 (1938); Kennedy v. Sampson, 511 F.2d 430, 437–42 (D.C. Cir. 1974).

[52] 109 S. Ct. 647 (1989).

(and assassination investigator) Earl Warren in concluding that the assumption of extrajudicial duties was not unconstitutional.

Reliance upon Functionalism

The functional approach, as we saw in Justice Sutherland's opinion in *Curtiss-Wright*, relies upon the institutional attributes of the branches as a standard for the allocation of power; powers are assigned based upon the functional advantages and disadvantages of one branch compared with the other. There appears to be no case in which the approach was solely relied upon by the Court, and indeed even passing references to functional considerations are fairly rare. One such case was *United States v. Nixon*,[53] where the Court noted that "[t]he President's need for complete candor and objectivity from advisers calls for great deference from the courts."[54] Similarly, in *Myers v. United States*,[55] the Court observed that a power to dismiss was necessarily lodged in the President to maintain discipline in the ranks of governmental employees.[56]

Analysis of the Court's Methodology

Weaknesses of Each Approach

The Supreme Court's vacillation among these approaches reflects a recognition that none of the four, taken alone, is equal to the task of resolving the full range of separation-of-powers conflicts. An examination of the weaknesses of each approach helps explain the absence of a more principled decisional framework. The Court has seldom employed only one such juridical device for resolving separation-of-powers issues; in *Bowsher v. Synar*,[57] for example, it employed three. For analytical purposes, however, each is considered below as an exclusive approach.

Textualism

The strict textualist approach to constitutional construction insists upon express textual authority for any assertion of constitutional power. Constitutional provisions are thus viewed as essentially "self-contained units, [to be] interpreted on the basis of their language . . . without significant injection of content from outside the provision."[58] The fundamental justification for textualism is usually the perception that the discretion to disregard textual limitations is inconsistent with a government of laws.

[53] 418 U.S. 683 (1974).
[54] *Id*. at 706.
[55] 272 U.S. 52 (1926).
[56] *Id*. at 132.
[57] 478 U.S. 714 (1986).
[58] J. Ely, Democracy and Distrust 12–13 (1980).

Although the differences between textualist and nontextualist approaches are most salient with respect to issues that touch fundamental rights,[59] the two approaches also yield significantly different results with regard to separation-of-powers disputes. In the *Steel Seizure Case*, for example, Justice Black relied upon the commander-in-chief clause and article I to dispose of the Executive's claim of authority to seize the nation's steel mills.[60] Justice Black could not conceive of any concept of "theater of war" or executive power that would support President Truman's assumption of what was essentially a legislative function. Hence, the seizure order could only have been issued by Congress, in which all "authority to make laws" was vested by the Constitution.[61] Justices Frankfurter and Jackson, concurring, doubted the power of the words' plain meaning. For Justice Frankfurter, "the considerations relevant to the legal enforcement of the principle of separations of powers seem . . . more complicated and flexible than may appear from what Mr. Justice Black has written."[62] Justice Jackson's concurring opinion seems implicitly to assume that the constitutional text alone cannot resolve all separation-of-powers disputes.[63]

The appeal of textualism is understandable. The job of judges is to interpret, not to rewrite, and they are most clearly doing that job when their decisions are grounded firmly in the Constitution's text.[64] But as *INS v. Chadha*[65] serves to point out, the illusory simplicity of the textualist approach obscures the real elements of the judges' work.[66] In *Chadha*, Chief Justice Burger relied largely upon the text of article I to find the legislative veto unconstitutional. The Court found that because the rules of the electoral branches in the legislative process were prescribed by "[e]xplicit and unambiguous provisions of the Constitu-

[59] *Id.* at 8.

[60] 343 U.S. at 585–89.

[61] *Id.* at 588–89.

[62] *Id.* at 589 (Frankfurter, J., concurring).

[63] *Id.* at 655–40 (Jackson, J., concurring).

[64] Another powerful argument in favor of interpretivism—that it avoids the more extreme countermajoritarian tendencies of judicial review because the constitutional text it relies upon has been accepted by a majority of the people—has been attacked as "largely a fake." *See* J. Ely, *supra* note 58, at 11.

[65] 462 U.S. 919 (1983).

[66] *See* A. Bickel, The Least Dangerous Branch 84–110 (1962), for a discussion of Justice Black and interpretivism. Bickel quotes Thomas Reed Powell on the Supreme Court of the 1920s:

> It sometimes seems that these judicial professions of automation are most insistent when it is most obvious that they are being honored in the breach rather than in the observance. They seem to appear less often when statutes are sustained than when they are condemned, less often when the court is unanimous than when there is strong dissent. Try as I will, I cannot bring myself to admire both the candor and the capacity of the men who write such things to be forever embalmed in the official law reports. They must lack one or the other, or I must suffer from some such serious lack in me.

Id. at 91 (citation omitted).

tion,'' no deviation from that method was allowable.[67] In his dissent, however, Justice White persuasively argued that ''[t]he constitutionality of the legislative-veto provision is anything but clearcut.''[68] He observed that the controversy was a direct result of the Constitution's silence ''on the precise question'' at issue.[69]

In the realm of separation-of-powers, therefore, no less than that of fundamental rights, the strict textualist approach masks the tangle of values and methodologies that compose the process of judicial decision making. Moreover, rigid textual adherence fails to account for the Constitution's silence with respect to some subjects, nor does it address the need to afford other ''enumerated powers the scope and elasticity'' necessitated by the practical implications of their exercise.[70] Applied to the few truly explicit constitutional provisions, textualism may be an appropriate means of judicial decision making. In the vast majority of separation disputes, however, the textualist approach represents result-oriented jurisprudence masquerading as commonsense reliance upon the constitutional text.

INTENTIONALISM

Unlike textualism, the intentionalist approach eschews complete reliance on the constitutional text and allows resort to other expressions of the Framers' intent in determining the meaning of the original document.[71] This intent is inferred from such sources as Madison's notes on the Constitutional Convention, the *Federalist* papers, records of the states' ratifying conventions, and the writings of participants.[72] Subsequent custom and practice are of no constitutional relevance.[73] The approach assumes that the states that ratified the work of the Constitutional Convention approved only the text before them, not a malleable instrument.

Although the pure intentionalist approach is not as limited in applicability as textualism, its weaknesses are no less evident. First, it is doubtful that the

[67] 462 U.S. at 955.

[68] *Id.* at 976 (White, J., dissenting).

[69] Justice White noted that ''[t]he issue divides scholars, courts, attorneys general, and the two branches of the National Government.'' *Id.*

[70] *Steel Seizure Case*, 343 U.S. at 640 (Jackson, J., concurring).

[71] Although this approach introduces more flexibility and discretion into the process of constitutional adjudication than is contemplated by strict interpretivism, it found support among the Framers. *See, e.g.*, 9 J. Madison, Writings 191, 372 (G. Hunt ed. 1900–10); 4 Debates in the Several State Conventions on the Adoption of the Federal Constitution 446 (J. Elliot 2d ed. 1836) (President Jefferson pledged to uphold the Constitution according to its meaning as ''found in the explanations of those who advocated . . . it'') (hereinafter cited as Debates).

[72] *See generally* Fisher, *Methods of interpreting the Constitution: The Limits of Original Intent*, 18 Cumb. L. Rev. 43 (1987); Kurland, *Judicial Review Revisited: ''Original Intent'' and the ''Common Will,''* 55 U. Cinn. L. Rev. 733 (1987).

[73] *See, e.g.*, R. Berger, Executive Privilege: A Constitutional Myth 88–101 (1974).

Framers themselves were strict intentionalists. They may have intended that their purposes, or at least some of their purposes, be viewed as tentative.[74] Madison, describing the organization of the new Executive to the Virginia ratifying convention, emphasized the difficulty in delineating its responsibilities and acknowledged that the "mode which was judged most expedient was adopted, till experience should point out one more eligible."[75] In addition, as Professor Sandalow has pointed out, the intentions of the Framers can be described on a number of different levels of generality: "[A]ll the decisions shaping constitutional law to contemporary values can be understood as coming within the general intentions of the framers. All that is necessary is to state those intentions at a sufficiently high level of abstraction."[76]

Second, fifty-five men took part in the Philadelphia Convention, and it is always dubious to infer the intent of an assembly from the statement of an individual.[77] Moreover, the records of the Philadelphia Convention, as well as those of the ratifying conventions, are incomplete. No verbatim notes were kept, and all meetings in Philadelphia were secret. Madison's notes were not published until 1840, and after the earlier publication of his *Journal*, he attempted to revise his account. The intentions of the Framers must, as Mr. Justice Jackson said, "be divined from materials almost as enigmatic as the dreams Joseph was called upon to interpret for Pharaoh."[78]

Third, it is doubtful that the Framers themselves intended that their intent be sought to resolve conflicts concerning the document's meaning.[79] The words of Thomas Jefferson bear note:

> Some men look at Constitutions with sanctimonious reverence, and deem them like the ark of the covenant, too sacred to be touched. They ascribe to the men of the preceding age a wisdom more than human, and suppose what they did to be beyond amendment. I knew that age well; I belonged to it, and labored with it. It deserved well of its country. It was very like the present, but without the experience of the present; and forty years of experience in government is worth a century

[74] *See, e.g.*, Brest, *The Misconceived Quest for the Original Understanding*, 60 B.U.L Rev. 204, 216 (1980).

[75] 3 Debates, *supra* note 71, at 531. A similar view was expressed by Justice White, dissenting in *Chadha*, who asserted that the Framers' wisdom lay in their anticipation "that the nation would grow and new problems of governance would require different solutions." 462 U.S. at 978. He argued that the Constitution was intended to prescribe "fundamental principles," while allowing "the flexibility to respond to contemporary needs." *Id.*

[76] Sandalow, *Constitutional Interpretation*, 79 Mich. L. Rev. 1033, 1045 (1981).

[77] *See id.* at 1041. This same difficulty inheres in attempts to infer congressional intent for purposes of determining acquiescence. In the area of statutory construction, the Court once adhered to the view that recourse to congressional debates was impermissible for the same reason. *See, e.g.*, Standard Oil v. United States, 221 U.S. 1, 50 (1911); United States v. Trans-Missouri Freight Ass'n, 166 U.S. 290, 318 (1897).

[78] *Steel Seizure Case*, 343 U. S. at 634 (Jackson, J., concurring).

[79] Powell, *The Original Understanding of Original Intent*, 98 Harv. L. Rev. 885 (1985).

> of book-reading; and this [the Framers] would say themselves, were they to rise from the dead. . . . Let us . . . avail ourselves of our reason and experience, to correct the crude essays of our first and unexperienced, although wise, virtuous, and well-meaning councils.[80]

Finally, the Framers' consent to the Constitution—whether divined from the text or other sources—does not establish the legitimacy of the system of government that exists two hundred years later. Few would argue that in a democratic society, decisions about the allocation of power made by a majority of the populace can be wholly displaced by the actions and beliefs of generations long dead.[81]

ADAPTIVISM

The adaptivist approach relies upon custom to determine the Constitution's meaning. It addresses the deficiencies of the first two methodologies by downplaying the primacy of the Constitution as originally conceived; the approach relies instead upon subsequent practice. Adherents to the adaptivist model emphasize the inability of the Framers to divine the exigencies likely to be confronted by the federal government in a dimly foreseen future. Karl Llewellyn, an eloquent advocate of the adaptivist perspective, found it "utterly fantastic that a document framed 150 years ago to initiate the operation of a government for three million agricultural, sea-board people could be presumed to control the present-day governing of an industrial nation of 130 million."[82] Dean Sandalow has written that constitutional law is not an exegesis, but "a process by which each generation gives formal expression to the values it holds fundamental in the operations of government."[83]

The flexibility and pragmatism that are the chief virtues of the adaptivist model suggest its deficiencies as well. In place of a "filiopietistic"[84] regard for the wisdom of the ancients, it substitutes a crypto-iconoclastic reverence

[80] Letter to Samuel Kercheval, July 12, 1816, *in* 15 Writings of Thomas Jefferson 40–42 (1903).

[81] *See* Brest, *supra* note 74, at 225 (footnote omitted). For Professor Berger's rejoinder, *see* Berger, *Paul Brest's Brief for an Imperial Judiciary*, 40 Md. L. Rev. 1 (1981).

[82] Llewellyn, *The Constitution as an Institution*, 34 Colum. L. Rev. 1, 3 (1934). This view has also found acceptance with a number of Supreme Court justices. Justice Holmes, for instance, argued that "the present has a right to govern itself," O.W. Holmes, Collected Legal Papers 139 (1920), *quoted in* Antieau, *Constitutional Construction: A Guide to the Principles and Their Application*, 51 Notre Dame Law. 358, 393 (1976), while Chief Justice Marshall insisted that the exposition of a constitution must, for the reasons expressed by Llewellyn, differ fundamentally from that of other, more particularized law. McCulloch v. Maryland, 17 U.S. (4 Wheat.) 415, 422 (1819).

[83] Sandalow, *supra* note 76, at 1068. He thus suggested that the Framers' intentions informed neither the minimum content nor the outer bounds of constitutional law. *Id.*

[84] McDougal & Lans, *Treaties and Congressional-Executive or Presidential Agreements: Interchangeable Instruments of National Policy: I*, 54 Yale L.J. 181, 214–15 (1945).

for the "street smarts" of contemporaries. It equates what *is* with what ought to be and regards patterns of practice as principles of law. Acts inconsistent with the intent of the Framers represent not a usurpation of power but in effect an alternative means of amending the Constitution. Washington recognized the occasional value of such an approach to the resolution of constitutional conflicts, but cautioned that it was also "the customary weapon by which free governments are destroyed."[85]

FUNCTIONALISM

It is easy to see why cases employing a functional approach are too few to indicate any doctrinal pattern. Indeed, in the most recent separation cases, the Court has seemed to take pains to *reject* the use of functional criteria. In an important passage in *INS v. Chadha*,[86] the Court said that "the fact that a given law is efficient, convenient, and useful in facilitating functions of government, standing alone, will not save it if it is contrary to the Constitution. Convenience and efficiency are not the primary objectives—or the hallmarks—of democratic government."[87] This repudiation of functionalism was reiterated in *Bowsher v. Synar*.[88]

Thus one cannot normally argue for a given allocation of power on the basis of functional considerations, for a simple reason: The Constitution has already taken those considerations into account. Functional considerations animated the Framers' debate in Philadelphia; functional considerations impelled them to draft the constitutional text as they did; functional considerations engendered the customs that have grown from the way government actually works. Functional considerations, in short, are for a Constitution's *makers*, not its interpreters. It is therefore impermissible to contend that the Senate is better suited to determine whether a given foreign government should be recognized and that the Senate, not the President, possesses the recognition power. This is a judgment that the Constitution makes for us. Similarly, it would not be satisfactory to think of the Constitution as now permitting the President, without statutory authority, to invade Mexico to collect delinquent American bank loans because the President is functionally better able to act quickly. Functional considerations inform constitutional interpretation, providing explanatory reasons *why* the Constitution allocates power as it does. But they are *not* criteria to be applied to resolve allocation disputes controlled by other sources of constitutional power. "[T]he Framers," the Court said in *Chadha*, "ranked other values higher than efficiency."[89]

[85] 35 The Writings of George Washington 228–29 (J. Fitzpatrick ed. 1940), *quoted in* Berger, *supra* note 73, at 100.

[86] 462 U.S. 919 (1983).

[87] *Id.* at 994.

[88] 478 U.S. 714, 721 (1986).

[89] INS v. Chadha, 462 U.S. 919, 944 (1983). "The hydraulic pressure inherent within each of

SUMMARY

None of the four approaches is capable of meeting reasonable objections leveled against its use as an exclusive methodology of constitutional interpretation. The pure textualist approach proceeds from the fiction that the language of the Constitution alone is dispositive; in contentious circumstances, it is not. On the other hand, the adaptivist approach prefers a Constitution that is all sail, threatening the very purpose of a written Constitution, and the intentionalist approach opts for a charter that is all anchor, presupposing a rigid constitutional order not subject to modification.[90] The functionalist approach, finally, stands upon the appealing premise "You too can be a Framer," permitting ephemeral administrative variables to supplant enduring constitutional norms.

The Court has apparently recognized the shortcomings of sole reliance on any one of the four approaches, and has therefore generally employed a combination of approaches. First, it seeks to resolve the controversy by reference to the constitutional text, as it has been interpreted in the case law. If the text is not found dispositive, the Court next looks to other sources of authority: custom, the Framers' intent, and (on rare occasions) functional considerations.

Recognition of the methodology's general contours, however, only begins the inquiry. Both litigants and courts must be able to discern a principled process or framework for applying text, custom, and intent consistently in separation disputes. An examination of the Court's decisions in this area, however, reveals no such apparent framework for identifying the source of authority that should be regarded as controlling in a case. The Court has shifted from one approach to another, or emphasized one while deemphasizing another, without articulating any principled basis for favoring the approach selected. And as Leonard Levy has pointed out in discussing the "jurisprudence of original intent," the Court is not alone in lacking a principled approach.[91]

In many cases, an approach other than the one employed would have seemed equally justified. In a dissenting opinion in *Myers*, for example, Justice Brandeis detailed the instances in which Congress had conditioned ex-

---

the separate Branches to exceed the outer limits of its power, even to accomplish desirable objectives, must be resisted." *Id.* at 951.

[90] Letter from Thomas B. Macaulay to H.S. Randall (May 23, 1857) ("Your Constitution is all sail and no anchor."), *reprinted in* G. Trevelynan, The Life and Times of Lord Macauley 409–10 (1975).

[91] "The evidence," he has written, "is abundant and easily obtainable to show that the Framers intended Congress to control the making and conduct of war, the Senate to control foreign policy, and the President to control the ceremonial functions of representing the nation in foreign relations, personally or through diplomats." Yet "leading supporters of a constitutional jurisprudence of original intent are advocates of inherent presidential powers in the field of foreign relations, a stance that sheds light on either their ignorance or their hypocrisy." L. Levy, Original Intent and the Framers' Constitution 31, 53 (1988).

ecutive removal of an official upon legislative concurrence.[92] Yet such precedents were accorded no weight by the Court's majority, who elected to view the Framers' intent as controlling.[93] In *Chadha*, the Court declined even to consider what weight should be given the practice of "legislative-veto" review of executive activities—even though the practice comprised hundreds of precedents over a history of nearly fifty years.[94] The long-standing use of executive agreements to settle international claims disputes was nonetheless found by the Court, in light of the provisions of the International Emergency Economic Powers Act, to be dispositive of the question of the validity of the United States–Iran Claims Settlement Agreement,[95] although significant authority exists for the position that such circumvention of the advice and consent of the Senate by using an executive agreement is at odds with the intent of the Framers.[96] The one analytic constant in such cases seems to be a recognition by the Court that its starting point must be the constitutional text—a sound theoretical instinct, but one that often produces little practical guidance.

Ambiguities in the Adjudication of Separation-of-Powers Disputes

The Court's practice of looking first to the constitutional text in separation disputes is prescribed by the plain-meaning rule, a fundamental rule of constitutional interpretation dictating that clear and unambiguous language of the Constitution must be given its plain meaning.[97] In fact, the rule derives from the notion of separated powers: If the Court ignored the plain meaning of the constitutional text, it would in effect be performing functions allocated to the legislative or executive branches and undercutting the rationale for a written Constitution. The Court has thus insisted that clear language must control. In 1819, for example, the Court was confronted with the question whether the thirty-year custom of state insolvency laws could affect the application of the contract clause. The Court held that it could not; according to Chief Justice Marshall, neither the practice of legislative bodies nor other extrinsic circumstances could control the Constitution's "clear language."[98]

[92] 272 U.S. 52 (1926).

[93] *Id.* at 175–76.

[94] 462 U.S. at 945.

[95] *Dames & Moore*, 453 U.S. 654 (1981).

[96] *See, e.g., Treaty Powers Resolution: Hearings on S. Res. 486 Before the Senate Comm. on Foreign Relations*, 94th Cong., 2d Sess. 20 (1976) (statement of Professor Arthur Bestor).

[97] Reid v. Covert, 354 U.S. 1, 8 (1957).

[98] Sturges v. Crowninshield, 4 U.S. (4 Wheat.) 362, 370–71 (1819). The contract clause provides that "[n]o State shall . . . [pass any] Law impairing the Obligation of Contracts." U.S. Const. art. I, § 10, cl. 1. *See also* McPherson v. Blacker, 146 U.S. 1, 27 (1892) ("resort to collateral aids to interpretation is [allowable only] where there is ambiguity or doubt, or where two views may well be entertained").

The problem is whether a provision is "clear." Varying degrees of ambiguity have led commentators to postulate the existence of various "tiers" in the Constitution.[99] Some such theories derive from the distinction proffered by Justice Frankfurter in *United States v. Lovett*.[100] The Constitution, Justice Frankfurter theorized, consists of two sets of provisions. Some provisions were a reaction against certain historical grievances and thus have meanings that are firmly established by that history. Other provisions set forth "broad standards of fairness" in terms such as "due process" or "equal protection" and allow a wide range of subsequent interpretation and expansion.[101]

Concededly, there are *some* specific provisions. These include those provisions that state specific numbers, such as terms of office or age requirements; provisions that designate a specific official to perform a specific function, such as the requirement that the Chief Executive give a State-of-the-Union address;[102] and provisions that relate to concepts not open to rational dispute.

Most of the Constitution's great mandates, however, are more general. Moreover, the problem of determining whether a particular controversy is resolved by the Constitution arises not only when the relevant clause is unclear but also when the subject is not even mentioned.[103] The difficulty—as well as the importance—of interpreting the Constitution's meaning with regard to these "interstitial" questions is illustrated by *Chadha*.[104] Faithful reference to the constitutional text is thus a principle of limited utility in resolving disputes that can reasonably be argued to fall in the Constitution's interstices. The effort is reduced to a guessing game concerning which express provision is conceptually nearest to the matter at issue; resort to extratextual sources of authority in such instances becomes all the more appealing.

[99] Corwin suggested that words in the Constitution which refer to "governing institutions, like 'jury,' 'legislature,' 'election,' " should be given their strict historical meanings, while those that speak "of power or of rights like 'commerce,' 'liberty,' 'property,' " should be interpreted to adapt to contemporary society. Corwin, *Judicial Review in Action*, 74 U. Pa. L. Rev. 639, 659–60 (1926). Similarly, Bickel advanced the idea that the Constitution contains two distinct sets of provisions: (1) those that are "open textured" and have thus required that the Court supply much of their complete meaning, such as "due process" and "equal protection," and (2) the "manifest constitution," which deals with structure and process and imposes on those whom it affects an "absolute duty to obey," subject only to subsequent amendment. A. Bickel, The Morality of Consent 29–30 (1975). *See also* C. Miller, The Supreme Court and the Uses of History 161–69 (1969).

[100] 328 U.S. 303 (1946).

[101] *Id.* at 321.

[102] U.S. Const. art. II, § 3.

[103] *See, e.g.*, McPherson v. Blacker, 146 U.S. 1, 27 (1892) (concerned with question of whether a particular clause was sufficiently ambiguous to warrant resort to other interpretive aids).

[104] Because the only permissible method of legislating is prescribed explicitly by the Constitution, Chief Justice Burger viewed the document's failure to delineate alternative methods as foreclosing their use. 462 U.S. at 956. Justice White, on the other hand, maintained in dissent that uncertainty over the device's validity derived from the Constitution's failure to address the subject. *Id.* at 978 (White, J., dissenting).

The difficulties inherent in constitutional interpretation only begin when a court finds that the Constitution does not address or is not clear about the matter in dispute. The court then must undertake the forbidding task of identifying the Framers' intent, the custom established by historical facts, or functional superiority. A court may infer the Framers' intent from a number of different sources. The choice of one source over another can yield different, even contradictory, results. Moreover, strong arguments can be made that such endeavors are fundamentally misguided.[105] Likewise, the use of custom requires the finding of historical facts, often through reliance on sources that are just as obscure as those used to divine the Framers' intent. There is clearly nothing approaching certainty in this fact-finding process. Facts, as Jerome Frank reminded us, are guesses,[106] and the guesswork is particularly troublesome in the law of interbranch relationships.[107] Finally, the practical advantages and disadvantages of assigning a task functionally to one political branch depends so much on subjective, value-laden assessments of the branches' relative strengths and weaknesses that an outcome-oriented analysis is hard to resist.

As I argue in Chapter 8, the imprecision, uncertainty, and complexity inherent in the resolution of a separation dispute—particularly acute for disputes over international issues—are not sufficient reasons for the courts to avoid the process of resolving such controversies. To do so would be to abandon process for outcome, to substitute power for law by rewarding that branch that is best able to work a fait accompli. It would sabotage any notion of the rule of law. "The rule of law," Professor Philip Kurland has written, "requires that government not act except according to preestablished rule. . . ."[108] When it does act, it is for the courts to decide whether it has done so according to preestablished rule. It is with this imperative in mind that I proffer the following methodology for assessing congressional versus presidential power with respect to a given foreign-affairs subject. The approach, although unarticulated as such by the Court, is one that normally yields the same results that the Court has

[105] *See* Tushnet, *Following the Rules Laid Down: A Critique of Interpretivism and Neutral Principles*, 96 Harv. L. Rev. 781, 793–804 (1983) (contending that certain and objective understanding of the Framers' intent is impossible because of the subjective interpolation necessary to give content to that intent).

[106] J. Frank, Courts on Trial 114–16 (1949).

[107] Indeed, much of the literature on the allocation of power among the branches suggests less a government of law and more a government of men than many would prefer. Raoul Berger, for example, characterized President Truman's asserted authority to order the seizure of steel mills in the *Steel Seizure Case* as a "presidential power-grab." R. Berger, *supra* note 73, at 3. Similarly, Theodore Sorensen has written that, in the area of foreign relations, the President cannot depend upon "harmonious cooperation" with his coequal branch, but must resort to either "submission," "leadership," or "defiance and domination." Sorensen, *Political Perspective: Who Speaks for the National Interest*? in The Tethered Presidency 10 (T. Franck ed. 1981).

[108] Kurland, *The Rise and Fall of the "Doctrine" of Separation of Powers*, 85 Mich. L. Rev. 592, 612 (1986).

reached, and it is easily summarized: (a) it requires initial reliance upon the constitutional text and case law; (b) it synthesizes custom with the intent of the Framers by according controlling constitutional weight to those executive or congressional practices that trace back to the days when the Framers ran the government and confronted the need to resolve the same conflicting interests that would confront their successors; and (c) it permits resort to function only as a last resort.

A Framework for Decision Making

Primary, Secondary, and Tertiary Sources of Power

Is there some hierarchy of sources that might suggest one as more (or less) probative than the others? In international law, as discussed in Chapter 1, the "doctrine of sources" is spelled out expressly in article 38 of the Statute of the International Court of Justice.[109] It is debated whether those sources are there listed in order of priority.[110] Another set of international-law sources, however, clearly *is* set out in hierarchical form—those used for treaty interpretation.[111] The peculiarities of treaty law render the substance of those sources largely irrelevant as tools for domestic constitutional interpretation. But what is interesting is the *categorization* of the sources; they are organized in clear levels of priority. One category comes first; a second may "be taken into account"; and a third is explicitly labeled "supplementary." By following this roadmap, a treaty interpreter knows where to look first, next, and last to determine a treaty's meaning.

Interpretation of the Constitution can never be reduced to neat formulas that calm all the storms that have raged for two centuries. Yet it should at least be possible, with this oldest written Constitution in the world, to suggest some modest notions of where one might turn first, second, and third in seeking after its meaning—particularly if those directions can be derived from the path that the United States Supreme Court has taken over those two centuries. I will call these primary, secondary, and tertiary sources of power, and will now proceed to suggest *what* sources fall within these categories.

Express Constitutional Provisions: The Primary Source

Happily, our hierarchy begins with a source whose primacy will be almost universally accepted: the constitutional text. The first reference of a constitu-

[109] 59 Stat. 1055 (1945), TS No. 993.

[110] However, two such sources—court cases and publicists' opinions—are expressly described as "subsidiary sources." *Id.*

[111] *See* Vienna Convention on the Law of Treaties, arts. 31–32, *opened for signature* May 23, 1969, UN Doc. A/Conf 39/27, *reprinted in* 63 Am. J. Int'l. L. 875 (1969).

tional interpreter must of course be to the document's text. If the Constitution expressly prohibits Congress from legislating in a given foreign-affairs controversy between Congress and the President, the inquiry is closed. The Court has no choice but to strike down the legislation. Few constitutional provisions, however, attain this level of specificity, and as discussed above, there is no clear line between those that do and those that do not. These problems suggest that the test for identifying express prohibitions must incorporate a high threshold if the concept is to have any operative utility.

These considerations indicate that something in the nature of a rational-basis test is appropriate. The test should prohibit "interpreting" a constitutional provision by reference to extrinsic materials—such as custom or intent—if no rational basis exists for any meaning but one.[112] When a rational basis does exist for more than one interpretation of the constitutional text, therefore, reference to extrinsic sources is permissible. A rational-basis test comports with the view of constitutional interpretation taken by the Supreme Court in *McCulloch v. Maryland*.[113] The test is also particularly appropriate in the foreign-relations context, which frequently involves disputes over whether, and how, government may adjust to changing circumstances. There seems to be little textual reason to distinguish between words such as *war* and *treaty* on the one hand and *due process* and *equal protection* on the other. Yet it is often contended that the first two have a static meaning but that the meaning of the latter two fluctuates over time. The concept of war has surely changed at least as much as the concept of due process since 1789.

Constitutional Cases and Custom: The Secondary Sources

THE CASE LAW

In the international legal system, cases decided by its highest tribunal, the International Court of Justice, are denied *stare decisis* effect.[114] A holding in

[112] McPherson v. Blacker, 146 U.S. 1, 27 (1892) ("The framers of the Constitution employed words in their natural sense; and where they are plain and clear, resort to collateral aids to interpretation is unnecessary and cannot be indulged in to narrow or enlarge the text. . . ."); *cf.* Bartels v. Iowa, 262 U.S. 404, 412 (1923) (Holmes, J., dissenting) (because he found that there was the possibility of a reasonable difference of opinion as to the Constitution's meaning, Justice Holmes would not have struck down the challenged governmental action on the basis of the provision in question).

[113] 17 U.S. (4 Wheat.) 316 (1819). In *McCulloch*, Chief Justice Marshall refused to impose a strict standard of review on Congress's necessary and proper clause power, recognizing that to do so would unduly restrict government's ability to adapt to unforeseen conditions. In a similar vein, Justice Jackson later identified the element common to "[t]he greatest expounders of the Constitution" as their insistence "that the strength and vitality of the Constitution stem from the fact that its principles are adaptable to changing events." R. Jackson, The Struggle for Judicial Supremacy 174 (1941).

[114] "The decision of the Court has no binding force except between the parties and in respect

one of its decisions is not considered binding with respect to future cases in which the same issue arises. Not so with respect to the United States Supreme Court: Its cases, all know, comprise *the* authoritative source for the meaning of the Constitution, to the point that Chief Justice Charles Evans Hughes could remark that "[t]he Constitution is what the judges say it is."[115] "The federal judiciary," the Court reminded some malingerers after *Brown v. Board of Education*,[116] "is supreme in the exposition of the law of the Constitution."[117] If research uncovers a controlling precedent, further inquiry is foreclosed. If not, we appropriately look to constitutional custom.

CUSTOM

Writing on international law, Pitt Cobbett compared custom to footsteps across a common that eventually become a widely used "path."[118] Similar paths have been established in constitutional law, perhaps most frequently in relations between the branches of the federal government. Many such paths have not been approved or even identified by the courts; frequently the issues involved have been regarded as nonjusticiable, as discussed in Chapter 8.[119]

---

of that particular case." Art. 59, Statute of the International Court of Justice, 59 Stat. 1055, T.S. No. 933, 3 Bevans 1153 (entered into force Oct. 24, 1945). In practice, the provision has been largely ignored, and the International Court frequently cites its own prior decisions.

[115] Speech in Elmira, New York (1907).

[116] 347 U.S. 483 (1954).

[117] Cooper v. Aaron, 358 U.S. 1, 17 (1956).

[118] 1 P. Cobbett, Leading Cases on International Law 5 (F. Grey ed. 1931). For a parallel discussion of the elements of custom in an international law context, see A. D'Amato, The Concept of Custom in International Law (1971).

[119] A "nonjusticiable" issue is one that does not admit of the possibility of judicial review. The "political-question doctrine," as articulated in Baker v. Carr, 369 U.S. 186 (1962), lays out the contours of justiciability. It is premised on the assumption that some controversies are, by their nature, not amenable to judicial resolution. The doctrine forbids judicial disposition of a dispute in the event that (1) the activity involved has been textually committed to a coordinate government branch; (2) resolution of the controversy would force the Court to make political determinations, beyond its experience; or (3) prudential considerations counsel against judicial intervention. *Id.* at 217. The doctrine has barred the adjudication of some controversies, *see* Gilligan v. Morgan, 413 U.S. 1 (1973), while many other cases in which the Court has reached the merits of a separation-of-powers dispute have required that it first surmount the threshold political question inquiry. *See, e.g.*, Goldwater v. Carter, 444 U.S. 996, 1002 (Rehnquist, J., dissenting), *denying cert. to* 671 F.2d 697 (1979). Moreover, one commentator has suggested that the doctrine represents an amalgam of independent concepts, such as the constitutional text, standing, and judicial limitations on equitable relief. Henkin, *Is There a "Political Question" Doctrine*? 85 Yale L.J. 597, 601–22 (1976). The concerns engendered by separation controversies may thus cause courts to refuse to entertain disputes, even though the doctrine is not explicitly relied upon. Professor Henkin's analysis of the political-question doctrine as a mere description of various juridical tools without any independent significance is similar to this chapter's description of separation principles. Each concludes that understanding and certainty in these areas would be advanced if the terms were disregarded and attention focused on the underlying rationales and approaches subsumed by those terms. For a discussion of the political question doctrine *see* Chapter 8.

But there is no doubt that such customs exist.[120] Those historical events that a branch claims should be treated as judicially cognizable precedent, justifying allocation of the disputed power to itself, represent customs in the separation-of-power context.

A Definition of Custom. In determining whether a custom exists, several factors are relevant: consistency, numerosity, duration, density, regularity, and normalcy.

Consistency. A practice may be considered "consistent" when distinct and often unrelated historical events are sufficiently similar. The process of analogizing past governmental actions to judicial precedents, however, must be conducted with caution. No generally recognized and well-established fact-finding procedure has emerged regarding governmental practices. Hence, arguments recur concerning which aspects of particular acts are significant or controlling. Moreover, judicial decisions explicitly set out the contextual elements on which they are based, whereas the circumstances surrounding historical occurrences must be found by a court before it can "apply" such events to the case before it. Because of these difficulties, the requirement of consistency may devolve into a philosophical inquiry into the substitutability of elements drawn from various contexts.[121] In the end, however, this is the same process that the courts use in analogizing cases.

In *Dames & Moore v. Regan*, the Court upheld the President's use of an executive agreement to settle all United States claims against Iran. The Court might well have noted that substantial controversy existed regarding the *general* practice of using executive agreements.[122] The lack of congressional acquiescence to this custom[123] could have required the Court to strike down the

[120] Such customs are integral to the functioning of every society. The impossibility of reducing all law to a specified set of legal provisions was discussed earlier in this century by the German jurist Eugen Ehrlich. *See* Ehrlich, *The Sociology of Law*, 36 Harv. L. Rev. 130, 133 (1922). He argued that most law was the immediate result of "spontaneous ordering[s] of social relations" and, as such, is constantly in flux. *Id.* at 136, 139.

[121] *See generally* W. Quine, Ontological Relativity and Other Essays 114 (1969).

[122] *See Congressional Review of International Agreements: Hearings on H.R. 4438 Before the Subcomm. on International Security and Scientific Affairs of the House Comm. on International Relations*, 94th Cong., 2d Sess. 3–5, 163–82 (1976) (statements of Thomas E. Morgan, Chairman, Committee on International Relations, and Monroe Leigh, Legal Adviser, Department of State).

[123] Senate objections to executive agreements as a usurpation of congressional power have been frequent. These objections include the constitutional debates of 1905–06 concerning Theodore Roosevelt's agreement for a United States takeover of Dominican Republic customs houses, an attack on an executive agreement with Panama relating to the Hoy-Vanilla Treaty, the 1952 criticism of the Yalta agreement by several senators, the Case Resolution of 1972 urging submission of the Azores and the Bahrain base agreements to the Senate, and Senator Case's proposed purse-strings retaliation when the Executive refused to comply with the 1972 resolution. L. Henkin,

agreement. By particularizing the practice to executive claims-settlement agreements, however, the Court defined a custom consisting of a handful of specific agreements about which little controversy had occurred, thus ensuring that the custom was supported by selected precedents.

Numerosity. In most cases, the act constituting the custom must be repeated more than once, and the greater the number of times the act has been repeated, the plainer the custom. In *Midwest Oil*, it was fundamental to the Court's decision that "scores and hundreds of [the executive] orders" in question had been made.[124] Likewise, in *Zemel v. Rusk*,[125] area restrictions on passports had been imposed by the Secretary of State "many times" since 1914, several times after 1926, and several more times after World War II, leading the Court to accord the custom significant weight.[126] More recently, in its decision upholding the executive agreement with Iran in *Dames & Moore*, the Court noted that "the President has entered into at least ten binding settlements with foreign nations" since World War II.[127]

In contrast, three comparable instances of executive plant seizures were not deemed probative in the *Steel Seizure Case*.[128] Similarly, although the Solicitor General in *Springer* was able to cite isolated examples of governmental corporations controlled by nonexecutive officers, the Court concluded that such a "limited number" of congressional acts could not support a legislative usurpation of an essentially executive function.[129] Finally, the limited import of numerosity alone is illustrated by *Chadha*, where the Court refused to consider the effect of over two hundred previously enacted statutes that also contained legislative vetoes.[130]

Foreign Affairs and the Constitution 426 n.16 (1972). *See generally* J. Paige, The Law Nobody Knows (1977) (surveying the expansion of executive power in foreign affairs and the congressional response to that expansion).

[124] 236 U.S. at 469 (upholding power of President to remove from private acquisition public lands that had been previously opened up to occupation by Congress).

[125] 381 U.S. 1 (1965) (affirming Secretary of State's authority to impose area restrictions on the validation of passports).

[126] *Id.* at 445.

[127] 453 U.S. at 680. The case demonstrates the degree to which numerosity, as well as historical precedent in general, may be manipulated. The factor is, of course, a function of the time frame selected for review, and the *Dames & Moore* Court selected only post–World War II practice. *Id.* Out of seventeen major international claims agreements entered into before World War II, however, fifteen were submitted to the Senate as treaties. *See* R. Lillich, International Claims: Their Adjudication by National Commissions 7–9 (1962).

[128] 343 U.S. at 588.

[129] 277 U.S. at 205.

[130] 462 U.S. 919 (1983); *accord* Bowsher v. Synar, 478 U.S. 714 (1986) (congressional control over execution of laws through removal power unconstitutional). Indeed, the Court at one point declared that the increasing use of congressional veto provisions had prompted it to subject the practice to even stricter scrutiny. *Id.*

Duration. This consideration relates to the period of time over which the act has been repeated. The longer the period, the more reason to view the repetition as custom. Concerning an eighty-five year history of presidents pardoning criminal contempts, the Court in *Ex parte Grossman* declared that "[s]uch long practice . . . and acquiescence in it strongly sustains the construction it is based on."[131] The ten similar agreements noted by the *Dames & Moore* Court extended back to 1952,[132] and the sort of area restriction upheld in *Zemel* traced back at least forty years.[133] In other cases, such as *Midwest Oil* and *Inland Waterways Corp. v. Young*,[134] the Court has also noted that the practice was "long-continued,"[135] without delineating the precise duration.

However, even long-established practices can run afoul of the Constitution. In *Fairbank v. United States*,[136] a stamp tax concerning exports was struck down—twelve years prior to the adoption of the sixteenth amendment—as violative of the Constitution, notwithstanding the imposition of stamp duties during two previous periods (from 1797 to 1802 and from 1862 to 1872).[137] Because the provisions of the Constitution bearing on the issue of taxation were clear, the Court declared that it could not "be overthrown by a legislative action, although several times repeated and never before challenged."[138] The elder Justice Harlan, joined by three other members of the Court, expressed in dissent his concern that a century-old practice should be so readily dismissed.[139]

Density. This factor focuses on the number of times an act has been repeated over the course of its duration; the greater the density, the more probative the custom. Like the other factors, however, density alone is not controlling. In the *Steel Seizure Case*, it was irrelevant that the three seizures cited as precedent had all occurred within a six-month period. Similarly, in *Chadha*, even though Congress had placed legislative-veto "mechanisms in nearly 200 separate laws over a period of fifty years," the use of the device was struck down by the Court.[140] Conversely, the absence of density was a factor in the *Myers* Court's decision to invalidate an 1876 statute requiring Senate consent for the removal of certain federal officials.[141] Although the statute had been in effect for fifty years, the Court found almost no instances of its being enforced or its

[131] 267 U.S. 87, 118–19 (1925).
[132] 453 U.S. at 680.
[133] 381 U.S. at 8–9.
[134] 309 U.S. 517 (1940).
[135] *Inland Waterways*, 309 U.S. at 524; *Midwest Oil*, 236 U.S. at 472.
[136] 181 U.S. 283 (1901).
[137] *Id.* at 312.
[138] *Id.* at 311.
[139] *Id.* at 319 (Harlan, J., dissenting).
[140] 462 U.S. at 968 (White, J., dissenting).
[141] 272 U.S. at 170–71.

violation challenged. The significance of the act's ''mere presence . . . on the statute book for a considerable time'' was thus negated by the lack of density.[142]

Regularity. If repetition of the act is irregular, so that there are comparatively long periods in which the practice has not been followed, there is less reason for the act to take on the authority of custom. Thus, the Court in *Midwest Oil* emphasized the continuity of the executive practice of withdrawing public lands from private acquisition in its decision to uphold that practice.[143] In contrast, when the Court struck down a congressional attempt to exclude a member-elect in *Powell v. McCormack*, it pointed out the irregular and erratic history of past congressional practice as well as the strong disagreement with the practice registered by many members of Congress.

Normalcy. If an act has been performed by a number of Congresses or presidents, greater reason exists to regard it as custom. Normalcy ensures that the act was not an aberration attributable to the personality of certain presidents or congressional leaders, or to other unique historical circumstances. This concern appears to have been the unarticulated basis of the Court's refusal in *Fairbank* to consider two prior periods during which similar stamp duties had been levied. From 1797 to 1802, exports were ''limited'' and duties were ''small''; and from 1862 to 1872, the large national debt made it ''not strange that the legislative action . . . passed unchallenged.''[144]

Summary. The consistency requirement must always be satisfied. However, not all of the remaining five elements discussed above must be present to justify the conclusion that a custom exists. The strength of one or more of those variables may overcome the weakness of another. Generally, a custom will thus fall somewhere along a continuum of strong to weak. It is not always possible, therefore, to conclude categorically that a given custom exists. Yet

[142] *Id.* at 171. The Court's decision could also be understood to stem from a concern that only acts and practices of other branches be given the effect of positive law. This would avoid the impracticalities and uncertainties involved in allowing either branch to restructure its powers and relations on the basis of unactualized policy pronouncements.

[143] 236 U.S. at 471.

[144] 181 U.S. at 311–12. Another example of the concern for normalcy can be found in the *Myers* Court's disregard of congressional legislation limiting the President's removal power. The legislation, according to the Court, was best understood as the result of ''heated political difference[s]'' between the electoral branches over the proper methods of reconstruction, which eventually led to impeachment proceedings against President Jackson. 272 U.S. at 175–76. Admittedly, actions that would fail the normalcy test because of the extreme circumstances surrounding them may go unchallenged at that time, either because of the political-question doctrine, *see supra* note 119, or as a result of political and societal pressures. The importance of this factor lies instead in the limitation it imposes on the subsequent extension of these actions beyond such exigencies.

a custom, to be considered probative, must have been understood and intended by both branches to represent a juridical norm; it cannot be simply a series of essentially random acts that happen to form a pattern of usage. This is the meaning of *opinio juris*.

Opinio Juris. The concept of *opinio juris sive necessitatis*, which apparently derives from the writings of the French jurist François Gény, describes a distinction between legal custom and acts of the sort that "remain outside the positive legal order."[145] Applied to custom in the separation-of-powers context, *opinio juris* requires three elements. First, the custom in question must consist of *acts*; mere assertions of executive or legislative authority to act are insufficient. Second, the other branch must have had *notice* of its occurrence. Third, that branch must have *acquiesced* in the custom; a custom possessed of *opinio juris* must have been intended by both political branches to represent a juridical norm. In the absence of *opinio juris*, custom is not properly relied upon by the courts. It is thus mistaken merely to string out bare references to historical incidents with no indication of the posture of the other branch; the attitude of the other branch is all-important in finding whether the incidents reflect a juridical norm.[146]

Action. Policy statements or claims of authority by one branch have no concrete existence that might supply substance and specificity to the meaning of the custom they purport to form; the "custom" remains a possibility rather than a reality. As Justice Brennan observed, dissenting in *Haig v. Agee*, congressional approval of a policy does not indicate approval of its specific application.[147] Problems with the delegation doctrine aside,[148] it is doubtful that

[145] F. Gény, Methode d'interprétation et sources en droit privé positif § 110 (1899). *See* A. D'Amato, *supra* note 118, at 49.

[146] This is precisely the methodology of the committees' minorities in their report on the Iran-Contra affair. "Presidents have exercised a broad range of foreign policy powers for which they neither sought nor received Congressional sanction through statute," the two committees' minority contended. S. Rept No. 100-216 & H. Rept. No. 100-433, 100th Cong., 1st Sess. 469 (1987). Yet incidents relied upon with the reverence of Supreme Court cases, regarding diplomacy, covert operations, and use of force, are described in a manner devoid of any indication of the posture of Congress. *Id.* at 463–69. As a rather embarrassing afterthought concerning "the historical examples given in the preceding section" of the report, the committees' minorities reflect that "a particular exercise of presidential power may have been acceptable in the past only because Congress had not yet spoken on the subject." *Id.* at 471. This is a damning admission, given the minority's acknowledgement that "[t]he major issues in the Iran-Contra investigation have to do with incidents [that] all fall into Jackson's third category." *Id.* at 471–72. The historical incidents cited may thus have no bearing whatever upon those composing the Iran-Contra episode.

[147] 453 U.S. at 315–16 (Brennan, J., dissenting).

[148] The Bumpers amendment to the Administrative Procedure Act is a recent, albeit unsuccessful, example of a congressional attempt to control the exercise of delegated power in the area of administrative law. The amendment would have allowed "a court to consider the agency interpre-

acquiescence in a policy, as distinct from a practice, has any place in the concept of *opinio juris*.[149] An act is required to identify specifically what the coordinate branch has acquiesced in.

Notice. Additionally, the requirement of an act ensures that actual notice has been received by the other branch. The daily practicalities of governing do not lend themselves to a thorough examination of and response to the myriad policy pronouncements emanating from the political branches and their components. Thus, in *Kent v. Dulles*,[150] the government's contention that "long-continued executive construction" of the Secretary of State's discretion to deny passports sufficed as a basis for inferring Congress's acquiescence was rejected by the Court, which insisted that "the key" was the more narrow manner in which the discretion was exercised.[151]

Insistence upon an actual executive assertion of power, as opposed to a mere claim, finds support in the Court's reasons for relying upon custom. Custom draws vitality as a source of authority from its utility as a reality tester; the act constituting it has been carried out over a period of time and found workable.[152] A policy statement is less likely than an act to draw a considered response from the other branches, and its ramifications cannot be appreciated or discerned. To equate policy with practice in this regard would thus confound the historical framework of analysis for consideration of custom and open the way for ill-conceived changes.

When a dispute does occur, it is important to establish that one branch was aware of the act's performance by the other. In cases relying on executive custom as a source of decisional authority, the Court has emphasized repeatedly that Congress had notice of the custom in question. The leading case in

---

tation, . . . [but would not] permit a court to presume that the interpretation of the agency is correct." 128 Cong. Rec. S2406 (daily ed. March 18, 1982) (statement of Sen. Bumpers); *see also* Rodgers, *A Hard Look at Vermont Yankee: Environmental Law Under Close Scrutiny*, 67 Geo. L.J. 699, 717 (1979) ("agencies are no longer trusted with the free-wheeling, answerable-to-none, brain-storming function" they previously enjoyed); Note, *Rethinking the Nondelegation Doctrine*, 62 B.U.L. Rev. 257, 258 n.11 (1982) (collection of various legislative and executive measures designed to limit and provide oversight of agency discretion). Although these efforts would not have altered the outcome of *Agee* or other recent cases, they do represent a desire in Congress—and the executive branch—for tighter controls on the exercise of delegated power.

[149] *See generally* A. D'Amato, *supra* note 118, at 87–98. "The . . . act is visible, real, and significant; it crystallizes policy and demonstrates which of the many possible rules of law the acting state has decided to manifest." *Id.* at 88.

[150] 357 U.S. 116 (1958).

[151] *Id.* at 125. Justice Brennan construed the required demonstration of exercised discretion in *Kent* "as a preference for the strongest proof that Congress knew of and acquiesced in" the practice. *Agee*, 453 U.S. at 315 (Brennan, J., dissenting).

[152] *See, e.g.*, *Chadha*, 462 U.S. at 972 (White, J., dissenting) (surveying history of legislative veto and concluding that veto "is more than efficient, convenient, and useful, [constituting] an important if not indispensable political invention" [citation omitted]).

this area, *Midwest Oil*, established congressional knowledge of executive land withdrawals from "notice of [the] practice" made ninety-two times and communicated to Congress.[153] Similar reliance is evidenced in *Dames & Moore*; the Court noted that the practice had been "long-continued" and "known to and acquiesced in by Congress."[154] Finally, although the action in *Agee* may have been supported more by policy than practice, it satisfied the notice requirement because the "history of administrative construction [had been] repeatedly communicated to Congress" by executive orders and regulations, specific presentations, and a 1960 Senate staff report.[155]

Of course, since "Congress" comprises thousands of employees, the meaning of *notice* in its case is not altogether clear. Is it reasonable to infer notice to Congress from notice accorded a handful of committee aides? In corporate law, similar problems arise in inferring notice for a large entity composed of many individuals. These problems have been resolved largely by reference to the corporate structure. Corporations can act only through their agents; thus, only service upon such agents will constitute sufficient notice to a corporation of a pending action.[156] By analogy, the guiding principle here should be whether the branch has learned of a disputed activity through the channels that were intended to receive information pertaining to that activity. It is therefore permissible to attribute notice to the entire Congress that, for example, certain covert operations are being performed if the intelligence committees of both Houses have been informed, even though this means that only a few individuals will have been apprised of the details.

The Court found an "elementary and fundamental requirement"[157] of American justice in the fourteenth amendment's guarantee of due process: Any party with an interest in a pending action must receive timely notice. This requirement satisfies the concern for fairness by effectively ensuring Congress's right to object to the proceedings.[158] Similar fairness considerations apply to relations among the branches of government: Without prior notice,

[153] 236 U.S. at 475, 481.

[154] 453 U.S. at 686 (quoting *Midwest Oil*, 236 U.S. at 474). This notice requirement has been expressed in numerous intervening cases. *See, e.g.*, Udall v. Tallman, 380 U.S. 1, 17–18 (1965) (Secretary of the Interior's interpretation of a statute had long been "a matter of public record and discussion," thus creating a presumption of notice on the part of the legislature); *Inland Waterways*, 309 U.S. at 524 (practice had been "long-continued" with the Comptroller of the Currency's knowledge).

[155] 453 U.S. at 299.

[156] Junk v. R. J. Reynolds Tobacco Co., 24 F. Supp. 716, 721 (W.D. Va. 1938). At common law, an "agent" to receive process meant a head officer of the corporation, Reader v. District Court, 98 Utah 1, 4; 94 P.2d 858, 860 (1939). Under modern statutes, it is usually "any agent authorized by appointment or by law to receive service of process." Fed. R. Civ. P. 4(d)(3).

[157] Mullane v. Central Hanover Bank & Trust Co., 339 U.S. 306, 314 (1950).

[158] *Id.*

one branch cannot reasonably be held to have acquiesced in the practice of another.

Acquiescence. Acquiescence by one branch in the actions of the other can be explicit. However, most separation-of-powers disputes involving foreign affairs will not involve clear congressional affirmations and will thus require a determination of whether consent can be inferred from silence or no action. Other areas of the law recognize that silence may constitute consent in certain circumstances,[159] whereas only a limited duty to express dissent is imposed in other situations.[160] With regard to individual rights, however, there are definite

[159] Silence is construed as consent primarily in two settings: against harm by intentional tortfeasors and in assertions of legal rights. In both cases, the failure to speak is unreasonable unless consent was intended. In the case of intentional torts, the maxim *volenti non fit injuria*—the volunteer suffers no harm—prevails on the assumption that no public interest exists when victims do not protect themselves to the extent that they are able. W. Prosser, The Law of Torts, § 18 (4th ed. 1971). Consent to an intentional tort may be manifested by silence or inaction if the surrounding circumstances indicate an intention to give consent. Restatement (Second) of Torts, § 892, Comment *b* (1979); *see, e.g.*, Mims v. Boland, 110 Ga. App. 477, 481, 138 S.E.2d 902, 907 (1964) (voluntary submission to medical exam construed as consent); Thibault v. Lalumiere, 318 Mass. 72, 60 N.E.2d 349, 350 (1945) (woman's failure to resist man's embrace construed as consent). Generally, courts find silent consent in situations in which a reasonable person would have voiced an objection, as measured by the prevailing customs of the community. Restatement (Second) of Torts, § 892, Comment *d* (1979).

Similarly, silence is construed as consent when a person fails, for a specified period, to assert a legal right. This is illustrated by the doctrine of adverse possession, which establishes a trespasser's ownership interest in property when that person holds it openly and notoriously for the statutory period, Mannilo v. Gorski, 54 N.J. 378, 387, 255 A.2d 258, 263 (1969), and the owner had the power to eject the trespasser, either through self-help or the courts. California v. United States, 235 F.2d 647, 661 (9th Cir. 1956). These two requirements presume that reasonable owners act or speak when someone wrongfully possesses their property; as with intentional torts, the failure to voice an objection is tantamount to consent.

[160] Although speech is generally required to prevent an inference of consent, narrow exceptions exist in certain areas of the law. *See, e.g.*, Southern California Accountics Co. v. C. V. Holder, Inc., 71 Cal. 2d 719, 456 P.2d 975, 79 Cal. Rptr. 319 (1969) (offeree's failure to respond to an offer generally should not be taken to indicate acceptance). Silence may be taken as an acceptance, however, if previous dealings between the parties—the functional equivalent of custom in separation of powers—indicate that the offeree would notify the offeror if he did not intend to accept. Restatement (Second) of Contracts, § 69 (1979). Contract law also treats silence as consent when it has the effect of misleading the other party. *See, e.g.*, Hughes v. Hancock Mut. Life Ins. Co., 163 Misc. 31, 297 N.Y.S. 116 (1937) (policy, which insurer asserted would go into effect without notice, held to have gone into effect because of insured's reliance on that assertion). Here the inquiry is also whether the party was reasonable in construing silence as acceptance.

Similarly, agency law generally requires that agents be affirmatively authorized by their principals; however, if an agent acts consistently in a realm not expressly designated to him and the principal, knowing this, fails to object, the principal's silence will be taken as authorizing the agent's actions. Dobbs v. Zink, 290 Pa. 248, 138 A. 758 (1927). Furthermore, a principal's silence with respect to a third party may have the effect of creating apparent authority in the agent. Restatement of Agency, § 49, Comment *b* (1933); *see, e.g.*, Sokoloski v. Splann, 311 Mass. 203, 207, 40 N.E.2d 874, 877 (1942) (store clerk held authorized to warrant merchandise without principal's verbal permission).

limitations on the meaning of silence as approbation or consent.[161] It should therefore be equally reasonable to infer consent in the relations between the political branches in similar circumstances. These exist when three conditions are satisfied: (1) absence of objection; (2) institutional capacity to object; (3) noninterference with protected freedoms.

Absence of Objection. The Court has insisted that a notice requirement be fulfilled before it will give weight to custom. Similarly, it has also required *absence of objection*—that the practice in question not have been objected to by the other branch. When such an objection has occurred, the Court has declined to find custom probative. Thus, the lack of congressional objection was a significant factor in both *Midwest Oil*[162] and *Myers*.[163] In contrast, the Court refused to consider the custom constituting the use of the legislative veto in *Chadha*, perhaps because eleven of thirteen presidents from Woodrow Wilson to Ronald Reagan have objected to the device.[164]

What constitutes objection will vary with each branch. Congressional objection will be found to fall, as Justice Rehnquist noted in *Dames & Moore*, along something of a spectrum.[165] Objection is manifested most clearly by the

[161] Silence in this area, particularly as it affects criminal defendants, will rarely be given the effect of consent to the curtailment of a right. For example, the right to remain silent under the fifth amendment will not be considered waived by a defendant's nondemonstrative silence in the face of an accusation. Miranda v. Arizona, 384 U.S. 436, 475 (1966). Prosecutors may not comment on a defendant's refusal to testify, nor can a court instruct a jury that the defendant's silence may be evidence of his guilt. Griffin v. California, 380 U.S. 609 (1965). Moreover, sixth-amendment rights to a jury trial and to counsel will likewise not be deemed waived based merely on the defendant's silence. *See* Fed. R. Crim. P. 23(A) (waiver of jury must be in writing); Girard v. Goins, 575 F.2d 160 (8th Cir. 1978) (defendant's acquiescence in proceeding to trial without jury does not constitute a waiver of right); Douglass v. First Nat'l Rlty. Corp., 543 F.2d 894, 899 (D.C. Cir. 1976) (defendant's failure to request jury is not a waiver of right); *see also Miranda*, 384 U.S. at 470 (defendant's failure to request counsel not a waiver of right).

The right to a jury trial in a civil action, guaranteed by the seventh amendment, may be waived by a party's mere acquiescence, as when the party is present and fails to make a timely demand for a jury. Duignan v. United States, 274 U.S. 195, 198 (1972); Bass v. Hoagland, 172 F.2d 205, 209 (5th Cir. 1949). According to Professor Wright, this indicates that the waiver test that applies to other constitutional rights—"an intentional relinquishment or abandonment of a known right or privilege"—is not applicable to jury trials in civil cases. 9 C. Wright & A. Miller, Federal Practice and Procedure § 2321 (1971) (footnote omitted). The conclusion to be drawn is that the right to trial in a civil action is somehow less "fundamental" than the other rights discussed above, and that the less fundamental a right, the more the individual must bear the burden of protecting it.

[162] *See* 236 U.S. at 481 (holding that congressional silence constituted authorization "to continue the practice until the power was revoked by some subsequent [congressional] action").

[163] *See* 272 U.S. at 163 (executive removal power upheld on basis of long-standing "affirmative recognition" of the practice by all three governmental branches).

[164] *See* Henry, *The Legislative Veto: In Search of Constitutional Limits*, 16 Harv. J. on Legis. 735, 737–38 n.7 (1979) (collection of citations to presidential statements).

[165] 453 U.S. at 669 (declaring that support for or objection to executive action may range from "explicit congressional authorization to explicit congressional prohibition").

enactment of a statute expressly prohibiting the action. Objection can exist, however, short of express prohibition, as when Congress rejects a bill or an amendment to a bill authorizing the disputed act. This occurred in the *Steel Seizure Case*, in which Congress declined to adopt an amendment that would have authorized the seizure of steel mills.[166] Similar congressional objection was registered in *Agee*, although the Supreme Court chose to ignore it. As noted by both the district court and the court of appeals, the executive branch had sought statutory authority from Congress in 1958 for the power to revoke passports on national-security or foreign-power grounds; the legislation died in committee in both the Senate and the House.[167]

As the facts of *Agee* suggest, however, the analysis is further complicated by the existence of a vertical spectrum of objection or consent, at least with respect to Congress. The objection might be made at the committee level or on the floor. Moreover, identical action might have been taken in the other house, in the conference committee, or in connection with action on the conference report in either house. An individual member might object, in a legislative context, such as a speech on the floor or in a committee meeting, or in a letter to the President or another executive official. Several members of Congress might, jointly or severally, take similar action. In short, there are gradations of objection, requiring case-by-case analysis to determine whether it is reasonable to infer objection by Congress as an institution, which would presumably involve a majority of the membership of each house.

Institutional Capacity to Object. Under certain circumstances, Congress may not have the *institutional capacity to object*. If this incapacity is due to executive action or nonaction, Congressional silence has no probative value. For example, the impossibility of imputing disagreement with an executive practice to a majority of each house may not mean that its members approved but that structural infirmities in congressional procedures made effective objection impracticable.[168] The absence of any institutional response by Congress to the seizure of the *Mayaguez*, for example, may simply have meant that, given the time constraints, no objection was feasible. The entire incident

[166] *See* 343 U.S. at 586.

[167] 453 U.S. at 317 n.7 (Brennan, J., dissenting) (citing Agee v. Muskie, 629 F.2d 80, 85 n.4 (D.C. Cir. 1980) and Agee v. Vance, 483 F. Supp. 729, 732 (D.D.C. 1980)).

[168] *See* Note, *Historical and Structural Limitations on Congressional Abilities to Make Foreign Policy*, 50 B.U.L. Rev. 51, 69 (1970):

> Congress has been a fragmented legislative institution since the time of World War I. This characteristic has restricted the flexibility of Congress when faced with modern security problems. An integrated, comprehensive analysis of executive policy formulation and administration demands of the legislature a degree of coordination and cohesiveness that Congress has lacked. Only the Executive has been able to ''orchestrate'' the diverse resources at its disposal to produce a ''coherent military strategy'' and an all-encompassing foreign policy. Congress has failed to make even those minor changes that would have minimized its handicaps.

Id. (footnotes omitted).

took place in less than forty-eight hours, ending *before* a report was transmitted to Congress under the War Powers Resolution.[169] Institutional capability in this context is largely a function of time constraints.

If the incapacity to act is a result of an act of an organ of Congress, congressional silence indicates acquiescence. Thus, if a certain congressional committee has blocked the reporting of a bill, a court may properly find congressional acquiescence. In such circumstances, the committee has exercised authority granted it by the full house, and its actions should therefore be attributed to the membership as a whole.

Noninterference with Protected Freedoms. A fundamental precept in the Court's scheme of constitutional construction has been the concern that "provisions for the security of person and property should be liberally construed."[170] As a consequence of its adherence to this principle of *noninterference with protected freedoms*, the Court has given greater scrutiny to customs that impinge on personal freedoms. An expression of this concern is the Court's consistent refusal to allow implementation of executive policy "when doubt exists as to whether the legislature in fact intended to impinge on a fundamental constitutional value."[171] The Court thus invalidated a passport revocation in *Kent v. Dulles*,[172] the revocation of a security clearance without a hearing in *Greene v. McElroy*,[173] a Coast Guard loyalty test focusing on political beliefs in *Schneider v. Smith*,[174] and federal civil service regulations discriminating against aliens in *Hampton v. Mow Sun Wong*.[175] In each case, although governmental regulation in a sensitive constitutional area was not prohibited altogether, the Court refused to permit it in the absence of "a specific, articulated legislative policy."[176]

It makes sense to refuse to find acquiescence when a personal freedom is abridged. Custom is only *evidence* of power, not power itself. When a finding of acquiescence would suggest that the exercise of power is in conflict with constitutional provisions that have traditionally been accorded a broad construction, the inference of consent is no longer justified. For this reason, in addition to those reasons already discussed, *Agee* was wrongly decided. Whether international travel is denominated a "right" under the first amend-

[169] *See* President's Letter to Speaker of the House and President Pro Tempore of the Senate Reporting on United States Actions in Recovery of the *S.S. Mayaguez*, Pub. Papers 669 (May 15, 1975).

[170] Reid v. Covert, 354 U.S. 1, 40 (1957); Gulf, C. & S.F. Ry. v. Ellis, 165 U.S. 150, 159 (1897); Boyd v. United States, 116 U.S. 616, 635 (1886).

[171] Neuborne, *Judicial Review and Separation of Powers in France and the United States*, 57 N.Y.U. L. Rev. 363, 419 (1982).

[172] 357 U.S. 116 (1958).

[173] 360 U.S. 474 (1959).

[174] 390 U.S. 17 (1968).

[175] 426 U.S. 88 (1976).

[176] Neuborne, *supra* note 171, at 421.

ment or a mere "liberty" under the fifth amendment, the Court should refuse to infer congressional intent to interfere unless the Congress has expressed its will unmistakably.

The Priority Custom Should Be Accorded. A prior case on point always controls; custom cannot supplant the interpretation of the Constitution by the Supreme Court. Where no prior case is apposite, however, and where *opinio juris* exists, it is appropriate to regard custom as a source of constitutional authority upon which the allocation of power might be based. Such a finding will, in most instances, allow a court to uphold the disputed practice and thus dispose of the challenge to it. An examination of Supreme Court decisions in this area reveals that only those constitutional customs, dating from the earliest days of the Republic, will be seen as giving rise to plenary power. In *Myers*, for example, the early starting point of the custom of unfettered removal power in the Executive was emphasized by the Court to overcome a fifty-year-old congressional enactment.[177] The practice, which predated the Constitution's adoption, was given this effect because it was found to represent an objective demonstration of the Framers' intent.[178]

Similarly, historical precedent tracing to the administration of George Washington was relied upon by the Court in *Schick v. Reed*[179] to uphold the power of the President to attach conditions to the commutation of a death sentence. The Court's determination "that the power flow[ed] from the Constitution alone, not from any legislative enactment, and that it cannot be modified, abridged or diminished by the Congress," was compelled by unbroken practice dating from 1790.[180] Applying this principle in *The Laura*,[181] the Court held that the statutory assignment to lesser executive officials of the power to remit certain forfeitures and penalties was permissible, noting that the "practice commenced very shortly after the adoption of the [Constitution]."[182] Going even further, the Court stated in *Powell v. McCormack* that the precedential value of prior incidents involving the challenged practice "tends to increase in proportion to their proximity to the Convention of 1787."[183] Thus in *Bowsher v. Synar*,[184] the Court, in striking down the

[177] 272 U.S. at 110 (tracing Executive's removal power to that exercised by Congress, both during the Revolution and under the Articles of Confederation).

[178] *Id.* at 161–75. The *Myers* Court reiterated the principle that "a contemporaneous legislative exposition of the Constitution when the founders of our government and framers of our Constitution were actively participating in public affairs, acquiesced in for a long term of years, fixes the construction to be given [the Constitution's] provisions." *Id.* at 175.

[179] 419 U.S. 256 (1974).

[180] *Id.* at 266.

[181] 114 U.S. 411 (1885).

[182] *Id.* at 414.

[183] 395 U.S. at 547.

[184] 478 U.S. 714, 724 n.3 (1985).

Gramm-Rudman-Hollings Act,[185] found the meaning of the separation-of-powers doctrine (as applied to the removal of federal officers) by referring to "debate in the First Congress of 1789, . . ." which it proceeded to review[186] in concluding that a direct congressional role in removal is constitutionally impermissible.[187] "The First Congress," the Court explained, "included 20 members who had been delegates to the Philadelphia Convention. . . ."[188] Finally, in *Mistretta v. United States*, the Court again emphasized that the custom upon which it relied (concerning judges' service on the Sentencing Commission) traced from the beginning: "Our 200-year tradition of extrajudicial service is additional evidence that the doctrine of separated powers does not prohibit judicial participation in certain extrajudicial activities."[189]

Perhaps custom has been used by the Court in this manner because a starting point virtually coincident with the birth of the Nation suggests that the Framers intended to permit such acts. The first President was, after all, the presiding officer at the Constitutional Convention. And, it has been pointed out, "[o]f the sixty-six men who served in the Senate during Washington's administrations, thirty-one had been members of the Continental Congress or of the Congress of the Confederation, twelve had helped draft the Constitution in the convention at Philadelphia, and ten had been members of state conventions which had ratified the federal instrument."[190]

There is no guarantee that such a custom was approved by the Framers and ratifiers. Alternative means of determining their intent, however, may be even more problematic—too unreliable and too prone to outcome-oriented analysis.[191] Reliance upon custom, backed by *opinio juris* and tracing to the earliest days of the Republic—"constitutional custom"—thus has the virtue of factoring the Framers' intent into constitutional analysis without giving force to intent that has not withstood the test of time and experience. It is thus properly regarded as a secondary source of power, not capable of displacing inconsistent constitutional text, but superior to an expression of the Framers' intent that has *not* enjoyed the blessing of two centuries' practice and also superior to mere functional considerations, which find support in neither the customs of our forebears nor the words of the Framers.

Cases involving constitutional custom have seldom been decided by the Court, probably because constitutional custom is usually so highly respected by both branches. Following President Carter's derecognition of the Republic of China in 1979, no one suggested that his exercise of the recognition power

[185] 2 U.S.C.S. §§ 901 et seq.

[186] Bowsher v. Synar, 478 U.S. 714, (1986).

[187] *Id.*

[188] *Id.*, n.3.

[189] 109 U.S. 647, 669 (1989).

[190] R. Hayden, The Senate and Treaties, 1789–1817, at 3 (1920).

[191] *Cf.* Tushnet, *supra* note 105.

was *ultra vires*, even though a measure was considered in the Senate challenging his authority to terminate the mutual security treaty.[192] The power of the President to recognize foreign governments, tracing to Washington's reception of Citizen Genet, is properly regarded as a constitutional custom. Similarly, the Senate's power to condition its consent to treaties might be regarded as a constitutional custom; the custom dates from Senate approval (with reservations) of the Jay Treaty in 1798. It is in this sense that Chief Justice William Howard Taft was correct: "So strong is the influence of custom that it seems almost to amend the Constitution."[193]

In general, the Court's use of custom as evidence of implied authorization has led to results consistent with the conceptual framework set forth above. In *Kent v. Dulles*, a case involving alleged congressional intent to interfere with a protected freedom, the Court rightly insisted upon express congressional authorization and, finding none, invalidated the denial of plaintiff's passport. Conversely, the plant seizure in the *Steel Seizure Case* was not supported by previous seizures of sufficient numerosity, duration, continuity, or normalcy to create a probative custom. Although *Chadha* might well have been decided as a protected-freedom case involving a bill of attainder, as the Ninth Circuit indicated in a thoughtful opinion written by then Judge Anthony Kennedy,[194] Chief Justice Warren Burger dismissed this notion in a footnote,[195] ignoring the congressional practice embodied in two hundred statutes enacted over a course of fifty years. Reliable application of the mode of analysis detailed in this chapter requires a closer inquiry into the elements of custom than that of *Chadha*.

Reliance upon custom as a source of constitutional power is, to be sure, inevitably backward-looking; historical analysis is by definition retrospective. For that matter, however, so is the principle of *stare decisis* upon which our law is based. A certain comfort attends the knowledge that a way of doing things has been tried and tested. As Justice Jackson noted, although the power of precedent "is only 'the path of the beaten track,' . . . the mere fact that a path is a beaten one is a persuasive reason for following it."[196]

FUNCTION AND INTENT: TERTIARY SOURCES OF POWER

It may be that with respect to a given question, the mode of analysis developed above will yield no hard and fast conclusion, that neither primary nor second-

[192] *See* S. Rept. No. 119, 96th Cong., 1st Sess. (1979) *reprinted in* 2 United States Foreign Relations Law: Documents and Sources 411 (M. Glennon & T. Franck eds. 1980).

[193] L. Fisher, President and Congress 36 (1972).

[194] Chadha v. Immigration & Naturalization Serv., 634 F.2d 408 (9th Cir. 1980).

[195] *See* 462 U.S. at 935 n.8.

[196] Jackson, *Full Faith and Credit—The Lawyer's Clause of the Constitution*, 45 Colum. L. Rev. 1, 26 (1945).

ary sources of power resolves a dispute. In such circumstances, reference to a third tier of sources is appropriate: the Framers' intent and the functional advantages and disadvantages of the two political branches, outlined in Chapter 1. Where the constitutional text is silent, there is no apposite precedent, and no custom exists, or where that custom, lacking *opinio juris*, fails to qualify as constitutional custom, it is sensible to refer to tertiary sources of constitutional power, to inquire into the intent of the Framers or to ask whether Congress or the President is better qualified to handle the task. There is, at that point, no other source of guidance. Yet it is worth reiterating that these are *tertiary* sources of constitutional power. They corroborate the conclusions established by primary and secondary sources. But for the reasons discussed above, the Framers' intent is not properly viewed as dispositive if a contrary constitutional custom prevails. Similarly, the abstract advantages or disadvantages of a certain allocation of power should not control if a concrete custom exists, tracing to the origins of the Union. An ounce of experience in governance is worth a pound of functionalist logic.

Conclusion

This chapter has set forth a methodology for resolving constitutional disputes between the Congress and the President on foreign-affairs issues.

First reference must be to the primary source, the constitutional text. One must determine whether the acts arguably composing the custom are expressly prohibited by a constitutional provision. The test should be whether a rational basis exists for more than one interpretation.

If there is a rational basis for finding that the text is ambiguous or silent, the next appropriate reference is to the secondary sources of constitutional case law and constitutional custom. Pertinent judicial precedents constitute the principal secondary source, and it is only in the absence of controlling precedent that recourse to other sources is justified. Assuming such absence, one looks for an apposite constitutional custom.

The process of identifying a constitutional custom is rooted in the methodology of international law. The variables of consistency, numerosity, duration, density, continuity, and normalcy should be considered to determine whether a practice rises to the level of a custom. If a custom is found, the next step is to determine whether it represents *opinio juris sive necessitatis*, meaning, in the context of this book, that it is intended by both political branches to represent a juridical norm.[197] In the absence of *opinio juris*, custom is not properly relied upon by the Court.

[197] In international law, *opinio juris* is a prerequisite to the formation of a rule of customary international law. A practice which nations generally follow, perhaps out of courtesy, but feel free to disregard does not impose a legal obligation because nations do not *believe* that they have a legal

Opinio juris can be found in a separation-of-powers context only if three conditions are fulfilled: first, the custom must consist of acts, not mere statements; second, the other branch must have notice that the act has been performed by the first branch; finally, the other branch must acquiesce. Acquiescence requires that the branch not object, that it be institutionally capable of objecting, that its objection would not be futile, and that the act not interfere with protected freedoms. A custom meeting these requirements is a *constitutional custom*.

Third, if neither constitutional text, constitutional case law, nor constitutional custom is dispositive, the Court is justified in referring to tertiary sources of power, the intent of the Framers or the comparative functional advantages of the two political branches.

The next chapter, concerning the war power, demonstrates how this framework is applied in a specific subject area.[198]

---

obligation to adhere to that practice. Evidence of *opinio juris* may be inferred from acts or omissions. *See* Restatement, § 102, Comment *c*.

[198] Space limitations do not permit its step-by-step application in each subsequent chapter, where discussion centers only on those steps in the analysis that are outcome determinative. But its application in each case would lead to the conclusions advanced.

Chapter Three

THE WAR POWER

The laws are silent amidst the clash of arms.
—Cicero[1]

THE CONSTITUTION ALLOCATES the power to use armed force. It does not address the relevant issues of morality or even public policy. It is worth noting, however, that the *process* by which that decision is made has been relied upon to support the morality of force. Hear, for example, the words of former Secretary of Defense Caspar W. Weinberger, debating whether there is a moral difference between American and Soviet foreign policy:

> There are significant differences between Grenada and Afghanistan. . . . [W]e think you can't have a moral foreign policy if the people cannot control it—if the people cannot change it. . . . [W]e really cannot do anything—we can't send a soldier anywhere, we can't spend a dime or a nickel or a shilling—that is not approved by our Congress. . . . So this is . . . a foreign policy that's based on consent of the governed and the opportunity and the ability of the people to change it at any time they wish. . . .
>
> Now who among the Soviets voted that they should invade Afghanistan? Maybe one, maybe five men in the Kremlin. Who has the ability to change that and bring them home? Maybe one, maybe five men in the Kremlin. Nobody else. And that is, I think, the height of immorality. . . .[2]

PLENARY PRESIDENTIAL WAR POWER

The scope of the President's plenary power to make war has been the subject of sustained controversy.[3] The wide divergence of opinion is illustrated by a

[1] Pro Milone.

[2] Remarks by Hon. Caspar W. Weinberger at the Oxford Union Debate, London, England (News Release, Office of Assistant Sec. of Defense [Pub. Aff.], Feb. 27, 1984) at 4–5. Weinberger was asked, in rebuttal, whether "the people who are tortured and killed and terrorized . . . think it is a more moral act because Congress approves of it and not some general?" He replied that "if [a policy] cannot be changed, it cannot possibly be considered moral." *Id.* at 6. The Secretary did not indicate how many individuals in the United States government decided to invade Grenada.

[3] *See, e.g.*, F. Wormuth & E. Firmage, To Chain the Dog of War (1986); E. Keynes, Undeclared War: Twilight Zone of Constitutional Power (1982); E. Corwin, The President: Office and Powers 1787–1957 (4th rev. ed. 1957): M. Pusey, The Way We Go to War (1969); A. Schle-

comparison of the most recent statement on the matter by Congress, section 2(c) of the War Powers Resolution, with the opinion of a recent legal adviser to the State Department. The Resolution states:

> (c) The constitutional powers of the President as Commander-in-Chief to introduce United States Armed Forces into hostilities, or into situations where imminent involvement in hostilities is clearly indicated by circumstances, are exercised only pursuant to (1) a declaration of war, (2) specific statutory authorization, or (3) a national emergency created by attack upon the United States, its territories or possessions, or its armed forces.[4]

WPR 2(c)

The State Department legal adviser:

> Besides the three situations listed in subsection 2(c) of the War Powers Resolution, it appears that the President has the constitutional authority to use the Armed Forces to rescue American citizens abroad, to rescue foreign nationals where such action directly facilitates the rescue of U.S. Citizens abroad, to protect U.S. Embassies and Legations abroad, to suppress civil insurrection, to implement and administer the terms of an armistice or cease-fire designed to terminate hostilities involving the United States, and to carry out the terms of security commitments contained in treaties. We do not, however, believe that any such list can be a complete one, just as we do not believe that any single definitional statement can clearly encompass every conceivable situation in which the President's Commander in Chief authority could be exercised.[5]

The Constitutional Text

Our starting point in this dispute, as discussed in the last chapter, is the primary source of constitutional power: the text of the Constitution. It is clear that the Constitution's textual grants of war-making power to the President are paltry in comparison with, and are subordinate to, its grants to Congress.[6]

The principal textual fount of the President's war-making power, whatever its scope, is the commander-in-chief clause: "The President shall be Commander in Chief of the Army and Navy of the United States, and of the Militia

singer, Jr., The Imperial Presidency (1973); F. Wormuth, The Vietnam War: The President Versus the Constitution (1968); Corwin, *The President's Power*, in The President: Role and Powers 361 (1965).

[4] War Powers Resolution, 87 Stat. 555, 50 U.S.C. §§ 1541–48 (1982 ed.) (hereinafter Resolution).

[5] *Compliance with the War Powers Resolution: Hearings Before the Subcomm. on International Security and Scientific Affairs of the House Comm. on International Relations*, 94th Cong., 1st Sess. 90–91 (1975) (hereinafter cited as *Hearings*).

[6] This is perhaps understating it a bit. "Something of the wonder that suffuses a child upon learning that a mighty oak sprang from a tiny acorn fills one who peers behind the tapestry of conventional learning and beholds how meager are the sources of presidential claims to monopolistic control of foreign relations." R. Berger, Executive Privilege: A Constitutional Myth 131 (1973).

of the several States. . . ."[7] In addition, article II, section 1, clause 1, of the Constitution vests the "executive Power" of the United States in the President. This clause has been cited by presidents as justification for their claims that United States treaty commitments authorized them to send troops abroad for purposes short of war, even when Congress had not enacted implementing legislation.[8]

In contrast, the grants to Congress of war-related powers are numerous: Congress is vested with the power "to lay and collect Taxes . . . to . . . provide for the common Defense,"[9] "[t]o define and punish . . . Offenses against the Law of Nations,"[10] "[t]o declare War,"[11] "[t]o raise and support Armies . . . ,"[12] "[t]o provide and maintain a Navy,"[13] "[t]o make Rules for the Government and Regulation of the land and naval Forces,"[14] "[t]o provide for calling forth the Militia to execute the Laws of the Union, suppress Insurrections and repel Invasions,"[15] and "[t]o provide for organizing, arming, and disciplining, the Militia, and for governing such Part of them as may be employed in the Service of the United States."[16]

Also important in this regard are general provisions vesting in Congress "[a]ll legislative Powers" granted to the federal government; power to make all laws "necessary and proper for carrying into Execution . . . all . . . powers vested by this Constitution in the Government of the United States"; and power to appropriate funds from the Treasury.[17] The first of these, in conjunction with the provision[18] placing the "executive Power" in the President, establishes Congress as the fount of federal laws and the President as their executor. The second, as the late Professor Alexander Bickel has noted, gives to Congress the sole power to implement not only its own powers but also those of the Executive:

> Whatever is needed to flesh out the slender recital of Executive functions must be done by Congress under the "necessary-and-proper" clause. Congress alone can make the laws which will carry into execution the powers of the Government as a whole, and of its officers, including the President.[19]

[7] U.S. Const. art. II, § 2, cl. 1.

[8] *See* L. Henkin, Foreign Affairs and the Constitution 55 (1972) (citing examples) (hereinafter cited as Henkin).

[9] U.S. Const., art. I, § 8, cl. 1.

[10] *Id.* cl. 10.

[11] *Id.* cl. 3.

[12] *Id.* cl. 12.

[13] *Id.* cl. 13.

[14] *Id.* cl. 14.

[15] *Id.* cl. 15.

[16] *Id.* cl. 16.

[17] U.S. Const., art. I, § 9, cl. 7.

[18] *Id.*, art. II, § 1, cl. 1.

[19] *War Powers Legislation: Hearings Before the Senate Comm. on Foreign Relations*, 92d Cong., 1st Sess. 551 (1971) (hereinafter cited as *War Powers Legislation*). It is easy to lose

Note, in this context, that section 2(b) of the War Powers Resolution cites the "necessary-and-proper" clause as authority for the Resolution, emphasizing that that clause authorizes Congress to implement "not only its own powers but also all other powers vested . . . in the Government . . . or in any department or officer thereof."[20]

The Case Law

The case law is devoid of support for the proposition that the commander-in-chief clause confers substantive policy-making authority upon the President. Several cases are often cited by proponents of plenary presidential war-making power, but there is little in them to warrant that claim.

Durand v. Hollins[21] is frequently relied upon as support for the notion that the President has plenary power to rescue endangered Americans abroad. The case, decided by the (United States) Court of Appeals for the Southern District of New York, arose in 1854. After a bottle was thrown at an American diplomat in Greytown, Nicaragua, the Secretary of the Navy ordered the *Cyane* to bombard the town. It did, inflicting heavy damage to a building owned by Durand, an American citizen, who sued Hollins, the commander of the *Cyane*. The court held for Hollins:

> It is to [the President that] the citizens abroad must look for protection of person and of property, and for the faithful execution of the laws existing and intended for their protection. For this purpose, the whole executive power of the country is placed in his hands. . . .
>
> Now, as it respects the interposition of the executive abroad, for the protection of the lives or property of the citizen, the duty must, of necessity, rest in the discretion of the president. Acts of lawless violence, or of threatened violence to the citizen or his property, cannot be anticipated and provided for; and the protection, to be effectual or of any avail, may, not unfrequently, require the most

balance by leaning too heavily on this deceptively sturdy provision. *See, e.g.*, Ely, *Suppose Congress Wanted a War Powers Resolution That Worked*, 88 Colum. L. Rev. 1379, 1392 n.40 (1988) (hereinafter "Ely"), who does so to the point of declining reliance upon Jackson's *Steel Seizure* analysis. The difficulty with this argument is that not everything Congress does in this regard would necessarily "carry into execution" a power of the Executive; in the war-powers context, for example, a president might argue that the War Powers Resolution actually *vitiates* the executive commander-in-chief power. *Compare* the testimony of Professor Arthur Schlesinger, The War Power After 200 Years: Congress and the President at a Constitutional Impasse: Hearings Before the Special Subcomm. on War Powers, Comm. on Foreign Relations, U.S. Senate, 100th Cong., 2d Sess. 40 (1989) (hereinafter "1988 Senate War Powers Hearings"): "[T]he President can act unless Congress acts; if Congress acts, its legislation would supersede an otherwise valid order of the President.

"The zone of twilight, in other words, is something Congress can enter at will."

[20] Resolution.

[21] 8 Fed. Cas. 111 (No. 4,186) (C.C.S.D.N.Y. 1860).

> prompt and decided action. Under our system of government, the citizen abroad is as much entitled to protection as the citizen at home. The great object and duty of government is the protection of the lives, liberty, and property of the people composing it, whether abroad or at home; and any government failing in the accomplishment of the object, or the performance of the duty, is not worth preserving.[22]

The case has been roundly criticized. It has been argued, correctly I believe, that the facts presented "no question of emergency intervention to save American citizens; it was rather a calculated retaliation after the fact."[23] The court makes no distinction between protecting and retaliating. The difference is crucial; protection often involves an emergency, whereas retaliation is frequently a considered reaction. In addition, the placement of American property on a par with American citizens would provide a rationale for presidential use of the armed forces in virtually any circumstances; almost every significant foreign conflict directly or indirectly threatens American property interests. Authority to protect any endangered citizen goes far toward eviscerating a congressional role in war making, for citizens find themselves present all too frequently at the site of global flash points.

The key issue for present purposes is whether the President acted in the face of congressional silence or congressional disapproval. On this the record is clear; no statute had been enacted prohibiting the act. The case thus does not deal with *plenary* constitutional power; it can stand at most for the proposition that the President has a concurrent power to initiate the use of force for protective purposes. Whether Congress could have proscribed the use of force in *Durand* was not an issue that confronted the court.

The *Prize Cases*[24] also represent an old standby in arguments for plenary presidential power to use the armed forces abroad. Here again, however, no plenary power was exercised, and further, the armed forces were used within the United States. The Court there considered the validity of President Lincoln's blockade of Confederate ports at the outset of the Civil War. It was carried out with congressional approval.[25] Moreover, the Court emphasized that war had been thrust upon the United States; indeed, to this day, the vast calamity of the Civil War, constituting as it did unprecedented military insurrection within the territorial boundaries of the United States, stands alone among historical precedents. That the Court upheld the President's power to

[22] *Id.* at 112.

[23] A. Schlesinger, The Imperial Presidency 57 (1973). *See also* Berger, *Protection of Americans Abroad*, 44 U. Cinn. L. Rev. 741, 742–43 (1975).

[24] 67 U.S. (2 Black) 635 (1862).

[25] "[B]y the Acts of Congress [of 1795 and 1807] he is authorized . . . to suppress insurrection against the government of . . . the United States." *Id.* at 668. Professor Ely reads the Prize Cases in much the same way. *See* Ely, *supra* note 19, at 1390 n.34.

deal militarily with this unique crisis says little about his power in other, inapposite factual settings.

Another Civil War case, *Ex parte Milligan*,[26] usefully points out (in dicta) that the power of Congress does not extend to "the command of the forces and the conduct of campaigns,"[27] but the decision has no bearing on which branch is possessed of the power to decide *whether* to conduct a military campaign. The Court also noted that "Congress has the power not only to raise and support and govern armies but to declare war. It has, therefore, the power to provide by law for carrying on war."[28] Senator Jacob Javits aptly observed that "if we have the power to provide by law for carrying on war, then we have the power to provide by law for not carrying on war. . . ."[29] Similarly, *Totten v. United States*,[30] though sometimes cited as support for plenary presidential "covert-operations" power, dealt with the breadth of presidential authority in time of war; the case involved an action in contract by the estate of a deceased Union spy, doubtless hired under congressional approval implied by the same statutes at issue in the *Prize Cases*. Thus *Totten* hardly suggests plenary presidential power to carry out covert or paramilitary activities in the face of statutory prohibition or limitation.

Cunningham v. Neagle[31] centered on the authority of a United States marshal who in guarding Justice Stephen J. Field of the Supreme Court, shot and killed Field's assailant. The plaintiff asserted that no statutory authority existed for the provision of Field's bodyguard. The Court held that it did. "Why do we have marshals at all," the Court asked, "if they cannot physically lay their hands on persons and things in the performance of their proper duties?"[32] There is much ensuing extraneous discussion concerning "the power of the president to take measures for the protection of a judge of one of the courts of the United States who, while in the discharge of the duties of his office, is threatened with a personal attack which may probably result in his death."[33] The Court based its holding on the finding of prior congressional authorization, not plenary executive power. Like the facts of the *Prize Cases*, therefore, those of *Cunningham v. Neagle*[34] are anomalous and give the case little precedential utility.

The *Slaughter House Cases*[35] contain a passing reference to presidential

[26] 71 U.S. (4 Wall.) 2 (1866).

[27] *Id.* at 139.

[28] *Id.*

[29] War Powers Legislation: Hearings Before the Comm. on Foreign Relations, U. S. Senate, 92d Cong., 1st Sess. 525 (1971).

[30] 92 U.S. 105 (1875).

[31] 135 U.S. 1 (1890).

[32] *Id.* at 61 (citing *Ex parte* Siebold, 100 U.S. 371, 394).

[33] *Id.* at 67.

[34] 135 U.S. 1 (1890).

[35] 83 U.S. (16 Wall.) 36 (1973).

"rescue" authority. An American citizen, the Court opined, may "demand the care and protection of the Federal government"[36] when endangered abroad. The thought comes almost as a bolt out of the blue, for the case deals with a subject having no bearing on foreign relations, let alone the use of force. The Court confronted the question of whether the fourteenth amendment's privileges or immunities clause prohibited Louisiana from granting a slaughterhouse monopoly in New Orleans. That plenary-powers proponents rely on this jurisprudential aside says much about the dearth of support for that view.

Myers v. United States,[37] although often cited as support by critics of congressional involvement in the decision to go to war, has nothing to do with the war power or with foreign-affairs powers generally. The case involved the constitutionality of a statute requiring the advice and consent of the Senate prior to the removal from office of a postmaster. Nothing in the Court's judgment as to the invalidity of the law is pertinent to unrelated laws such as the War Powers Resolution.

More relevant to the scope of presidential war-making power are the several cases dealing directly with it. *Little v. Barreme*[38] has been discussed in Chapter 1; it is worth recollecting that Chief Justice Marshall grounded his validation of the restrictive statute upon the will of Congress, declining even to address the issue of exclusive presidential power. W. W. Willoughby found the teaching of *Little* unambiguous: "Not even the order of the President himself," he wrote, "the constitutional commander-in-chief of the army and navy, if that order be without authority of law, is sufficient to justify the performance of the act commanded."[39] *Bas v. Tingy*[40] and *Talbot v. Seeman*[41] also dealt with incidents arising during the undeclared naval war with France from 1798 to 1801. The Court in those cases took the same approach, holding that Congress, although it had not formally declared war against France, had authorized involvement of the armed forces in hostilities—subject to statutorily specified limitations that were binding upon the President. "The whole powers of war being, by the Constitution of the United States, vested in Congress, the acts of that body can alone be resorted to as our guide," Marshall wrote in *Talbot*.[42] Its power to declare unlimited or perfect war implied the power to authorize limited or imperfect war. "An imperfect war, or a war, as to certain objects, and to a certain extent, exists" between the United States and France,

[36] *Id.* at 79.

[37] 272 U.S. 52 (1926).

[38] 6 U.S. (2 Cranch) 170 (1804).

[39] W. Willoughby, 3 The Constitutional Law of the United States § 1008 at 1536 (2d ed. 1929).

[40] 4 Dall. (U.S. 1800).

[41] 1 Cranch 1 (U.S. 1801).

[42] *Id.* at 28.

Justice Paterson wrote in *Bas*.[43] "As far as Congress tolerated and authorized the war on our part, so far may we proceed in hostile operations."[44] Justice Burford Washington agreed that the hostilities constituted "imperfect" or "partial" war, conferring power to act only upon specified persons in specified circumstances.[45] Justice Samuel Chase concurred in the view that the United States was engaged in "partial" war.[46] Congress, in other words, had the unquestioned power to set limits upon presidential war-making power. To the same effect is *Brown v. United States*,[47] discussed in Chapter 7.

Two commentators—one early, another contemporary—pithily summarized the law. Justice Joseph Story put it thus:

> The power to declare war may be exercised by Congress, not only by authorizing general hostilities, . . . [but also by authorizing] partial hostilities. . . . The latter course was pursued in the qualified war of 1798 with France, which was regulated by divers acts of Congress, and of course was confined to the limits prescribed by those acts.[48]

Abraham Sofaer described the early cases as follows:

> The Supreme Court upheld the legality of undeclared war because Congress had chosen to proceed in that manner, not because of any executive power. Furthermore, the Court specifically declared that Congress could control the conduct of war even to a high degree, and that when it did so the executive acted unlawfully if it exceeded the legislature's limits.[49]

Custom

The other secondary source of constitutional power is constitutional custom. Early presidents generally respected the primacy of Congress in the war-powers area.[50] Although they were vigorous and expansive in their use of executive power, they deferred to legislative authority and deliberately sought con-

[43] 4 Dall. 45 (U.S. 1800).

[44] *Id.*

[45] *Id.* at 40.

[46] *Id.* at 45.

[47] 12 U.S. (8 Cranch) 110 (1814).

[48] J. Story, 3 Commentaries on the Constitution § 1169 (1833).

[49] Sofaer, *The Presidency, War, and Foreign Affairs: Practice Under the Framers*, 40 Law & Contemp. Problems 12, 37 (1976) (citing Little v. Barreme, 6 U.S. (2 Cranch) 170 (1804), and Brown v. United States, 12 U.S. (8 Cranch) 110 (1814)).

[50] *See War Powers Legislation*, *supra* note 19, at 75 *et seq.* (testimony of Professor Richard B. Morris of Columbia University); Presidential Statements Acknowledging Need for Explicit Congressional Exercise of the War Power, app. A to Statement of Leon Friedman, Special Counsel, ACLU, *id.* at 805–8; Berger, *War, Foreign Affairs, and Executive Privilege*, 72 Nw. U. L. Rev. 309 (1977).

gressional approval for actual military conflict.[51] They claimed no monetary, diplomatic, or military power to act in the national interest in the absence of an emergency,[52] nor did any suggest that Congress was significantly limited in its control over assigned executive powers.[53] Two examples are particularly relevant in that they reflect not only presidential deference to the congressional war-making power but also presidential recognition of the need for congressional authorization of the funds necessary to any use of the armed forces. Confronted with a dispute with Spain on the Florida border, President Jefferson requested instruction from Congress:

> That [course] which [the Spanish] . . . have chosen to pursue will appear from the documents now communicated. They authorize the inference that it is their intention to advance on our possessions until they shall be repressed by an opposing force. Considering that Congress alone is constitutionally invested with the power of changing our condition from peace to war, I have thought it my duty to await their authority for using force in any degree which could be avoided. I have barely instructed the officers stationed in the neighborhood of the aggressions to protect our citizens from violence, to patrol within the borders actually delivered to us, and not to go out of them but when necessary to repel an inroad or to rescue a citizen or his property; and the Spanish officers remaining at New Orleans are required to depart without further delay. . . .
>
> . . . But the course to be pursued will require the command of means which it belongs to Congress exclusively to yield or to deny. To them I communicate every fact material for their information and the documents necessary to enable them to judge for themselves. To their wisdom, then I look for the course I am to pursue, and will pursue with sincere zeal that which they shall approve.[54]

Even President Andrew Jackson, a man not shy of war, similarly looked to Congress for guidance and "means" when American shipping was plagued by Argentine marauders near the Falkland Islands:

> In the course of the present year one of our vessels, engaged in the pursuit of a trade which we have always enjoyed without molestation, has been captured by a band acting, as they pretend under the authority of the Government of Buenos Ayres. I have therefore given orders for the dispatch of an armed vessel to join our squadron in those seas and aid in affording all lawful protection to our trade which shall be necessary, and shall without delay send a minister to inquire into the nature of the circumstances and also of the claim, if any, that is set up by that Government to those islands. In the meantime, I submit the case to the consider-

[51] Sofaer, *The Presidency, War, and Foreign Affairs: Practice Under the Framers*, 40 Law & Contemp. Problems 12, 37 (1976).

[52] *Id.* at 36.

[53] *Id.* at 37.

[54] Message from Thomas Jefferson to the Senate and House of Representatives, Dec. 6, 1805, in 1 Messages and Papers of the Presidents 389–90 (J. Richardson ed. 1897) (emphasis added).

ation of Congress, to the end that they may clothe the Executive with such authority and means as they may deem necessary for providing a force adequate to the complete protection of our fellow-citizens fishing and trading in these seas.[55]

In recent decades, presidents have assumed the power to involve the armed forces in "full scale and sustained warfare."[56] A 1966 State Department memorandum states that "[s]ince the Constitution was adopted there have been at least 125 instances in which the President has ordered the armed forces to take action or maintain positions abroad without obtaining prior Congressional authorization, starting with the 'undeclared war' with France (1798–1800)."[57] It has been demonstrated, however, that most of these instances were relatively minor uses of force.[58] Thus, no custom of statutorily unauthorized presidential use of armed forces qualifies as the basis for a juridical norm. Among other things, in all but the narrowest of circumstances, such use has been the subject of vigorous congressional objection. As Professor Alexander Bickle put it, "There are very few instances in our history where a President has taken the law into his own hands against the will of Congress."[59] No constitutional custom can be found because the requisite element of acquiescence is lacking.

Intent of the Framers

One may be inclined to infer from the asymmetrical textual grants of authority that the Framers' intent concerning the scope of presidential power was also limited. Such an inference would be correct. Original constitutional materials indicate that the Framers intended a narrowly circumscribed presiden-

[55] 1 State of the Union Messages of the Presidents 1790–1966, at 352 (F. Israel ed. 1966) (emphasis added).

[56] S. Rep. No. 797, 90th Cong., 1 Sess. 24 (1967). As of 1975, the number of casualties suffered by the United States in Vietnam (359,859) exceeded that suffered in World War I (320,710), the Korean War (157,530), and every other war in which the United States participated except World War II (in which the United States suffered 1,078,062 casualties). The World Almanac & Book of Facts 476 (1975).

[57] Office of the Legal Adviser, U.S. Dep't of State, The Legality of the United States Participation in the Defense of Vietnam, *reprinted in* 75 Yale L.J. 1085, 1101 (1966).

[58] *See* Mora v. McNamara, 389 U.S. 934, 936 (1967) (Douglas J., dissenting) (quoting statement of Under Secretary of State Nicolas Katzenbach); Corwin, *The President's Power*, in The President: Role and Powers 361 (1965) (the "vast majority" of the instances "involved fights with pirates, landings of small naval contingents on barbarous or semi-barbarous coasts [to protect American citizens], the dispatch of small bodies of troops to chase bandits or cattle rustlers across the Mexican border"); Wormuth, *The Vietnam War: The President Versus the Constitution*, in 2 The Vietnam War and International Law 711, 740–54 (1969). Examining these and other authorities, Professor Berger concludes that " 'only since 1950 have Presidents regarded themselves as having authority to commit the armed forces to full scale and sustained warfare.' " Berger, *supra* note 50, at 67 (quoting S. Rep. No. 797, 90th Cong., 1st Sess. 24 (1967)).

[59] War Powers Legislation: Hearings Before the Comm. on Foreign Relations, U.S. Senate, 92d Cong., 1st Sess. 560 (1971).

tial war-making power, with the commander-in-chief clause conferring minimal policy-making authority.[60] The Framers' concept of the commander in chief as "first general" apparently derives from the relationship between the Continental Congress and General Washington during the Revolutionary War. The commission given Washington as commander in chief reflects the subordination of that officer to the will of Congress. After reciting their "especial trust and confidence" in Washington and enjoining him to cause "strict discipline and order to be observed in the army and that the soldiers are duly exercised and provided with all convenient necessaries," the commission concluded:

> And you are to regulate your conduct in every respect by the rules and discipline of war (as herewith given you) and punctually to observe and follow such orders and directions from time to time as you shall receive from this or a future Congress of the said United Colonies or a committee of Congress for that purpose appointed.[61]

There is no evidence that the Framers intended to confer upon the President any independent authority to commit the armed forces to combat, except in order to repel "sudden attacks." Early drafts of the Constitution gave Congress the power to "make war." This apparently was an intentional reversal of the English procedure and a return to what was perceived as the English system prior to 1066 when Parliament, not the King, made war. Edmund Wilson, writing in 1791, observed that "[a]s the law is now received in England, the king has the sole prerogative of making war. On this very interesting power, the constitution of the United States renews the principles of government, known in England before the conquest."[62]

In what apparently was the Philadelphia Convention's primary debate on the war power, on August 17, 1787, Samuel Butler proposed vesting the power to declare war in the President alone. Elbridge Gerry responded that he never expected to hear in a republic a motion to empower the Executive alone to declare war. Oliver Ellsworth said that it should be easier to get out of war than into it. George Mason agreed; he was, he said, for clogging rather than facilitating war, but for facilitating peace. He was against giving the power of war to the Executive, he said, because the Executive was not safely to be trusted with it.[63] On the motion of James Madison and Elbridge Gerry *declare*

[60] Professor Arthur Schlesinger testified that the "Framers understood the commander in chief clause . . . as conferring merely ministerial function, not as creating an independent and additional source of executive authority. The commander in chief clause definitely did not bestow war-making power on the chief executive." 1988 Senate War Powers Hearings, *supra* note 19, at 1230–31.

[61] The Washington Papers 124–25 (S. Padover ed. 1955).

[62] J. Wilson, 1 Works 434 (1791).

[63] 1 The Records of the Federal Convention of 1787, at 317 (M. Farrand rev. ed. 1937) (hereinafter cited as Farrand).

was substituted for *make*.[64] The reason given in Madison's notes was to "[leave] to the Executive the power to repel sudden attacks."[65] Rufus King added that " 'make' war might be understood to 'conduct' it which was an Executive function."[66]

Writing in 1793, Madison, the principal architect of the Constitution, addressed the executive power to make war:

> Every just view that can be taken of this subject, admonishes the public of the necessity of a rigid adherence to the simple, the received, and the fundamental doctrine of the constitution, that the power to declare war, is fully and exclusively vested in the legislature; that the executive has no right, in any case, to decide the question, whether there is or is not cause for declaring war; that the right of convening and informing congress, whenever such a question seems to call for a decision, is all the right which the constitution has deemed requisite or proper. . . .[67]

Madison wrote Jefferson that he believed that "the constitution supposes, what the History of all Gov[ernmen]ts demonstrates, that the Ex[ecutive] is

[64] 2 The Records of the Federal Convention of 1787, at 318–19 (M. Farrand ed. 1911).

[65] *Id.* at 318.

[66] *Id.* at 319. It has been argued that the change from "make" to "declare" recognized "the warmaking authority of the President, implied by his role as executive and commander-in-chief and by congressional power to declare, but not make, war." Ratner, *The Coordinated Warmaking Power—Legislative, Executive and Judicial Roles*, 44 S. Cal. L. Rev. 461,467 (1971). But as Professor Raoul Berger of Harvard Law School pointed out, the commander-in-chief clause conferred only the first generalship of the forces, and the "executive powers . . . do not include the rights of war and peace." Berger, *War-Making by the President*, 121 U. Pa. L. Rev. 29, 41 (1972) (citing 1 The Records of the Federal Convention of 1787, at 66–67 (M. Farrand ed. 1911)) (hereinafter cited as Berger). Professor Berger concludes that "[o]nly in a very limited sense—command of the armed forces plus authority to repel sudden attacks—can one accurately refer to a presidential war-making power." *Id.* He also makes a cogent argument, based on original materials, that "sudden attacks" was not meant to include threats of attack, for in such cases the ability of Congress to respond promptly would obviate the need for immediate presidential action that the change from "make" to "declare" had recognized. *Id.* at 43–45.

Section 2(c) of the War Powers Resolution conforms precisely, it will be noted, with Professor Berger's views. The Senate version of the Resolution, on the other hand, would have allowed the President to use force to evacuate United States citizens and nationals in certain emergency situations, S. 440, 93d Cong., 1st Sess. § 3(3) (1973), and to "forestall direct and imminent" threats of attack on the United States, its territories and possessions, and its armed forces abroad, *id.* §§ 3(1)–(2). But the Senate version did not indicate that such uses were the constitutional prerogative of the President. Addressing the "forestall direct and imminent" threats provision of this bill, Professor Berger concluded that it represented a constitutionally permissible delegation of power. Berger, *supra*, at 45–47. The evacuation provision might have been similarly viewed; on the other hand, there is some reason to believe that the Framers intended that the President be able to use force to rescue United States citizens abroad when there is no time for Congress to authorize such use and Congress has not explicitly prohibited it. See *supra* note 54 (message of President Jefferson).

[67] 6 The Writings of James Madison 174 (G. Hunt ed. 1906).

the branch of power most interested in war, & most prone to it. It has accordingly with studied care, vested the question of war in the Legisl[ature].''[68] He was nonetheless concerned that the people might still be ''cheated out of the best ingredients in their Govt, the safeguards of peace which is the greatest of their blessings.''[69] Congress might forestall this eventuality, he believed, by ''insist[ing] on a full communication of the intelligence on which measures are recommended.''[70] ''Those who are to conduct a war,'' Madison wrote elsewhere, ''cannot in the nature of things, be the proper or safe judges, whether a war ought to be commenced, continued or concluded.''[71]

Thomas Jefferson, in an oft-quoted letter to Madison in 1789, wrote: ''We have already given in example one effectual check to the dog of war by transferring the power of letting him loose from the Executive to the Legislative body, from those who are to spend to those who are to pay.''[72] Alexander Hamilton, among the Founders a relative admirer of the Executive, concurred:

> The history of human conduct does not warrant that exalted opinion of human virtue which would make it wise in a nation to commit interests of so delicate and momentous a kind as those which concern its intercourse with the rest of the world to the sole disposal of a magistrate, created and circumstanced, as would be a president of the United States.[73]

In the Federalist No. 69, he explained the commander-in-chief clause:

> [T]he President is to be Commander in Chief of the army and navy of the United States. In this respect his authority would be nominally the same with that of the King of Great Britain, but in substance much inferior to it. It would amount to nothing more than the supreme command and direction of the military and naval forces, as first General and Admiral of the confederacy; while that of the British King extends to the declaring of war and to the raising and regulating of fleets and armies; all which, by the Constitution under consideration, would appertain to the Legislature.[74]

Professor Henkin has noted in this connection that generals, ''even when they are 'first,' do not determine the political purposes for which troops are to be used; they command them in the execution of policy made by others.''[75] The ''others,'' of course, consisted of Congress; James Wilson's comments at the

[68] *Id.* at 313.
[69] *Id.*
[70] *Id.*
[71] 6 J. Madison, Writings 148 (G. Hunt ed. 1900–10).
[72] 15 The Papers of Thomas Jefferson 397 (J. Boyd ed. 1958).
[73] The Federalist No. 75, at 505–6 (A. Hamilton) (J. Cooke ed. 1961).
[74] The Federalist No. 69, at 465 (A. Hamilton) (J. Cooke ed. 1961).
[75] Henkin, *supra* note 8, at 50–51.

Pennsylvania ratifying convention seemed to sum up his colleagues' belief concerning the power to initiate hostilities:

> This system will not hurry us into war; it is calculated to guard against it. It will not be in the power of a single man, or a single body of men, to involve us in such distress; for the important power of declaring war is vested in the legislature at large: this declaration must be made with the concurrence of the House of Representatives. . . .[76]

In sum, the power to declare war meant the power, in Hamilton's words "*when the nation is at peace*, to change that state into a state of war; whether from calculations of policy or from provocations or injuries received: in other words, it belongs to Congress only, *to go to war*."[77]

Functional Analysis

Functional considerations, the final tertiary source, suggest that presidential authority exists in emergency situations representing bona fide threats to the survival of the nation. Congress in such circumstances would probably have no time to meet; the President in such circumstances can act quickly. It is hard to hypothesize congressional restrictions limiting this sort of purely protective presidential response. It is equally difficult to imagine congressional restrictions that would pose any significant restraint to valid use of the armed forces to respond to attacks upon United States forces located abroad. Similar considerations would apply to other uses of the armed forces suggested in the legal adviser's list. It could be that the President does indeed have a plenary power to respond defensively in such situations, but the question has never arisen in practice and likely never will. Thus there seems little point in devoting much attention here to whether the President has plenary power in such situations. It might suffice to say that his or her sole powers do extend to operational battlefield decisions concerning the means to be employed to achieve ends chosen by Congress.

Conclusion

The most reasonable conclusion, taking into account the constitutional text, case law, constitutional custom, the Framers' intent, and functional considerations, is that the President's plenary power to introduce the armed forces into hostilities abroad is extraordinarily narrow. *Plenary*, again, is used as a term of art; it signifies a power to act in the face of congressional disapproval (e.g.,

[76] 2 Debates in the Several State Conventions on the Adoption of the Federal Constitution 528 (J. Elliot ed. 1859, 1861).

[77] A. Hamilton, The Examination, *in* H. Syrett, 25 The Papers of Alexander Hamilton 456 (1961–79) (emphasis in original).

beyond the sixty-day period set out in the War Powers Resolution, discussed next). There is nothing in these sources of constitutional power that would indicate the constitutional authority for a president to disregard the congressional policy determinations concerning the duration or purposes for which the armed forces may be used in combat. The constitutional model was aptly summarized by Senator Fulbright:

> The analogy has been used of whether or not a ship is to take a trip. It is the Congress [that has] authority to decide and not the President, but the Congress is not the captain of the ship. Once we decide to go into a war then nobody questions the right of the President to direct it. He is to guide the ship. . . .[78]

These sources further suggest conclusions concerning two additional issues. First, does the Constitution pose limits on the President's concurrent power to use the armed forces where Congress has prescribed no limits? Second, does the Constitution prescribe any limits concerning the *scope* of force that may be employed, once requirements concerning initial justification have been met?

Is the President possessed of *concurrent* power, an "initiating power," that permits action unless and until Congress limits or prohibits the action? If so, what is its scope; what sorts of acts may be initiated? Stated somewhat differently, the question might be framed this way: Does the Constitution pose limits on the President's power to use the armed forces where Congress has prescribed no limits?

The sources reviewed above indicate that it is for Congress to determine the policy reasons for which armed force will be used. The President is precluded from doing so. This preclusion obtains in nonemergency situations, circumstances that permit and require policy formulation. The President cannot, for example, constitutionally use armed force to harass or overthrow a government that he happens not to like. Such acts require a policy determination of the sort clearly allotted to Congress by the declaration-of-war clause.

Before discussing circumstances in which the President is constitutionally permitted to use the armed forces in hostilities without congressional authorization, let us note that we have thus far been considering only one of two dimensions of the war power. The first is whether the use of force is constitutionally permitted *ab initio*. The second concerns the permissible *scope* of the war power. We have not considered whether, given a constitutional use of the armed forces in hostilities, that use might nonetheless be subject to constitutional constraints concerning the *degree* of force that can be employed. It is important to note the possibility of such limits before treating other conceivable justifications. If, for example, the Department of State legal adviser is

[78] War Powers Legislation: Hearings Before the Comm. on Foreign Relations, U. S. Senate, 92d Cong., 1st Sess. 504 (1971).

correct that the President possesses the independent power to use the armed forces to "protect U.S. Embassies and Legations abroad," it does not necessarily follow that he or she possesses the constitutional power to use whatever measure of force he or she chooses. The degree of force employed is itself the subject of constitutional limits; it must be proportional—"strictly circumscribed by the circumstances which justify its initiation."[79]

The sources reviewed suggest that when the President acts on his own constitutional authority, the force employed must be strictly tied to and justified by the circumstances initially permitting the use of force. If the President does indeed possess the constitutional power to "protect U.S. Embassies and Legations abroad," therefore, that does not mean that he or she may, say, use nuclear weapons against a country in response to its government's indifference to attacks on United States diplomatic persons or property. Nor does it mean that if he does indeed possess the power to "rescue American citizens abroad," he also possesses the power to overthrow the government of a country that is unable or unwilling to protect them. Use of force against such a government would not be justified by the emergency protective rationale pursuant to which force is deployed.

Having noted that initial use of force and its permissible scope are different issues, it is possible to return now to the discussion of circumstances in which the President has constitutional authority, acting in the face of congressional silence, to *initiate* the use of the armed forces in hostilities. The legal adviser's list is not a bad start. To express the converse of the proposition set out above, the President does have the power to use the armed forces, in the face of congressional silence, in emergency situations involving the imminent threat of grievous harm to American citizens and nationals. Consistent with the sources outlined above, however, several limitations apply.

First, all diplomatic remedies must have been exhausted. As in domestic jurisprudence, one is not required to undertake futile efforts, but the constitutional structure implies the propriety of armed force only as a last resort. Accordingly, it is important that within the limits of reason, a president attempt to settle a dispute peacefully before introducing the armed forces into hostilities without statutory authorization.

Second, the use of force must be strictly limited to and justified by the purpose of rescuing the endangered citizens. "Rescue" cannot be a pretext for other unauthorized missions. The use of force must be terminated when the limited protective objective is achieved—not, as occurred in the Grenadian invasion, continued for purposes unrelated to the rescue mission.

[79] This language comes from Terry v. Ohio, 392 U.S. 1 (1968), an opinion upholding "stop-and-frisk" searches. A similar two-part analysis exists in fourth amendment law. The search must be both justified at the outset and restricted in scope. Circumstances justifying a stop will support only a pat-down for weapons. *Id.* In contrast, a stronger factual showing, of the sort permitting a full arrest, will accordingly permit a broader search. *See generally* F. Miller, R. Dawson, G. Dix & R. Parnas, Criminal Justice Administration 228–42 (1986).

Third, a principle of proportionality must be respected. Likely gains to be achieved through use of force must outweigh likely losses. Thus the use of a Marine battalion to rescue, say, a jailed American journalist from a Soviet prison obviously is not permitted. The President's act must be purposefully calculated to save lives, not jeopardize them. President Gerald Ford's reckless use of armed force to rescue the crew of the container ship *Mayaguez* is a case in point; it is hard to justify the loss of forty-one lives to save thirty-nine.

Fourth, people who voluntarily enter ultrahazardous areas, such as Lebanon in the mid-1980s, should be deemed to assume the risk. One who travels to a region where physical danger is reasonably foreseeable has no reasonable expectation of rescue by United States armed forces. Such operations carry with them the ever-present risk of causing further harm to fellow citizens by embroiling the nation in full-scale hostilities. No American traveling abroad has a "claim" to rescue, any more than the President has a "duty" to rescue that person. The exercise of presidential rescue authority is discretionary, not ministerial.[80]

Subject to these limits, it can reasonably be argued that the President has a limited concurrent or "initiating" power to use armed force to rescue endangered Americans abroad.[81] A similar initiating power exists for threats against other United States entities, such as embassies, consulates, and military installations. Yet similar restraints apply. The armed forces must have a legal right to be where they are. The President cannot bootstrap his or her way into broader constitutional authority by unconstitutionally invading a foreign nation and then claiming to respond to attacks on those same forces. The prevention of violence directed at an American embassy or American diplomats is primarily the responsibility of the government of the country where an embassy is located. If violence against the embassy staff is foreseeable, the proper response is not to wait until the attack occurs but to withdraw endangered personnel until conditions permit their safe return.

An "initiating" power, it bears repeating, is ultimately subject to congressional limitation. The President may act only as long as the Congress remains silent. Those acts are "contingently constitutional." Congress can legislate a termination. The President's exercise of power is justified by the emergency. Once Congress has time to act, the emergency, *and the President's initiating war powers*, are by definition terminated.

THE WAR POWERS RESOLUTION

In the aftermath of the long and bitter debate over United States military involvement in Vietnam, Congress determined "to fulfill the intent of the fram-

[80] *See* Chapter 6, dealing with claims that the President has a "duty" to carry out the terms of mutual-security treaties by introducing armed forces into hostilities.

[81] *But see* Berger, *The Protection of Americans Abroad*, 44 U. Cinn. L. Rev. 741 (1975), arguing that the President has no such power.

ers of the Constitution . . . [by ensuring] that the collective judgment of both the Congress and the President''[82] would apply to future exercises of the war-making powers. The War Powers Resolution was the product of growing concern that the role of Congress in effecting ''national commitments'' had been permitted to atrophy.[83] Enacted over President Nixon's veto in 1973,[84] the

[82] Resolution, *supra* note 4, § 2(a).

[83] *See* S. Res. 85, 91st Cong., 1st Sess. (1969), expressing the sense of the Senate that a national commitment of the United States should result ''only from affirmative action taken by the executive and legislative branches of the United States Government by means of a treaty, statute, or concurrent resolution of both Houses of Congress specifically providing for such commitment.'' The resolution defined a ''national commitment'' as ''the use of the armed forces of the United States on foreign territory, or as a promise to assist a foreign country, government, or people by the use of the armed forces or financial resources of the United States.'' *Id.* Hearings on war powers legislation were held on it in 1967 and again in 1969, when the Senate adopted a slightly different version. Yet ''[i]t soon became evident,'' Senator Fulbright testified before the Murphy Commission, ''that the Executive was not prepared to comply with congressional affirmations of constitutional principle that do not carry the force of law.'' Committee on Foreign Affairs, United States House of Representatives, The War Powers Resolution: A Special Study of the Committee on Foreign Affairs 24 (undated committee print).

The next year, 1970, ten different versions of war-powers legislation were introduced in the House of Representatives. *Id.* at 48. Senator Jacob Javits and several other Senators initiated such legislation in the Senate. *Id.* at 52. Hearings were held in the House, and legislation was passed, *id.* at 66, but the Senate took no action on it that year. In 1971, however, the Senate Foreign Relations Committee held hearings, and by the middle of that year, war-powers measures had been introduced by five Senators. In 1972, war-powers legislation was reported by the Committee and passed by the Senate, and although the House again held hearings on and repassed its own version, the conference committee was unable to fashion a compromise. Finally, in 1973, both houses again passed such legislation; this time, a compromise was reached, and the conference report was adopted by both houses—only to be vetoed by President Richard Nixon.

For an excellent review of the Resolution's ''antecedents'' along with thoughtful commentary on its workability, *see* P. Holt, The War Powers Resolution: The Role of Congress in U.S. Armed Intervention (1978).

[84] Joint Resolution of Nov. 7, 1973, Pub. L. No. 93-148, 87 Stat. 555. In his veto message, the President explained that ''[w]hile I am in accord with the desire of the Congress to assert its proper role in the conduct of our foreign affairs, the restrictions which this resolution would impose upon the authority of the President are both unconstitutional and dangerous to the best interests of our Nation.'' Message from Richard Nixon to the House of Representatives, Oct. 24, 1973, in 9 Weekly Compilation of Presidential Documents 1285 (1973). The President's constitutional objection was essentially that the Resolution ''would attempt to take away, by a mere legislative act, authorities which the President has properly exercised under the Constitution for almost 200 years.'' *Id.* at 1286.

The President's conclusion that the Resolution would be ''dangerous to the best interests of our Nation'' derived from his opinion that it ''would seriously undermine this Nation's ability to act decisively and convincingly in times of international crisis.'' Message from Richard Nixon to the House of Representatives, Oct. 24, 1973, in 9 Weekly Compilation of Presidential Documents 1285, 1286 (1973). He hypothesized that had the Resolution been in effect in recent years, ''[w]e may well have been unable to respond in the way we did during the Berlin crisis of 1961, the Cuban missile crisis of 1962, the Congo rescue operation in 1964, and the Jordanian crisis of 1970—to mention just a few examples.'' *Id.* The President's veto message apparently was written before enactment of the Resolution and not modified thereafter. It seems clearly to respond to the Senate version, having assumed that the conference report would retain prior restraints. It did not.

Resolution restricts the duration of any involvement of United States armed forces in "hostilities" or in "situations where imminent involvement in hostilities is clearly indicated by the circumstances," when the introduction of those forces occurs without a declaration of war.[85] It requires the President to submit a report to Congress within forty-eight hours after any such introduction of the armed forces,[86] and to terminate the involvement within sixty days after the report was or should have been submitted,[87] or sooner "if the Congress so directs by concurrent resolution."[88] The Resolution also requires the President to consult with Congress before and during such involvements[89] and to report to Congress when forces are deployed in certain other situations.[90] These are the only provisions of the Resolution that restrict presidential use of the armed forces.[91] A "Purpose and Policy" section[92] expresses the understanding of Congress as to the scope of the President's constitutional power independently to introduce the armed forces into hostilities,[93] but it contains no mandatory language.[94]

The Resolution, then, imposes only what may be termed "subsequent limitations" upon the President's use of the armed forces. This contrasts with the Senate version of the Resolution, rejected by the conference committee, which would also have imposed "prior restraints."[95] It stated in operative terms,

[85] Resolution, *supra* note 4 § 4(a)(1). For the sake of convenience, and unless otherwise indicated, the word *hostilities* "will hereinafter encompass "situations where imminent involvement in hostilities is clearly indicated by the circumstances," as well as hostilities per se.

[86] *Id.* § 4(a). The report must set forth the circumstances necessitating, the legal authority for, and the estimated duration of the involvement. *Id.* § 4(a)(A)(C). In addition, the President must report periodically on the status of the involvement. *Id.* § 4(c).

[87] *Id.* § 5(b). The sixty-day period may be extended up to thirty days if the President determines and certifies to Congress in writing that the safe removal of the troops so requires. *Id.* This automatic termination does not apply if Congress has declared war, specifically authorized the involvement, extended the sixty-day period, or is "unable to meet as a result of armed attack upon the United States." *Id.*

[88] *Id.* § 5(c).

[89] *Id.* § 3.

[90] *Id.* § 4.

[91] Other provisions of the Resolution require that Congress give expedited consideration to a concurrent resolution terminating hostilities, *id.* § 7, and to proposals to extend the sixty-day limit on involvement, *id.* § 6; prohibit the inference that any law or treaty authorizes introduction of the armed forces into hostilities, unless such law or treaty "states that it is intended to constitute specific statutory authorization [for the introduction] within the meaning of this joint resolution," *id.* § 8(a), and states that the Resolution is not intended to alter the constitutional authority of the President or Congress or grant any authority to the former that "he would not have had in the absence of this joint resolution." *Id.* § 8(d).

[92] *Id.* § 2.

[93] *Id.* § 2(c).

[94] For a thorough and accurate account of the emergence of the "compromise" version, *see* T. Eagleton, War and Presidential Power: A Chronicle of Congressional Surrender (1974).

[95] One of the best analyses of the comparative institutional responsibilities of Congress and the President in the realm of war making is the report of the Senate Foreign Relations Committee on the Senate version of the Resolution, S. Rep. No. 220, 93d Cong., 1st Sess. (1973).

rather than merely as the understanding of Congress, the circumstances in which the armed forces may be introduced into hostilities without a declaration of war.[96] The Senate version differed from the Resolution in two other important respects. It explicitly allowed the President to introduce the armed forces to evacuate United States citizens and nationals abroad in certain emergency situations,[97] and by avoiding reference to the Constitution in defining the circumstances in which the President could independently engage the armed forces, it avoided indicating to some that the President has a constitutional right to act independently in those circumstances.[98]

[96] The bill, introduced by Senator Jacob Javits, provided in § 3 that

> [i]n the absence of a declaration of war by Congress, the Armed Forces of the United States may be introduced in hostilities, or in situations where imminent involvement in hostilities is clearly indicated by the circumstances, only—
>
> (1) to repel an armed attack upon the United States, its territories and possessions; to take necessary and appropriate retaliatory actions in the event of such an attack; and to forestall the direct and imminent threat of such an attack;
>
> (2) to repel an armed attack against the Armed Forces of the United States located outside of the United States, its territories and possessions, and to forestall the direct and imminent threat of such an attack;
>
> (3) to protect while evacuating citizens and nationals of the United States, as rapidly as possible, from (A) any situation on the high seas involving a direct and imminent threat to the lives of such citizens and nationals, or (B) any country in which such citizens and nationals are present with the express or tacit consent of the government of such country and are being subjected to a direct and imminent threat to their lives, either sponsored by such government or beyond the power of such government to control; but the President shall make every effort to terminate such a threat without using the Armed Forces of the United States, and shall, where possible, obtain the consent of the government of such country before using the Armed Forces of the United States to protect citizens and nationals of the United States being evacuated from such country; or
>
> (4) pursuant to specific authorization. . . .

S. 440, 93d Cong., 1st Sess. § 3 (1973).

[97] *Compare id.* § 3(3), with Resolution § 2(c).

[98] *Compare* S. 440, 93d Cong., 1st Sess. § 3 (1973) *with* Resolution § 2(c). Section 2(c) of the Resolution reflects a compromise reached in conference committee between § 3 of the Senate bill and the House bill, H. J. Res. 542, 93d Cong., 1st Sess. (1973), which contained no provision similar to either of those sections. (Otherwise, the two bills were essentially similar, except that the Senate bill's counterpart of Resolution § 5(b) provided a basic thirty-day limit, S. 440, 93d Cong., 1st Sess. § 5 (1973), while that of the House bill, H.J. Res. 542, 93d Cong., 1st Sess. § 4(b) (1973), allowed 120 days.) The prior restraints provision of the Senate bill was opposed on primarily two grounds. Some considered the President's powers to be more extensive than those recognized by that provision. Senator Strom Thurmond, for example, expressed this view during debate on the bill:

> The legislation provides only four situations in which an immediate response is allowed, and it may well be questioned whether it is possible to define and describe in advance all possible potential emergency situations to which the President might be called on to respond.
>
> . . . It should also be pointed out that some constitutional law experts maintain that the independent authority of the President under the Constitution is substantially broader than the four categories specified in the bill.

119 Cong. Rec. 25,104 (1973). Similarly, Senator Griffin believed that § 3 was "an arbitrary restriction" on the President's constitutional powers. *Id.* at 25,099.

The word *invoke* is occasionally applied to the War Powers Resolution, but the concept is misleading because it suggests that the Resolution contains some authority to be "invoked" and that adherence to its procedure is discretionary. The Resolution explicitly states that "[n]othing in this joint resolution . . . shall be construed as granting any authority to the President with respect to the introduction of the United States Armed Forces into hostilities . . . which . . . he would not have had in [its] absence."[99] The filing of a report under section 4(a)(1) thus gives the President no additional authority. During the sixty-day period in which the armed forces are engaged in hostilities, the President can derive no authority from the Resolution.

The notion of "invoking" the Resolution also wrongly implies presidential discretion in the submission of reports. In fact, the wording of section 4(a)(1) is clear, and no discretion exists; if events occur that constitute "hostilities or . . . situations where imminent involvement in hostilities is clearly indicated by the circumstances," a report must be submitted. That the sixty-day period commences when a report is "required to be submitted" reinforces this conclusion. This provision makes clear that presidential noncompliance with the

---

Others expressed a contrary fear—that "spelling out" powers not recognized by the Constitution would only support further presidential usurpation of the war-making powers by providing statutory language on which unconstitutional military operations could be based. Senator Fulbright observed:

> The list of conditions spelled out in Section 3 of the bill is, in my opinion, about as precise and comprehensive a list as can be devised, and its purpose, I fully recognize, is not to expand Presidential power but to restrict it to the categories listed. Nevertheless, I am apprehensive that the very comprehensiveness and precision of the contingencies listed in Section 3 may be drawn upon by future Presidents to explain or justify military initiatives which would otherwise be difficult to explain or justify. A future President might, for instance, cite "secret" or "classified" data to justify almost any conceivable foreign military initiative as essential to "forestall the direct and imminent threat" of an attack on the United States or its armed forces abroad.

S. Rep. No. 220, 93d Cong., 1st Sess. 34–35 (1973) (supplemental views of J. W. Fulbright).

The absence of prior restraints in the House bill and in the Resolution itself, on the other hand, was opposed on the ground that it rendered ineffectual any legislation purporting to inhibit presidential initiation of wars unwanted by Congress. Thus Senators Thomas Eagleton and Gaylord Nelson, cosponsors of the Senate bill, voted against the Resolution. Senator Eagleton explained:

> If we are reluctant to deal with the constitutional issue of prior authority, then we will continue to be confronted in years to come with the prospect of desperately trying to stop misbegotten wars.
>
> War powers legislation that is meaningful has to deal with the fundamental causes of the constitutional impasse that plagued the Nation for the past decade. It must, in my judgment, in the most precise legal language, carefully spell out those powers which adhere to the Executive by reason of his status as Commander in Chief and his obligation to act in emergencies to repel attacks upon the Nation, its forces, and its citizens abroad. For the rest, such legislation must make clear that all remaining decisions involved in taking the Nation to war are reserved to the elected representatives of the people—as the Constitution so says, the Congress.

119 Cong. Rec. 33,557 (1973). Representative Elizabeth Holtzman also voted against the Resolution, stating that "it does not prevent the commencement of an illegal war, but allows one to continue for from 60 to 90 days." *Id.* at 33,872 (1973).

[99] Resolution, § 8(d)(2).

reporting requirement of section 4(a)(1) will not defeat the operation of the Resolution; the running of the period will still be triggered if the specified events occur. Congress, under such circumstances, might elect to provide by law that the period has been triggered on a certain date. Nothing in the Resolution, however, suggests that congressional inaction will in any way toll the running of the time limit.

Indeed, it would have made no sense for Congress to require that if the President violates the law by failing to report, the onus would then be on Congress to pass a law "invoking" (presumably triggering) the time period. The option of enacting a statute that limits presidential authority to use the armed forces was available to Congress before it enacted the War Powers Resolution—and is still available. Congress can always enact a law imposing a sixty-day limit on such use; there would have been no purpose in enacting the War Powers Resolution if its only effect were to announce statutorily that Congress has the authority to enact a sixty-day limit on use of the armed forces in hostilities.

The legislative history of the Resolution makes this plain. There is nothing in that history to suggest that in the event the armed forces are introduced into hostilities or into situations where imminent involvement in hostilities is clearly indicated by the circumstances, the President has the option of submitting or not submitting a report under section 4(a)(1). Nor is there anything to suggest that if the President fails to comply with that statutory obligation, Congress must then say statutorily (over a veto) that such a report was required. The wording of this section is a compromise between the Senate and House versions. The Senate version made no reference to a report to trigger the period. Rather, it provided that the commencement of the period occurred on "the date of the introduction of [the] Armed Forces in hostilities or any" "situation where imminent involvement in hostilities is clearly indicated by the circumstances."[100] The House version provided that "[w]ithin one hundred and twenty calendar days after a report is submitted or is required to be submitted, . . . the President shall terminate any commitment. . . ."[101] Opponents of the Resolution in both houses claimed that the effect of the time limit, in the words of Congressman Mailliard, "would be to permit the exercise of congressional will through inaction."[102] The argument (addressed below in the discussion of the Resolution's validity) underscores the apparently undisputed legislative intent that no congressional action would be required to trigger the running of the period. As accurately described by one of the

[100] S. 440, 93d Cong., 1st. Sess., § 5 (1973).

[101] H. J. Res. 542, 93d Cong., 1st Sess., § 4(b).

[102] Cong. Rec. H5306 (June 25, 1973) (daily ed.). Similar objections were raised by Reps. Stratton, Cong. Rec. H5308 (June 25, 1973) (daily ed.), Frelinghuysen, Cong. Rec. H5309 (June 25, 1973) (daily ed.), Whalen, Cong. Rec. H5319, (June 25, 1973) (daily ed.), and Ford, Cong. Rec. H6242, (July 18, 1973) (daily ed.)

Resolution's House sponsors, Congressman Pete DuPont, "if nothing happens, the military action stops. . . ."[103]

Validity

TIME LIMITS

In *Lowry v. Reagan*,[104] the Reagan Administration contended that "every Administration since the enactment of the War Powers Resolution . . . has taken the position that the automatic withdrawal provisions of the War Powers are unconstitutional."[105] Not so. Aside from the Nixon Administration,[106] only the Reagan Administration took that position, and only the Reagan Administration violated it.

The Administration's reasons, never spelled out in detail, would probably not have been persuasive. Under the analytical approach set forth in Chapter 1—initially by Chief Justice Marshall in *Little v. Barreme*,[107] reiterated by Justice Jackson in *Youngstown Sheet & Tube Co. v. Sawyer*,[108] and formally adopted by Justice Rehnquist in *Dames & Moore v. Regan*[109]—the time limits of the War Powers Resolution, as well as the "prior restraints" set forth in the earlier Senate version, seem clearly constitutional. The scope of the President's initiating power is a function of the concurrence or nonconcurrence of the Congress; once Congress acts, its negative provides "the rule for the case."[110] That analytical framework provides a general foundation for the Resolution's mandate of consultation and reporting and a time limit upon the use of force abroad—all of which, absent a statement by Congress, might fall within a "zone of twilight."[111] This was Corwin's analysis too: "Clearly such legislation did not require a constitutional amendment, since it only spells out how a power already granted to Congress is to be exercised. . . . [O]n the basis of the precedent of the *Steel Seizure* case . . . it is probable that the Court would uphold the act of Congress."[112] In an important but largely unnoticed opinion of the Carter Justice Department, the Office of the Legal Counsel agreed:

[103] Cong. Rec. H6268, (July 18, 1973) (daily ed.).

[104] 676 F. Supp. 333 (1987).

[105] Declaration of Michael H. Armacost, *id.* at 28.

[106] *See supra* notes 83, 84.

[107] 6 U.S. (2 Cranch) 170 (1804).

[108] 343 U.S. 579 (1952).

[109] 453 U.S. 654 (1981).

[110] *Youngstown*, 343 U.S. at 634 (Jackson, J., concurring).

[111] *Id.* at 637. As indicated in this chapter, I continue to believe that the Resolution should be amended to include prior restraints, backed by funding prohibitions.

[112] E. Corwin, The Constitution and What It Means Today 110 (H. Chase & C. Ducat, eds., 14th ed. 1978).

> We believe that Congress may, as a general constitutional matter, place a 60-day limit on the use of our armed forces as required by the provisions of [section 5(b)] of the Resolution. The Resolution gives the President the flexibility to extend that deadline for up to 30 days in cases of "unavoidable military necessity." This flexibility is, we believe, sufficient under any scenarios we can hypothesize to preserve his constitutional function as Commander-in-Chief. The practical effect of the 60-day limit is to shift the burden to the President to convince the Congress of the continuing need for the use of our armed forces abroad. We cannot say that placing that burden on the President unconstitutionally intrudes upon his executive powers.
>
> Finally, Congress can regulate the President's exercise of his inherent powers by imposing limits *by statute*.[113]

"[A]lthough the Resolution may plausibly be challenged as insufficiently restoring Congress' constitutionally contemplated role in war-making," Professor Tribe has written, "it can hardly be said to take from the Executive Branch any power delegated to it by the Constitution or to enlarge upon powers constitutionally delegated to Congress."[114]

Whether the Resolution can be challenged on *constitutional* grounds as "insufficiently restoring" Congress's role seems doubtful. The time period may represent bad policy in granting the President, as Senator Thomas Eagleton charged, "a 60- to 90-day open-ended blank check."[115] Indeed, the Resolution has also been challenged as *unconstitutional* for this reason; the time period, it is suggested, constitutes an invalid delegation of legislative power—the power to declare war—to the President.[116] Similar contentions have been made with respect to the Gulf of Tonkin Resolution, which provided that "the United States is . . . prepared, *as the President determines*, to take all necessary steps, including the use of armed force, to assist any member" of SEATO.[117] These arguments seem hard to sustain in light of the core holding of

[113] *Presidential Power to Use the Armed Forces Abroad without Statutory Authorization*, 4A Op. Office of the Legal Counsel, Department of Justice 185, 196 (1980).

[114] L. Tribe, American Constitutional Law § 4–7 at 236 (1988).

[115] 119 Cong. Rec. S33556 (daily ed. Oct. 10, 1973). The criticism is more compelling when made from a policy rather than a constitutional standpoint. Although the Resolution disclaims an intent to confer upon the President any authority which he would not have had in its absence, Resolution § 8(d)(1), such a disclaimer is meaningless if the practical effect of § 5(b) is to recognize implicitly executive authority to use the armed forces in hostilities for up to sixty days without congressional approval. In light of the absence of prior restraints and the oblivion into which § 2(c) has been cast, presidents seemed to assume congressional concurrence for such action.

[116] *See, e.g.*, F. Wormuth & E. Firmage, To Chain the Dog of War 216 (1986); Ides, *Congress, Constitutional Responsibility and the War Power*, 17 Loy. L.A.L. Rev. 599 (1984). The delegation doctrine is discussed in Chapter 1 in connection with United States v. Curtiss-Wright, 299 U.S. 304 (1936), and in Chapter 6 in connection with United States mutual-security treaties.

[117] Pub. L. 88-408, H. J. Res. 1145, 73 Stat. 384 (1964) (emphasis added). For suggestions

United States v. Curtiss-Wright[118] that the delegation doctrine applies with lesser force in foreign affairs than domestic affairs. Indeed, the Court has never struck down a foreign-affairs statute as violative of the doctrine. Professor Henkin has thus written that "[f]or constitutional purposes it seems indisputable" that the President had the approval of Congress in the Gulf of Tonkin Resolution.[119] Under the existing case law, this conclusion is hard to dispute, although the rationale underpinning the delegation doctrine supports its application to foreign-affairs matters,[120] and if it is so applied, a broad, standardless grant of war-making power to the President would be unconstitutional.[121]

On the other hand, it is argued that the Resolution is unconstitutional in giving an enemy notice that a president has only sixty to ninety days to use armed force. Aside from lacking support historically,[122] that is a meat-ax argument against all constitutional constraints upon executive war power,[123] for unless that power is seen as unlimited, at some point the President must come to Congress for statutory approval. These critics' quarrel is not with Jacob Javits but with James Madison.[124]

---

that the law raised constitutional difficulties, *see* L. Tribe, American Constitutional Law 234 (2d ed. 1988); Van Alstyne, *Congress, the President, and the Power to Declare War: A Requiem for Vietnam*, 121 Pa. L. Rev. 1, 14–15 (1972).

[118] 299 U.S. 304 (1936).

[119] L. Henkin, *supra* note 8, at 101.

[120] *See* Chapter 6.

[121] *Accord* L. Tribe, American Constitutional Law 234 (2d ed. 1988).

[122] *See* the testimony of two former Chairmen of the Joint Chiefs of Staff:

> SENATOR PRESSLER Now, do you believe that our adversaries have changed their military planning any because of the existence of the War Powers Act? . . .
>
> GENERAL [DAVID C.] JONES I doubt that they have changed their plans. . . .
>
> GENERAL [JOHN W.] VESSEY I would echo that. . . .

1988 Senate War Powers Hearings, *supra* note 19, at 125.

[123] Indeed, some of the Resolution's critics seem to believe that the Executive is not constitutionally constrained in that way. *See, e.g.*, testimony of Hon. Brent Scowcroft, 1988 Senate War Powers Hearings, *supra* note 19, at 122.

> SENATOR BIDEN [W]ould [the President] have the authority . . . to invade Nicaragua with American troops?
>
> GENERAL SCOWCROFT Yes. It may not be prudent if he does not have the support of the Congress, of the country, and a debacle could ensue. But yes.
>
> SENATOR BIDEN . . . [W]ould the President have the authority to invade . . . Poland? . . .
>
> GENERAL SCOWCROFT Yes.

[124] An example is State Department Legal Adviser Abraham Sofaer, who could barely list the parade of horribles set to march by the time limits: they interfere with the "successful completion" of the President's initiative; they "may signal a divided nation, giving adversaries a basis for hoping that the President may be forced to desist"; they provide "an undesirable occasion for interbranch or partisan rivalry. . . ." 1988 Senate War Powers Hearings, *supra* note 19, at 1059–60. The curious thing about these arguments is that every one of them is an argument, not against the War Powers Resolution, but against constitutional limitations on presidential war-making power. Each of these arguments is an argument for untrammeled presidential discretion to use the armed forces whenever, wherever, and for whatever purpose the President may choose. Indeed,

The time limits therefore seem beyond constitutional challenge. The ''definition'' of the President's powers, however (set out in section 2(c)), seems unduly narrow. It fails to recognize presidential power to rescue endangered American nationals abroad. As discussed above, a strong case can be made that the President does possess such a power, albeit a narrow one; force may be used to rescue endangered Americans, subject to the limitations discussed above. Such authority was recognized in the Senate version of the War Powers Resolution,[125] and the conference committee would have been wise to retain a carefully limited provision to that effect in the conference report. Because the military operations conducted in the evacuations of Phnom Penh and Saigon, the seizure of the *Mayaguez*, the Iranian hostage crisis, and the Grenada invasion were all rescue missions, however, the section has largely been ignored, not only by executive officials but by Congress.

During the United States military operations in the Persian Gulf, officials of the Reagan Administration voiced the opinion with some frequency that the Resolution is unconstitutional.[126] These views were not formally communi-

---

on close analysis, it becomes clear that that is precisely his view: ''explicit legislative approval for particular uses of force has never been necessary,'' he candidly states. *Id.* at 1050. The President thus could have used armed force in World War I, World War II, or Vietnam without any declaration of war or any other legislative approval. This view of war-making power is of course not new, but it should suffice at this point in our history to note that the divine-right-of-kings approach was ventilated and rejected in 1789.

As to Sofaer's argument that the time limits interfere with the successful completion of the President's initiative, or former Senator John Tower's argument that the Resolution ''jeopardizes the President's ability to respond quickly, forcefully . . . to protect American interests abroad,'' *id.* at 65, *compare* the testimony of two former chairmen of the Joint Chiefs of Staff:

> GENERAL [DAVID C.] JONES I really do not believe that the War Powers Resolution has had any conscious [effect] on war planning at all. . . .
>
> GENERAL [JOHN W.] VESSEY I think that's right. . . . I have looked down the list of the other 35 or so incidents that one might say have taken place where armed forces have been deployed since the War Powers Resolution has been enacted, and I do not believe that the War Powers Resolution had any impact on the planning for any of those.

Id. at 124, 125. A former (and current) national security adviser, General Brent Scowcroft, responded: ''I would agree with my colleagues.'' *Id.* at 125. Asked what effect the Resolution has had on United States policy, whether it has caused Presidents to ''be more cautious,'' General Scowcroft responded: ''I guess I would have to say that it has had virtually no impact.'' *Id.* at 126.

[125] S. 440, 93d Cong., 1st Sess. § 3(3) (1973).

[126] *See, e.g.*, comments of Secretary of Defense Caspar Weinberger: ''We have always felt it was unconstitutional, an infringement by the Congress on the constitutional authority of the President to conduct foreign policy and to be the commander in chief of the forces.'' N.Y. Times, Sept. 24, 1987, at 1. Marlin Fitzwater, the White House spokesman, echoed that thinking in a news briefing but denied that the Administration was trying to provoke a test in federal courts.

Weinberger repeated his challenge on the ''MacNeil-Lehrer News Hour'' on September 22, 1987. ''[W]e cannot,'' he said, repeating a frequently made assertion, ''accede to, or grant the constitutionality or validity of a statute that every president has felt to be unconstitutional, that every president's legal advisors have told him was unconstitutional.'' Secretary Weinberger did

cated to Congress, however, as a ground for noncompliance with the Resolution. The Carter Administration argued that the Executive may disregard a statute that it considers unconstitutional.[127] The Supreme Court has not addressed the issue; although lower courts have held that the President may decline to defend a statute regarded as constitutionally infirm,[128] they have also held that neither the faithful execution clause of the Constitution[129] nor the President's oath of office[130] permit noncompliance with an act of Congress because of a belief that it is unconstitutional.[131] The scant scholarly opinion that exists supports this view.[132]

If the Resolution was found unconstitutional as applied in certain circumstances,[133] that would not necessarily justify its invalidation *in toto* or even the invalidation of the provision in question. In dealing with treaties thought to suffer some constitutional infirmity, the courts have been disposed to deny enforcement to the suspect provision rather than to strike down the treaty or treaty provision as unconstitutional.[134] Similarly, a statute raising certain first amendment overbreadth problems that render it void on its face may in effect be "rewritten" by the courts to alleviate constitutional difficulties.[135] This approach seems more in keeping with the traditional deference shown the legislature by the courts. Under such an approach, if a portion of the Resolution

---

not specify which provision had been regarded as unconstitutional. In fact, as noted above, only President Nixon challenged the constitutionality of the time limits.

[127] Letter of Attorney General Benjamin R. Civiletti to the Chairman of the Senate Subcomm. on Limitations of Contracted and Delegated Authority, July 30, 1980, 4A Op. of Office of the Legal Counsel, Dep't of Justice 55 (1980).

[128] West Indian Co., Ltd. v. Government of the Virgin Islands, 844 F.2d 1007 (3d Cir. 1988).

[129] U.S. Const., art. II, § 3.

[130] U.S. Const., art. II, § 2, cl. 8.

[131] Lear Siegler, Inc., Energy Products Div. v. Lehman, 842 F.2d 1102 (9th Cir. 1988).

[132] *See, e.g.*, Miller, *The President and the Faithful Execution of the Laws*, 40 Vand. L. Rev. 389 (1987). Corwin firmly agreed:

> The fact the President takes an oath "to preserve and protect" the Constitution does not authorize him to exceed his own powers under the Constitution on the pretext of preserving and protecting it. The President may veto a bill on the ground that in his opinion it violates the Constitution, but if the bill is passed over his veto, he must, by the great weight of authority, ordinarily regard it as law until it is set aside by judicial decision, since the power of interpreting the law, except as it is delegated by the law itself, is not an attribute of "executive power."

E. Corwin, The Constitution and What It Means Today 156 (H. Chase & C. Ducat, eds., 14th ed. 1978) (citations omitted).

[133] For the reasons discussed above, such a finding is hard to imagine with respect to any provision of the Resolution except the time limits.

[134] *See, e,g.*, City of New Orleans v. United States, 35 U.S. (10 Pet.) 662 (1836) (treaty provision violating fifth amendment just-compensation clause denied enforcement); Rocca v. Thompson, 223 U.S. 317 (1912) (treaty provision creating federalism problems denied enforcement); United States *ex rel.* Martinez Angosto v. Mason, 344 F.2d 673 (5th Cir. 1975) (treaty provision raising fourth amendment problems denied enforcement).

[135] *See, e.g.*, Brockett v. Spokane Arcades, Inc., 472 U.S. 491 (1985).

was deemed violative of the Constitution, the courts might appropriately "perform reconstructive surgery"[136] to render inoffensive the part of the Resolution held unconstitutional.

LEGISLATIVE VETO

One operative provision of the War Powers Resolution does raise grave constitutional questions. Section 5(c), allowing Congress by concurrent resolution to force the President to withdraw the armed forces from hostilities, is clearly invalid after the Supreme Court's decision in *Immigration and Naturalization Service v. Chadha*.[137] The Court found that presentation clause[138] requirements must be met whenever legislative action has the "purpose and effect of altering the legal rights, duties and relations of persons, including the . . . Executive Branch . . . outside the legislative branch."[139] Adoption of a concurrent resolution under section 5(c) would have the purpose and effect of altering the rights and duties of the President.[140] Justice White, in dissent, was doubtless correct in reading the majority opinion as invalidating the legislative veto in the War Powers Resolution.[141] Supreme Court decisions since *Chadha* have read its prohibition broadly and support this conclusion.[142]

To be sure, arguments can be made to the contrary, but none is persuasive. It might be argued that the legislative veto contained in section 5(c) is distinguishable from that in *Chadha*[143] in that the latter pertained to the exercise of a statutorily delegated power, whereas in the case of the War Powers Resolution (and, arguably, the Impoundment Control Act[144]), the legislative veto applies to the exercise of a power that derives not from any statute[145] but entirely

[136] This is the term used by Professor Laurence Tribe in describing the process that occurs in first amendment cases. *See generally* L. Tribe, American Constitutional Law § 12-28 at 1027 (1988).

[137] 462 U.S. 919 (1983).

[138] U.S. Const., art. I, § 7, cl. 3.

[139] *Chadha*, 462 U.S. at 952.

[140] It is not that the President has a "right" or "duty" to use the armed forces in hostilities, but rather that a duty to *withdraw* them would obtain upon the adoption of a concurrent resolution. And the invalidity of this procedure does not, of course, imply a plenary presidential power to use armed force in any given circumstances. Congress *can* legislate limits to such use, provided they are enacted in accordance with the presentation clause.

The *Chadha* prohibition does not apply to policy declarations and statements of political intent, such as the legislative review procedures in the Central American agreement reached between the President and the congressional leadership. *See* Glennon, *The Good Friday Accords: Legislative Veto by Another Name*? 83 Am. J. of Int'l. L. 554 (1989).

[141] *Id*. at 974 (White, J., dissenting). Justice White concluded that "[t]he Court's Article I analysis appears to invalidate all legislative vetoes irrespective of form or substance." *Id*.

[142] *See* L. Tribe, American Constitutional Law § 4-3, at 217 (2d ed. 1988).

[143] The legislative veto at issue in *Chadha* was contained in § 244(c)(2) of the Immigration and Nationality Act, 8 U.S.C. § 1254(c)(2) (1976).

[144] Congressional Budget and Impoundment Control Act of 1974, 31 U.S.C. § 1403.

[145] Resolution, §§ 8(a)(1), 8(d)(2).

from the Constitution.[146] This argument, however, proves too much and only fortifies the conclusion that *Chadha* applies to the War Powers Resolution: If Congress is unable to attach the "string" of a legislative veto to a statutorily delegated power, surely it is on far weaker ground when it attempts to do so in connection with a power not delegated by it but conferred by the Constitution.[147]

A broader argument against the application of *Chadha* is that it would be inconsistent with previous cases that affirm the power of Congress to express its will in other contexts without adhering to the requirements of the presentation clause. In the *Steel Seizure Case*, for example, the Court found that Congress had expressed its opposition to presidential seizure of the steel mills by rejecting an amendment that would have authorized that seizure; the President never had the opportunity to veto the congressional rejection of that amendment since it was not contained in the legislation presented to him.[148] Similarly, in *Dames & Moore v. Regan*, the Court inferred congressional approval of the Iranian Claims Settlement Agreement from the failure of Congress to disapprove.[149]

In each case, the courts necessarily reasoned that "the legal rights, duties and relations of persons . . . outside the legislative branch"[150] were affected by congressional action accomplished without strict adherence to presentation clause procedures. Yet there is no suggestion in *Chadha* that the Court intended to overrule either case or to limit the power of Congress so to express its will. Although the Court disapproves of a "binding" expression of congressional opinion through simple or concurrent resolution and will give such expression no legal effect, it seems willing to infer congressional intent from sources far less precise.[151] Accordingly, whereas a concurrent resolution adopted under section 5(c) can have no mandatory effect in requiring presidential withdrawal of the armed forces, such a resolution could nonetheless suffice under Justice Jackson's analysis to place the President's power at its lowest ebb. Indeed, it is hard to see why a concurrent resolution adopted with-

[146] Professor Ely seems to buy into this argument, buttressing it by the parallel between the Resolution's "package" effect that approximates the emergency-powers paradigm envisaged by the Framers. *See* Ely, *supra* note 19, at 1396.

[147] *Accord* Note, *The Future of the War Powers Resolution*, 36 Stan. L. Rev. 1407, 1453 (1984); *Presidential Power to Use the Armed Forces Abroad without Statutory Authorization*, 4A Op. Office of the Legal Counsel, Department of Justice 185, 196 (1980).

[148] Youngstown Sheet & Tube Co. v. Sawyer, 343 U.S. 579, 586 (1952).

[149] 453 U.S. at 682.

[150] *INS v. Chadha*, 462 U.S. at 952 (1983).

[151] The Court's holding in *Chadha* that Congress can speak legislatively only by following the requirements of the presentation clause finds support in some older cases suggesting that it is impermissible for a court to consult legislative debates to determine the meaning of a statute. *See, e.g.*, Standard Oil v. United States, 221 U.S. 1, 50 (1910); United States v. Trans-Missouri Freight Ass'n, 166 U.S. 290, 318 (1896). The law today is clearly to the contrary.

out reference to the War Powers Resolution should not be accorded such effect.[152]

Finally, regarding the time limits, the argument advanced by George Will and others—that what Congress cannot accomplish through action it cannot accomplish through inaction—applies to far more than the "inaction" incident to the expiration of the sixty-day limit.[153] All sunset legislation conferring statutory authority on the President for a limited period of time—and, indeed, the eighteenth-month Lebanon compromise itself—is impermissible under Will's Constitution. However reckless the *Chadha* court may have been in failing to distinguish the several different categories of legislative vetoes,[154] nothing in its opinion suggests that the hundreds of statutes conferring statutory authority for limited periods were intended to fall within its sweep.[155]

IMPLIED STATUTORY AUTHORIZATION

A more novel approach to the constitutionality of the time limits was proposed by State Department legal adviser Abraham Sofaer in testimony before the House Foreign Affairs Subcommittee in 1986. Properly interpreted, he argued, the time limits are essentially meaningless. "In recent weeks," Sofaer testified, "the question has been raised publicly as to the President's right to take military action without the express approval of Congress."[156] He assured the Subcommittee that President Reagan's air strike against Libya fell within the Chief Executive's independent authority under the Constitution. He added that, in any event, "the President is not simply acting alone, under his inherent constitutional authority."[157] Why? Because Congress has effectively approved such operations through enactment of various laws and because the provision of the Resolution that precludes the Executive from inferring authority from

[152] The incoherence of the case law had a dizzying effect on the commentary. *Compare, e.g.*, Ely, *supra* note 19, at 1395 ("section 5(c) does not appear to be unconstitutional") *with* Ely, *id.* at 1386, n.25 ("[s]ection 5(c) probably *would* be declared unconstitutional" [emphasis in original]).

[153] Will, *War Powers Act and Common Sense*, L.A. Times, Sept. 15, 1983, § 2 at 7, col. 1; Moore, *Rethinking the "War Powers" Gambit*, Wall St. J., Oct. 27, 1983, at 30, col. 3.

[154] For a collection of citations to statutes exhibiting the variety of legislative vetoes that exist, see *Chadha*, 462 U.S. at 1003–1013 (appendix to opinion of White, J., dissenting).

[155] Such sunset laws may have been within the intent of the Framers. *See* 2 The Records of the Federal Convention of 1787 at 587 (M. Farrand ed. 1966) (quoting Madison as recognizing the possibility that limits in the duration of laws would be used by Congress), cited in *Chadha*, 462 U.S. at 954 n.18. The *Chadha* Court recognized that durational limits on authorizations "would be a constitutionally permissible means of limiting the power of administrative agencies." *Id.* at 955 n.19.

[156] War Powers, Libya, and State-Sponsored Terrorism: Hearings Before the Subcomm. on Arms Control, International Security and Science of the House Comm. on Foreign Affairs, 99th Cong., 2d Sess. 10, 29 (1986) (testimony of State Department Legal Adviser Abraham D. Sofaer) (hereinafter "Sofaer testimony").

[157] *Id.* at 29.

other legislation[158] is unconstitutional.[159] Sofaer proceeded to suggest that if the sixty-day time period of the Resolution expired,[160] the President could nonetheless continue to infer such authority from appropriations measures and other legislation.[161]

Professor Archibald Cox, testifying two days later, said he was "aghast" at Sofaer's theory of implied statutory authority.[162] Understandably so. If Sofaer is correct, if it is permissible for the President to infer congressional approval to introduce the armed forces into hostilities from general legislation authorizing or appropriating funds for the military, then what little coercion there is in the War Powers Resolution dissolves. For in Sofaer's view, Congress in 1973 wrote empty words. Whatever the constitutional validity of the sixty-day time limit, that requirement will never actually apply because Congress apparently will be deemed to have enacted authorization contemplated by the Resolution.[163]

A novel theory,[164] to be sure, but one that succeeds only insofar as it distorts and ignores. In the name of narrow interpretation, it ignores the most fundamental canons of statutory interpretation—that every word be given effect,

[158] Section 8(a)(1) of the Resolution provides:

> Authority to introduce United States Armed Forces into hostilities or into situations wherein involvement in hostilities is clearly indicated by the circumstances shall not be inferred . . . from any provision of law . . . , including any provision contained in any appropriations Act, unless such provision specifically authorizes the introduction of United States Armed Forces into hostilities or into such situations and states that it is intended to constitute specific statutory authorization within the meaning of this joint resolution.

[159] *See* Sofaer testimony, *supra* note 156, at 18.

[160] Section 5(b) of the Resolution requires the President to terminate any use of armed forces in hostilities within sixty days (or ninety days in the event of "unavoidable military necessity") after their introduction into hostilities has been reported to Congress under § 4(a)(1).

[161] Sofaer stated his views in the following colloquy:

> MR. BERMAN So then you believe that, in fact, the executive branch can infer from appropriations measures, other legislation, etc., . . . enacted subsequently to the War Powers Act, that that introduction of hostile activity [*sic*] or whatever reference you made to it, is all right, notwithstanding the sixty-day limitation of the War Powers Act?
>
> MR. SOFAER Yes. And Congressman, let me just say that philosophically I feel that way because I think it is preferable, from the viewpoint of a lawyer advising his client to look to more limited claims of authority, claims based on a partnership between the President and Congress, rather than to more extravagant, broader claims, based on unilateral authority. . . . I'm naturally drawn, in advising my client, to evidence that Congress will approve of what he's going to do. . . .

See Sofaer testimony, *supra* note 156, at 46.

[162] *Id.* at 141.

[163] Section 5(b) provides that the President is not required to withdraw the armed forces if Congress "has declared war or has enacted a specific authorization for such use of United States Armed Forces."

[164] This apparently was the first time that the constitutional validity of § 8(a)(1) of the Resolution has been challenged by the executive branch.

that Congress is presumed not to have enacted a nullity, that an interpretation that saves is preferred to one that destroys.

In the name of respect for the congressional will, Sofaer's theory ignores the intent of Congress. The theory apparently proceeds on the assumption that a disclaimer of authority cannot be simply stated once, but must be reiterated in every single piece of legislation from which authority might conceivably be inferred. Yet Congress, in enacting legislation, is deemed to know what laws already exist; its intent is considered to embrace all acts *in pari materia*. Section 8(a) is in effect a statement by Congress that it wants the War Powers Resolution to be seen as related to every piece of authorizing and appropriating legislation, at least to the extent that that legislation might be read as approving the introduction of armed forces into hostilities. Section 8(a) was intended, the Senate Foreign Relations Committee explained, "to counteract the opinion in the *Orlando v. Laird* decision of the Second Circuit holding that passage of defense appropriation bills, and the extension of the Selective Service Act, could be construed as implied Congressional authorization of the Vietnam war."[165]

In the name of "partnership," Sofaer thus ignores the authority of Congress to define its own intent. Section 8(a) is, again, a statement of how certain statutes should be read. That provision is in effect an instruction to the Executive and the courts. It tells those branches not to apply their usual presumption—the presumption that Congress desires the statute last in time to control. Congress has effectively said that here it wishes the *first* in time to control—unless it specifically signals a contrary intent. There is no reason why the last in time must control if Congress indicates otherwise, nor is there any reason why Congress must leave its intent to be guessed at by the Executive or the courts. Indeed, Congress has used this very method before to preclude those branches from guessing wrong.[166]

Given Sofaer's theory of implied statutory approval, the war-powers partnership between Congress and the Executive, as contemplated by the legal adviser, was comparable to a tap-dancing duo of a chipmunk and an elephant. To the elephant, it would be a smashing success.

Effectiveness

That the Resolution is mostly constitutional, however, does not mean that it is either wise or effective. Fifteen years after its enactment—after Lebanon, Grenada, and the Persian Gulf—and after the *Chadha* decision, it has become clear that whatever congressional intent underlay the War Powers Resolution,

[165] S. Rep. No. 220, 93d Cong., 1st Sess. 20 (1973) (War Powers).

[166] *See, e.g.*, § 15 of the Act of Aug. 1, 1956, as amended, Pub. L. No. 84-885, 70 Stat. 890 (codified at 22 U.S.C. § 2680(a)(1)(b)) (prohibiting appropriations not authorized by law to be made to the State Department and precluding nonspecific supersession of that prohibition).

any expectation that its procedures would actually lead to collective Legislative-Executive judgment in the war-making process was mistaken.

That belief was mistaken because the Resolution's sponsors seriously misjudged the role Congress is required to play under the Resolution's procedural framework. Worse, they misjudged the ability of Congress to play its assigned role. Finally, they misjudged the likely response of the Supreme Court to the provision of the resolution that was central to its procedural framework—the legislative veto.[167] Those misjudgments rendered largely Pyrrhic the widely hailed victory of Congress in "recapturing" its share of the war-making power.[168]

The first and most serious misjudgment derived from a seemingly minor drafting error, unnoticed when the Resolution was enacted, that turned out to be fatal to its proper operation. The sponsors had intended to require the President, upon introducing the armed forces into hostilities,[169] to transmit to Congress a written report on that action within forty-eight hours.[170] He or she would then have sixty days to keep them in hostilities.[171]

The problem results from the failure of the Resolution to require the President to specify the kind of report he is filing. A "hostilities" report is only one of three kinds of reports required by the Resolution, and the other two do not set the clock ticking.[172] The latter two apply in situations that could also require a "hostilities" report; for example, when forces are introduced "into the territory, airspace or waters of a foreign nation, while equipped for combat,"[173] and when forces are introduced "in numbers which substantially enlarge United States armed forces equipped for combat already located in a foreign nation."[174] Thus, when President Reagan informed Congress on September 29, 1983, that he had stationed 1,200 Marines in Lebanon, his report did not specify under which of the three requirements it was being submitted.[175] Similarly, in August 1983, when the Marines suffered twenty casualties in ten days of fighting, the President's report did not indicate which kind it

[167] Resolution, *supra* note 4, § 5(c).

[168] *See, e.g.*, the remarks of Senator Jacob K. Javits, the Resolution's chief sponsor in the Senate, upon its enactment: "At long last . . . Congress is determined to recapture the awesome power to make war." 119 Cong. Rec. 36, 187 (1973).

[169] The term *hostilities*, as used in this book, includes "situations where imminent involvement in hostilities is clearly indicated by the circumstances." *See* Resolution, *supra* note 4, § 4(a)(1).

[170] *Id.* § 4(a).

[171] *Id.* § 5(b). Under the Resolution, Congress retained the power to order, by concurrent resolution, the withdrawal of U.S. forces from hostilities. *See id.* § 5(c).

[172] *See id.* § 5(b). The Resolution provides that the time commences when a report is "required to be submitted," but it established no procedure for that determination to be made if the President fails to do so. *Id.*

[173] *Id.* § 4(a)(2).

[174] *Id.* § 4(a)(3).

[175] *See* President's Letter to the Speaker of the House and the President Pro Tempore of the Senate, 18 Weekly Comp. Pres. Doc. 1232 (Sept. 29, 1982) (hereinafter Weekly Comp.).

was,[176] nor did the report filed upon the invasion of Grenada.[177] Thus, no one can determine whether the sixty-day period had been triggered by any of the reports. Consequently, Congress, frustrated by the President's easy circumvention of the law and eager to save face by appearing to assert its constitutional war-making prerogative, took it upon itself to declare that in both cases the sixty-day time limit had been triggered.

Or at least tried. Following the fighting in Lebanon, the "compromise" worked out with the White House purported to declare the sixty-day limit in effect as of August 31, 1983.[178] Because a new eighteen-month limit was set by that Act, however, the declaration was only an academic assertion; the only relevant result—the expiration of the sixty-day limit—would never occur. Yet the House Committee on Foreign Affairs maintained that the President's signature would imply "endorsement of the War Powers Resolution."[179]

As a matter of law, this is simply not so. Numerous presidents have indicated upon signing legislation that their signatures would not estop a later executive challenge to the constitutionality of the bill. The practice of signature accompanied by "reservation" occurred with some frequency in the case of legislation containing legislative vetoes.[180] But as Congress found in *Chadha*, all those signatures meant little. In that case, the Supreme Court was confronted with the same claim in the context of the legislative veto—that presidential signature had conferred legitimacy. The Court construed the argument as effectively tantamount to a contention that Congress and the Executive, "acting in concert and in compliance with Article I, can decide the constitutionality of a statute,"[181] which it quickly dismissed: "The assent of the Executive to a bill which contains a provision contrary to the Constitution does not shield it from judicial review."[182]

The attempt to declare the time limit operative following the invasion of Grenada was even less successful.[183] Both houses voted to do so, but conveniently got stalled by a procedural impasse, and no triggering provision was sent to the White House.[184]

[176] *See* President's Letter to the Speaker of the House and the President Pro Tempore of the Senate, 19 *id*. at 1186 (Aug. 30, 1983).

[177] *See* President's Letter to the Speaker of the House and the President Pro Tempore of the Senate, *id*. at 1493 (Oct. 25, 1983).

[178] Multinational Force in Lebanon Resolution, Pub. L. No 98-119, 97 Stat. 805 (1983).

[179] H.R. Rep. No. 385, 98th Cong., 1st Sess. 5 (1983).

[180] *See* Henry, *The Legislative Veto: In Search of Constitutional Limits*, 16 Harv. J. Legis. 735, 737–38 n.7 (1979) (collecting citations to presidential statements).

[181] *INS v. Chadha*, 462 U.S. at 942 (1983).

[182] *Id*. at 942 n.13.

[183] For a highly critical analysis of the Administration's legal rationale for the invasion *see* Quigley, *The United States Invasion of Grenada: Stranger Than Fiction*, 18 Univ. of Miami Inter-American L. Rev. 271 (Winter 1986–87).

[184] United States forces invaded Grenada on Oct. 25, 1983. On Oct. 27, the House Foreign

Even if the efforts at triggering the sixty-day limit were successful, the very act of engaging in them amounted to an implicit admission that the Resolution had failed. The Resolution's central objective was to create a self-activating mechanism to control abuse of presidential discretion in the event Congress lacked the backbone to do so, as the sponsors believed had happened during the Indochinese War.[185] Thus, in 1973 the sixty-day time period seemed to have the advantage of shifting to the White House the burden of justifying military actions by requiring their termination—automatically—despite congressional inaction.

But by 1983, these expectations proved ephemeral. The element of "automaticity," as Senator Javits liked to call it,[186] was grounded entirely upon the foundation of a written "hostilities" report submitted by the President. In the absence of such a report—and in the absence of the Executive's good-faith adherence to the spirit of the Resolution, which the sponsors also had mistakenly expected[187]—the whole procedural edifice turned out to be a house of cards.

When the cards collapsed with the Lebanon Peace-keeping Resolution, Grenada, and the Persian Gulf, the principal reason was that the congressional role proved to be vastly different from that expected in 1973. Congress expected that because legislative action would occur as the expiration of the sixty-day period approached, members of Congress would be able to overcome the rally-round-the-flag mentality that suffuses legislative consideration of sudden war-powers issues.[188] Now, however, the congressional role actually required under the Resolution apparently entails less detachment. "When Congress declares that . . . the War Powers Resolution is in effect," former Senator Javits wrote, "it answers the more fundamental question of who makes war."[189] In other words, as the House Foreign Affairs Committee put it in its report on the Lebanon Peace-keeping Resolution, "the War Powers

---

Affairs Committee voted to declare that U.S. troops had become involved in "hostilities" as of the date of the invasion. H.R.J. Res. 402. On Oct. 28, the Senate voted 64–20 to add a rider to legislation raising the national-debt ceiling that similarly invoked the Resolution. *See* 129 Cong. Rec. S14,876 (daily ed. Oct. 28, 1983). On Nov. 1, the House passed H.R.J. Res. 402 by a vote of 403–23–7, purporting to invoke the resolution as of Oct. 27. H.R.J. Res. 402, 9th Cong., 1st Sess. (1983). Neither provision, however, was agreed to by the other house.

[185] *See, e.g.*, Letter of Nov. 1, 1973 from Thomas E. Morgan, Chairman, House Committee on Foreign Affairs, to Congress, *reprinted in* 119 Cong. Rec. 35,868 (1973) (responding to presidential veto message of the War Powers Resolution). Answering President Nixon's contention that the resolution was not clear on the sixty-day time limit, Representative Morgan said that "the provisions of the Resolution are triggered by a specific, tangible act by the President—i.e., introduction of troops into hostilities." *Id.*

[186] *See, e.g.*, 119 Cong. Rec. 33,550 (1973).

[187] *See, e.g.*, 118 *id.* at 11,489, 12,146 (1972).

[188] *See, e.g.*, 119 *id.* at 33,859 (1973) (remarks of Rep. Zablocki); 118 *id.* at 11,026 (1972) (remarks of Sen. Javits).

[189] N.Y. Times, Oct. 23, 1983, § 6 (Magazine), at 108.

Resolution was crafted to enable the Congress, as well as the President, to determine when a [hostilities] report should be submitted.''[190]

But, again, this is not so: Congressional leaders never contemplated that *Congress* itself would be compelled statutorily to declare that the Resolution was in effect. That was thought to be the obligation of the *President*.[191] Therefore, instead of responding to a presidential request for statutory approval pursuant to an already-triggered sixty-day limit, Congress found itself compelled at the outset of the process to establish that the time limit had been triggered. Former House Foreign Affairs Committee Chairman Clement Zablocki opined that the War Powers Resolution would become a dead letter if Congress did not pass a bill implementing it.[192] Precisely the opposite is true. If Congress needs to ''implement'' the Resolution, then it becomes a dead letter. For the point of the Resolution was to create self-activating limits on presidential war-making powers. Yet the very existence of the Resolution seemed to generate a congressional perception that authorization of presidential war making was somehow necessary to preserve congressional constitutional prerogatives.

By the time of the invasion of Grenada, it had become apparent that something was dreadfully wrong. President Reagan again flouted the spirit of the reporting requirement by refusing to submit a ''hostilities'' report that would trigger the time limit. Congress, boxed in by the face-saving Lebanon precedent, confronted a procedure that had been stood upon its head. Predictably, its members again undertook the task of trying to establish that the sixty-day period was in effect.[193] Thus, instead of facing dispassionately a wave of patriotic fervor that had already crested, its members found themselves involved in the process at the outset and confronting a roaring tidal wave of pro-military sentiment. They sought, in effect, precisely the same remedy that had existed prior to the enactment of the War Powers Resolution, the imposition of a time limit enacted over a presidential veto. Plus ça change . . .

Any lingering doubts concerning the inefficacy of the Resolution were removed by President Reagan's successful flouting of its requirements when units of the armed forces were introduced into hostilities in the Persian Gulf. On July 22, 1987, the first Navy escort operations began for two reflagged Kuwaiti ships. Iran had previously taken the public position that the escort

190 H.R. Rep. No. 385, *supra* note 179, at 4.

191 *See* Chapter 1.

192 N.Y. Times, Sept. 29, 1983, at A8.

193 Rather pathetically, a number of House members introduced legislation stating that ''Congress hereby determines that the requirements of section 4(a)(1) of the War Powers Resolution became operative on October 25, 1988, when United States Armed Forces were introduced into Grenada.'' H.R. J. Res. 402, 98th Cong., 1st Sess. (1983). The President had transmitted a report the day before describing the invasion. The War Powers Resolution: Relevant Documents, Correspondence, Reports: Prepared by the Subcomm. on Arms Control, International Security and Science of the House Foreign Affairs Comm., U.S. House of Representatives (Comm. print, May 1988). The legislation was never reported by the Committee.

operations of the United States were protecting the ships of Kuwait, which Iran viewed as an ally in its war against Iraq. It had also installed Silkworm missiles by the Strait of Hormuz, where they were capable of hitting any ship that traversed the Strait. On July 24, a mine, believed by the Administration to have been laid by Iran, exploded and did serious damage to the *Bridgeton*, one of the reflagged vessels being escorted by the U.S. Navy.

Subsequent actions of the Administration further reinforced the conclusion that the armed forces had been introduced into hostilities in the Gulf. By September 1987, more than twenty United States warships and ten thousand armed forces personnel had been ordered to the Gulf to conduct and support the escort operations. On September 21 of that year, two United States helicopters fired on an Iranian ship that was laying mines in international waters in the Persian Gulf. The next day, as part of a follow-up to the events in which three Iranian sailors were killed, the Navy seized the Iranian ship, which had been set afire, and captured twenty-six Iranian sailors. Similarly, on April 14, 1988, the frigate *Samuel B. Roberts* hit two mines, injuring ten crew members, two of them seriously. "The ship sustained significant hull and structural damage," Pentagon officials said. They asserted that the mines had been put there recently by Iran.[194] In retaliation, United States naval forces again bombarded Iranian oil platforms. An extended clash ensued in which six Iranian vessels were crippled or sunk and one American helicopter was apparently shot down. Two Iranian frigates fired missiles at United States aircraft, and an Iranian guided-missile patrol boat fired on the cruiser *Wainwright*.[195] Finally, on July 3, 1988, when the cruiser *Vincennes* shot down an Iranian airliner, killing 269 people, Vice President George Bush defended the action by accusing the Iranians of "sending an airliner over a combat zone. . . ."[196] The plane, he said, flew "over a warship engaged in battle. . . ."[197] No report was submitted.

Members of Congress, concerned about the Administration's apparent violation of the reporting requirement of the War Powers Resolution proceeded along two avenues: judicial and legislative. One hundred and ten members of Congress brought an action seeking an order requiring the filing of a report or a declaratory judgment finding that a report was required to have been submitted at the outset of the escort operations. In *Lowry v. Reagan*,[198] the district court declined to reach the merits,[199] dismissing the suit on grounds of the

[194] N.Y. Times, Apr. 16, 1988, at 5.

[195] N.Y. Times, Apr. 19, 1988, at 1, 4.

[196] N.Y. Times, Aug. 4, 1988, at A6.

[197] N.Y. Times, Aug. 3, 1988, at 5.

[198] 676 F. Supp. 333 (D.D.C. 1987).

[199] The court said, in passing, that President Reagan had, in a communication to Congress, "stated his belief that the War Powers Resolution is unconstitutional." *Id.* at 336. That was not exactly what President Reagan said. He wrote that he was "mindful of the historical differences

political-question doctrine and the doctrine of remedial discretion. The case was appealed; in its appellate brief, the Justice Department made sweeping claims of executive war-making power, contending, for example, that "[t]he Constitution commits to the executive branch the conduct of American diplomatic and foreign affairs,"[200] and that "whether hostilities exist or are imminent involves the President's responsibilities as 'Commander in Chief of the Army and Navy' . . . and as 'sole organ of the nation in its external relations.' "[201]

Throughout these events, members of Congress also pushed for legislation to "invoke" the Resolution,[202] but none was enacted. From a statutory perspective, the effort was futile, for the President's potential veto had to be overridden, and this was never politically feasible. Part of the impetus, at least in the Senate, apparently came from a belief that consideration of one of the measures[203] under the expedited parliamentary procedure prescribed by the Resolution[204] would have the effect of triggering the Resolution's time limits. According to the theory, an internal parliamentary determination of one house could somehow effectively substitute for a statutory determination of both houses.[205] Even some opponents of the legislation agreed that its mere consideration would trigger the time limit.[206] Indeed, some argued that passage by

---

between the legislative and executive branches of government, and the positions taken by all of my predecessors in office, with respect to the interpretation and constitutionality of certain provisions of the War Powers Resolution. . . ." Report Dated Sept. 23, 1987, from Pres. Ronald Reagan to Hon. Jim Wright, Speaker of the House of Representatives, *reprinted in* The War Powers Resolution—Relevant Documents, Correspondence, Reports Prepared by the Subcom. on Arms Control, International Security and Science of the Comm. on Foreign Affairs, U.S. House of Representatives [Committee Print], 100th Cong., 2d Sess. 100 (May 1988 ed.). Thus the President did not indicate to which of the Resolution's provisions, if any, he actually had constitutional objections; perhaps his reference was to § 5(c) pertaining to the legislative veto. As noted in this chapter, such an objection would be well founded.

200 Brief for the Appellee at 20, Lowry v. Reagan, Appendix A.

201 *Id.* (citing United States v. Curtiss-Wright, 299 U.S. 304, 319 (1936)).

202 *See, e.g.*, H.R.J. Res. 310, 100th Cong., 1st Sess (1987); S.1343, 100th Cong., 1st Sess. (1987); H.R.J. Res. 295, 100th Cong., 1st Sess. (1987); S. Res. 217, 100th Cong., 1st Sess. (1987).

203 S. Res. 217, 100th Cong., 1st Sess. (1987).

204 Resolution, § 6.

205 For the argument that the date on which a "hostilities" report "is required to be submitted" can be determined "by a vote of the house in which the authorizing legislation is to be introduced," *see* Adler, *Senator Adams' Gambit Paves the Way for Vote on Tanker-Escort in the Persian Gulf*, 13 First Principles No. 1 at 4, 6 (Feb./Mar. 1988); remarks of Senator Brock Adams, "Implementing Foreign Policy: Congress and the Executive," panel discussion, American Society of International Law, Annual Meeting, Washington, D.C. (Apr. 1988).

206 The Senate Majority Leader, Robert Byrd, raised a point of order against the expedited consideration of the measure because "it places the Senate in the awkward position of either having the War Powers Resolution invoked by the Parliamentarian or of disposing of an important policy question through a procedural device." 134 Cong. Rec. S7167 (daily ed. June 6, 1988).

the Senate of similar legislation under the Resolution's expedited procedure *had* triggered the time limit.[207] It is surprising that this theory could have been taken seriously after *INS v. Chadha*.[208] It is clear beyond question that the vote of one house of Congress—even when a statute purports to give that vote legislative effect (and none did here)—cannot have the "purpose and effect of altering the legal rights, duties and relations of . . . the . . . Executive Branch. . . ."[209] The purpose of the vote, of course, would have been precisely to alter the duties of the Executive.

As a consequence of the role reversal between the President and Congress at the "triggering" stage, the Resolution has thus failed as a mechanism for creating consensus. A number of "hawks" supported the Resolution in the belief that the requirement of a congressional vote on whether to continue after sixty days would either generate public support or bring hostilities to an end.[210] But again matters did not work out as expected. Congressional support for the Executive's Lebanon initiative did not translate into public support, in part because Congress focused less on the wisdom of the policy than on the need to pretend to trigger the time limit. Indeed, while the debate on the compromise caused a pro-Executive coalition to form in Congress, it ironically seemed to foster a public consensus that the action was mistaken—perhaps because it appeared unsuccessful.[211]

That Congress has an operative institutional memory is another false assumption on which the Resolution was based. Permeating its consideration of the Resolution was the belief that Congress would remember recent institutional reversals (Vietnam and the Gulf of Tonkin Resolution) and learn from its errors. In fact, Congress learned little and forgot everything. "This is the first time since the enactment of the War Powers Resolution on November 7, 1973, that Congress has faced the task of considering a specific authorization for the involvement of United States armed forces in hostilities," the Republican-controlled Senate Foreign Relations Committee said in its report on the Lebanon Peace-keeping Resolution.[212] "Members of Congress are therefore confronted with the need to decide a novel issue regarding the role appropriate of the legislative branch: how far should Congress go in defining the authority being granted to the President in a situation of hostilities?"[213]

In fact, this was not the first time since the enactment of the Resolution that

[207] *Id.* at S7166 (remarks of Senator Byrd). Senator John Warner agreed: "The War Powers Resolution has been triggered, one body of the Congress has triggered it, or said it should be triggered." He proceeded to criticize the House of Representatives, which "sits and does nothing" on the legislation. *Id.* at S7171.

[208] 462 U.S. 919 (1983).

[209] *Chadha*, 462 U.S. at 952.

[210] *See, e.g.*, 118 Cong. Rec. 11,532 (1972) (remarks of Sen. Talmadge).

[211] N.Y. Times, Oct. 29, 1983, at 9, col. 1 (NYT/CBS poll).

[212] S. Rep. No. 242, 98th Cong., 1st Sess. 10 (1983).

[213] *Id.*

Congress had considered such legislation. On April 18, 1975, the Vietnam Contingency Act[214] was reported by the Senate Foreign Relations Committee, authorizing the introduction of the armed forces into hostilities in Vietnam, incident to the evacuation of Saigon.[215] It contained tight restrictions defining the authority granted to the President. It permitted use of the armed forces "in a number and manner essential to and directly connected with the protection of . . . United States citizens and their dependents while they are being withdrawn from South Vietnam."[216] It required the President, upon any such use of the forces, to submit a report under the War Powers Resolution and to certify that there was a direct and imminent threat to the lives of such citizens, that every effort had been made to terminate the threat diplomatically, and that the evacuation was being carried out as rapidly as possible.[217]

The issues debated in 1975 concerning the scope of the authority to be conferred upon the President were virtually identical to those debated in connection with the Lebanon compromise, and much useful insight could have been gained through a considered recollection of that episode. But the amnesia of the Republican-controlled Committee regarding its own recent history raised serious questions about the accuracy of its claim that the compromise "was adopted after very careful consideration."[218]

Those questions were underscored in 1983 by the confusion of the Republican majority of the Committee about the scope of the congressional war power. By way of explaining (or apologizing for) the loose reins placed on executive discretion in Lebanon, the Committee suggested (in a majority report submitted by Chairman Richard Lugar) that it might not have had the power to do more:

> A different approach to the drafting of a specific authorization is to enact particular limitations or criteria which circumscribe the scope of the commitment. Such specifications might include the duration, location, size, cost and mission of U.S. deployment, as well as requirements based upon future developments. Presidents have traditionally resisted such constraints as infringements on the Commander-in-Chief power, but no definitive Resolution of such questions has ever been achieved.[219]

Whether such issues are ever "definitively resolved" is open to debate. But as noted in Chapter 1, similar questions were addressed in 1804 in *Little v. Barreme*.[220] The Committee discussed *Little* at some length in 1971 when it

[214] S. 1484, 94th Cong., 1st Sess. (1975).
[215] H.R. Rep. No. 88, 94th Cong., 1st Sess. (1975).
[216] S. 1484, 94th Cong., 1st Sess., § 3(a) (1975).
[217] *Id.*, § 3(b), (c).
[218] S. Rep. No. 242, *supra* note 212, at 13.
[219] *Id.* at 10.
[220] 6 U.S. (2 Cranch) 170 (1804).

held hearings on the initial drafts of war-powers legislation.[221] Considering the unprepossessing understanding of the pro-Executive majority of the Foreign Relations Committee regarding the constitutional underpinnings of the legislative war power, one could hardly expect that it would have urged a responsible role on Congress.

Clearing the Judicial Path

The ability of Congress as a collective entity to play the role required of it under the current version of the War Powers Resolution is thus doubtful. A different approach is called for, one that does not rely exclusively upon the political process as a means of forcing a recalcitrant president into compliance but provides the impetus for individual members to proceed in the courts when the limits of the Resolution are transgressed. The Resolution can and should be amended in at least two ways to assist individual legislators wishing to seek judicial recourse to challenge a presidential violation.

First, as discussed in Chapter 8, in *Crockett v. Reagan*,[222] the Court of Appeals for the District of Columbia Circuit held that the question of whether a report is required to be submitted under section 4(a)(1) of the Resolution is, at least with respect to combat activities in El Salvador, a political question.[223] The district court also relied upon that doctrine in dismissing the action in *Lowry v. Reagan*.[224] Although both courts erroneously applied the doctrine,[225] in principle there should be little that Congress can do to overcome the political-question impediment where it is constitutionally imposed. In those circumstances, it is beyond the power of Congress to tell the courts by statute not to regard the issue as a political question.[226] Similarly, any joint Legislative-Executive effort to "formulate" a "test case" in a "nonconfrontational context" is almost surely misdirected.[227] A nonbinding sense-of-the-Congress

[221] *War Powers Legislation: Hearings on S. 731, S.J. Res. 18 and S.J. Res. 59 Before the Senate Comm. on Foreign Relations*, 92d Cong., 1st Sess. 142–43, 197, 353, 466, 469, 495 (1971).

[222] Crockett v. Reagan, 720 F.2d 1355 (D.C. Cir. 1983), *aff'g* 558 F. Supp. 893 (1982).

[223] *Id.*

[224] 676 F. Supp. 333 (1987). For the unpublished opinion of the court of appeals, *see* Appendix A. *See* Chapter 8.

[225] *See* Chapter 8.

[226] In *Baker*, the Court stated that "the nonjusticiability of a political question is primarily a function of the separation of powers," *Baker*, 369 U.S. at 210, seemingly implying that the political-question doctrine is at least in some applications *constitutionally* mandated and that it is in those instances beyond the power of Congress to order the Court to decide a political question. *See also* Sierra Club v. Morton, 405 U.S. 727, 732 n.3 (1972).

[227] Sen. Arlen Specter (R, Pa.) argued that "there has been some discussion between the Senate leadership and the White House to formulate a test case that would go to the Supreme Court of the United States which would decide this question in a nonconfrontational context." N.Y. Times, Mar. 29, 1984, at A6, col. 1. If the President and congressional leaders made a direct appeal to

statement, on the other hand, would be permissible; there is no reason why the War Powers Resolution could not be amended to set forth the opinion of Congress that disputes concerning its violation should be adjudicated by the courts. In a case that might otherwise be thought to cause "embarrassment" to Congress within the meaning of *Baker*, such guidance should presumably be taken into account by a court in deciding whether to reach the merits.

On the other hand, it may be possible to limit the application of the political question by statute in those instances where the application of the doctrine is not constitutionally mandated. In some circumstances, the courts find a case nonjusticiable for prudential rather than constitutional reasons.[228] In those cases, Congress may be able to compel justiciability.[229] A case in point involved the act-of-state doctrine, which holds that the courts of one country will not sit in judgment on the acts of the government of another within its own territory.[230] The Supreme Court has in effect considered the doctrine a subset of the political-question doctrine.[231] In enacting the "Second Hickenlooper Amendment,"[232] Congress drastically limited the application of the act-of-state doctrine. Yet the validity of the Amendment was upheld by the Second Circuit in *Banco Nacional de Cuba v. Farr*,[233] even though the act-of-state doctrine is a species of the political-question doctrine that has "constitutional underpinnings."[234] If Congress can limit the application of one form of the political question, even though it has "constitutional underpinnings," it should arguably be able to limit other forms as well, such as those that might otherwise prevent the adjudication of claims under the War Powers Resolu-

---

the Supreme Court to take up the War Powers Resolution, Senator Specter said, he believed it would do so. It is hard to see how the Court could entertain such an action, however, without overturning long-standing precedent. Since 1793, the Supreme Court has maintained that it has no constitutional power to render advisory opinions. In that year, President Washington sought to have the Court answer certain legal questions in the absence of any immediate controversy. However, the Court unanimously declined to do so. *See* P. Bator, P. Mishkin, D. Shapiro & H. Wechsler, Hart & Wechsler's The Federal Courts and the Federal System 64–66 (2d ed. 1973). Accordingly, the Court has consistently held that the "case or controversy" requirement of article III of the Constitution is not satisfied unless a bona fide dispute exists and the parties are genuinely adverse. *See* United States v. Johnson, 319 U.S. 302, 305 (1943) (a suit "is not in any real sense adversary" if it is "collusive").

[228] *See generally* A. Bickel, The Least Dangerous Branch 183–95 (1962).

[229] For an elaboration of this argument *see* Franck & Bob, *The Return of Humpty-Dumpty: Foreign Relations Law After the Chadha Case*, 79 Am. J. Int'l. L. 912, 957–59 (1985).

[230] *See* Underhill v. Hernandez, 168 U.S. 250, 252 (1897). *See also* the discussion in Chapter 7.

[231] Banco Nacional de Cuba v. Sabbatino, 376 U.S. 398 (1964) ("the validity of a foreign act of state in certain circumstances is a 'political question' not cognizable in our courts." *Id.* at 787–88.).

[232] 22 U.S.C. § 2370(e)(2) (1982).

[233] 383 F.2d 166, (2d. Cir. 1968), *cert. denied* 390 U.S. 956, *rehearing denied* 390 U.S. 1037 (1968).

[234] Banco Nacional d. Cuba v. Sabbatino, 376 U.S. 398, 423 (1964).

tion. In fact, legislation was introduced that would do precisely that.[235] It did not distinguish between prudential and constitutional applications of the doctrine. But since the courts seldom do so, Congress can hardly be expected to be more precise.[236]

Second, as also discussed in Chapter 8, the potential impediment imposed by the requirement of standing should be removed by statute. Judge Bork, in a concurring opinion filed in *Crockett*, expressed the belief that the congressional plaintiffs lacked standing.[237] The law of standing with regard to congressional plaintiffs is not entirely settled;[238] however, the issue can be mooted by amending the War Powers Resolution to create expressly a cause of action to challenge its violation.[239]

Proposed Amendments

The adoption of amendments such as those suggested above is probably impossible in the current political climate; any amendment directed at strengthening the congressional hand would surely face a presidential veto. In addition, recent events have demonstrated that the same complacency that has long afflicted congressional thinking about the Resolution is more than ever an obstacle. If the day ever comes when amendment of the Resolution is feasible, in addition to those discussed above, a number of others should be considered.[240]

First, the Resolution should be amended to set forth a definition of *hostilities*. In the absence of such a definition, officials of the Executive and mem-

[235] *See* H.R.J. Res. 462, 100th Cong., 2d Sess. (1988), and H.J. Res. 157, 101st Cong., 1st. Sess. (1989), introduced by Rep. Peter DeFazio.

[236] For a discussion of the political-question doctrine *see* Chapter 8.

[237] *Crockett*, 720 F.2d at 1357 (Bork, J., concurring).

[238] *See* T. Franck and M. Glennon, Foreign Relations and National Security Law 799–855 (1988).

[239] The Supreme Court has indicated that Congress does have the power to confer standing by statute:

> Moreover, Congress may grant an express right of action to persons who otherwise would be barred by prudential standing rules. Of course, Art. III's requirement remains: the plaintiff still must allege a distinct and palpable injury to himself, even if it is an injury shared by a large class of other possible litigants. . . . But so long as this requirement is satisfied, persons to whom Congress has granted a right of action, either expressly or by clear implication, may have standing to seek relief on the basis of the legal rights and interests of others, and, indeed, may invoke the general public interest in support of their claim.

Warth v. Seldin, 422 U.S. 490, 500–01 (1975). *See also* Sierra Club v. Morton, 405 U.S. at 732 n.3, 737; FCC v. Sanders Radio Station, 309 U.S. 470, 477 (1940). *Compare* 2 U.S.C. § 437h(a) (1970 ed., Supp. IV) (facilitating judicial review of Federal Election Campaign Act) *with* Buckley v. Valeo, 424 U.S. 1 (1976) (construing that provision as "intended to provide judicial review to the extent permitted by Art. III," *id.* at 11–12).

[240] A number of the amendments advanced herein have been incorporated into H.R.J. Res. 157, 101st Cong., 1st Sess. (1989), introduced by Rep. Peter DeFazio.

bers of Congress engaged in a running argument whether military activities in Lebanon constituted *hostilities*. When ten marines died in a twenty-day period after having been fired upon regularly by hostile forces, it seemed utterly disingenuous to claim, as the Reagan Administration did, that the hostilities test was not met. Nevertheless, the term is not self-defining, and because the Resolution provides no guidance on this meaning,[241] a gradual escalation of hostilities can generate serious confusion about when the time limit is triggered. Similarly, the Resolution does not clearly indicate whether a variety of activities are intended to fall within the hostilities test, such as exposure to minefields, missile attack, chemical or biological agents, or neutron rays. The Justice Department has construed the Resolution as not applicable to "sporadic military or paramilitary attacks on our armed forces stationed abroad."[242] If Congress is serious about removing uncertainty and closing the door to semantic circumvention by the Executive, it must define *hostilities*.

Second, time after time, consultation has been perfunctory at best, largely because the Executive has been allowed to get away with perfunctory consultation. Aside from raising a political stink when such failure occurs—which congressional leaders have been loath to do for fear of being mistakenly seen by the public as somehow critical of a military initiative—a Congress truly serious about consultation would amend the Resolution to specify precisely who is to be consulted, to make clear that "in every possible instance" does not include instances that present alleged security problems, and perhaps to prohibit certain uses of the armed forces in the absence of genuine consultation. One proposal regarding the consultation process that should *not* be adopted is that pertaining to a single consultative committee consisting of the congressional leadership. The drawbacks of this suggestion are discussed at length in Chapter 8.

Third, the reporting requirement is unacceptably vague. As noted above, this has led to the Resolution's virtual unraveling. Although the Executive's record here is clearly at odds with the Resolution's spirit, presidential reports, at least until the Persian Gulf, have complied with its letter. This anomaly arises because the Resolution sets forth not one reporting requirement but three. Only one, that required by section 4(a)(1), triggers the sixty-day limit;

[241] There is, however, legislative history on the matter. The House Committee report describes the origin of the formulation in connection with § 2 of the House bill. The word *hostilities* was substituted for *armed conflict*, the report said, because it was "considered to be somewhat broader in scope." H.R. Rep. No. 93-287, 93d Cong., 1st Sess. (1973). The report continued: "[I]n addition to a situation in which fighting has actually begun, *hostilities* also encompasses a state of confrontation in which no shots have been fired but where there is a clear and present danger of armed conflict. *Imminent hostilities* denotes a situation in which there is a clear potential either for such a state of confrontation or for actual armed conflict." *Id*. (emphasis in original).

[242] *Presidential Power to Use the Armed Forces Abroad without Statutory Authorization*, 4A Op. Office of the Legal Counsel, Department of Justice 185, 194 (1980). "Such situations," the Department elaborated, " do not generally involve the full military engagements with which the Resolution is primarily concerned." *Id*.

those required by sections 4(a)(2) and 4(a)(3) are merely informational (although in the original House version of the Resolution they too triggered the limitations). As discussed earlier, the problem arises when the three situations overlap; facts that would require a report under section 4(a)(1) might also require a report under one of the two succeeding paragraphs, and the Resolution contains no requirement that the President specify which of the three reports he or she is submitting. Only the *Mayaguez* report (submitted after the military operations had terminated because they lasted less than forty-eight hours) referred expressly to section 4(a)(1).[243] Consequently, the other reports effectively left unanswered the critical question whether the sixty-day limit had been triggered. The appropriate remedy was that set forth in the Use of Force Act, a staff-prepared committee print considered by the Senate's Special Subcommittee on War Powers in 1988.[244] The Act would have simply eliminated paragraphs (2) and (3) of section 4(a), two provisions that have turned out to be unneeded.

Fourth, the "prior restraints" contained in the original Senate version of the bill should be inserted. The approach of subsequent limitations alone has proven feckless. Aside from removing the argument of implicit authorization for up to sixty or ninety days, the imposition of a set of flat prohibitions would add needed teeth to the Resolution. If Congress really means what section 2(c) says, it should expand its scope to make it realistic,[245] and it should make it mandatory.[246] It should also back it up with a funding prohibition.[247] There would be several advantages in this course: (a) It would prevent unwanted presidential military excursions at the outset by denying funds to a president who intended to operate beyond the congressionally recognized limits of his power. (b) It would obviate the need for Congress, in order to prevent unauthorized presidential use of armed force, hurriedly to legislate ad hoc authorizations, limitations, and prohibitions every time the occasion arose; the scope of the President's authority to use the armed forces in an emergency situation would already be defined. (c) For the reasons set forth in Chapter 8, prior

[243] I wrote in 1975, following the *Mayaguez* incident, that "had hostilities gradually increased, serious disagreements could have arisen as to whether the sixty-day period had been triggered by the report." "Even if one assumes good faith on the part of a President, a gradual escalation of hostilities could generate honest differences of opinion as to the date on which the report was required to be submitted." Glennon, *Strengthening the War Powers Resolution: The Case for Purse-Strings Restrictions*, 60 Minn. L. Rev. 1, 36 (1975). I concluded that "disagreements concerning the legal underpinnings of the Resolution have not been resolved since its enactment. They simply have not been forced to the surface by events." *Id.* at 38.

[244] 1988 Senate War Powers Hearings, *supra* note 19, at 289. For the text of Committee Print No. 1, which is not printed in the hearings, *see* Appendix B.

[245] *See supra* text at notes 79–81.

[246] For a proposal along these lines *see* H. J. Res. 157, 101st Cong., 1st sess. (1989), introduced by Rep. Peter DeFazio.

[247] Section 8 of the proposed Use of Force Act, for example, would cut off funds for any use of force inconsistent with the Act. See Appendix B.

restraints tied to the purse strings would be more resistant to constitutional challenge and would thus provide a needed predictability that they would be respected in times of crisis. Including prior restraints backed by funding cut-offs will in short ensure that during the next involvement of the armed forces in hostilities, the Resolution will not be largely irrelevant.[248]

Along with prior restraints concerning *when* force can be used, the Resolution should include restraints on *scope* of force, limits on the *degree* of force that can be employed, a subject discussed above.[249] Section 4(b) of the proposed Use of Force Act would have prohibited any use of force for purposes of aggression and any use inconsistent with the principles of necessity and proportionality.[250] These are seminal concepts in the jurisprudence of international law concerning use of force; the proposed Act would have had the effect of incorporating them into United States statutory law.

An alternative to the Senate approach of ''prior restraints'' that would accomplish the same objective but might be less vulnerable constitutionally is statutorily *authorizing* specified uses of armed force, simultaneously specifying precise limits to such use. The War Powers Resolution confers no authority upon the President; as section 8 makes clear, it merely places limits upon the authority that otherwise might lie unregulated. The proposed Use of Force Act, on the other hand, would have affirmatively delegated power to the President to use armed force in certain instances.[251] The distinction is critical. Congress can authorize ''imperfect'' war, in which authority is conferred upon the President subject to statutorily specified limitations, including limits on *scope* of the sort discussed above. Writing in *Bas v. Tingy* in 1800, Justice Paterson said that the war between the United States and France was not an unlimited war, but ''a war for certain objects, and to a certain extent.''[252] He continued: ''[A]s far as Congress tolerated and authorized the war on our part, so far may we proceed in hostile operations.''[253] Similarly, Justice Washington underscored the validity of congressionally imposed limits incident to the delegation of power:

> [H]ostilities may subsist between two nations more confined in its nature and extent; being limited as to places, persons, and things. . . . [T]hose who are author-

[248] Professor Ely's concern that presidents would disobey such restraints, Ely, *supra* note 19, at 1394–95, seems unpersuasive for the reasons that he gives for *expecting* presidential compliance with the Resolution's time limits. *See id.*, 1421 (''If police officers, and even racial bigots, can be conditioned by the rule of law to operate within fetters they initially condemned as impossibly constricting, can't we expect as much of the President and Congress?'').

[249] *See supra* text, at notes 79–81.

[250] *See* Appendix B.

[251] *See* § 4(a), Appendix B. As set forth in Committee Print No. 1, however, the authority conferred was far too broad.

[252] 4 U.S. 37, 45 (1800).

[253] *Id.*

ized to commit hostilities, act under special authority, and can go no farther than to the extent of their commission.[254]

Similar analysis can be found in *Talbot v. Seaman*.[255]

Where Congress delegates authority, therefore, limits imposed incident to that delegation are constitutionally valid. This important premise undergirds the approach of the Use of Force Act.

Fifth, the restraints established by the Resolution should be made to apply to paramilitary operations and CIA personnel, at least where (as in Central America) the "secret war" was a matter of open knowledge.[256] Senator Eagleton offered an amendment to this effect while the Resolution was considered in the Senate, but the amendment was rejected by a vote of 53 to 34.[257] The Church Committee recommended the imposition of time limits similar to those set forth in the Resolution.[258]

Sixth, amendments to the standing rules of the two houses of Congress should be adopted, causing points of order to lie against the consideration of legislation containing funds to carry out prohibited military activities.[259]

Seventh, the courts should be warned not to interpret a variety of congressional acts as approval of a given use of force.[260]

Finally, it must be emphasized again that if the Resolution is to be enforceable, it must be amended to encourage the judicial resolution of disputes about its application.[261] Section 10 of the Use of Force Act, for example, would have attempted to get the courts to resolve disputes over the application of the

[254] *Id.* at 40.

[255] 1 Cranch (5 U.S.) 1, 36 (1801).

[256] Restraints on "covert" activities similar to those contained in the War Powers Resolution concerning members of the armed forces arguably already exist in the Neutrality Act. 18 U.S.C. § 960 (1976). A federal district court decided that § 960 may have been violated by President Reagan's support of guerrilla attacks on Nicaragua. Dellums v. Smith, 577 F. Supp. 1449 (N.D. Cal. 1984). However, the Ninth Circuit dismissed the suit for want of jurisdiction. Dellums v. Smith, 797 F.2d 817 (9th Cir. 1984). The limitations of the Neutrality Act logically belong with those of the War Powers Resolution, and any omnibus amending legislation should combine the two.

[257] 119 Cong. Rec. 25,079 (1973).

[258] Senate Select Comm. to Study Governmental Operations with Respect to Intelligence Activities, Foreign and Military Intelligence: Final Report (Book I), S. Rep. No. 755, 94th Cong., 2d Sess. 449 (1976) (hereinafter Final Report).

[259] A similar approach to executive agreements was attempted by Senator Dick Clark in 1976. *See* S. Res. 486, 94th Cong., 2d Sess. (1976); Treaty Powers Resolution, Hearings Before the Comm. on Foreign Relations, U.S. Senate, 94th Cong., 2d. Sess. (1976). *See generally* Chapter 4; L. Johnson, The Making of International Agreements: Congress Confronts the Executive 140–47 (1984). This approach was pursued in § 8(b) of the Use of Force Act, 1988 Senate War Powers Hearings, *supra* note 19, at 289.

[260] The proposed Use of Force Act did this in § 9(d). *See* Appendix B.

[261] *See* testimony of Michael J. Glennon, 1988 Senate War Powers Hearings, *supra* note 19, at 1180–81.

Act.[262] It would have created standing on the part of members of Congress to challenge noncompliance with the Act,[263] which clearly can be done by statute.[264] It then would have proceeded to direct the courts not to dismiss such an action on grounds of nonjusticiability unless that action is required by the Constitution.[265] Similarly, it would have directed the courts to decide such a case as expeditiously as possible, consistent with the requirements of the Constitution.[266] Because these provisions would spur the judiciary to action only to the extent constitutionally permissible, the provisions avoid constitutional pitfalls by their own terms. Three final amendments concerning judicial review made by the proposed section 10 should also be adopted. First, the provision would have spelled out the remedies a court may employ if it finds that a report was required to be submitted but was not.[267] Second, it would have directed an expedited judicial procedure.[268] And third, section 10 would have provided for direct appeal to the Supreme Court.[269]

Further Comments

The Resolution has been an experiment, and like many experiments, it has led to discoveries. Never before had Congress attempted to enact a systematic framework governing the exercise of a cornerstone presidential power. In many ways, the experiment was the best that could have been attempted. In some ways, it worked. During certain crises, for example, the Resolution may have caused some executive officials to focus on the need for congressional involvement in a way that they would not otherwise have done.[270] Mostly, however, the Resolution has failed. Those failures are identifiable, and they can be rectified. In 1977, the Senate Foreign Relations Committee held hearings to review the effectiveness of the Resolution during its first four years.[271] Many of the deficiencies that recently proved fatal to its effective operation

[262] *See* Appendix B.

[263] *See* § 10(a), Appendix B.

[264] *See, e.g.*, TVA v. Hill, 437 U.S. 153, 164, n.15 (1978); Trafficante v. Metropolitan Life Ins. Co., 409 U.S. 205 (1972).

[265] *See* § 10(b)(1), Appendix B. Similarly, it seems clear that Congress has power to preclude the courts from getting off the hook through reliance upon the doctrine of remedial discretion. *See, e.g.*, Moore v. U.S. House of Representatives, 733 F.2d 946, 954 (D.C.Cir. 1984), *cert. denied*, 469 U.S. 1106 (1985).

[266] *See* § 10(c) of the Use of Force Act, Appendix B.

[267] These were three: (1) direct the President to submit a report; (2) declare that the time period has commenced on the date of the court's judgment; or (3) make such a declaration with respect to a previous date. *See* § 10(d), Appendix B.

[268] *See* § 10(c), Appendix B.

[269] *See* § 10(e), Appendix B.

[270] *See* Atwood, *The War Powers Act Doesn't Work*, Wash. Post, Oct. 2, 1983, at C8, col. 1.

[271] *War Powers Resolution: Hearings Before the Senate Comm. on Foreign Relations*, 95th Cong., 1st Sess. (1977) (hereinafter *1977 Hearings*).

were then evident.[272] But no action was taken because no crisis compelled action.

A crisis finally focused attention on the Resolution's substantial shortcomings. Unfortunately, the conclusions drawn were largely erroneous. As a consequence of United States military action in the Persian Gulf, several leading senators introduced legislation that would repeal the Resolution's core provisions—its time limits.[273] Senators Robert Byrd, Sam Nunn, John Warner, and George Mitchell proposed instead that a "permanent consultative group" consisting of leaders in both houses, be established; the group would meet in time of crisis and upon the introduction of the armed forces into hostilities by the President, would be empowered to introduce legislation approving or disapproving the action. The legislation would be considered pursuant to an expedited procedure, designed (like that originally written into the Resolution) to prevent filibusters, committee bottlenecks, and other procedural roadblocks. Thus the Byrd-Nunn proposal would cut down the current framework to an expedited procedure—one is already in the present law[274]—and a consultation procedure. (It purported to include a funding cutoff as well, but the provision was more smoke than substance.[275])

Senator Byrd, explaining his objections to the Resolution, complained that it is "unworkable" and "robs the President of . . . credibility" because, even though "it might be in the best interest of the country that [the armed forces] not be withdrawn," if Congress "just sits back and does nothing," they must be withdrawn.[276] Senator Nunn was also dissatisfied with the time limit, which "gives foreign governments and renegade groups a lever for influencing U.S. policy debates. . . . our adversaries believe they can simply out-wait us." Moreover, "it is ineffective" because "any congressional action is subject to veto"; it "encourages Lebanon-type compromises" that limit the time of troop deployments, and it "encourages confrontation rather than consultation between Congress and the President."[277]

[272] *See, e.g.*, Senate Comm. on Foreign Relations, Comm. Print No. 2, 95th Cong., 1st Sess. (Comm. Print 1977), *reprinted in 1977 Hearings, supra* note 276, at 338.

[273] *See* S.J. Res. 323, 100th Cong., 2d Sess. (1988).

[274] *See* Resolution, § 6.

[275] Section 5 of S.J. Res. 323, 100th Cong., 2d Sess. (1988) would have amended the Resolution to deny any use of funds for activities which would have violated any law enacted under the Resolution's amended expedited procedure. For the reasons discussed in Chapter 8, it makes good sense to ground limitations on military activities on funding cutoffs. Yet in this form a funding prohibition was a hollow one. The funding cutoff would of course not take effect unless another law were enacted. That law, incorporated by reference in the Resolution, could set its own terms with respect to use of funds; it could easily waive the cutoff, or cut down the scope of its application. There is little reason to include a cutoff in an eviscerated Resolution rather than in the statute actually limiting or ending military operations; that statute will of course be vetoed, and its chances of passage will not be enhanced by placing a funding cutoff that it triggers in the Resolution rather than in it.

[276] 134 Cong. Rec. S7167 (daily ed., June 6, 1988).

[277] Nunn, *War Powers*, Baltimore Sun, Mar. 7, 1988, at 7.

Should the Resolution be repealed as these senators have in effect proposed? Perhaps—but not for their reasons. Senator Byrd's objection is really directed at congressional involvement in war-powers decision making. The way to give the President the credibility Byrd desires is to permit him to commit the armed forces to combat without risk of congressional countermand. For better or worse, that is not the system given us by the Constitution. If it is indeed in the best interests of the country that the forces remain, why cannot Congress be counted on to come to that conclusion?

Nunn's objections too were more properly directed at the Constitution. It is the Constitution that places limits on presidential power—limits that could work to the advantage of our adversaries, who surely know, as do all informed Americans, that we live under a government of limited power and that at some point, the President cannot act (or continue to act) without congressional authorization.

Senator Nunn's real objection seemed to be that because the President has successfully ignored the Resolution and Congress has not effectively played out its true role of reiterator of the preexisting statutory requirements of the Resolution, the Resolution is a failure; another way of looking at it, however, is that more effective *enforcement* is required.

Finally, is a "Lebanon-type compromise" necessarily bad? Should we be concerned that Congress finally mustered the courage to place a statutory time limit upon involvement in the Lebanon quagmire? One might well conclude that the encouragement of this sort of outcome represents a virtue of the Resolution rather than a vice. Similarly, "confrontation" under certain circumstances may be entirely appropriate. As a process, the exercise of constitutional checks is inherently fractious. The process presumes a shifting equilibrium; as one branch asserts itself beyond its proper sphere, the other must also assert, or the equilibrium is destroyed. To call for an end to confrontation is thus to call for an end to balanced power, for acrimony is a regrettable but unavoidable element in the process by which a system of separated powers rights itself.

Perhaps the nation would have been better off if the Resolution had not been enacted. When a President introduced the armed forces into hostilities prior to the Resolution's enactment, the Constitution permitted Congress three options: approval, disapproval, and silence. The Resolution removed one of those options—silence. In effect, it required Congress to support or oppose military operations. The operations in the Persian Gulf, however, suggested a congressional desire to remain silent. The desire was awkwardly pursued; the Resolution renounced the option of silence, and Congress could not, without seeming hypocritical, remain silent without repealing the Resolution. Yet it must be acknowledged that silence in such circumstances does serve understandable political ends. If the President chooses to "go it alone," Congress incurs limited political cost if the operation goes awry. Not having been "in on the take-off,'' it will not be ''in on the landing.'' Perhaps the option of silence had more to commend it than Congress in 1973 realized.

The Resolution has had other untoward effects, principal among them its tendency to deflect public attention from underlying constitutional questions. Rather than inquiring whether a military action is within the President's constitutional power, the tendency is to question whether he has complied with the War Powers Resolution, or worse, whether Congress will ''invoke'' it.[278] The public perception (the public misperception) is that the Resolution *gives* the President sixty days to use the armed forces in hostilities as he sees fit. The text of the Resolution says that this is not so; it provides expressly that ''[n]othing in this joint resolution . . . shall be construed as granting any authority to the President with respect to the introduction of the United States Armed Forces into hostilities . . . which authority he would not have had in the absence of this joint resolution.''[279] Yet the perception remains. Perhaps with statutes, unlike politics, it pays to look at what is said, not at what is done. The difficult issue the Resolution raises is whether modification should be effected in response to public misperception.

That the enactment of the Resolution has been of dubious benefit does not necessarily mean that its repeal would be wise. Repeal of the Resolution at this point—or repeal under amendatory fig leaves, as the Byrd-Warner proposal would effect—could well be seen as signaling congressional surrender. Rather than providing opponents of congressional involvement in war-making ammunition for years to come, a better course would be to modify the Resolution so that it makes for a genuine war-powers partnership between the President and Congress.

Conclusion

Since the enactment of the Resolution, its shortcomings have been addressed through processes that are largely political and that have served its objectives poorly. The alternative is to rectify those deficiencies through legislative processes. For contrary to the intention and belief of its sponsors, the Resolution has not succeeded in separating legal and political processes. If any lesson is to be learned from the first fifteen years of the Resolution's history, it is that

[278] Several commentators have noted that the Resolution, by focusing congressional attention upon issues of legal procedure and constitutional power, has also diverted congressional attention from the substance of policy. *See, e.g.*, testimony of Professor Thomas Franck, 1988 Senate War Powers Hearings, *supra* note 19, at 215. I concur, but I do not believe that this congressional focus has been unprofitable: the whole point of the procedural argument is whether congressional views *count*; there would be little reason to waste time debating a subject, or passing a law on it, if the Executive were completely free to disregard the congressional view.

[279] Resolution, § 8(d)(2).

no congressional reclamation of the war power can succeed unless that reclamation is in the end based more on law than on men.

No modification of the Resolution will in itself "insure that the collective judgment of both the Congress and the President will apply to the introduction of United States Armed Forces into hostilities. . . ."[280] Fifteen years later, it has become clear that the Resolution's sponsors were naive to believe that any law could achieve that objective.[281] The most that a statute can do, however artfully drawn, is to facilitate the efforts of individual members of Congress to carry out their responsibilities under the Constitution.[282] To do that requires understanding, and it also requires courage; it demands an insight into the delicacy with which our separated powers are balanced and the fortitude to stand up to those who equate criticism with lack of patriotism. For a Congress composed of such members, no War Powers Resolution would be necessary; for a Congress without them, no War Powers Resolution will be sufficient.

[280] Resolution, § 2(a).

[281] One sponsor who seemingly came to doubt the Resolution's wisdom was Senator Frank Church. Reflecting upon its operation in 1977, he said:

> I supported that undertaking and I voted for the bill because it came in the aftermath of the Vietnam experience and it seemed that Congress should at least endeavor to prevent another war initiated and pursued on the basis of executive decision.
>
> Still, I have had my doubts that it is possible to accomplish such an objective by statute, not only because it is so hard to foresee future circumstances, but because my reading of history indicates the following. . . .
>
> First, if the President, as Commander-in-Chief, uses the Armed Forces in an action that is both swift and successful, then there is no reason to expect the Congress to do anything but applaud.
>
> If the President employs forces in an action which is swift, but unsuccessful, then the Congress is faced with a fait accompli, and although it may rebuke the President, it can do little else.
>
> If the President undertakes to introduce American forces in a foreign war that is large and sustained, then it seems to me that the argument that the War Powers Resolution forces the Congress to confront the decision is an argument that overlooks the fact that Congress in any case must confront the decision, because it is the Congress that must appropriate the money to make it possible for the sustained action to be sustained.
>
> So, I wonder really whether we have done very much in furthering our purpose through the War Powers Resolution.

A Review of the Operation and Effectiveness of the War Powers Resolution: Hearings Before the Comm. on Foreign Relations, U.S. Senate, 95th Cong., 1st Sess. 172 (1977).

[282] Professor Schlesinger recalled the words of Lord Bryce: "The student of institutions as well as the lawyer is apt to overrate the effect of mechanical contrivances in politics." 1988 Senate War Powers Hearings, *supra* note 19, at 1244.

Chapter Four

THE TREATY POWER

Neither the President nor the Senate, solely, can complete
a treaty; they are checks upon each other, and are so
balanced as to produce security to the people.
—James Wilson[1]

THE AIM OF DIPLOMACY, said Sir Edward Grey, is to enlarge the area of confidence between governments.[2] Absent that confidence, international order breaks down; as international discord increases, nations become more isolated and wary of cooperation, more willing to "go it alone" and to resort to guile and coercion as means of achieving foreign-policy objectives. On the other hand, the gradual growth of a body of reciprocally held assumptions alleviates fears of diplomatic deception and generates a measure of predictability ultimately conducive to international harmony.[3]

The pursuit of stronger and clearer mutually shared expectations is complicated by legislative involvement in foreign-policy formulation.[4] Multi-branched participation in that process may help form or strengthen a national consensus and may also lessen the likelihood of unpopular policies.[5] But a nation with more than one governmental hand at the foreign-policy helm can incur costs in credibility. The hand that signs is not the hand that delivers; what looks like a good bargain to diplomats at the negotiating table may look altogether different to legislators in the cold light of constituents' mail. Thus the domestic value of pluralistic governmental decision making competes with the international value of reciprocal expectations.[6]

[1] 2 J. Elliot, ed., The Debates in the Several State Conventions on the Adoption of the Federal Constitution As Recommended by the General Convention at Philadelphia In 1787, at 507 (2d. ed. 1888).

[2] Richard, *Foreign Perspective: With Whom Do You Deal? Whom Can You Trust*? in The Tethered Presidency 21 (T. Franck ed. 1981) (quoting Sir Harold Nicolson as having quoted Sir Edward Grey).

[3] *See generally* H. Nicolson, Diplomacy (1963); T. Franck & E. Weisband, Word Politics: Verbal Strategy Among the Superpowers (1971); L. Henkin, How Nations Behave (2d ed. 1979).

[4] For a comparative survey of constitutional provisions and national practices concerning legislative participation in the treaty-making process, *see* L. Wildhaber, Treaty-Making Power and Constitution (1971).

[5] *See generally* T. Franck & E. Weisband, Foreign Policy by Congress (1979); Bennet, *Congress in Foreign Policy: Who Needs It?* 57 Foreign Aff. 40 (1978).

[6] *See generally* Christopher, *Ceasefire Between the Branches: A Compact in Foreign Affairs*,

The tension between these values is particularly evident in the making of international agreements by the United States, a nation whose Constitution mandates a fairly strict separation of powers. The revival of congressional involvement in international agreement making—perhaps the most important diplomatic tool for clarifying shared expectations—has further highlighted that tension. Generated principally by crises—Vietnam, Watergate, Iran-Contra—the reassertion by Congress of its foreign-policy prerogatives raises new questions concerning the respective scope of legislative and executive powers in international agreements. This chapter and the next explore some of the issues created by this value tension, which is reflected in the making, unmaking, interpretation, and termination of international agreements.

Conditioning Senate Consent to Treaties

The Disputed Annex to the Spanish Bases Treaty

The authority of the Senate to condition its consent to treaties, although not set forth expressly in the Constitution,[7] is now well settled.[8] Recently, however, concern has arisen in the Senate about the continued viability of that power, traceable to a little-noticed dispute that followed the Senate's consent in 1976 to the Treaty of Friendship and Cooperation with Spain.[9]

After transmittal of that Treaty to the Senate,[10] the Foreign Relations Committee held hearings on the agreement. These hearings brought out serious concern about Spanish progress toward democracy.[11] Consequently, the Committee appended a five-part "declaration" to its resolution of ratification[12] that stated that the Senate "hopes and intends that this Treaty will serve to support

60 Foreign Aff. 989 (1982); Richard, *supra* note 2; Tower, *Congress Versus the President: The Formulation and Implementation of American Foreign Policy*, 60 Foreign Aff. 229 (1981/82).

[7] The Constitution merely provides that the making of a treaty requires the advice and consent of the Senate, U.S. Const. art. II, § 2, cl. 2.

[8] *See, e.g.*, Restatement, § 303, Comment *d* (stating that the Senate may condition its consent to a treaty, provided the condition has a plausible relation to the treaty's content or implementation); L. Henkin, Foreign Affairs and the Constitution 133–34 (1972) (stating that the Senate's constitutional right to impose reservations as a condition for consent is universally accepted); 14 M. Whiteman, Digest of International Law 138 (1970); Note, *The Reservation Power and the Connally Amendment*, 11 N.Y.U. J. Int'l. L. & Pol. 323, 327 (1978) (tracing the Senate practice of adding reservations to treaties to 1794).

[9] Treaty of Friendship and Cooperation, United States–Spain, Jan. 24, 1976, 27 U.S.T. 3005, T.I.A.S. No. 8630.

[10] S. Exec. Doc. E, 94th Cong. 2d Sess. (1976).

[11] *Spanish Base Treaty: Hearings on Executive E Before the Senate Comm. on Foreign Relations*, 94th Cong. 2d Sess. (1976).

[12] S. Exec. Rep. No. 5, 94th Cong., 2d Sess. 11 (1976).

and foster Spain's progress toward free institutions.''[13] The Senate later approved the resolution of ratification as reported by the Committee.[14]

Several weeks thereafter, the Department of State reported strong opposition in the Cortes (the Spanish parliament) to the Senate declaration and indicated to the Senate Foreign Relations Committee that the government of Spain would not ratify the Treaty were the Senate declaration included in the United States instrument of ratification. During consultation with various members of the Committee, the State Department proposed inclusion of the declaration in an annex to the Treaty, to be incorporated by reference in the instrument of ratification and transmitted simultaneously.[15] ''Attaching the Senate resolution to the instrument by means of an annex referred to in the instrument of ratification,'' the Department said, ''is the equivalent of incorporating the resolution in the instrument.''[16] The Senators approved, and the Treaty was ratified by the President.

Effect on the Panama Canal Treaties

With fresh memories of this episode, the Senate Foreign Relations Committee took up the Panama Canal Treaties.[17] The Committee appended to each resolution of ratification an ''understanding'' that ''[t]he President shall include all amendments, conditions, reservations, and understandings incorporated by the Senate in this resolution of ratification in the instrument of ratification to be exchanged with the Government of the Republic of Panama.''[18] The Senate's concern that the material it had added might be transmitted separately from the instrument of ratification is understandable: The requirements of international law concerning treaty ratification, in light of United States ratification practice, raise serious doubts whether a separately transmitted Senate condition would be binding on the other party. International law, at least as interpreted by the United States government, requires that all reservations and other terms and conditions attached to a nation's ratification of a treaty be formulated in writing and communicated to the other party or parties to the

[13] *Id.*

[14] S. Res. 401, 94th Cong. 2d Sess. (1976); *see also* 122 Cong. Rec. 19,390 (1976) (ratification vote).

[15] For a general discussion of the diplomatic contretemps, see Meron, *The Treaty War: The International Legal Effect of Changes in Obligations Initiated by the Congress*, in The Tethered Presidency, *supra* note; *Panama Canal Treaties: Hearings Before the Senate Comm. on Foreign Relations*, 95th Cong. 2d Sess. 122–23 (1978) (hereinafter cited as *Panama Canal Hearings*).

[16] Letter from Robert J. McCloskey, Assistant Secretary of State for Congressional Relations, to John J. Sparkman, Senate Foreign Relations Committee Chairman (undated) (on file with the author).

[17] *See* S. Exec. Rep. No. 12, 95th Cong. 2d Sess. 10–11 (1978) (alluding to concern over the Spanish Treaty incident).

[18] *Id.* at 10.

treaty.[19] Traditionally, the United States has communicated such Senate conditions in the instrument of ratification,[20] and other nations might presumably rely on this practice. Given the requirement that the President make the Senate's qualifications on consent effective if he wishes to bring the treaty into force,[21] it is most sensible that a Senate condition be incorporated in the instrument of ratification.[22]

Rule of the Restatement

The *Restatement*, however, would impose a less rigorous requirement. Section 314, concerning reservations and understandings, provides as follows:

> (1) When the Senate of the United States gives its advice and consent to a treaty on condition that the United States enter a reservation, the President, if he makes the treaty, must include the reservation in the instrument of ratification or accession, or otherwise manifest that the adherence of the United States is subject to the reservation.
>
> (2) When the Senate gives its advice and consent to a treaty on the basis of a particular understanding of its meaning, the President, if he makes the treaty, must do so on the basis of the Senate's understanding.[23]

Comment *b* recognizes that the President "must give effect to conditions imposed by the Senate on its consent."[24] It notes, accordingly, that the President

[19] *See e.g.*, Letter from Douglas J. Bennet, Jr., Assistant Secretary of State for Congressional Relations, to John J. Sparkman, Chairman of the Senate Foreign Relations Committee (Jan. 26, 1978), *reprinted in Panama Canal Hearings*, *supra* note 15, at 49.

[20] *See* Letter from Herbert J. Hansell, Legal Adviser to the Department of State, to Michael J. Glennon, Legal Counsel to the Senate Foreign Relations Committee (June 8, 1979), *reprinted in* 2 United States Foreign Relations Law 199 (M. Glennon & T. Franck eds. 1980) (hereinafter cited as Foreign Relations Law).

[21] Restatement (Second) of the Foreign Relations Law of the United States, § 133, Comment *c* (1965); Restatement, § 314, Comment *b*.

[22] 14 M. Whiteman, *supra* note 8, at 138–39. *See also* Memorandum from the Office of the Legal Adviser of the Department of State, Mar. 22, 1971, to J. W. Fulbright, Chairman of the Senate Foreign Relations Committee, *reprinted in* S. Exec. Rep. No. 5, 93d Cong., 1st Sess. 15–16 (1973):

> In United States law a condition placed by the Senate on its approval of a treaty—whether by reservation or by understanding—and included by the President in the instrument of ratification takes effect as domestic law along with the treaty itself. This is a necessary result of the shared constitutional role of the President and the Senate in the treaty-making process.
>
> An instrument of ratification or adherence executed by the President of the United States sets forth the text of the reservation, understanding, or other instrument as given in the Senate resolution. . . .
>
> Reservations, understandings, or declarations of intent or interpretation, in order to have international effect, are incorporated in the case of a bilateral treaty. . . .

Id.

[23] Restatement, § 314.

[24] *Id.* § 314, Comment *b*.

''generally includes a verbatim recitation of any proposed reservation, statement of understanding, or other declaration relevant to the application or interpretation of the treaty contained in the Senate resolution of consent, both in the instrument notifying the other state or the depositary of United States ratification or accession, and in the proclamation of the treaty.''[25] Without explanation or elaboration, however, the comment then states flatly that ''[t]he President may also communicate a Senate qualification separately.''[26]

The *Restatement* seems mistaken in permitting such discretion. An absolute requirement of inclusion in the instrument of ratification is appropriate to ensure identical expectations by both nations concerning rights and obligations imposed by the treaty. Transmission of material included by the Senate in its resolution of ratification by means of an ''annex'' not incorporated by reference or a diplomatic note only increases the possibility of misunderstanding. This applies even more to provisions that expressly or implicitly alter provisions of a treaty.

If broader presidential discretion is to be recognized, however, it should be limited to the authority to exclude from the instrument of ratification only material added by the Senate that in the Senate's view does not represent a ''condition'' to its consent. The President may have the power to transmit separately from the instrument of ratification a ''statement'' or ''declaration'' merely expressing the sense of the Senate and not altering treaty terms. Such authority would arguably derive from the President's power as ''sole organ of the United States''[27] for the purpose of communicating with foreign governments, a power long recognized by the Senate.[28] The *Restatement* maintains that the Senate cannot condition its consent upon the firing of a cabinet officer,[29] presumably on the notion that dismissal is a plenary presidential power; the same might be said of the power to communicate with foreign governments[30] or negotiate treaties.[31] Because conditions have the same force

[25] *Id.*

[26] *Id.*

[27] *See infra* note 30.

[28] *See e.g.*, S. Exec. Rep. No. 12, *supra* note 17, at 9–10. The President's power in this regard seems settled. ''As 'sole organ,' '' Professor Henkin has written, ''the President determines . . . how, when, where and by whom the United States should make or receive communications, and there is nothing to suggest that he is limited to time, place, or forum.'' L. Henkin, *supra* note 8, at 47.

[29] Restatement, § 303, Comment *d.*

[30] *But see* Chapter 1, discussing the limits of that power. *See also* Berger, *The President's Unilateral Termination of the Taiwan Treaty*, 75 NW. U. L. Rev. 577, 590 (1980).

[31] Pursuant to its ''advice'' power, the Senate clearly can express its sense as to what sort of agreement it wishes the Executive to negotiate or not to negotiate. In considering the INF Treaty, for example, the Senate adopted a declaration that, in any subsequent agreement, it ''should'' be the position of the United States that no restrictions ''should'' be established on certain cruise missiles. 134 Cong. Rec. S6615 (daily ed. May 25, 1988). While the President may disregard this admonition, he does so at his peril. The Senate cannot, however, *bind* the President with respect to future negotiations. During that same debate, Senator Jesse Helms offered an amend-

domestically and internationally as the text of the treaty,[32] it follows that the same principles apply to the treaty text. The President and the Senate could not, for example, approve a treaty prohibiting a future president from negotiating another treaty on a given subject. As submitted to the Senate, the Panama Canal Treaty did precisely that, prohibiting the United States from negotiating with third states concerning the construction of another canal.[33] The Foreign Relations Committee recommended, and the Senate adopted, an understanding "to make clear that the provision may not be construed as precluding a future President from exercising his constitutional power to confer with other governments."[34] (The purpose of the treaty provision, the Committee believed, was to "ensure that the United States not . . . *enter into*" such an agreement.)[35]

The difficulty with this argument is that it would cause presidential power to turn on an empty semantic distinction or would make the President the sole judge of the Senate's substantive intent. It is established that the legal effect of any matter added by the Senate depends upon its substance, not its denomination.[36] But the President, under this analysis, would be empowered to exclude from the instrument of ratification material intended by the Senate to be included[37] and, conversely, would be required to include material that the Senate had not intended to be transmitted.[38] The alternative—allowing the Presi-

---

ment, rejected by the Senate, providing that the United States "shall" be guided by certain principles and considerations in continued negotiations with the Soviet Union. 134 Cong. Rec. S6785 (daily ed. May 26, 1988). Such a restriction, as Senator Alan Cranston pointed out, would have been unconstitutional. *Id.* at S6787.

[32] Restatement, § 314, Comment *b*.

[33] Treaty Concerning the Permanent Neutrality and Operation of the Panama Canal, United States–Panama, Sept. 7, 1977, art. XII(2), subpar. (b), T.I.A.S. No. 10,029 (1977).

[34] Exec. Rept. 95-12, 95th Cong., 2d Sess. 9 (1978).

[35] *Id.* (emphasis in original).

[36] 14 M. Whiteman, *supra* note 8, at 140.

[37] *See* Chapter 7.

[38] The so-called Niagara Reservation could be viewed as such a condition. In 1950, the United States and Canada reached an agreement governing the use of the Niagara River, designed to protect the scenic beauty of Niagara Falls and to allow diversion of waters from the river for generation of hydroelectric power. Convention on Uses of the Waters of the Niagara River, United States–Canada, Feb. 27, 1950, 1 U.S.T. 694, T.I.A.S. No. 2130. The Senate, uncertain as to how the American share of the waters should be utilized, adopted a "reservation" to the treaty providing that the question would be resolved by an act of Congress and that the water would not be utilized in the interim. The government of Canada accepted the reservation, and the treaty entered into force. Henkin, *The Treaty Makers and the Law Makers: The Niagara Reservation*, 56 Colum. L. Rev. 1151, 1155–58 (1956). Congress then failed to take action on the issue over the next five years, a delay that proved too much for "the energetic Mr. [Robert] Moses of the New York Power Authority," who brought suit to have the reservation declared null and to have a license for hydroelectric development issued to the authority. *Id.* at 1159. The United States Court of Appeals for the District of Columbia Circuit held that the reservation was not really part of the treaty, as it dealt with a matter of purely domestic concern, and therefore was not legally

dent to look to the substance of the added material—creates equally great difficulties in that it increases executive discretion to the point of authorizing the separate transmittal of material that in the President's exclusive judgment, was falsely labeled a "reservation," a formulation of authority that would not comport with traditional United States ratification practice.[39] The better view is that the President is required to communicate a Senate condition as a part of the instrument of ratification unless the Senate expressly waives the requirement.

Regardless of the position taken by the *Restatement* on the scope of presidential authority in the face of Senate "silence," it should nonetheless be clear that presidential discretion is diminished if the Senate consents to a treaty on the express condition that specified material be transmitted with the instrument of ratification, as it did, without objection by the executive branch, in approving the Panama Canal Treaties.[40] Such a condition (subject to the possible implication of the President's "communication" power)[41] would rest upon approximately the same constitutional footing as a condition providing that the Senate or Congress participate in the termination process.[42] If the Senate can validly accomplish the latter by conditioning its consent to a treaty, as the *Restatement* concludes it "presumably" can,[43] then presumably it can thus accomplish the former as well. Each condition would be "applicable to the treaty before it" and have a "plausible relation to its adoption."[44]

---

enforceable; the Supreme Court, however, vacated the appeals court's judgment. Power Auth. v. Federal Power Comm'n, 247 F.2d 538 (D.C. Cir.), *vacated as moot sub nom.* American Pub. Power Ass'n v. Power Auth., 355 U.S. 64 (1957).

[39] *See* 14 M. Whiteman, *supra* note 8, at 138–39.

[40] *See* Chapter 7.

[41] *See supra* note 30 and accompanying text.

[42] The question whether the Senate may condition its consent to a treaty by prescribing the procedure the President must follow in terminating it gave rise to considerable controversy in the aftermath of President Carter's unilateral termination, effective January 1, 1980, of the Mutual Defense Treaty between the United States and the Nationalist Chinese on Taiwan (Treaty of Mutual Defense, United States–China, Dec. 2, 1954, 6 U.S.T. 433, T.I.A.S. No. 3178). The Department of Justice, relying upon the President's position as the nation's "sole representative in foreign affairs," argued that the President alone can determine whether a treaty should be terminated. The Department cited in support the dictum of Justice Sutherland in *Curtiss-Wright*, 299 U.S. at 319, that the President is the "sole organ" of the United States in foreign policy.

The Senate Foreign Relations Committee did not accept this view, believing that either the Senate acting alone (by attaching a condition to a treaty) or the Congress as a whole (by statute) could constitutionally limit the President's authority to terminate a treaty. The Committee based its reasoning on the separation of powers analysis in Justice Jackson's concurring opinion in the *Steel Seizure Case*. The American Law Institute supports the Senate's position in Restatement, § 339, Comment *a*. *See generally* Glennon, *Treaty Process Reform: Saving Constitutionalism Without Destroying Diplomacy*, 52 U. Cinn. L. Rev. 84.

[43] Restatement, § 339, Comment *a*.

[44] *Id.* § 339, Reporters' Note 3.

Effect of Senate Conditions

The legal effect of Senate conditions in the United States instrument of ratification depends on the response of the other signatory. The United States is effectively placed in the position of making a "counteroffer,"[45] and United States practice is accordingly to place the other signatory on notice of such conditions prior to the exchange of instruments of ratification.[46] Refusal of the other state to exchange instruments of ratification constitutes rejection of the treaty.[47] Under such circumstances, the treaty and the Senate's conditions are therefore without effect, both domestically and internationally. On the other hand, if the other signatory expressly accepts the Senate's conditions upon exchange of the instruments, both the text of the treaty and the Senate's conditions take effect internationally and, if the treaty is self-executing, become the law of the land.[48]

Is the other signatory to the treaty, upon exchanging instruments of ratification with United States representatives, nonetheless bound by those conditions if it makes no comment regarding the Senate's conditions? The question gave rise to some debate during consideration of SALT II by the Senate Foreign Relations Committee. The author advised the Committee that "[i]f the Soviet Union proceeds with the exchange of instruments of ratification its silence constitutes assent to the treaties as modified by the United States."[49] Eugene V. Rostow,[50] however, sharply disagreed in testimony before the Committee[51] and in a subsequent letter.[52] "[A] reservation has the same legal effect as a

[45] *See, e.g.*, T. Elias, The Modern Law of Treaties 28 (1974).

[46] 14 M. Whiteman, *supra* note 8, at 138.

[47] T. Elias, *supra* note 45, at 28–29; 14 M. Whiteman, *supra* note 8, at 140–41.

[48] As the "supreme law of the land," U.S. treaties enjoy equal status with federal statutes. U.S. Const. art. VI, cl. 2. The Supreme Court has held, however, that insofar as a treaty is a contract, its duties must be carried out by a political branch of the government and not by the judiciary. Foster v. Neilson, 27 U.S. (2 Pet.) 253, 314 (1829). Thus, treaty terms requiring legislative action are not enforced by the courts until Congress has enacted the appropriate legislation.

There is some controversy whether a treaty becomes law for domestic purposes on the date it enters into force or on the date the President formally proclaims it. Restatement, § 312, Reporters' Note 4. The question is of minor importance, as Presidents are generally swift to issue such proclamations. *See id.* § 312, Comment *k*.

[49] Memorandum from Michael J. Glennon and Frederick S. Tipson to members of the Senate Foreign Relations Committee (June 25, 1979), *reprinted in* 4 *SALT II Treaty: Hearings on Ex. Y Before the Senate Comm. on Foreign Relations*, 96th Cong., 1st Sess. 18, 23 (1979) (hereinafter cited as *SALT II Hearings*.)

[50] Professor Rostow appeared as chairman of the Committee on the Present Danger, a group opposed to ratification of the SALT II Treaty.

[51] 4 *SALT II Hearings*, *supra* note 49, at 1–15.

[52] *Id.* at 15–17. The letter was also signed by Professor Rostow's Yale Law School colleagues, Joseph W. Bishop, Robert H. Bork, Leon Lipson, Myres S. McDougal, and William M. Reisman.

letter from my mother,'' he said.[53] Elaborating, Professor Rostow suggested that an amendment to the text of a treaty is of greater legal force than a reservation[54] and that in any event, ''silence would not be acceptance.''[55]

Rostow is mistaken in his conclusion that the legal effect of treaty reservations is less than that of amendments. ''If a treaty is ratified or acceded to by the United States with a reservation effective, . . . the reservation is part of the treaty and is law of the United States.''[56] Rostow's error may derive from the confusing interface between principles of domestic ratification law and those of international law. In domestic law, the Senate may condition its consent to treaties in either of two ways. It may amend its resolution of ratification by adding material (normally called a reservation, understanding, interpretation, declaration, or statement), or it may amend the resolution by inserting a condition that the text of the treaty be amended. Strictly speaking, the Senate does not ''amend'' the treaty text; it consents to ratification by the President on the condition that the President amend the text upon ratification.[57] Each form of alteration is equally binding on the President, however, if he or she chooses to exchange instruments of ratification.[58] Similarly, international law regards a reservation to a bilateral treaty as tantamount to a proposed amendment.[59] The principal reason that the Senate sometimes prefers the ''reserva-

[53] *Id.* at 13; *see also* 2 *SALT II Hearings*, *supra* note 49, at 393–94.

[54] Professor Rostow engaged in the following colloquy with Senator Joseph Biden:

SENATOR BIDEN . . . If the reservation is adopted by the U.S. Senate, and the Soviets go forward with the treaty accepting our stated interpretation—

MR. ROSTOW That is the same drama we had in 1972. That is exactly the problem of the unilateral interpretations in 1972, which were sold to you and the Senate as grounds for abrogating the treaty. The Soviets paid no attention to our unilateral interpretations, and we did nothing about it when they were violated.

SENATOR BIDEN I am told by counsel that a reservation becomes a full part of the treaty. Assume that counsel is right that it does, would you have a problem?

. . . MR. ROSTOW I made a list of other problems on which we think amendments or reservations are necessary and I certainly should prefer amendments. I am happy to know that your counsel thinks that a reservation becomes part of the treaty, and I will be glad to talk with him about it afterward.

2 *SALT II Hearings*, *supra* note 49, at 393–94.

[55] 4 *id.* at 14.

[56] Restatement, § 314, Comment *b*.

[57] *See infra* note 58.

[58] As noted above, the label used by the Senate is legally irrelevant. 14 M. Whiteman, *supra* note 8, at 140. Thus, a Senate amendment to its resolution of ratification providing that a given article of the treaty is without force and effect would be every bit as effective as an actual ''amendment to the text'' of that treaty striking the article.

[59] The use of the terms *amendment* and *reservation* is thus somewhat confusing. As pointed out above, the Senate cannot itself amend a treaty. Nor can it really enter a reservation; rather, it can impose, as a condition for its advice and consent, the requirement that the President enter a reservation. Restatement, § 303, Reporters' Note 3. In either event, the President must, *under international law*, return to the other signatory to ask consent to a new treaty. *See* 1 L. Oppenheim, International Law 914 (H. Lauterpacht 8th ed. 1955) (calling a reservation ''the refusal of an offer

tion'' mode to the ''amendment'' mode is diplomatic. Domestic political considerations in the nonreserving state may make it easier for its government to accept a treaty alteration that is less glaring.[60] Thus, the *Restatement* defines ''reservation'' as including any ''unilateral statement made by a state when signing, ratifying, accepting, approving, or acceding to an international agreement, whereby it purports to exclude or modify the legal effect of certain provisions of that agreement in their application to that state.''[61]

Whether nonobjection constitutes tacit acceptance of a reservation to a bilateral treaty is more difficult. While tacit acceptance of reservations to multilateral treaties has received considerable attention,[62] that of reservations to bilateral treaties has not. The universal acceptance of reference to contract law supports the principle that a reservation to a bilateral treaty puts the reserving state in the position of rejecting the treaty and proposing a counteroffer.[63] Thus, one may refer to contract law for answers to ancillary questions such as when a counteroffer has been accepted. Principles of contract law would suggest that if the other state proceeds to the affirmative act of exchanging instruments of ratification after having been placed on notice that an alteration is demanded, it has accepted the counteroffer. Because of the dearth of authority in traditional sources of customary international law, however, the matter is not free from doubt.

The question is largely academic because the United States generally obtains the express acceptance of Senate conditions by the other party, at least

---

and the making of a fresh offer''); Parry, *The Law of Treaties*, in Manual of Public International Law 175, 194 (M. Sorensen ed. 1968) (stating flatly that ''[a] reservation constitutes a proposal of an amendment of the treaty text'').

The Vienna Convention on the Law of Treaties uses the term *reservation* to encompass both types of Senate conditions, providing in article 2(1)(d) that '' 'reservation' means a unilateral statement, *however phrased or named*, made by a State, when signing, ratifying, accepting, approving or acceding to a treaty, whereby it purports to exclude or to modify the legal effect of certain provisions of the treaty in their application to that State.'' Vienna Convention on the Law of Treaties, May 23, 1969, UN Doc. A/Conf. 39/27, *reprinted in* 63 Am. J. Int'l L. 875 (1969), 8 I.L.M. 679 (1969) (emphasis added) (hereinafter cited as Vienna Convention).

[60] To cite one example, the Senate Foreign Relations Committee recommended to the Senate that changes to the Panama Canal Treaties other than those recommended by the Committee itself not take the form of amendments. S. Exec. Rep. No. 12, *supra* note 17, at 13.

[61] Restatement, § 313, Comment *a*.

[62] Brazil, *Some Reflections on the Vienna Convention on the Law of Treaties*, 6 Fed. L. Rev. 223 (1975); Comment, *Reservations to Multilateral Treaties: How International Doctrine Reflects World Vision*, 23 Harv. Int'l L.J. 71 (1982); *see generally* Vienna Convention, *supra* note 59. While § II of the Vienna Convention is entitled simply ''Reservations''—a shortening of the title ''Reservations to Multilateral Treaties'' used in an earlier draft—the President of the Vienna Conference, Professor Ago, said that the change should be understood as reflecting the fact that all reservations are, by definition, to multilateral treaties since, strictly speaking, a so-called reservation to a bilateral treaty constitutes a proposal for a new treaty and not a true reservation at all. Brazil, *supra* at 230–31.

[63] *See, e.g.*, Parry, *supra* note 59, at 194.

with respect to major bilateral treaties. Both sides sign a protocol of exchange of the instruments of ratification, which spells out the legal effect to be accorded all material in those instruments and thus effectively binds each party explicitly to any conditions entered by the other.[64]

The practice of executing a protocol of exchange, hitherto a relatively obscure stage in the process of treaty ratification, can be expected to gain greater prominence as attention focuses increasingly on the need for precision in treaty commitments. The evolution of the practice was hastened greatly during the Senate's consideration of the Panama Canal Treaties[65] and the SALT II Treaty.[66] A condition added to the so-called Panama Canal Neutrality Treaty required, apparently for the first time, that a protocol of exchange be executed and that it include a particular condition.[67] Curiously, however, the "inclusion" requirement applied only to that one condition and not to other material added by the Senate.[68]

The Senate Foreign Relations Committee took a great step toward clarifying this increasingly confused situation in its resolution of ratification concerning the SALT II Treaty.[69] The resolution dispensed with the outmoded lexicon of ratification law and instead of using such labels as "amendments," "reservations," and "understandings," set forth three explicit categories of conditions: (1) those that need not be formally communicated or agreed to by the Soviet Union; (2) those to be formally communicated to the Soviet Union but not necessarily agreed to; and (3) those that would require the explicit agreement of the Soviet Union.[70] This tripartite structure, the Committee noted, "should avoid the ambiguities and potential misunderstandings inherent in the traditional designation."[71] It continued:

> Those designations may still be useful as indicators of a sponsor's intent. But as to whether Soviet involvement is required either through formal notice or agreement, the designations themselves would not have to carry the entire weight in-

[64] *See* S. Exec. Rep. No. 14, 96th Cong., 1st Sess. 33 (1979); Restatement, § 314, Comment *b*; 14 M. Whiteman, *supra* note 8, at 139. *See generally id.* at 138.

[65] Treaty concerning the Permanent Neutrality and Operation of the Panama Canal, United States–Panama, Sept. 7, 1977, T.I.A.S. No. 10,029; Treaty on the Panama Canal, United States–Panama, Sept. 7, 1977, T.I.A.S. No. 10,030.

[66] S. Exec. Doc. Y, 96th Cong. 1st Sess. (1979).

[67] *See* 124 Cong. Rec. 7187 (1978).

[68] *Senate Additions to the Panama Canal Treaties*, Dep't St. Bull., No. 2014, May 1978, at 52, 53.

[69] S. Exec. Rep. No. 14, *supra* note 64, at 72–78.

[70] *Id.* The Committee's chairman, Senator Frank Church, and ranking minority member, Senator Jacob Javits, previously had received assurances in an exchange of letters with Secretary of State Cyrus Vance that the President would respect the Senate's wishes on this matter, as expressed in the resolution. *Id.* at 31–32.

[71] *Id.* at 35.

> dicating the Senate's intentions. Placement in a particular section of the Resolution of Ratification should leave no doubt on this score.[72]

Happily, the new terminology seems to have stuck; during Senate consideration of the INF Treaty, "condition" seemed to supplant entirely the old labels of "reservation" and "understanding."[73]

Treaty Interpretation

Can the President "interpret" a treaty in a manner at odds with the meaning communicated by the Senate when it approved the treaty? This question generated heated controversy between the Senate and the Reagan Administration regarding the ABM Treaty[74] and, later, the INF Treaty.[75]

The *Restatement* notes that the President has broad authority to construe the words of treaties.[76] The Senate is said to have no role in the interpretive process.[77] Its role has been seen as confined to the advise-and-consent function conferred by the Constitution.[78]

Yet it is clear that the President's interpretive power is limited. He cannot make an altogether new treaty and dispense with the requirement of Senate advice and consent by calling that treaty an "interpretation" of an earlier one. Nor can he amend an earlier treaty and escape the requirement of Senate approval (to what is in reality a new treaty) by calling the amendment an "interpretation."[79] The President's semantic denomination of his act cannot by itself control the procedure constitutionally required. At some point, his authority ends and the Senate's begins; at some point, an interpretation becomes a new treaty or an amendment to the old one. But when?

[72] *Id.*

[73] *See generally* Exec. Rep. 100-15, 100th Cong., 1st Sess. (1988) (INF Treaty).

[74] Treaty Between the United States of America and the Union of the Soviet Socialist Republics on the Limitation of Anti-Ballistic Missile Systems, May 26, 1972, 23 U.S.T. 3435, T.I.A.S. No. 7503 (hereinafter referred to as the ABM Treaty). For an excellent review of the substantive arguments on both sides of the ABM controversy *see* "The Anti-Ballistic Missile Treaty Interpretation Dispute," Committee on International Arms Control and Security Affairs of the Association of the Bar of the City of New York, 43 Record of the Ass'n of the Bar of the City of N.Y. 300 (1988).

[75] Treaty between the United States of America and the Union of the Soviet Socialist Republics on the Elimination of their Intermediate-Range and Shorter Range Missiles, Treaty Doc. No. 100-11 (1988) (hereinafter referred to as the INF Treaty).

[76] Section 326(1) of the *Restatement* provides that the President "has authority to determine the interpretation of an international agreement to be asserted by the United States in its relations with other states." Restatement, § 326(1).

[77] *Id.*, Reporters' Note 1.

[78] Art. II, § 2, cl. 2 provides that the President "shall have power, by and with the advice and consent of the Senate, to make treaties, provided two-thirds of the Senators present concur."

[79] "The President's power to terminate an international agreement does not imply authority to modify an agreement or to conclude a new one in its place." Restatement, § 339, Comment *a*.

At the outset, it is useful to recall that the United States' *domestic* obligations under an international agreement need not correspond to its *international* obligations. This principle is clear under customary international law and of course is true with respect to every nation. Perhaps the best example of an agreement giving rise to disparate obligations in the two legal systems is an agreement entered into in violation of a nation's domestic law. Under international law, such an agreement can be binding internationally, notwithstanding the domestic violation. Indeed, such an agreement *is* binding internationally unless the agreement violates a "fundamental rule" of domestic law and that violation is "manifest."[80] At the same time, the domestic rule is, *ex hypothesi*, contravened. Domestically, such an agreement is thus void; internationally, it is binding.

This consideration is important to bear in mind because during the dispute concerning interpretation of the ABM Treaty, the State Department legal adviser, Abraham Sofaer repeatedly cautioned the Senate against endorsing a principle that would "[deprive] our nation of the benefits of mutuality of obligation in its treaty relations."[81] "The United States," the adviser testified, "would be put at a significant disadvantage if the President is subject to stricter constraints, as a result of internal understandings of the Senate, than those which apply to other parties."[82] It is important, he appeared to suggest, that the Senate not endorse a principle that could result in one obligation for the United States and another for a treaty partner. This argument was repeated during the debate on the INF Treaty.[83]

Surely all nations have a "tidiness" interest; it ill behooves a nation that takes law seriously to flirt with juridical schizophrenia by permitting itself to undertake dissonant domestic and international obligations. Yet the legal adviser seemed (wrongly) to assume that the possibility of disparity was some novel idea propounded by a few senators, rather than a contingency inherent in the nature of the relationship between the two legal systems. Moreover, he seemed (wrongly) to assume that harmony between the two legal regimes is the *only* interest at stake. Surely a far greater interest is involved: The interest of every state—the United States in particular—in preserving the integrity of the domestic legal order must prevail against concerns about mere orderliness. The United States Constitution places limits on the President's power. Whatever international law may say about the *international* nature of an obligation

[80] *See* article 46, Vienna Convention, *supra* note 59.

[81] *The ABM Treaty and the Constitution: Joint Hearings Before the Senate Committee on Foreign Relations and the Senate Committee of the Judiciary*, 100th Cong., 1st Sess. 372 (1987) (statement of Abraham Sofaer, State Dept. Legal Adviser).

[82] *Id.*

[83] *See, e.g.*, Sofaer's address to the American Law Institute, *reprinted in* 134 Cong. Rec. 6724 (daily ed. May 26, 1988) (stating the Administration's belief that "only one treaty can exist, the one to which the Senate gives its advice and consent." *Id.* at 6742).

undertaken by the United States, those limits apply domestically and must be respected unless Congress legislates to change the obligation.[84]

In the ABM dispute, curiously, the Reagan Administration was not truly concerned about a lack of mutuality of *international* obligations. Its argument to the Senate was that United States and Soviet negotiators did indeed have a meeting of the minds in 1972 and that the meaning of the Treaty in force in 1987 was the Treaty on which the negotiators had secretly agreed, not the meaning described to the Senate in 1972 by the Executive's spokesmen, not the meaning identified in 1972 by the two Senate opponents of the Treaty as a reason for voting against it. That meaning, which would have prohibited testing and development of the exotic space-based laser technologies composing the Strategic Defense Initiative or ''Star Wars,'' may have been *inferred* by the Senate, but the Senate was wrong—or more precisely, misled. ''[E]rrors sometimes occur,'' the legal adviser testified, ''people sometime [*sic*] exaggerate, and misunderstandings take place.''[85] His fundamental argument, therefore, was that however clear the ratification record of the treaty, however clear the subsequent practice of the parties, the secret negotiating record was dispositive as to the Treaty's meaning.[86]

But dispositive in which legal system—international law or domestic constitutional law? *Time* magazine reasonably drew the conclusion that the legal adviser's reference was to both systems; he was, after all, giving testimony concerning the propriety of a measure that undertook to describe principles of treaty interpretation ''[u]nder the United States Constitution.''[87] Yet, in a letter to the editor of *Time*, the legal adviser disclaimed any intent to address the domestic issues:

> You say that I ''claimed that nothing the Administration tells the Senate during the ratification process is binding.'' My testimony, however, was addressed to the effect of the Senate's ratification record on international *obligations* toward the other party to a treaty, not the obligations of the President toward the Senate under the United States constitutional structure.[88]

With all due respect to Sofaer, this is simply not true. His testimony is replete with commentary concerning the ''obligations of the President toward the

[84] *See* Chapter 7 concerning international law as law of the United States.

[85] *See* Sofaer testimony, *supra* note 81, at 373.

[86] Administration supporters of the ''broad'' interpretation and Senate proponents of the ''narrow'' interpretation both contended that the text of the Treaty supported their interpretation, and allowed that, in the event of ambiguities, reference to extrinsic sources was permissible. Certain senators opposing the Administration, however, disputed the propriety of reference to an untransmitted secret negotiating record to resolve textual ambiguities.

[87] § 2(2)(A), Senate Resolution 167, 100th Cong., 1st Sess. (1987).

[88] Time, April 27, 1987, at 10.

Senate under the United States constitutional structure.''[89] And the legal adviser continued to confound international and constitutional law precepts in his criticism[90] of the Foreign Relations Committee's report on the INF Treaty,[91] which contained lengthy analysis in support of the ''Biden Condition'' requiring that the Treaty be interpreted in accordance with the common understanding shared by the Executive and the Senate at the time of its ratification.[92]

Much of the confusion can be eliminated by distinguishing between the different effects under the different systems; the distinction serves to highlight three central issues arising within the domestic legal system.

[89] Sofaer commented on the Framers' intent with respect to the Treaty Clause. *The ABM Treaty and the Constitution: Joint Hearings Before the Senate Committee on Foreign Relations and the Senate Committee of the Judiciary*, 100th Cong., 1st Sess. 123 (1987). He proceeded to address Professor Henkin's remarks on the role of the President and the Senate. *Id.* at 124. He raised a core constitutional question: ''What is the treaty that is the law that the President must faithfully execute?'' *Id.* at 124. He then talked about constitutional requirements concerning the inclusion of Senate-added conditions in the resolution of ratification and constitutional requirements concerning their inclusion by the President in the instrument of ratification. *Id.* at 126–27. He described certain elements of the ratification record as ''purely domestic documents.'' *Id.* at 127. He talked about the President's ''responsibilities to enforce the laws and to conduct the foreign affairs of the United States. . . .'' *Id.* at 128. He addressed the ''allocation of powers'' that ''the nation has developed.'' *Id.* at 129. Finally, Sofaer asserted explicitly that ''when [the Senate] gives its advice and consent to a treaty, it is to the treaty that was made, irrespective of the explanations it is provided.'' *Id.* at 130.

[90] Address by Abraham Sofaer, American Law Institute (May 19, 1988), *reprinted in* 134 Cong. Rec. 6740 (daily ed. May 26, 1988).

[91] *Id.*

[92] The Condition was initiated by Senator Joseph R. Biden and modified slightly in a technical amendment by Senator Robert Byrd when the Treaty was approved by the Senate. It provided as follows:

> The Senate's advice and consent to ratification of the I.N.F. Treaty is subject to the condition, based on the treaty clauses of the Constitution, that:
>
> 1. The United States shall interpret the treaty in accordance with the common understanding of the treaty shared by the President and the Senate at the time the Senate gave its advice and consent to ratification;
>
> 2. Such common understanding is based on: a) first, the text of the treaty and the provisions of this resolution of ratification; and b) second, the authoritative representations which were provided by the President and his representatives to the Senate and its committees, in seeking Senate consent to ratification, insofar as such representations were directed to the meaning and legal effect of the test of the treaty; and
>
> 3. The United States shall not agree to or adopt an interpretation different from that common understanding except pursuant to Senate advice and consent to a subsequent treaty or protocol, or the enactment of a statute; and
>
> 4. If, subsequent to ratification of the treaty, a question arises as to the interpretation of a provision of the treaty on which no common understanding was reached in accordance with paragraph 2, that provision shall be interpreted in accordance with applicable United States law.

134 Cong. Rec. 6724 (daily ed. May 26, 1988). The condition was adopted by the Senate by a vote of 72 to 27. *Id.* at 6783–84.

First, is it within the President's *constitutional* power to enter into a treaty different from the one approved by the Senate? In effect, that different treaty is not a treaty but an executive agreement; the issue is whether that executive agreement falls within the scope of his sole power under the Constitution. The President's very act of transmitting the *treaty* for Senate advice and consent implies the answer: Constitutionally, if the treaty can be entered into as an executive agreement, why seek Senate approval? There can be little quarrel with the statement of Senate Resolution 167: "if, following Senate advice and consent, the President proceeds to ratify a treaty, the President may ratify only the treaty to which the Senate advised and consented."[93] This is in essence the rule incorporated in the "Biden Condition" to the INF Treaty and approved by a federal district court.[94]

Second, what weight is the negotiating record to be accorded in interpreting the President's constitutional obligations?

Before addressing the substantive issue, it is worth looking closely at exactly what the term *negotiating record* means. In reality, no genuine negotiating record was compiled when the ABM Treaty was ratified.[95] Rather, the

[93] 100th Cong., 1st Sess. (1987). The "ABM Treaty Interpretation Resolution," as it was called, was the subject of extensive joint hearings before the Foreign Relations and Judiciary Committees. *See* The ABM Treaty and the Constitution: Joint Hearings Before the Senate Committees on Foreign Relations and Judiciary, 99th Cong., 2d Sess. (1987). It was reported by the Committee on Foreign Relations on Sept. 22, 1987. *See* S. Rept. No. 100-164 (1987). Although the Resolution was not taken up by the Senate, the principles it outlined formed the basis of the treaty interpretation Condition added by the Senate to the INF Treaty. *See* S. Rept. No. 100-15 (INF Treaty).

[94] Rainbow Navigation, Inc. v. Dept. of the Navy, 669 F. Supp. 339 (D.D.C. 1988). In United States v. Stuart, 109 S. Ct. 1183 (1989), the Supreme Court, in construing a tax treaty with Canada, stated: "The clear import of the treaty language controls unless 'application of the words of the treaty according to their obvious meaning effects a result inconsistent with the intent or expectations of its signatories.' " *Id.* at 1191. To determine the United States' and Canada's "intent and expectations," the Court looked exclusively to the Senate debates, without suggesting any requirement that the Senate's intent be reduced to a condition. Justice Scalia took strong issue with the Court's methodology, relating that he had been "unable to discover a single case" taking that approach. *Id.* at 1195 (Scalia, J., concurring). As Professor Detlev Vagts has pointed out, however, there are in fact several earlier cases on point, and they are not difficult to find. *See* Vagts, *Senate Materials and Treaty Interpretation: Some Research Hints for the Supreme Court*, 83 Am. J. Int'l. L. 546 (1989). *See also International Law: The Year in Review*, 83 Am. Soc'y Int'l L. Proc. (1989).

[95] Former Senator J. W. Fulbright, chairman of the Committee on Foreign Relations in 1972 and floor manager of the ABM Treaty, appeared before the Foreign Relations and Judiciary Committees during the Mar. 11, 1987, hearing. He testified that he did not have access to the negotiating record:

SENATOR SARBANES . . . [Y]ou did not have access to the negotiating record when you acted on this treaty, did you?

FORMER CHAIRMAN FULBRIGHT No.

SENATOR SARBANES You did not know what was in the negotiating record.

FORMER CHAIRMAN FULBRIGHT No, we didn't.

"record" assembled was put together only recently—through an office-to-office survey conducted by personnel of the State Department legal adviser, Abraham Sofaer. Normally, *negotiating record* is a term of art used to describe an *agreed* negotiating record, since it is only the joint intent of the parties that has significance under international law. Notes unilaterally compiled cannot control a treaty's meaning.

In addition, there is no guarantee that Sofaer's staff was able to find all the pieces of the purported record. Sofaer candidly described this process in testimony before the House Foreign Affairs Committee in 1985. He said that he and his staff "obtained from various sources *everything that we could find* that might be relevant to the issue of future systems and components."[96] Yet all must realize that the process of assembly was fragmentary and that the resulting collage may represent far less than a complete, accurate picture of what actually transpired during the ABM Treaty negotiations.

Finally, even if (as seems unlikely) every piece of that disjointed record was recovered, what reason is there to believe that the American negotiators chose to reduce to writing all relevant materials bearing upon this question? Evidently the members of the American negotiating team never believed that their instructions, responses, and various musings would someday be viewed as dispositive concerning the Treaty's meaning; otherwise, would they not have taken more care in assembling a single complete and cohesive record?

For these reasons, therefore, reference to the "negotiating record" of the ABM Treaty presented threshold fact-related difficulties. Even if those difficulties could be overcome, substantive constitutional hurdles concerning its relevance remained. The "ABM Treaty Interpretation Resolution," Senate Resolution 167, addressed those issues directly: "[T]he Senate's understanding of a treaty cannot be informed by matter of which it is not aware, such as private statements made during the negotiations that were not communicated to the Senate."

SENATOR SARBANES So, on what basis, then, did you proceed to ratify the treaty?

FORMER CHAIRMAN FULBRIGHT On the basis of our understanding of what the treaty meant, and it was, of course, given to us. We had witnesses, the Secretary of State and others, from the officials who did have access or who knew about the negotiating record, as to what they said it meant.

There was very little dissent at the time. I cited the dissent. There were two votes against it, and the reason they voted against it was because of the very fact that is at issue today, it was so restrictive. They believed . . . it was restricting, as we use the term today, too restricting, and they voted against it.

All the rest of them took, I would say, what we would call the restrictive interpretation and voted for it—88 against 2.

See supra note 89, at 42.

[96] *ABM Treaty Interpretation: Hearings Before the Subcommittee on Arms Control, International Security and Science of the House Committee on Foreign Affairs*, 99th Cong., 1st Sess. 7 (1985).

This formulation is eminently reasonable. Although it does not expressly address the issue, it would presumably permit a secret negotiating record not transmitted to the Senate when it approved a treaty to be taken into account when that record is not inconsistent with the Senate's understanding of a treaty's meaning. However, that would be disallowed where the Senate understood otherwise, as reflected in the treaty's legislative history. Then the Senate's understanding would control, as indeed it should. Legislative intent is reflected by legislative history, and an untransmitted negotiating record is by definition not part of the legislative history.

Third, how is the Senate's understanding to be assessed? Again, the question is asked for *constitutional* purposes. To say, as the legal adviser did,[97] that formal communication to the other party is required is to say what need be done to firm up an *international* obligation. At issue here is the President's obligation vis-à-vis the Senate. In this domestic context, there is no reason to insist that the Senate make formal its understanding of the treaty's meaning. As Senate Resolution 167 put it, "[T]he understanding of the Senate is manifested by any formal expression of understanding by the Senate, as well as by other evidence of what the Senate understood the treaty to mean, including Senate approval or acceptance of, or Senate acquiescence in, interpretations of the treaty by the executive branch communicated to the Senate. . . ."[98]

Conditions imposed by the Senate may thus be explicit, as they are when formally reduced to express reservations, understandings, or other statements, or they may be implicit, as they were in the case of the ABM Treaty, where their content is to be gleaned from statements by senators and statements by administration representatives in which the senators present acquiesced. The form of the Senate's understanding of a treaty's meaning is constitutionally irrelevant; *substance* controls. As Professor Louis Henkin testified before the Committee:

> The President can only make a treaty that means what the Senate understood the treaty to mean when the Senate gave its consent. That is indisputable when the Senate has made its understanding plain in the form of a proposed reservation or explicit understanding.
>
> The same principle governs when the Senate's understanding of a treaty provision is not expressed in a formal resolution, but is apparent from the Senate's deliberations leading to its expression of consent.
>
> The Senate's understanding of the treaty to which it consents is binding on the President. He can make the treaty only as so understood. He cannot make the treaty and insist that it means something else.[99]

[97] *See* Sofaer, *supra* note 89, at 357.
[98] *Id.*
[99] *Id.* at 82.

Professor Henkin addressed directly the question whether the Senate is required to "formalize" its understanding of a treaty's meaning:

> I do not think the formality of a reservation or understanding by the Senate is a constitutional requirement. The Constitution says nothing of the kind.
>
> I think what the Constitution clearly implies is that it is what the Senate understands the treaty to mean, that that is what the treaty means for purposes of its consent.[100]

It therefore seems entirely sensible to believe, as Senate Resolution 167 indicated, that if the Senate proceeds to approve a treaty based on a certain understanding, that understanding controls. This is the rule of section 314 of the *Restatement*, which imposes no requirement that the Senate's understanding be reduced to a formal condition. It is reiterated in comment *d.*[101] A contrary rule would seem illogical. The reason that the understanding is not reduced to a formal condition is that the Senate considers the meaning of the treaty obvious; formal conditions are appropriate where the meaning is not obvious. The Administration's position would require that the Senate clarify—indeed, clarify formally, through an explicit condition to its consent—precisely what it is that the Senate views as *beyond* reasonable disagreement. Normally, of course, the Senate conditions its consent to a treaty to make some change in the treaty. There is thus no reason for the Senate to condition its consent to a treaty when it believes that the treaty's meaning is clear. Yet in the Reagan Administration's view, it is those matters about which a genuine consensus exists that most require formal clarification. The argument is difficult to take seriously, for it assumes the very point in controversy; it assumes that the ABM Treaty in 1972 was properly accorded a "broad" interpretation and that it was up to the Senate to change that interpretation if it so wished.

Constitutionally, the President cannot, by relying upon a secret negotiating record not transmitted to the Senate, "interpret" the treaty in a manner at odds with the Senate's earlier understanding. The President is bound by the Constitution to take care that the laws be faithfully executed, and to act on the basis of such an interpretation would breach that requirement.

For such an act is not truly an "interpretation" at all; it is a violation of the Constitution's treaty clause. When the President acts beyond the scope of his constitutional authority to interpret a treaty, he is in effect either amending that treaty or making a new one. The President cannot *call* a new treaty an interpretation of an old one and thereby dispense with the constitutional re-

[100] *Id.* at 87–88.

[101] Restatement, § 314, Comment *d*:

Although the Senate's resolution of consent may contain no statement of understanding, there may be such statements in the report of the Senate Foreign Relations Committee or in the Senate debates. In that event, the President must decide whether they represent a general understanding by the Senate and, if he finds that they do, must respect them in good faith.

quirement of Senate advice and consent. Similarly, the President cannot *call* an amendment to a treaty an interpretation of that treaty and thus dispense with that requirement. The President's power of treaty interpretation is limited, limited by the treaty clause. The Constitution permits the President, acting alone, to interpret only existing treaties, not to make new ones. To remain within the scope of his constitutional power, the President must be genuinely engaged in the act of treaty *interpretation*. He cannot by himself engage in treaty *creation*.

Where is the line drawn? Senate Resolution 167 drew the line in the same place as the Vienna Convention on the Law of Treaties[102] and the *Restatement*,[103] both of which state that a treaty is to be construed in good faith, in accordance with the ordinary meaning to be given its terms in light of their context and its object and purpose. When the President does so, he acts within the scope of his constitutional power. When his construction of a treaty cannot be so described, it represents not construction or interpretation, but the making of a new treaty. This he can do only with the advice and consent of the Senate.

Sound functional reasons support this conclusion. If the negotiating record was deemed controlling, the damage to the institution of the Presidency—and the conduct of American diplomacy—would be immeasurable. The Senate would feel compelled to demand the negotiating record to every treaty to satisfy itself that nothing therein contradicted the public assurances of the administration. Or, the Senate would feel compelled to incorporate into its approval of every treaty a reservation for every jot and tittle in the administration's public statements about what the treaty means, lest those statements later be disavowed in favor of a secret negotiating record.

The impact on American diplomacy would be devastating. "Treaties so laden," said Senator Nunn, "would sink under their own weight. It would be extremely difficult to achieve bilateral agreements and virtually impossible for the United States to participate in multilateral treaties."[104] It could also mean the end of confidential treaty negotiations, a tradition that traces to the earliest days of the Republic and widely thought essential to the candid exchange of views by negotiators.

These ghosts came back to haunt the Reagan Administration when the INF Treaty[105] came before the Senate for its advice and consent, leading to the adoption of the Biden Condition.[106] President Reagan gave no indication at the

[102] *See* art. 31(1).

[103] *See* § 325(1).

[104] The ABM Treaty and the Constitution: Joint Hearings Before the Senate Committees on Foreign Relations and Judiciary, 100th Cong., 1st Sess. 62 (1987).

[105] Treaty between the United States of America and the Union of the Soviet Socialist Republics on the Elimination of Their Intermediate-Range and Shorter-Range Missiles, Dec. 8, 1987, Exec. Rep. 100-15 (1988).

[106] *See supra* notes 92 and 93.

time of its consideration that he might elect to disregard it. Nonetheless, following his ratification of the Treaty in Moscow, he seemed to imply that he would not be bound by it:

> [A] condition in a resolution to ratification can[not] alter the allocation of rights and duties under the Constitution, nor could I, consistent with my oath of office, accept any diminution claimed to be effected by such a condition in the constitutional powers and responsibilities of the presidency.[107]

Shortly afterwards, the *Wall Street Journal*[108] and the Heritage Foundation[109] launched a critique of the Biden Condition. Their analysis misapprehended the substance of the Condition as thoroughly as it did the requirements of the Constitution.

The Condition is merely a rule of interpretation, governing how the INF Treaty is to be construed as domestic law. The Condition provides, as Senate Resolution 167 provided, that the treaty means what the President tells the Senate it means. If this principle seems self-evident, it is, and it has been for nearly two hundred years—until the Reagan Administration asserted that a President can claim that a treaty means something altogether different from what his representatives told the Senate when it was approved.

The argument for such presidential authority, embraced uncritically by the *Journal* and the Heritage Foundation, apparently rests upon the claim that "the President alone has the right to determine U.S. international treaty obligations."[110] This would have confused the Framers, who seemed to express themselves clearly on the issue. The Constitution provides that "the President shall have power, by and with the advice and consent of the Senate, to make treaties, provided two-thirds of the Senators present concur."[111] It would have stunned Alexander Hamilton—no wallflower on the subject of presidential power—who considered it "utterly unsafe and improper" to entrust the power of making treaties to the President alone.[112] Pursuant to this shared power, the Senate since the earliest days of the Republic has conditioned its consent to treaties. It often approves ratification subject to the condition that the President change the treaty. No President has ever challenged the Senate's power to do so; as the Foreign Relations Committee has said, that power has become part of "customary constitutional law."[113]

The Senate might well have insisted that the INF Treaty be changed. Instead, the Senate chose a more restrained course, one that did not endanger the Trea-

[107] 134 Cong. Rec. S7664 (daily ed. June 13, 1988).
[108] "Sofaer's Revenge," Wall St. Journal, June 15, 1988, at 22.
[109] Rivkin, *GOP Must Share Blame for Byrd Amendment*, *id.* at col. 3.
[110] *Id.*
[111] Art. II, § 2, cl. 2.
[112] *See also infra* note 120.
[113] Exec. Rep. No. 95-12, 95th Cong., 2d Sess. 11 (1978) (Panama Canal Treaties).

ty's ratification. It conditioned its consent upon adherence to a canon of construction tailored to this specific agreement.[114] Rather than inject the Senate into the process of interpretation that occurs after the Senate's consent, therefore, the Condition simply shaped the meaning of the document to which the Senate consented. The President remains free, as with all other treaties, to interpret the INF Treaty to which the Senate consented. But he cannot interpret a treaty other than the one to which the Senate consented, subject to the Biden Condition, for to do so would be to make a new treaty.[115]

Upon bringing the INF Treaty into force, the President was therefore bound to give effect to the Senate's Condition. "[A] condition having a plausible relation to the treaty, or to its adoption or implementation, is presumably not improper, and if the President proceeds to make the treaty he is bound by the condition."[116] If the President doubted the validity of a Senate condition, he "would then have to decide whether he could assume that the Senate would have given its consent without the condition."[117] He could not assume that the Senate would have consented to the INF Treaty without the Biden Condition. That the Condition was just that—a condition on which the Senate based its approval—is clear from the report of the Foreign Relations Committee:

> [T]he President may not act upon the Senate's consent without honoring this Condition. Nothing that he or his Administration does, by statement or action, whether before or after the act of ratification, can alter the binding effect of any condition which the Senate places upon its consent to treaty ratification. If the President brings the INF Treaty into force, the Condition takes effect.[118]

If President Reagan intended to challenge the wisdom or constitutionality of the Biden Condition, the time to act upon that doubt was before he ratified the Treaty. After ratification, Mr. Reagan's legal scrutiny might more properly

[114] That the canon—the Biden Condition—has constitutional underpinnings seemingly bolsters its validity.

[115] President Reagan claimed that "the principles of treaty interpretation recognized and repeatedly invoked by the courts cannot be limited or changed by the Senate alone." 134 Cong. Rec. S7664 (daily ed. June 13, 1988). This may or may not be correct, depending upon what principles he was referring to. Principles concerning ultimate constitutional authority obviously cannot be changed by Senate condition. The Senate could not, for example, accord itself final say as to the meaning of a treaty; treaty interpretation is, in the first instance, the task of the President and in the end, the job of the courts. But principles concerning the construction of treaty terms clearly can be governed by Senate conditions. The Senate might provide, for example, that in the event of a conflict between two treaty provisions, the one specified will govern. Or it might provide by condition that a certain provision is to be construed broadly or that a certain term of art will be accorded the same meaning it has in another treaty. Because the Senate can, in short, *alter* the meaning of a treaty provision by requiring modification before presidential ratification, it can also alter that meaning by imposing a canon that governs how that meaning is derived. The prescribed canon then is merely another provision subject to presidential interpretative authority.

[116] Restatement, § 303, Comment *d.*

[117] Restatement, § 303, Reporters' Note 4.

[118] Exec. Rep. No. 100-15, 100th Cong., 2d Sess. 100 (1988) (INF Treaty).

have been directed to the constitutional requirement that he "take care that the laws be faithfully executed."[119] A treaty is a law,[120] and a Senate condition is part of a treaty.[121]

Treaty Termination

President Carter's decision to terminate the mutual-security treaty with the Republic of China brought into question the extent of the President's power to terminate a treaty without Senate concurrence. Can the President, on his own authority, end an international agreement that had the full solemnity of the treaty-making advice and consent of the Senate?[122]

For years, presidents have opposed congressional proposals to limit the use of executive agreements to enter into international agreements, on the theory that American credibility would be undermined.[123] But the tables turned curiously when, upon President Carter's announced intent to terminate the mutual-security treaty, members of Congress charged the Executive with undermining United States credibility abroad.[124] Senators previously among the foremost defenders of presidential power suddenly found themselves trying to cut it down to size,[125] supported by legal commentators whose previous works belied their newfound adulation for separation of powers.[126] Result-oriented jurisprudence seldom rode higher.

[119] U.S. Const., art. II, § 3.

[120] The President "is charged with the Execution of the Laws, of which Treaties form a part. . . ." A. Hamilton, Pacificus, *in* 15 H. Syrett, The Papers of Alexander Hamilton 35 (1961–79).

[121] Restatement, § 313.

[122] For a recent study of the treaty termination question, *see* D. Adler, The Constitution and the Termination of Treaties (1986).

[123] An example of the Executive's concern arose in 1977, when the Senate Foreign Relations Committee asked for the Administration's comments on a proposal of Senator Clark's to amend internal Senate procedure to deny funding to an executive agreement which it believes should be a treaty. The State Department expressed concern "not only that the adoption of such a procedure might become a source of discord between the Senate and the Executive, but that important international undertakings might be jeopardized because of institutional conflict between the two Houses." Letter from Douglas J. Bennet, Jr., Assistant Secretary of State for Congressional Relations, to John J. Sparkman, Chairman of the Senate Foreign Relations Committee (Dec. 30, 1977), reprinted in 1 Foreign Relations Law, supra note 20, at 453, 455.

[124] *See, e.g.*, 123 Cong. Rec. 28, 296 (1977) (speech by Sen. Goldwater opposing unilateral presidential treaty termination).

[125] *Compare* Goldwater, President's Constitutional Primacy in Foreign Relations and National Defense, 13 Va. J. Int'l. L. 463 (1973) (arguing for presidential leadership in foreign affairs) *with* Goldwater, *supra* note (calling presidential treaty termination without congressional approval unconstitutional).

[126] *Compare* McDougal & Lans, *Treaties and Congressional-Executive or Presidential Agreements: International Instruments of National Policy*, 54 Yale L.J. 181, 336 (1945) (affirming power of President to terminate treaties with or without prior congressional authorization) *with Treaty Termination: Hearings on S. Res. 15 Before the Senate Committee on Foreign Relations*, 96th Cong., 1st Sess. 387, 394 (1979) (statement of Professor Reisman to the Senate Foreign

The matter reached the Supreme Court in 1979 in *Goldwater v. Carter*.[127] The Court divided sharply on the propriety of judicial involvement in the case. Six Justices concluded that the case should be dismissed but failed to agree in their reasoning.[128] Oral arguments were never heard, and only one Justice expressed an opinion on the substantive issues.[129]

The ambivalence of the Court highlights the difficulty of reconciling domestic political pluralism with international expectations.[130] Four principal positions shaped the debate. The State Department argued that the President can abrogate[131] any treaty at any time.[132] The sponsors of Senate Resolution 15

Relations Committee, on behalf of himself and Professor McDougal, stating that "the President cannot terminate these treaties on his own initiative, without an authorization") (hereinafter cited as Treaty Termination Hearings).

[127] 444 U.S. 996 (1979).

[128] Justice Rehnquist was joined by Chief Justice Burger and Justices Stewart and Stevens in reviewing the question as political and therefore nonjusticiable. Justices White and Blackmun explicitly reserved judgment on the question's justiciability, while Justice Brennan thought that it was justiciable. Justice Powell thought the question justiciable but not yet ripe; he preferred to postpone Court involvement until the potential Executive-Legislative conflict developed into actual confrontation. Despite his disagreement with the Rehnquist group on justiciability, Justice Powell joined them in voting for dismissal, as did Justice Marshall, who gave no reason for his vote. Thus, although a clear six-vote majority existed for dismissal, the Court was split 4–4 between those holding treaty terminations non-justiciable and those refusing so to hold, with Justice Marshall, by his silence, leaving the deadlock unresolved.

[129] Goldwater v. Carter, 444 U.S. 996, 1007 (1979) (Brennan, J., dissenting). Justice Brennan concluded that the President had the authority to terminate the treaty.

[130] No doubt the Court's ambivalence also contributed to the avalanche of commentary on the subject. *See, e.g.*, Berger, *The President's Unilateral Termination of the Taiwan Treaty*, 75 Nw. U. L. Rev. 577 (1980); Bestor, *Respective Roles of Senate and President in the Making and Abrogation of Treaties—The Original Intent of the Framers of the Constitution Historically Examined*, 55 Wash. L. Rev. 1 (1979); Gable, *Taiwan Relations Act: Legislative Re-Recognition*, 12 Vand. J. Transnat'l L. 511 (1979); Goldwater, *Treaty Termination Is a Shared Power*, 65 A.B.A.J. 198 (1979); Henkin, *Litigating the President's Power to Terminate Treaties*, 73 Am. J. Int'l L. 647 (1979); Kennedy, *Normal Relations with China: Good Law, Good Policy*, 65 A.B.A.J. 194 (1979); *Legal Implications of the Recognition of the People's Republic of China: A Panel*, 72 Am. Soc'y Int'l L. Proc. 240 (1978); Pappas, *The Constitutional Allocation of Competence in the Termination of Treaties*, 13 N.Y.U. J. Int'l. & Pol. 473 (1981); Comment, *The Law of Treaty Termination as Applied to the United States De-Recognition of the Republic of China*, 19 Harv. Int'l L.J. 931 (1978); Comment, *Treaty Termination by the President without Senate or Congressional Approval: The Case of the Taiwan Treaty*, 33 Sw. L.J. 729 (1979); Comment, *Resolving Treaty Termination Disputes*, 129 U. Pa. L. Rev. 1189 (1981); Comment, *The Constitutional Twilight Zone of Treaty Termination:* Goldwater v. Carter, 20 Va. J. Int'l L. 147 (1979); Note, *Unilateral Termination of the 1954 Mutual Defense Treaty Between the United States of America and the Republic of China Pursuant to the President's Foreign Relations Power*, 12 Vand. J. Transnat'l L. 133 (1979).

[131] The Senate Foreign Relations Committee, in its treatment of the issue, used the word *terminate* to refer to treaty denunciations that are authorized by international law, and "abrogate" to refer to those that are not. This book uses the terms in the same way.

[132] Memorandum from the legal adviser of the Department of State to the Secretary of State (Dec. 15, 1978), *reprinted in* 2 Foreign Relations Law, *supra* note 20, at 377–404.

contended that Senate consent is required prior to the termination of any mutual-security treaty.[133] The Senate Foreign Relations Committee concluded that the President could terminate a treaty acting alone, but (1) only in accordance with international law; (2) only if such termination would not "result in the imminent involvement of United States Armed Forces in hostilities or otherwise seriously and directly endanger the security of the United States"; and (3) only if unopposed by the Congress or the Senate.[134] Finally, Justice Brennan, the only member of the *Goldwater* Court to address the issue, seemed to side with the State Department, finding the termination

> a necessary incident to Executive recognition of the Peking government, because the defense treaty was predicated upon the now abandoned view that the Taiwan government was the only legitimate political authority in China. Our cases firmly establish that the Constitution remits to the President alone the power to recognize and withdraw recognition from foreign regimes.[135]

Justice Brennan's opinion gave no indication that his conclusion was limited to treaty terminations authorized by international law.

[133] S. Res. 15, 96th Cong., 1st Sess. (1979) provided: "Resolved, that it is the sense of the Senate that approval of the United States Senate is required to terminate any mutual defense treaty between the United States and another nation." *Id*. The Senate never adopted this resolution.

[134] S. Rep. No. 119, 96th Cong., 1st Sess. 9–10 (1979). The report summarizes the circumstances in which, under "customary international law, as reflected generally in the Vienna Convention, *supra* note 59, a state may terminate a treaty, as follows:

(1) in conformity with the provisions of the treaty;
(2) by consent of all the parties after consultation with the other contracting states;
(3) where it is established that the parties intended to admit the possibility of denunciation or withdrawal;
(4) where a right of denunciation or withdrawal may be implied by the nature of the treaty;
(5) where it appears from a later treaty concluded with the same party and relating to the same subject matter that the matter should be governed by that treaty;
(6) where the provisions of the later treaty are so far incompatible with those of the earlier one that the two treaties are not capable of being applied at the same time;
(7) where there has been a material breach by another party;
(8) where the treaty has become impossible to perform;
(9) where there has been a fundamental change of circumstances;
(10) where there has been a severance of diplomatic or consular relations and such relations are indispensable for the the application of the treaty;
(11) where a new peremptory norm of international law emerges which is in conflict with the treaty;
(12) where an error was made regarding a fact or situation which was assumed by that state to exist at the time when the treaty was concluded and formed an essential basis of its consent to be bound;
(13) where a state has been induced to conclude a treaty by the fraudulent conduct of another state; and
(14) where a state's consent to be bound has been procured by the corruption or coercion of its representatives or by the threat or use of force.

[135] Goldwater v. Carter, 444 U.S. 996, 1007 (1979) (Brennan, J., dissenting).

The *Restatement* appears to take a position close to that of the Senate Foreign Relations Committee.[136] The *Restatement* provides, in relevant part:

> Section 339. Authority to Suspend or Terminate International Agreement: Law of the United States.
>
> Under the law of the United States, the President has the power:
>
> (a) to suspend or terminate an agreement in accordance with its terms;
>
> (b) to make the determination that would justify the United States in terminating or suspending an agreement because of its violation by another party or because of the supervening events, and to proceed to terminate or suspend the agreement on behalf of the United States; or
>
> (c) to elect in a particular case not to suspend or terminate the agreement.[137]

Its conclusion thus seems to be that while presidential treaty ''termination'' is permissible, treaty ''abrogation'' is not;[138] for example, abrogation could not have been effectuated with respect to the mutual-security treaty with Taiwan without one year's notice, in accordance with the terms of article X of that treaty.[139] The comments on section 339 support the view that the President, acting alone, cannot abrogate a treaty: ''The President's power to terminate an international agreement does not imply authority to modify an agreement or to conclude a new one in its place.''[140] ''The President's authority to terminate or suspend international agreements is implied in his office as it has developed over almost two centuries.'' The Reporters' Notes, by referring to termination as opposed to abrogation, are consistent with a denial of presidential abrogation authority.[141] The President's power as ''sole organ of the federal government in the field of international relations,'' they continue, ''. . . would seem to include the authority to decide on behalf of the United States to terminate a treaty that no longer serves the national interest. . . .''[142] Three cases are cited in support: *Charlton v. Kelly*;[143] *La Abra Silver Mining Co. v. United States*;[144] and *Frelinghuysen v. Key*.[145]

None of these cases supports sole presidential treaty abrogation.[146] The Su-

[136] *See supra* note 134.

[137] Restatement, § 339.

[138] *Id.*

[139] Treaty of Mutual Defense, Dec. 2, 1954, United States–China, 6 U.S.T. 433, T.I.A.S. No. 3178.

[140] Restatement, § 339, Comment *a*.

[141] Restatement, § 339, Reporters' Note 1.

[142] *Id.* (quoting United States v. Curtiss-Wright Corp., 299 U.S. 304, 310 [1936]).

[143] 229 U.S. 447 (1913).

[144] 175 U.S. 423 (1899).

[145] 110 U.S. 63 (1884).

[146] In Charlton v. Kelly, 229 U.S. 447, (1913), Charlton, an American wanted for the murder of his wife in Italy, argued that the Italian-American extradition treaty was no longer in force due to breaches by the Kingdom of Italy. The Court held that as the treaty had not been denounced by the Executive, it was one the courts were obliged to enforce. In La Abra Silver Mining Co. v. United States, 175 U.S. 423 (1899), the United States Government had successfully presented La

preme Court has never upheld the authority of the President to terminate a treaty lacking a termination clause on the basis of his sole judgment that it ''no longer serves the national interest.'' Indeed, in a number of cases, it has effectively upheld the authority of the Congress to control the termination process, at least insofar as that process applies to the domestic effectiveness of a treaty (the only question on which the domestic courts of any country can rule).[147] The *Restatement*'s unqualified observation that the President may ''elect in a particular case not to suspend or terminate the agreement''[148] thus seems questionable.

The Senate rejected the Committee's recommendation, with some senators expressing the belief that the fourteen grounds enumerated were too extensive.[149] In fact, the Committee's enumeration may not have been sufficiently exhaustive to encompass all circumstances in which sole presidential action is appropriate. Few would contend, for example, that congressional approval is required following a judicial determination of a treaty's unconstitutionality; in such an instance, consultation should occur with the Congress, or with the Senate, to determine whether the court's opinion indeed invalidates the treaty and whether amendments to the treaty are desirable.[150]

Abra's claim against the Mexican Republic to an international claims commission. Later, having grounds to believe the claim had been fraudulent, Congress by statute directed the Executive to return to Mexico any funds obtained as a result of fraud, even though the treaty establishing the claims commission had said that the commission's decisions would be final. The Court held that it was ''the absolute legal duty of the Secretary of State'' to obey the statue, adding, ''[i]t was competent for Congress to impose that duty upon him and he could not refuse to obey the mandate of the law.'' *Id.* at 462. In supporting its reasoning, the Court pointed out that ''it has been adjudged that Congress by legislation, and so far as the people and authorities of the United States are concerned, could abrogate a treaty made between this country and another country which had been negotiated by the President and approved by the Senate.'' *Id.* at 460. Similarly, Frelinghuysen v. Key, 110 U.S. 63 (1884), involved an earlier stage in the La Abra controversy, which dragged on for over thirty years. President Arthur, concerned that American honor would be tarnished if this country were a party to perpetrating a fraud on a friendly power, ordered that no further payments be made on the La Abra claim, pending further negotiations. The Court, taking pains to show that the President's action was not at odds with the will of Congress, *id.* at 74–75, held that the President had the discretion to act as he had ''under these circumstances.'' *Id.* at 75. While nothing in *Frelinghuysen* would seem to derogate from congressional authority, anything in it contrary to the Court's later holding in the same controversy in *La Abra* presumably was overruled by the later opinion.

[147] *See, e.g.*, Fong Yue Ting v. United States, 149 U.S. 698, 720–21 (1893); The Chinese Exclusion Case, 130 U.S. 581, 600 (1889); Whitney v. Robertson, 124 U.S. 190, 194 (1888); Edye v. Robertson, 112 U.S. 580, 599 (1884); The Cherokee Tobacco, 78 U.S. 6l6, 621 (1870). In addition, one of the cases cited in support of executive authority, La Abra Silver Mining Co. v. United States, 175 U.S. 423 (1899), actually seems to affirm congressional primacy. *Id.* at 460.

[148] Restatement, § 339(c).

[149] *See, e.g.*, 125 Cong. Rec. 13,679 (1979) (speech by Sen. Harry F. Byrd, Jr.).

[150] The Justice Department expressed to the Senate Foreign Relations Committee its opinion that ''[t]he President cannot amend a treaty in any significant way by means of an executive agreement or parallel declaration of understanding after it has received the advice and consent of

The reasons advanced for rejecting its approach are illuminating. (Those reasons are detailed in the report of the Senate Foreign Relations Committee on the Byrd Resolution,[151] its report on the Taiwan Enabling Act,[152] and the opinion of the court of appeals in *Goldwater v. Carter*,[153] which, although vacated by the Supreme Court, contains much useful analysis.)

First, the argument for congressional primacy grounded on the supremacy clause[154] fails on several counts. That argument is that because treaties, like statutes, are the supreme law of the land, treaties, like statutes, cannot be terminated by the President alone. But as the Committee pointed out, treaties are *not* like statutes in one significant respect: "Although the Congress has the last word in determining whether a statute is enacted, the Senate merely authorizes the ratification of a treaty; it is the President's role that is determinative."[155] The Committee continued:

> [The President] decides at the outset whether to commence treaty negotiations. He decides whether to sign a treaty. He decides whether to exchange instruments of ratification after a treaty has been approved by the Senate. At each of these stages, it is the President who has the power to determine whether to proceed—*and thus whether treaty relations will ultimately exist*.[156]

Thus, as was suggested by the court of appeals, the text of the supremacy clause may fairly be read only as a *status*-prescribing provision, not as a *procedure*-prescribing provision. That it assigns the same status—supreme law of the land—to each of the instruments denominated does not mean that it commands that the same procedure be followed in their termination.

Second, there is no reason why the termination of "mutual defense treaties"— or any other category of treaties, such as those representing a long-standing United States policy or a policy of supreme national importance—should be seen as subject to different constitutional principles than all other treaties. None of the constitutional sources of power discussed in Chapter 2 supports the contention that one termination procedure applies to one set of treaties and another termination procedure to another set. As the court of appeals said in *Goldwater v. Carter*, "There is no judicially ascertainable and manageable method of making any distinction among treaties on the basis of

---

the Senate (unless, of course, the treaty sets forth a procedure for amendment or implementation in that way)." Letter from Larry A. Hammond, U. S. Deputy Assistant Attorney General, to Frank Church, Senate Foreign Relations Committee Chairman (undated), *reprinted in Treaty Termination Hearings*, *infra* note 158, at 217, 220.

[151] S. Rep. No. 119, 96th Cong., 1st Sess. (1979) *reprinted in* 2 M. Glennon & T. Franck, United States Foreign Relations Law 411–52 (1980).

[152] S. Rep. No. 7, 96th Cong., 1st Sess. (1979).

[153] 617 F.2d 697 (D.C. Cir. 1979), *cert. granted and dismissal directed*, 444 U.S. 996 (1979).

[154] U.S. Const. art. VI, § 2.

[155] S. Rep. No. 7, 96th Cong., 1st Sess. 18 (1979).

[156] *Id.* (emphasis in original).

their substance, the magnitude of the risk involved, the degree of controversy which their termination would engender, or by any other standards. We know of no standards to apply in making such distinctions.''[157] The constitutional text does not address the matter. No Supreme Court case has reached the merits of the controversy. Although the Department of State argued vigorously that historical precedent supported a plenary presidential power to terminate the mutual-security treaty with the Republic of China,[158] neither it nor its opponents even began to address the critical question of *opinio juris*—the shared belief of the political branches that the executive practice represented a juridical norm. It is thus difficult to find any constitutional custom on the matter; nor is there even the appearance of a *practice* of treaty abrogation, which apparently has occurred only once in American history, in 1798, in connection with treaties of alliance with France.[159] The intent of the Framers is thoroughly ambiguous. The most reasonable mode of analysis, therefore, since the application of all other primary, secondary, and tertiary sources fails to resolve the issue, is to resort to functional considerations.

The issue, thus, is which of the political branches is best suited to make the determination that the Declaration should be terminated, taking into account factors such as the need for swiftness versus deliberation and secrecy versus diverse viewpoints.[160]

A functional approach is obviously imprecise, involving as it does a subjective judgment concerning attributes of the two branches. Yet even the most cursory consideration would suggest that the argument for excluding Congress (or the Senate) from treaty termination is weak. The decision to withdraw from a treaty is almost never precipitated by an emergency that requires, say, secrecy or dispatch; it represents a question that looms on policy horizons for some months, one that might benefit from the ventilation of diverse opinion in congressional hearings and debate.[161] What is true of treaty negotiations is in this context largely true of termination as well. ''Thus we see,'' John Jay said,

[157] 617 F.2d 697, 707 (D.C. Cir. 1979), *cert. granted and dismissal directed*, 444 U.S. 996 (1979). The Committee, too, doubted that any such distinction is constitutionally supportable. S. Rep. No. 119, 96th Cong., 1st Sess. at 8 (1979).

[158] Treaty Termination: Hearings Before the Comm. on Foreign Relations, United States Senate, 96th Cong., 1st Sess. 50 (1979) (testimony of State Dep't Legal Adviser Herbert Hansell).

[159] Treaty Termination: Hearings Before the Comm. on Foreign Relations, United States Senate, 96th Cong., 1st Sess. 310 (1979) (testimony of Prof. Abram Chayes).

[160] See Chapter 2 for a discussion of the characteristics to be considered.

[161] It has been suggested, for example, that the Panamanian government has mismanaged portions of the Canal already turned over to it and that that mismanagement may constitute breach of the Treaty. N.Y. Times, Mar. 7, 1988, at 1. If such breaches did occur and were ''material,'' under international law, the United States would be permitted to denounce the Treaty. Because the principal performance obligation of the United States—transfer of the Canal to Panama—does not arise until 1999, however, and because the consequences of denunciation are so grave, involvement of Congress would seem all the more appropriate.

"that the constitution provides that our negotiations for treaties shall have every advantage which can be derived from talents, information, integrity, and deliberate investigations on the one hand, and from secrecy and dispatch on the other."[162]

Functional considerations thus suggest the propriety of some form of Congressional involvement at some stage in the resolution of the issue. But these considerations do not imply that *initial* resolution of the question by the President is improper. The act falls within the concurrent powers of the President; it is a matter concerning which the President's power is *initiative* and the power of the Congress (or the Senate) is *reactive*.[163] Under such an approach, the best conclusion is that, *in the face of congressional silence*, treaty termination by the President does not impinge upon the constitutional prerogatives of the Senate or Congress. As Professor Abram Chayes has put it, "The structure of the overall distribution of the foreign affairs powers, then, seems, at least on first appraisal, to argue for the existence of an independent presidential initiative in treaty termination."[164]

This was the approach of the Committee in reporting the Taiwan Relations Act.[165] The Senate Foreign Relations Committee there cited with approval[166] the tripartite analysis employed by Justice Jackson in his much-praised concurring opinion in the *Steel Seizure Case*.[167] After outlining the three categories,[168] the Committee stated:

> Under this formulation, termination by the President of the U.S.–R.O.C. Defense Treaty would fall within the "zone of twilight" of category (2) and the President would, accordingly, appear to possess the constitutional authority to do so absent any statute enacted by the Congress or resolution adopted by two-thirds of the

[162] Federalist No. 64 (Jay) (Cooke, ed. 1961) 436.

[163] For a similar analysis, *see Treaty Termination Hearings*, *supra* note 159, at 306 (testimony of Prof. Abram Chayes).

[164] Treaty Termination: Hearings Before the Comm. on Foreign Relations, United States Senate, 96th Cong., 1st Sess. 311 (1979) (testimony of Prof. Abram Chayes). Chayes emphasizes, however, a point made throughout this book—that the breadth of presidential power is a function of the posture of Congress. "The key question . . . is whether the President can act on his own in the first instance to give notice of termination without securing some form of congressional approval in advance. I put aside, once more, the issue of what he could do in the face of contrary congressional action." *Id.*

[165] 22 U.S.C. § 3301 (Supp. 1980).

[166] S. Rep. No. 7, 96th Cong., 1st Sess. 18–19 (1979).

[167] Youngstown Sheet & Tube Co. v. Sawyer, 343 U.S. 579, 635–37 (1952) (Jackson, J., concurring).

[168] Under Justice Jackson's analysis, presidential action can be classified into one of three categories: the first, in which the President's power is at a "maximum," encompassing action pursuant to congressional authority; the second, the so-called "zone of twilight," encompassing actions regarding which Congress has not expressed an opinion; and the third, in which his power is at its "lowest ebb," encompassing actions taken contrary to the will of Congress. *Id. See* Chapter 1.

Senate directing contrary action: such measures would place the President's action in category (3). Similarly, his actions would have fallen with category (3) had the Congress enacted a statute prohibiting him, prospectively, from terminating a treaty by himself, or had the Senate done so by so providing in a reservation to the treaty itself or in a two-thirds resolution.

. . . It appears to the Committee, therefore, that the constitutional prerogatives of the Congress and the Senate have not been invaded in that neither the Congress nor the Senate has elected to exercise the powers granted it by the Constitution to participate in the process of treaty termination. Had either done so, a different conclusion would likely obtain.[169]

Apparently concerned about the scope of Senate or congressional power asserted in the last sentence, the Justice Department indicated to the Committee that a "fundamental error" was found in its discussion of the *Steel Seizure Case*, and suggested that treaty termination "is a power that the President exercises alone":

Whether Congress may act depends on the nature of the President's independent powers. Jackson cites Myers v. United States, 272 U.S. 52 (1926), in a footnote to this discussion. There . . . the Constitution is silent upon removal of executive officers but removal was held to be a sole presidential power. The Constitution is silent on many points regarding foreign affairs but it does not follow that concurrent power exists. The most obvious is the power to speak for the nation as its representative in foreign affairs. . . . It is clear that this is a power that the President exercises alone even though the Constitution does not deal specifically with the subject.[170]

The Committee, following enactment of the Taiwan Relations Act, next confronted the issue in Senate Resolution 15. In its report on the Resolution, the Committee responded as follows:

[I]t cannot accept the notion advanced by Administration witnesses that the President possesses an "implied" power to terminate any treaty, with any country, under any circumstances, irrespective of what action may have been taken by the Congress by law or by the Senate in a reservation to that treaty. Such an argument in this context is at odds with the most fundamental precepts underlying the separation of powers doctrine. . . .[171]

The *Restatement* takes the position of the Committee. The Reporters' Notes observe that the Senate "has not attempted to grant its consent to a treaty on

[169] S. Rep. No. 7, 96th Cong., 1st Sess. 19 (1979) (emphasis added).

[170] Letter from Larry A. Hammond, U.S. Deputy Assistant Attorney General, to Frank Church, Senate Foreign Relations Committee Chairman (undated), *reprinted in Treaty Termination Hearings*, *supra* note 158, at 217.

[171] S. Rep. No. 119, 96th Cong., 1st Sess. 6 (1979).

condition that the treaty be terminable only with its consent or in accordance with some other prescribed procedure.'' But a condition ''applicable to the treaty before it and having a plausible relation to its adoption,'' the Reporters concluded, ''would presumably be valid . . . and if the President proceeded to make the treaty, he would be bound by the condition.''[172]

The position of the *Restatement* is sound. The Justice Department's rationale—a textbook example of bootstrapping[173]—is, on close analysis, an undifferentiated argument against the Senate's power to condition its consent to treaties.[174] Such executive branch arguments, claiming sweeping presidential

[172] Restatement, § 339, Reporters' Note 3.

[173] The Justice Department argued as follows:

> Under our Constitution the power to do the greater, i. e., reject the treaty, does not necessarily include the power to do the lesser by any means whatever. It is well-settled that Congress cannot attach an unconstitutional condition to a benefit or power merely because it has authority to withhold the benefit or power entirely. . . . For example, Congress could, if it chose, bar aliens from our shores, but could not admit them under conditions which deprive them of constitutional rights such as the right to a fair trial. Wong Wing v. United States, 163 U.S. 228, 237 (1896). The issue here is very like the question addressed by the Supreme Court in the Myers Case. 272 U.S. 52 (1926). There the Court made clear that the existence of an advice and consent power in the Senate did not, by inference, also give the Senate the power to exert control over the removal of officers once approved. 272 U.S. at 164.

Treaty Termination Hearings, *supra* note 158, at 217–18 (letter from Hammond, *supra* note 170). The Department, of course, is assuming the very point in contention by arguing that the Congress cannot ''attach an unconstitutional condition.'' Similarly, reference to Myers v. United States, 272 U.S. 52 (1926), assumes *ipse dixit* that attachment by the Senate of a termination condition to a treaty is constitutionally on the same footing as an exercise by the Senate of the removal power. Given the conclusion of the Supreme Court that the treaty power extends to ''all proper subjects of negotiation between our government and the governments of other nations,'' Geofroy v. Riggs, 133 U.S. 258, 266 (1890), there can be little doubt, as the Committee argued, that a termination procedure would constitute such a subject. S. Rep. No. 119, 96th Cong., 1st Sess. 10–11 (1979).

Similarly flawed is the Justice Department's argument that a Senate reservation on treaty termination relates to a ''purely domestic'' issue, and is therefore invalid under the Niagara reservation case, Power Auth. v. Federal Power Comm'n, 247 F.2d 538 (D.C. Cir.), *vacated as moot sub nom.* American Pub. Power Ass'n v. Power Auth., 355 U.S. 64 (1957). The Committee correctly noted that ''it is simply unconvincing to contend that a prospective treaty partner would be uninterested in how the United States will, internally, go about deciding whether to terminate its treaty obligations.'' S. Rep. No. 119, 96th Cong., 1st Sess. 12 (1979). The *Restatement*, which criticizes the *Power Authority* decision, does not support the Justice Department argument. The Reporters noted:

> The effectiveness of such a Senate proviso . . . does not depend on its becoming law of the land as a part of the treaty. Such a proviso is an expression of the Senate's constitutional authority to grant or withhold consent to a treaty, which includes authority to grant consent subject to a condition. The authority to impose the condition implies that it must be given effect in the constitutional system.

Restatement, § 303, Reporters' Note 4.

[174] The Committee responded by noting that, since granting conditional approval to the Jay Treaty in 1795, the Senate has very often granted conditional consent. ''No such condition has ever been held invalid by the Supreme Court, and no President, so far as the Committee is aware,

power that would overturn nearly two centuries of historical precedent, ultimately result in an erosion of executive authority. Members of Congress who may be relatively indifferent about the outcome of a particular substantive issue may nonetheless care deeply about institutional prerogatives and thus support restrictive measures merely to establish the principle of legislative precedence.[175] A narrow, carefully reasoned executive objection, particularly one that flows from policy rather than constitutional concerns, is generally far more effective in avoiding needless confrontation than a broad claim to constitutional power.

Precision and restraint are especially appropriate where the Executive is unlikely to persist in its objection. However willing the Executive may be to object in the abstract to a hypothetical Senate condition concerning termination procedure, it is unlikely to interpose strenuous objections in a particular case. The reasons are, obviously, political. An indication by a president that he or she views a given Senate condition as unconstitutional, or the suggestion that he or she will feel free to ignore it, would virtually guarantee Senate rejection of a treaty.[176] Three recent significant treaties reported by the Senate Foreign Relations Committee—the two Panama Canal Treaties[177] and the SALT II Treaty[178]—were reported with conditions at least as broad as the termination condition discussed by the Committee during consideration of the treaty-ter-

---

has ever indicated his intent, upon ratifying a treaty, to disregard a provision upon which the Senate conditioned its consent.'' S. Rep. No. 119, 96th Cong., 1st Sess. 11–12 (1979) (footnotes omitted).

[175] When the Senate approved the Spanish Base Treaty, Jan. 24, 1976, United States–Spain, 27 U.S.T. 3005, T.I.A.S. No. 8360, it included a ''declaration'' in the resolution of ratification expressing the hope that the treaty would further the progress of democratic institutions in Spain. Members of the Spanish Parliament were offended by what they considered the declaration's patronizing tone, and the United States Department of State reported that Spain would not ratify the treaty if the declaration were included in the formal instrument of ratification. Fortunately a solution was found which saved face both for the Senate and the Spanish government by which the declaration was included in an ''annex.'' This annex was referred to in, but not made part of, the instrument. The incident is discussed generally in Meron, *The Treaty Power: The International Legal Effect of Changes in Obligations Initiated by the Congress*, in The Tethered Presidency (T. Franck ed. 1981); *Panama Canal Treaties: Hearings Before the Senate Foreign Relations Committee*, 95th Cong., 2d Sess. 122–23 (1978) (remarks by Michael J. Glennon, Legal Counsel to the Committee). The incident made the Senate Foreign Relations Committee cautious about ensuring that material the Senate wanted included in subsequent instruments of ratification would be included, a concern the Committee referred to in its report on the Panama Canal Treaties. *See* S. Exec. Rep. No. 12, 95th Cong., 2d Sess. 10–11 (1978).

[176] Note, in this connection, President Reagan's objections to the ''Biden Condition'' to the INF Treaty, discussed earlier in this chapter. His suggestion that he might disregard the Condition was made a week *after* he ratified the Treaty.

[177] Treaty concerning the Permanent Neutrality and Operation of the Panama Canal, United States–Panama, Sept. 7, 1977, T.I.A.S. No. 10,029; Treaty on the Panama Canal, United States–Panama, Sept. 7, 1977, T.I.A.S. No. 10,030.

[178] S. Exec. Y. 96th Cong., 1st Sess. (1979).

mination issue.[179] But none of the conditions of Senate consent to those treaties generated executive opposition, perhaps because they reflected, and were seen by the Executive to reflect, legitimate Senate concern for the continued viability of its role in the treaty-ratification process.

The approach outlined above is vastly different from saying that the President acts with plenary constitutional power in terminating a treaty. To say that would be to exclude Congress and the Senate from a reactive role. The President's power is not exclusive. Where the Senate specifies a procedure for termination, the President is compelled constitutionally to adhere to that procedure. Such a condition normally has the effect, constitutionally, of placing the President's power at its lowest ebb, for to terminate a treaty in such circumstances would be in direct opposition to the express will of the Senate.[180] Thus the *Restatement* correctly recognizes that "[i]f the United States Senate, in giving consent to a treaty, declares that it does so on condition that the President shall not terminate the treaty without the consent of Congress or of the Senate, or that he shall do so only in accordance with some other procedure, that condition presumably would be binding on the President if he proceeded to make the treaty."[181] As the reporters of the *Restatement* conclude, notwithstanding occasional suggestions to the contrary,[182] such a condition must be given effect in the constitutional system, even though arguably it is solely of domestic import.[183]

If the Senate can prescribe a specific termination procedure as a condition to its consent to a treaty, there is no reason to believe that Congress could not prescribe such a procedure by statute. This was the position of the Committee in its report on the Byrd Resolution.[184] Nor is there any reason to believe that a statute overturning the transmittal of a notice of termination would be ineffective, at least if it was enacted before the effective date of the notice of

[179] S. Rep. No. 119, 96th Cong., 1st Sess. (1979) (S. Res. 15, Treaty Termination).

[180] *See supra* note 167 and accompanying text. During the Senate Foreign Relations Committee's hearings on the Byrd Resolution, the Justice Department took the position that the President's power to terminate treaties is exclusive. *See Treaty Termination Hearings*, *supra* note 158 (letter from Larry A. Hammond to Frank Church, Chairman, arguing that "[i]t is clear that this is a power that the President exercises alone even though the Constitution does not deal specifically with the subject"). On close analysis, the Justice Department position is little more than an undifferentiated argument against the Senate's power to condition its consent to treaties. *See* S. Rep. No. 119, 96th Cong., 1st Sess. 11–12 (1979); Glennon, *Treaty Process Reform: Saving Constitutionalism Without Destroying Diplomacy*, 52 U. Cinn. L. Rev. 84, 96–97 (1983).

[181] Restatement, § 339, Comment *a*.

[182] *See* Power Authority v. Federal Power Commission, 247 F.2d 538 (D.C.Cir. 1957), *vacated as moot sub nom.*, American Pub. Power Ass'n v. Power Auth., 355 U.S. 64 (1957).

[183] Restatement, § 303, Reporters' Note 4. Whether this particular condition would in fact be of purely domestic concern is of course doubtful, and the practical utility of the test is questionable. *See* Henkin, *The Treaty Makers and the Law Makers: The Niagara Power Reservation*, 56 Colum. L. Rev. 151 (1956).

[184] S. Rep. 15, 96th Cong., 1st Sess. 2 (1979).

termination.[185] It too would place the President's power at lowest ebb. Although this procedure would "deal in" the House of Representatives on the treaty power, not all members of the Senate Foreign Relations Committee were troubled.[186]

This approach does not mean that the congressional power to direct the withdrawal of a notice of termination is without constitutional limits. Such a directive may not interfere with the exercise of one of the President's *specific* plenary powers. For example, Congress could not have overturned by law President Carter's notice of termination of the mutual-security treaty with the Republic of China, because such a law would have interfered with the President's plenary power to recognize and derecognize foreign nations; a formal

[185] Under international law, such an instrument may be revoked at any time before it takes effect. Art. 64, Vienna Convention on the Law of Treaties, May 23, 1969, U.N. Doc. A/Conf. 39/27, *reprinted in* 8 I.L.M. 679 (1969) (hereinafter Vienna Convention). The United States has taken the position that a notice of termination may be withdrawn at any time before its effective date. *See* Lowenfeld & Mendelsohn, *The United States and the Warsaw Convention*, 80 Harv. L. Rev. 497, 550 (1967); *In re* Air Crash in Bali, 684 F.2d 1301, 1305 (9th Cir. 1982).

In the absence of a specific time period provided in the treaty, a party is required to give not less than twelve months' notice of its intention to terminate a treaty. Vienna Convention, *supra* note 59, at art. 56, para. 2.

[186] Some Senators expressed their feelings as follows:

THE CHAIRMAN Congress can pass a law prescribing how either a given treaty can be terminated or a class of treaties. If the President joins in it, that, then, has the force of law. If the President vetoes it, then the Congress can override the President's veto and it will still have the force of law.

SENATOR SARBANES Is it clear to you that a treaty can be terminated over the opposition of the President?

SENATOR JAVITS By law.

THE CHAIRMAN By law. . . . We are saying if the Congress passes a joint resolution over the President's veto, then he should not terminate that treaty. He would be inviting trouble.

But I would take it a step further. I would hazard that if the Congress overrode a veto with a joint resolution which, under the Constitution, would have the force of law, the congressional position would be upheld in the courts as a constitutional proposition. I think I can make an awfully persuasive case for that position.

MR. HENKIN You are right, Senator. But I think one might distinguish general termination procedures from a particular agreement. I think the emphasis ought to be on particular agreements where Congress can make a special case. Then you avoid the rigors of that stark confrontation.

SENATOR SARBANES I agree with that point. . . . If you make the joint resolution general, then what you are doing is dealing in the House of Representatives on the treaty powers in a role on which I think some question can be raised as to whether it is an appropriate role for them.

MR. GLENNON I would point out that this, in effect, establishes a procedure not only for the repeal of treaty provisions but for the repeal of Senate reservations, as well, by a majority of the Senate acting in concurrence with a majority of the House and the President.

THE CHAIRMAN If by the passage of a law that is inconsistent with a provision of a treaty, the treaty or the reservation can be undone, then it seems to me that it follows that a direct repeal should also be a valid way to undo a treaty provision.

S. Rep. No. 119, 96th Cong., 1st Sess. (1979).

treaty relationship with a state is inconsistent with the status of nonrecognition.

Just as Congress's concurrent power to *react* is not unfettered, neither is the President's concurrent power to *initiate* without limits. The power to initiate a treaty termination, it must again be emphasized, exists only when the President acts pursuant to legislative approval or in the face of legislative silence. He may not initiate the termination of a treaty if that action is prohibited by law or by treaty. Treaty *termination* is therefore different, constitutionally, from treaty *abrogation*. A treaty is *terminated* when it is brought to an end in accordance with its terms. A treaty is *abrogated* when it is brought to an end in violation of its terms. In the case of abrogation, the Senate has, in effect, explicitly stated its opposition to the President's act by expressing its advice and consent to a term of the treaty—its termination clause—which the President has disregarded. His power is then at its lowest ebb. Accordingly, the *Restatement* recognizes presidential power to terminate but not to abrogate,[187] and the Senate Foreign Relations Committee, in its report on the Byrd Resolution, recognized presidential power to initiate the termination of a treaty only when permitted by international law.[188]

The distinction between termination and abrogation is therefore important constitutionally because treaty *termination* is permitted by international law, whereas treaty *abrogation* is not. The customary norm of *pacta sunt servanda*, which makes treaties binding and requires that they be performed by the parties in good faith,[189] is violated when a treaty is abrogated. This norm has been called the glue that holds the international system together, and it is binding upon the President as a matter of domestic law.[190]

These considerations suggest two further conclusions concerning the scope of presidential authority. First, some treaties that lack termination clauses may not be terminable. Article 56 of the Vienna Convention on the Law of Treaties provides that such a treaty is ''not subject to denunciation or withdrawal unless . . . it is established that the parties intended to admit the possibility of denunciation or withdrawal; or . . . a right of denunciation or withdrawal may be implied by the nature of the treaty.''[191] The United Nations Charter has been said to represent such a treaty. The mutual-security treaty with Taiwan obviously was not, since it contained a six-month notice requirement. There is therefore no reason to believe that the President exceeded the scope of his

[187] Restatement, § 339.

[188] S. Rep. No. 96-119, 96th Cong., 1st Sess. (1979) (President may initiate the termination process in any of the fourteen situations permitted by the Vienna Convention on the Law of Treaties).

[189] *See* Vienna Convention, *supra* note 59, at art 56.

[190] *See* Chapter 7.

[191] Vienna Convention, *supra* note 59, at art. 56.

concurrent ''initiative'' power in transmitting notice of termination of the Taiwan treaty.

Second, very different principles apply to treaty abrogation. The issue of abrogation arose in connection with the 1984 modification[192] of the 1946 Declaration by which the United States accepted the compulsory jurisdiction of the International Court of Justice.[193] It also arises in connection with the seventy or so treaties that confer jurisdiction on the International Court in accordance with article 36(1) of the Statute of the International Court of Justice.[194] The Executive's abrogation of the 1946 Declaration on October 7, 1985, raised the possibility that some of these jurisdictional provisions might also have been the subject of termination efforts. If such review had taken the form of renegotiation of the treaty and if renegotiation had led to that treaty's termination, the principles discussed herein would have applied: Treaty termination in accordance with its terms and in the face of congressional silence would place the President's act, constitutionally, in Justice Jackson's ''zone of twilight.''

If on the other hand the parties had agreed merely to an amendment to the treaty, a very different issue would have been raised. The constitutional power of the President to effect an amendment is far more limited than his power to carry out complete termination. This was acknowledged by both the Department of State[195] and the Department of Justice[196] during the dispute concerning termination of the mutual-security treaty with Taiwan. Although not addressed directly by the *Restatement*, the reasoning seems implicit in the proposition that ''[t]he President's power to terminate an international agreement does not imply authority to modify an agreement or to conclude a new one in its place.''[197] Were the President to amend an agreement on his own, he would in effect be terminating an old agreement and entering into a new one.

Perhaps for reasons such as these, the Reagan Administration made no effort to negotiate across-the-board removal of provisions in treaties providing for the adjudication of disputes by the ICJ under its compulsory jurisdiction. Indeed, it had apparently recognized earlier that treaty amendment lies beyond the scope of the President's sole authority. In announcing that the United

[192] *See generally* Glennon, Nicaragua v. United States: *Constitutionality of U.S. Modification of ICJ Jurisdiction*, 79 Am. J. Int'l. L. 682 (1985).

[193] 61 Stat. 1218 (1947).

[194] Article 36(1) provides that ''[t]he jurisdiction of the Court comprises all . . . matters specially provided for . . . in treaties and conventions in force.'' *See generally* Morrison, *Treaties as a Source of Jurisdiction for the International Court of Justice with Special Reference to the Practice of the United States of America*, in L. Damrosch, ed., The International Court of Justice at a Crossroads (1987).

[195] *Treaty Termination: Hearings*, *supra* note 158.

[196] *Id.* at 220–21.

[197] Restatement, § 339, Comment *a*.

States would not sign the 1982 Law of the Sea Convention,[198] President Reagan enumerated its ''unacceptable elements'' and said that the United States wanted a treaty that would ''[n]ot allow for amendments to come into force without approval of the participating states, including, in our case, the advice and consent of the Senate.''[199] ''[T]his is clearly incompatible with the United States approach to such treaties,'' the President later said.[200] These concerns were reiterated by Ambassador James Malone, who complained that the Convention allowed for the adoption of amendments in a manner that ''effectively bypass[es] U.S. approval, including congressional [*sic*] advice and consent.''[201]

The Executive had thus declined to argue that it possessed plenary power to amend a treaty in violation of its terms. Such a power would vitiate the Senate's right to approve a treaty conditionally. For under such an argument, any Senate reservation, together with any other unwanted provisions, could be unilaterally removed by the President. For similar reasons, the constitutional rationale proffered by representatives of the Department of State to justify the 1984 modification of the 1946 Declaration is unpersuasive. They argued that although the President cannot amend a treaty to *expand* United States liability, he may constitutionally amend a treaty to *constrict* United States liability.

First, the argument creates false categories. It is easy to hypothesize an amendment that does neither. The oft-mentioned (before termination of the Declaration) possibility of an amendment that would have ''traded'' the Connally Reservation[202] for a ''use-of-force'' or ''political-question'' exception is a good example. Who can say whether the net effect of such an amendment would have been to expand or to constrict United States liability? Under this ''test,'' the amendment process becomes an extended excursion into casuistry.

Second, even if one can distinguish the two categories, the assumption that a compact formally approved by the Senate can be caused to take an entirely new and different form without Senate or legislative approval still has no constitutional basis. If the Senate conditioned its consent to a treaty upon *increased* United States liability, by what authority might the President disregard the Senate's action? The power of the Senate to grant its conditional consent to a treaty, the Senate Foreign Relations Committee noted in 1978, is

[198] United Nations Convention on the Law of the Sea, *opened for signature* Dec. 10, 1982, reprinted in *The Law of the Sea: United Nations Convention and the Law of the Sea*, U.N. Sales No. E.83V.5 (1983).

[199] 82 Dep't State Bull. No. 2060 at 54 (Mar. 1982).

[200] 82 Dep't State Bull. No. 2065 at 71 (Aug. 1982).

[201] 82 Dep't State Bull. No. 2067 at 49 (Oct. 1982). *See also* 82 Dep't State Bull. No. 2062 at 62 (May 1982) (similar statement by Ambassador Malone).

[202] I.C.J. Statute, art. 36(2)(b) (the Connally Amendment allows the United States to determine which disputes are within its domestic jurisdiction).

part of customary constitutional law in the United States.[203] Surely there is no constitutional basis for distinguishing between Senate conditions and "original" treaty text for purposes of presidential amendment authority.

It seems reasonable to conclude, therefore, that the President cannot act alone to amend a treaty to eliminate a grant of jurisdictional authority contained therein.

FULL SENATE REVIEW OF THE TREATY PROCESS

The Senate should undertake a general review of the entire treaty-making process with an eye toward reporting a simple resolution setting forth its views on the kinds of issues discussed in this chapter. Such a resolution, if adopted pursuant to the Senate's "advice" power, might represent constitutionally something more than simply the "sense" of the Senate as to what treaty procedures are appropriate. The power to advise has never developed as the Framers intended,[204] although it was invoked as the basis for the Senate's call for consultations concerning the form of an agreement.[205] "The [Senate Foreign Relations] committee rejected use of the word 'consult' because," the Committee said in its report, "while having no different operative effect, 'consult' would suggest an ad hoc procedure which is entirely consensual rather than constitutional, and the committee believes it essential to make clear that a constitutional basis underlies the procedure contemplated herein."[206]

The provisions of such a resolution could be made effectively binding with respect to specific treaties through incorporation by reference. Such incorporation could, for example, obviate the need to reiterate applicable interpretative principles or directions to the President such as those set forth in the SALT II resolution of ratification. That resolution spelled out which Senate material was to be included in the protocol of exchange (Category I), which was to be included in the instrument of ratification (Category II), and which did not need to be transmitted (Category III).[207] These three categories might be generally useful in refining the process further. The Senate could authoritatively attach a label to each of the three categories, so that anything called a "reservation"

[203] Senate Comm. on Foreign Relations, Report on Executive N, S. Rep. No. 12, 95th Cong., 1st Sess. 11 (1978).

[204] The original expectation of the Framers was that the Senate would function as a sort of executive council to the President in the formation of treaties. The expectation was abandoned very early, as President Washington found it impractical to coordinate detailed formulations of policy with twenty-six independent-minded senators. L. Henkin, *supra* note 8, at 131.

[205] S. Res. 536, 95th Cong., 2d Sess. (1978).

[206] S. Rep. No. 1171, 95th Cong., 2d Sess. 4 (1978).

[207] S. Exec. Rep. No. 14, 96th Cong., 1st Sess. 72–78 (1979). The Committee's chairman, Senator Frank Church, and ranking minority member, Senator Jacob Javits, previously had received assurances in an exchange of letters with Secretary of State Cyrus Vance that the President would respect the Senate's wishes on the matter, as expressed in the resolution. *Id.* at 31–32.

or ''understanding'' might be deemed a Category I condition, anything called a ''statement'' a Category II condition, and anything called a ''declaration'' a Category III condition. The Committee belief, expressed in the Committee's report on the SALT II Treaty, that the old labels create unnecessary confusion will mean little unless a new procedural framework is instituted.[208] Senators are likely, in floor amendments to treaties if not in Committee amendments, to return to their old ways and use traditional labels.

Incorporating such a clarifying resolution by reference in resolutions of ratification would not be without precedent. The International Security Assistance and Arms Export Control Act of 1976 set forth, in section 601, an ''expedited procedure'' intended to be incorporated in subsequently enacted statutory provisions that might establish additional legislative vetoes.[209] A resolution of the sort described here, which might aptly be denominated the Treaty Powers Resolution,[210] might also incorporate relevant concepts from the *Restatement*, thus providing clear guidance for foreign diplomats who look with bewilderment at the United States ratification process.

In addition to dealing with the treaty-termination issue, approval of the Vienna Convention, and the adoption of the Senate's own ''restatement'' of United States treaty practice, a fourth element is essential to a thorough update of the treaty-making process. Rule XXX of the Standing Rules of the Senate,[211] which governs the consideration of treaties in the Senate, needs revision. The rule describes a ''Committee of the Whole'' procedure, adopted when the Senate was a much smaller body. As a result of that procedure, the Rule provides an incentive to propose amendments to the text of the treaty, rather than amendments to the resolution of ratification (such as reservations, understandings, declarations, etc.).[212] Only amendments to the text can be offered in the Committee of the Whole, and because the Committee meets before the Senate considers amendments to the resolution, a senator wishing to modify a treaty may feel compelled to offer an amendment to the text on the theory that he needs ''two bites at the apple''; the second bite—proposal of an amendment to the resolution—may fail. The Senate rules thus inadvertently encourage the adoption of textual amendments that could otherwise take the form of modifications with lower political visibility and thus less chance of causing rejection of the instrument of ratification by the other signatory.

[208] *See generally id.* at 27–35.

[209] International Security Assistance and Arms Export Control Act of 1976, Pub. L. No. 94-329, 90 Stat. 729 (1976).

[210] *See e.g.*, S. Res. 24, 95th Congress, 1st Sess. (1977) (Treaty Powers Resolution); *see also supra* note 20.

[211] S. Doc. 98-10, Standing Rules of the Unites States Senate, 98th Cong., 1st Sess. (1983).

[212] Such amendments are variously denominated; terms used include *reservation*, *understanding* and *declaration*. The label applied by the Senate to its amendment is legally irrelevant. *See* 14 M. Whiteman, *supra* note 8, at 138–39.

This obstacle to treaty relations can and should be eliminated. The problem was "read out of" Rule xxx by Vice President Marshall in 1919 during consideration of the Treaty of Versailles; Senator Henry Cabot Lodge offered a reservation in the Committee of the Whole against which a point of order was made. The Vice President, presiding, overruled the point of order, and the ruling was not appealed.[213] Sixty years later, however, during Senate consideration of the Panama Canal Treaties, the Senate Parliamentarian advised Vice President Mondale, based upon more recent precedents, that amendments to the resolution of ratification should not be held in order in the Committee of the Whole, and the Vice President so ruled.[214] The Rule should be changed to allow amendments to the treaty and the resolution to be offered simultaneously. The neatest way of accomplishing this may be to abolish the Committee of the Whole proceeding, which serves no useful purpose and merely complicates a procedure that is already unnecessarily arcane.

Conclusion

Congress is too often forced by events into a reactive role; hearings conducted in response to the press of events, such as those held in 1979 on the Treaty Termination Resolution, seldom allow as much time for staff preparation and committee briefing as, say, those reviewing the operation and effectiveness of the War Powers Resolution in 1977.[215] The time is now ripe for comprehensive review and reform of the process of making international agreements. Such a review and reform would now be free from the charged political climate that invariably surrounds these issues when raised during the consideration of particular international agreements. Reform is now timely as well as imperative. Like the worst urban blight, American practices with respect to international agreements have developed without design or direction and demand an intelligent modernization sensitive to the imperatives of domestic constitutional constraint and the needs of diplomacy.

[213] 1919 Cong. Rec. 8013–22; F. Riddick, Senate Procedure: Precedents and Practices, United States Senate 827 (1973).

[214] 124 Cong. Rec. 2696 (1978).

[215] War Powers Resolution: Hearings before the Senate Foreign Relations Committee, 95th Cong., 1st Sess. (1977).

Chapter Five

PRESIDENTIAL POLICY AND EXECUTIVE AGREEMENTS

> The constitutional role of the Congress has too often been short-circuited because it was viewed—in the executive branch and even by some members of Congress—as an impediment to the expeditious adoption of substantive policies commanding the support of a majority. Thus, when in our recent history the substance of those policies lost that support, the procedures once available as checks had atrophied, and the Congress was forced to struggle to reclaim its powers. The lesson was learned the hard way: procedural requirements prescribed by the Constitution must not be disregarded in the name of efficiency, and the substance of a policy, however attractive, can never justify circumventing the procedure required by the Constitution for its adoption.
>
> —The Senate Foreign Relations Committee[1]

PLENARY EXECUTIVE DIPLOMATIC POWERS

The previous chapter has discussed specific aspects of the treaty-making process in which Senate participation is constitutionally appropriate. Participation by the Senate (or Congress) in certain other aspects of that process is not constitutionally permitted.[2] The core presidential power, perhaps, is negotiation. *Curtiss-Wright*, it will be recalled, noted in dicta that the President "alone negotiates. Into the field of negotiation, the Senate cannot intrude; and Congress itself is powerless to invade it."[3] Commenting on the breadth of this authority, the Senate Foreign Relations Committee said: "A President may voluntarily commit himself not to enter into certain negotiations, but he cannot circumscribe the discretion of his successors to do so, just as they may not be

[1] S. Rep. No. 96-119 at 5–6 (1979) (treaty termination).

[2] For an excellent review of the subject of international agreements, *see* S. Prt. 98–205, Comm. on Foreign Relations, 98th Cong., 2d. Sess., Treaties and Other International Agreements: The Role of the United States Senate (Study Prepared by the Congressional Research Service, Library of Congress) (Comm. Print 1984).

[3] United States v. Curtiss-Wright Corp., 299 U.S. 304, 319 (1936).

limited in doing so by treaty or by law.''[4] Thus, President Ford's 1975 promise to Israel that the United States would not negotiate with the Palestine Liberation Organization[5] unless certain conditions were met could not constitutionally bind subsequent Presidents, and a 1985 statute reiterating that prohibition[6] was similarly unconstitutional, as President Reagan indicated upon signing the Continuing Resolution in which it was contained.[7]

Another example of authority exclusively executive—one that has received far less discussion than the power to negotiate—is the articulation of policy intentions not rising to the level of international obligations.

Nonbinding Adherence to a Treaty

The most prominent recent example of such a declaration is that made by the Carter Administration with respect to the so-called Interim Agreement, part of the SALT I Treaty package.[8] Immediately prior to the expiration date of the Interim Agreement and with no hope of reaching prompt agreement on a successor instrument, the United States and the Soviet Union indicated their intent to continue to adhere to its terms. Secretary of State Cyrus Vance, on September 23, 1977, issued the following statement:

> In order to maintain the status quo while SALT II negotiations are being completed, the United States declares its intention not to take any action inconsistent with the provisions of the Interim Agreement on Certain Measures with Respect to the Limitations of Strategic Offensive Arms which expires October 3, 1977, and with the goals of these ongoing negotiations, provided that the Soviet Union exercises similar restraint.[9]

The next day, September 24, the official Soviet news agency, Tass, reported in English from Moscow that the Soviet government had made the following statement:

> In accordance with the readiness expressed by both sides to complete within the near future the work on a new agreement limiting strategic offensive arms in the interests of maintaining the status quo while the talks on the new agreement are being concluded, the Soviet Union expresses its intention to keep from any actions incompatible with the provisions of the Interim Agreement [on] some measures

[4] Exec. Rep. No. 95-12 at 10 (1978) (Panama Canal Treaties).

[5] Memorandum of Agreement Between the Governments of Israel and the United States (Sinai Accords), Sept. 1, 1975, *reprinted in* 1 M. Glennon & T. Franck, United States Foreign Relations Law: Documents and Sources 268 (1980).

[6] § 530, Pub. L. No. 95-591; 100 Stat. 3341 (1986).

[7] N.Y. Times, Oct. 13, 1988, at 8.

[8] Interim Agreement on the Limitation of Strategic Offensive Arms, United States–Soviet Union, May 26, 1972, 23 U.S.T. 3462, T.I.A.S. No. 7504.

[9] *Statement by Secretary of State Cyrus Vance, Sept. 23*, 77 Dept. St. Bull. 642 (1977).

pertaining to the limitations of strategic offensive arms which expired on October 3, 1977, and ending with the goals of the talks that are being conducted provided that the United States of America shows the same restraint.[10]

Such unilateral declarations can constitute binding international obligations under certain circumstances. Declarations made in 1905 by Chinese diplomats concerning future railway construction in Manchuria were later held by the League of Nations Commission of Inquiry to constitute a binding commitment with the force and effect of "a formal agreement."[11] In the *Eastern Greenland* case of 1933, declarations of the Minister of Foreign Affairs of Norway made to his Danish counterpart were held by the Permanent Court of International Justice to be binding upon Norway.[12] Most recently, the International Court of Justice, in the 1974 *Nuclear Tests* cases,[13] held that a series of public statements by the President of France, the French Ambassador to New Zealand, the French Foreign Minister, and the French Minister of Defense constituted legally binding commitments by France to refrain from atmospheric nuclear testing.[14]

Under the World Court's analysis, the *sine qua non* of a binding unilateral declaration is intent. Unless "it is the intention of the State making the declaration that it should become bound," the Court said, no legal obligation obtains.[15] Thus, "if given publicly— even though not made within the context of international negotiations—an understanding with an intent to be bound" confers a legal obligation.[16]

Perhaps intent to make an agreement was present with respect to the simultaneous statements of the United States and the Soviet Union regarding the Interim Agreement.[17] The concept of *objective intent* is a commonplace in United States law.[18] "Conscious parallelism" between two parties' actions

[10] 1 M. Glennon & T. Franck, United States Foreign Relations Law 34 (1980).

[11] Garner, *The International Binding Force of Unilateral Oral Declarations*, 27 Am. J. Int'l L. 493, 497 (1933) (quoting the League of Nations Commission of Inquiry).

[12] Legal Status of Eastern Greenland (Den. v. Nor.), 1933 P.C.I.J., ser. A/B No. 53.

[13] Nuclear Test Cases (Austl. v. Fr.), 1974 I.C.J. Rep. 253; Nuclear Tests (N.Z. v. Fr.); 1974 *id.* 457 (Judgments of Dec. 20, 1974).

[14] *Id.* at 474–75. *Compare* Franck, *Word Made Law: The Decision of the ICJ in the Nuclear Test Cases*, 69 Am. J. Int'l L. 612 (1975) (viewing the cases as legitimately extending a principle developed in an earlier line of cases and as providing a useful new vehicle for international commitments) *with* A. Rubin, *The International Legal Effects of Unilateral Declarations*, 71 *id.* at 1 (1977) (criticizing the cases as contrary to existing law and as likely to inhibit world leaders in communicating their intentions).

[15] Nuclear Test Cases (N.Z. v. Fr.), 1974 I.C.J. Rep. at 472.

[16] *Id.*

[17] *See supra* text at notes 11–14.

[18] In contract law, an objective standard is virtually always used to determine intent. Judge Learned Hand said that the law will not depart from the objective measure of intent, even "if it were proved by twenty bishops" that a party's intent was different from that suggested by the objective standard. Hotchkiss v. National City Bank, 200 F. Supp. 287, 293 (S.D.N.Y. 1911). The law of torts deems a person to have intended the effects a reasonably prudent person would

can be evidence of objective intent,[19] and it takes little imagination to find conscious parallelism in the statements of the United States and the Soviet Union. Indeed, as a domestic legal matter, it would be disturbing if a President could escape altogether the constitutional consequences of concluding a binding international agreement simply by calling it something else.[20]

To assume that an agreement existed, however, does not dispose of the issue. United States jurisprudence notwithstanding, it seems clear that international law, at least at this point in its development, considers only subjective intent. The International Court of Justice strongly implied in the *Nuclear Tests* cases[21] that a nation's characterization of its acts is controlling. It emphasized that a state is "legally required to follow a course of conduct *consistent with*

---

have foreseen as inevitable from his actions. Thus, a bicyclist who runs down a pedestrian on a wide, nearly empty sidewalk is liable for the intentional tort of battery, despite his insistence that the collision was an accident. Mercer v. Corbin, 117 Ind. 450, 20 N.E. 132 (1889). Even criminal law, which usually insists on proof of intent, deems a killing to have been in "a heat of passion" only if an ordinary person would have been provoked to homicide by the circumstances. The leading English case is Bedder v. Director of Public Prosecutions, [1954] 2 All E.R. 801 (H.L.), in which the Court refused to consider the special susceptibility of an impotent man.

[19] *See* United States v. Paramount Pictures, Inc., 334 U.S. 131 (1948); Interstate Circuit, Inc. v. United States, 306 U.S. 208 (1939).

[20] Professor Philip Kurland has protested against "the executive usurpation of Congressional authority in working out secret—or at least unapproved—agreements with foreign countries," and questioned why it is that "for some reason or other we are always reminded that because it is a Constitution we are expounding we need not be concerned with what it says." Kurland, *The Impotence of Reticence*, 1968 Duke L.J. 619, 626.

Kurland feared that the "disease" afflicting the separation of powers doctrine "appeared to be terminal." *Id.* at 261. Since 1968, however, despite much talk in Congress, nothing substantial has been done. *See Treaties and Executive Agreements*, 71 Am. Soc'y Int'l L. Proc. 235 (1977). For the principal congressional proposals, see H.R. 4438, 94th Cong., 1st Sess. (1975) (Morgan-Zablocki); *Congressional Review of International Agreements: Hearing on H.R. 4438 Before the Subcomm. on International Security and Scientific Affairs of the House Comm. on International Relations*, 94th Cong., 2d Sess (1976); S. Res. 24, 95th Cong., 1st Sess. (1977) (Clark Treaty Powers Resolution); *Treaty Powers Resolution: Hearings Before the Senate Comm. on Foreign Relations*, 94th Cong. 2d Sess. (1976) (hearings on earlier version of Clark Resolution); *Treaty Termination: Hearings on S. Res. 15 Before the Senate Comm. on Foreign Relations*, 96th Cong., 1st Sess. (1979). During this period, Congress did pass the Case Act, 1 U.S.C. § 1126 (1976), requiring the Executive to transmit all executive agreements to the Senate Foreign Relations Committee. Had the joint Soviet-American statements on SALT I constituted an international agreement, it would have been required, of course, that they be transmitted under the provisions of the Case Act.

[21] 1974 I.C.J. Rep. 253; 1974 *id.* 457. See also the opinions of Senators Dick Clark and George McGovern that the United States had not entered into an agreement with the Soviet Government by virtue of the parallel unilateral policy declarations by the two Governments:

> The arguments are made that under American antitrust law an agreement would be found to exist, as it would under American contract law. This may be, but we would point out that international law, perhaps shortsightedly, has not adopted the test applied by our antitrust statutes, and that no court in this country has ever found a contract where no party intended one to exist and where all parties *ab initio* expressly refused to be bound.

S. Rep. No. 499, 95th Cong. 1st Sess. 13–14 (1977).

the declaration.''[22] The United States declared that its statement concerning the Interim Agreement is ''non-binding and non-obligatory,''[23] so it seems clear that the element of subjective intent was lacking. This is true whether the statement is regarded as part of an agreement or as a unilateral declaration. Under international law, either can be binding or nonbinding, depending apparently on the nation's characterization of its intent.

The *Restatement* does not address the question whether objective intent will be sufficient to render a statement obligatory. It simply states that ''[s]ince an international agreement is one intended to be legally binding and having legal consequences,''[24] the pertinent *Restatement* provisions do ''not apply to agreements not intended to have such legal character or consequences.''[25] But it observes that ''non-binding agreements'' have been ''made at various times in United States history'' and notes the 1977 United States–Soviet action without suggesting that it may have constituted a binding agreement.[26]

The *Restatement*'s benign treatment of nonbinding international actions is justified. To be sure, there is a danger that nonbinding agreements or unilateral declarations will be used to circumvent constitutionally required procedures for making agreements. But this problem is not truly analogous to the circumvention of the treaty process by executive agreement.[27] A president who circumvents the requirement of Senate advice and consent by making an executive agreement with another nation generally achieves, at least on the international level, the same result—a binding agreement.[28] But a president who sidesteps the Senate by issuing a nonbinding declaration parallel to a declaration issued by another nation pays a price: In the event of noncompliance, he cannot accuse the other state of a *legal* violation.[29] Nevertheless, nonbinding international statements do serve a purpose.

[22] 1974 I.C.J. Rep. at 267 (emphasis added). The State Department instructions to United States diplomatic personnel on the criteria to be used in determining what constitutes an international agreement provide in part as follows: ''The central requirement is that the parties intend their undertaking to be of legal, and not merely political or personal, effect. Documents intended to have political or moral weight, but not intended to be legally binding, are not international agreements.'' Airgram from the Department of State to all U.S. Diplomatic Posts, Mar. 9, 1976 (State Dep't reference No. A-1394), *reprinted in* Foreign Relations Law, *supra* note 10, at 15.

[23] *See* Letter from Herbert J. Hansell, State Department Legal Adviser, to John J. Sparkman, Chairman, Senate Foreign Relations Committee, Sept. 28, 1977, *reprinted in* S. Rep. No. 499, *supra* note 21, at 9–10 (quoting Paul Warnke, *id.* at 9 n.2).

[24] Restatement, § 301, Comment *e*.

[25] *Id.*

[26] *Id.*, § 301, Reporters' Note 2.

[27] *See supra* note 20.

[28] *Compare* Restatement, § 303 (describing such presidential actions as international agreements) *with* § 321 (stating that all international agreements are binding on the parties).

[29] Professor Schachter has commented that nonbinding agreements do remove the matters dealt with from domestic jurisdiction and give rise to a right of the parties to raise questions of noncompliance. *See* Schachter, *The Twilight Existence of Nonbinding International Agreements*, 71 Am. J. Int'l L. 296 (1977).

The flexibility to employ such diplomatic tools is an important ingredient in the process of forming stronger and clearer reciprocal international expectations. The Final Act of the Helsinki Conference,[30] for example, has served an extraordinarily useful purpose as a nonbinding statement of principle concerning future conduct, and though nonobligatory, its authority has suffered little. Yet its adoption would have been doubtful had ratification as a multilateral agreement been required, and principles of constitutionalism would have derived little strength from such a complication. The same applies to the 1989 Vienna accord concerning freedom of association, religion, travel, and emigration.[31] The head of the Arms Control and Disarmament Agency during the Reagan Administration understandably viewed this approach as "the most promising of innovative thoughts," not because of the possibility of Senate circumvention, but because it could "help avoid endless problems over what programs to exclude, which to include, and how to verify them."[32]

Duties of a Signatory

A somewhat different issue was raised by United States adherence to the terms of the SALT II Treaty, submitted to the Senate on June 22, 1979,[33] but never approved by the Senate. A resolution of ratification was reported by the Committee on Foreign Relations on November 9, 1979.[34] In the absence of Senate action, however, under Rule XXXVII of the Standing Rules of the Senate,[35] the Treaty was taken off the Executive Calendar at the beginning of the Ninety-seventh Congress in January 1981 and returned to the Committee on Foreign Relations.

Nonetheless, President Ronald Reagan, who during the 1980 campaign referred to the Treaty as "fatally flawed,"[36] stated on May 31, 1982: "As for existing agreements, we will refrain from actions which undercut them so long as the Soviet Union shows equal restraint."[37]

If the Chief Executive, as a matter of nonbinding policy, can adhere to the

[30] Final Act of the Conference on Security and Cooperation in Europe, Aug. 1, 1975, 73 Dep't St. Bull., 323 (1975). *See generally* R. Bilder, Managing the Risks of International Agreement (1981).

[31] The final nonbinding document was adopted by thirty-five nations at the Conference on Security and Cooperation in Europe. N.Y. Times, Jan. 17, 1989 at A1, A6.

[32] K. Adelman, *Arms Control with and without Agreements*, 63 For. Aff. 240, 259 (1984).

[33] S. Exec. Doc. Y, 96th Cong., 1st Sess. (1979).

[34] S. Exec. Rep. No. 14, 96th Cong., 1st Sess. 26 (1979).

[35] Rule XXXVII, Standing Rules of the United States Senate, *reprinted in* Senate Comm. on Rules and Administration, 95th Cong., 1st Sess., Standing Rules of the United States Senate and Provisions of the Legislative Reorganization Acts of 1946 and 1970 and the Budget Control Act Relating to the Operation of the Senate 65–67 (Comm. Print 1977).

[36] Lindsey, *Reagan Urges Ban on Arms Pact Unless Soviet Withdraws Troops*, N.Y. Times, Jan. 26, 1980, at 10.

[37] Memorial Day, 1982, 18 Weekly Comp. Pres. Doc. 730 (May 31, 1982).

terms of an agreement no longer in effect, as President Carter did[38] with the Interim Agreement,[39] then it would seem that, a fortiori, he can also adhere as a matter of policy to the terms of an agreement that has not yet taken effect. In both instances, the President would be acting pursuant to whatever independent authority he might bring to bear. Indeed, with respect to a signed but unratified agreement, an additional source of authority arguably exists; no event has occurred that has diminished whatever authority flows from the President's signature. In contrast, the President's signature to a treaty (or agreement) that has been ratified but has since expired no longer confers any authority.[40] But what power, if any, actually flows from the signature?

The question is addressed by article 18 of the Vienna Convention on the Law of Treaties,[41] which provides as follows:

> A State is obliged to refrain from acts which would defeat the object and purpose of a treaty when:
> (a) it has signed the treaty or has exchanged instruments constituting the treaty subject to ratification, acceptance, or approval, until it shall have made its intention clear not to become a party to the treaty; or
> (b) it has expressed a consent to be bound by the treaty, pending the entry into force of the treaty and provided that such entry into force is not unduly delayed.[42]

The treaty clause of the Constitution, however, provides that the ''President . . . shall have power, by and with the advice and consent of the Senate, to make treaties provided two thirds of the Senators present concur. . . .''[43] Would article 18 of the Convention, by its requirement that a signatory to a treaty ''refrain from acts which would defeat the object and purpose'' of the treaty,[44] undermine the constitutional role of the Senate by allowing the President to incur treaty obligations without the Senate's approval?

[38] *Statement by Secretary of State Cyrus Vance, Sept. 23*, 77 Dept. St. Bull. 642 (1977).

[39] Interim Agreement on the Limitation of Strategic Offensive Arms, *supra* note 8.

[40] According to Justice Jackson's analysis of presidential powers in the *Steel Seizure Case*, the President's power is most restricted where he acts contrary to the will of Congress. *Youngstown*, 343 U.S. at 637 (Jackson, J., concurring). Where Congress—or the body charged with approving treaties, the Senate—has approved a treaty to be effective a given length of time and no longer, it might be presumed that it is contrary to the Senate's expressed will that the treaty remain in effect past the expiration date, unless the termination date is to be regarded as mere surplusage.

[41] Vienna Convention on the Law of Treaties, May 23, 1969, U.N. Doc. A/Conf. 39/27 *reprinted in* 63 Am. J. Int'l L. 875 (1969), 8 I.L.M. 679 (1969), art. 18.

[42] *Id.*

[43] U.S. Const. art II, § 2, cl. 2.

[44] The Convention does not specify what acts would have that effect. The Restatement applies a standard of irreversibility: ''Testing a weapon in contravention of a clause prohibiting such a test might violate the purpose of the agreement, since the consequences of the test might be irreversible.'' *Id.* at § 312, Comment *i*. On the other hand, ''[f]ailing to dismantle a weapon scheduled to be dismantled under the treaty might not defeat its object, since the dismantling could be effected later.'' *Id.*

The answer depends upon what rule would apply in the absence of article 18. If the rule of article 18 would effect no change in the status quo, it would represent no threat to the constitutional order. On the other hand, if the rule of article 18 embodies a precept of customary international law that has emerged only recently, the constitutional and international legal systems may not be in harmony.

The Convention,[45] though not ratified by the United States, has been said to represent merely a codification of customary international law with respect to treaties.[46] That view may be oversimplified, however; other authorities have pointed out that while some provisions of the Convention merely set forth existing international legal principles, other provisions represent an effort at law reform, reflecting the notions of the draftsmen about what "progressive development" ought to take place.[47] Into which category does article 18 fall?

Several commentators conclude that "[w]hether Article 18 as it now stands is declaratory of prior customary international law is uncertain. There is some authority for that conclusion, but the matter is not free from doubt."[48] However, the better view appears to be that article 18 codified international law as it existed at the time the Vienna Convention was adopted. The question gave rise to considerable controversy during the long process of drafting the Convention.[49] Some scholars, it is true, believe that the article represents progressive development.[50] Others, however, believe that the article represents codification,[51] and there is impressive support for their view. The International

[45] Vienna Convention, *supra* note 41.

[46] 3 *Panama Canal Treaties: Hearings Before the Senate Comm. on Foreign Relations*, 95th Cong. 1st Sess. 520 (1977) (statement of Professor Dean Rusk).

[47] Professor Rusk would appear to be in the distinct minority in applying this view to the treaty as a whole rather than to certain sections of it. Professor Holloway quotes with approval the statement of Sir Hersch Lauterpacht, who as special rapporteur played a major part in preparing the Convention, that the International Law Commission "is not limited to registering uniform practice. If that were its purpose, its work would be partly nominal and partly redundant." K. Holloway, *infra* note 127, at 58. *See also* Goldie, *The International Law Commission and Progressive Development of International Law*, 28 Fed. B.J. 25, 26 (1968); Jacobs, *Innovation and Continuity in the Law of Treaties*, 33 Mod. L. Rev. 502, 509 (1970); Sinclair, *Vienna Conference on the Law of Treaties*, 19 Int'l & Comp. L.Q. 47, 49–50 (1970).

[48] L. Henkin, R. Pugh, O. Schachter, & H. Smit, International Law 604 (1980).

[49] *See* Glennon, The Senate Role in Treaty Ratification, 77 Am. J. Int'l L. 257, 274 n.108 (1983).

[50] *See* C. Hyde, International Law 1432–33 n.13 (2d. rev. ed. 1945); I. Brownlie, Principles of Public International Law 489 (1966); I. Sinclair, *supra* note 49, at 39; Nisot, *L'Article 18 de la Convention de Vienne sur le droit des traités*, 6 Rev. Belge Droit Int'l 498 (1970–71); D. O'Connell, International Law 223 (1970); *cf.* J. Mervyn Jones, Ratification and Full Powers 81 (1949) (submitting that the rule may be somewhat overstated); Morvay, *The Obligation of a State Not to Frustrate the Object of a Treaty Prior to its Entry into Force*, 27 Zeitschrift Für Ausländisches Öffentliches Recht und Völkerrecht 451, 458 (1967) (stating that the rule formulated by the Vienna Convention either goes beyond customary law or states it in the broadest possible way).

[51] *See* Restatement, § 312; 1 D. Anzilotti, Cours De Droit International 372–73 (G. Gidel trans.

Law Commission, in preparing the draft of the Convention, appeared to take this view.[52] International tribunals recognized a signatory's obligation pending ratification to refrain from acts that would frustrate a treaty's purpose long before the Vienna Convention was adopted.[53] The United States,[54] the United Kingdom,[55] and other nations have long recognized such an obligation.[56]

Accordingly, it seems clear that if the United States subscribes to article 18 through ratification of the Vienna Convention, it would not undermine the role

---

1929); S. Crandall, Treaties, Their Making and Enforcement 343–44 (2d ed. 1916); 3 P. Fauchille, Traité De Droit International Public 319–20 (1926); 1 O. Hoijer, Les Traités Internationaux 136 (1928); K. Holloway, *infra* note 127, at 28; 1 L. Oppenheim, International Law 909; Cavagliere, *Règles générales du droit de la paix*, Recueil des Cours 311, 520 (1929 I); Hassan, *Good Faith in Treaty Formation*, 21 Va. J. Int'l L. 443, 452 (1981); Rogoff, *supra* note 49, at 271–72; *cf.* A. McNair, Law of Treaties 199 (1961) (suggesting that the signing of a treaty may limit freedom of action pending the entry into force of the treaty, but expressing reservations as to the conclusiveness of evidence for the proposition).

[52] "That an obligation of good faith to refrain from acts calculated to frustrate the object of the treaty attaches to a State which has signed a treaty subject to ratification appears to be generally accepted." Reports of the International Law Commission to the General Assembly [1966], at 202, UN Doc. A/6309/Rev. 1.

[53] Case Concerning Certain German Interests in Polish Upper Silesia, 1926 P.C.I.J., Ser. A, No. 7, at 30; Megalidis v. Etat turc, 8 Trib. Arb. Mixtes 386, 395 (1929) (holding that "il est de principe que déjà avec la signature d'un Traité et avant sa mise en vigueur, il existe pour les parties contractantes une obligation de ne rien faire qui puisse nuire au Traité en diminuant la portée de ses clauses").

[54] Secretary of State John Hay, expressing his dissatisfaction over Colombian failure to act in accordance with the United States–Colombia Panama Canal Treaty, which Colombia had signed but not ratified, asserted that in signing a treaty, states "bind themselves, pending its ratification, . . . to do nothing in contravention of its terms." 2 C. Hyde, *supra* note 50, at 1432–33 n.13.

[55] In 1857, Great Britain's law officers advised the Foreign Office that "[n]o act can be properly done by Her Majesty whilst the ratification of the Treaty is under consideration, which may at all affect any of the stipulations of the Treaty." Report by J. D. Harding, Attorney General, and R. Bethell, Queen's Advocate, to the Secretary of State for Foreign Affairs, May 15, 1857 (original on file in the Public Record Office in London, Law Officers' Reports Section, F.O. 83 2242), *reprinted in* A. McNair, *supra* note 51, at 200.

[56] The Final Act of Berlin of Feb. 26, 1885—which provided that "en attendant la ratification, les Puissances signatoires de cet Acte général s'obligent à n'adopter aucune mesure qui serait contraire aux dispositions dudit [*sic*?] Acte"—was, according to Sir Hersch Lauterpacht, "no more than declaratory of an existing principle." Lauterpacht, *Law of Treaties*, [1953] 2 Y.B. Int'l L. Comm'n 90, 110 UN Doc. A/CN.4/Ser. A/1953/Add.1.

Professor Holloway states that the Latin American states follow the same principle. *See* K. Holloway, *infra*, note 127, at 46 n.28.

Before the French and American revolutions, ambassadors were regarded as personal agents of their sovereigns, acting with full power to bind their royal clients, who were not free to disavow commitments their ambassadors made in pursuance of their delegated authority. The concept that a state might refuse to ratify a treaty signed on its behalf evolved gradually during the nineteenth century. *See generally* J. Mervyn Jones, *supra* note 50, at 12, 74–78. Given the existence of authority as early as 1857 for the rule eventually embodied in article 18 and the lack of early authority for a contrary rule, it seems that the first commentators and practitioners to address the question reached the conclusion of the Vienna Convention. *See supra* notes 167–78.

of the Senate in the treaty-making process. The constitutional allocation of power is consistent with a structure appropriate for carrying out the rule set forth in article 18. The President clearly possesses the authority to sign treaties and in view of the effect accorded signature by international law, he may constitutionally infer from that signature the further authority to act so as not to defeat the object or purpose of a signed treaty. "The rule of constitutional interpretation announced in *McCulloch v. Maryland*," the Supreme Court has said, "that that which was reasonably appropriate and relevant to the exercise of a granted power was to be considered as accompanying the grant, has been so universally applied that it suffices merely to state it."[57] A contrary rule in this context would undermine the ability of the United States to function in the community of nations.

But this does not mean that presidential power is unlimited in either scope or duration. It is important to distinguish between the President's *obligation* to observe the provisions of signed treaties awaiting ratification and his *authority* to do so. Customary international law imposes certain duties upon the United States and therefore upon the President as its agent in matters of foreign affairs. But international law can confer no power on the President; only the United States Constitution can do so.[58] It is the Constitution that authorizes him or her to carry out certain international obligations of the United States. In refraining from acts that would defeat the purpose of a signed treaty, he thus cannot exceed his own independent powers—although those powers are again properly viewed as encompassing the authority to carry out obligations incurred by the United States by virtue of its status as a treaty signatory. Similarly, if the treaty is rejected by the Senate, the President's signature is no longer available as a source of authority, and any adherence, binding or non-binding, must thereafter flow from his independent powers.

A thornier question arises if the Senate effectively rejects the treaty through inaction; it is unclear at what point authority no longer flows from signature. It may be that signature diminishes as a source of authority for article 18 purposes the longer a treaty remains before the Senate, since inaction can constitute effective rejection. After all, article 18(a) provides that obligations flow from signature only until a state "shall have made its intention clear not to become a party to the treaty."[59]

Precisely when a state's intention becomes clear is not readily determinable. Given this uncertainty, if it wishes to signal a definite end to obligations under article 18, the Senate is best advised simply to return the treaty to the Presi-

[57] Marshall v. Gordon, 243 U.S. 521, 537 (1917).

[58] *But see* United States v. Curtiss-Wright Export Corp., 299 U.S. 304 (1936), discussed in Chapter 2.

[59] *See* Glennon, The Senate Role in Treaty Ratification, 77 Am. J. Int'l L. 257, 274 n.108 (1983).

dent. As this normally is achieved by the adoption of a resolution,[60] the debate on such a resolution would represent an effective referendum on whether authority under article 18 should be continued. If such a resolution was defeated, the President's political position in declining to undermine the treaty would surely be bolstered. In addition, defeat could remove any doubt about his legal position in the event that a long time had elapsed since the transmittal of the treaty to the Senate.[61]

Should the President wish to signal a definite end to obligations called for by article 18 under a signed treaty,[62] he would be best advised to request its return from the Senate and to indicate in a formal message to the Senate that he does not intend to cause the United States to become a party. In the alternative, in the case of a bilateral treaty, the President might simply notify the other signatory that the United States does not intend to pursue ratification. Because the President (should the Senate give its consent) retains the discretion to decline to proceed to ratification, it might seem sensible that the President can withdraw a treaty from the Senate without its consent; after all, Senate consideration of the treaty would be pointless if it was clear from the outset that ratification by the President would not follow. Nonetheless, practicality

[60] Orders and unanimous consent requests also have been used for this purpose. The Senate has returned treaties to the Executive at the request of the Executive, but also on its own initiative. Given the President's authority to decline to ratify a treaty approved by the Senate, it might nonetheless be argued that he thus possesses, a fortiori, the lesser authority to forestall Senate approval by withdrawing a treaty. No instance has been identified in which an executive request for the return of a treaty has been rejected, however, or in which the Executive "withdrew" a treaty from the Senate without its consent. Memorandum from Congressional Research Service, Library of Congress, to Senate Foreign Relations Committee, Mar. 23, 1977, *reprinted in* 1 Foreign Relations Law, *supra* note 10, at 60–64; Senate Practice with Respect to Withdrawal of Treaties, Staff Memorandum, Senate Foreign Relations Committee, June 18, 1963 (on file with author); *accord* F. Riddick, Senate Procedure: Precedents and Practices, U.S. Senate 829 (1973); 14 M. Whiteman, Digest of International Law 61–62 (1970). The question seems primarily political rather than legal; if a President indicates an intent not to ratify, the Senate will seldom, if ever, go through the legally feckless act of according its consent.

[61] Under such circumstances, the President might claim that he was following the express will of Congress. The argument might be made that to observe the terms of a treaty until the defeat of a "resolution of return" would effectively change the fraction of the Senate required for approval from two-thirds to one-half. The answer, of course, is that international law as embodied in article 18 of the Vienna Convention does not place the treaty in force; it simply proscribes action that would defeat the object and purpose of the treaty. The difference is critical. Thus, for example, if President Reagan were to sign a strategic-arms-reduction treaty but face a reluctant Senate, article 18 would not give him authority to scrap prohibited missiles pending ratification, as their temporarily continued existence would not defeat the purpose of the treaty. "Failing to dismantle a weapon scheduled to be dismantled under the treaty," write the Reporters of the Restatement, "might not defeat its object, since the dismantling could be effected later." Restatement, § 312, Comment *i*. The test, they suggest, is whether the consequences of the action in question "might be irreversible." *Id*. Thus, "[t]esting a weapon in contravention of a clause prohibiting such a test might violate the purpose of the agreement." *Id*.

[62] *See* Rogoff, *supra* note 49.

argues against such presidential authority, since at that point the Senate, not the President, has custody of the official treaty documents; they are not then within the President's control. Perhaps for this reason, custom apparently supports a requirement that the President seek Senate consent for the withdrawal of a disfavored treaty. Between 1947 and 1963, forty-five treaties were withdrawn, in each case pursuant to a request of the President (which was met by the Senate's unanimous consent, order, or resolution).[63]

Status of the SALT Agreements

The SALT II Treaty was never withdrawn from the Senate; the popularity of the treaty may have made this a politically complicated course. Rather, the Reagan Administration simply announced its intent not to pursue ratification. "The proposal has been abandoned by this administration," Secretary of State Alexander Haig testified before the Senate Foreign Relations Committee. "We have so informed the Soviet Union. . . ."[64] The Administration might conceivably have changed its mind at some point, but to the extent that the United States can make clear its intention not to become a party to a treaty, it would appear to have done so with respect to SALT II. The United States is therefore not bound under the rule of Article 18 to refrain from acts that would defeat the object or purpose of SALT II, although the President may of course do so voluntarily.

This course apparently was chosen by President Reagan in his Memorial Day declaration that the United States would "refrain from actions which would undercut . . . [existing agreements] so long as the Soviet Union shows equal restraint."[65] Ironically, however, the President may have inadvertently gone beyond a mere statement of nonbinding policy. Unlike Secretary of State Cyrus Vance's similar statement concerning United States adherence to the terms of the SALT I Interim Agreement,[66] President Reagan's declaration was not made with the express caveat that it was not intended to be binding. Consequently, under the rule of the *Nuclear Tests* cases,[67] the President's statement may well have created a binding (if conditional) obligation under international law.[68]

[63] "Senate practice with respect to withdrawal of treaties," staff memorandum, Comm. on Foreign Relations, U.S. Senate, June 18, 1963 (unpublished; on file with author).

[64] *Nuclear Arms Reduction Proposals: Hearings Before the Senate Comm. on Foreign Relations*, 97th Cong. 2d Sess. 121 (1982) (statement of Secretary of State Alexander Haig).

[65] *See supra* note 37.

[66] *Statement by Vance*, *supra* note 9, at 642.

[67] 1974 I.C.J. Rep. 253, 457.

[68] Perhaps even more troubling, in this context, is the remark of President Carter with regard to SALT II: "I consider it *binding* on our two countries." The President's news conference of March 14, 1980, 16 Weekly Comp. Pres. Doc. 484, 488 (Mar. 14, 1980) (emphasis added). President Carter, of course, did not say whether he regarded the obligation as *legally* or *morally*

If so, the measure reported by the Senate Foreign Relations Committee—stating as a matter of law that the United States "shall continue to refrain from actions which would undercut the SALT I and SALT II agreements, provided the Soviet Union shows equal restraint"[69]—would, if enacted, merely have caused the President's obligations under domestic law to correspond to those imposed by international law.[70] It would not have interfered with the President's foreign-affairs powers because a binding commitment would already have existed as a result of his declaration. To the contrary, the real issue is whether the issuance of such a declaration is within the scope of the President's independent powers.[71]

If, on the other hand, his declaration is viewed as a nonobligatory policy statement, the matter becomes more difficult. Clearly, Congress can prohibit the President by law from taking steps that would have been prohibited under SALT I and SALT II. The Committee's proposal might thus be seen merely as a statutory limitation on the President's authority to take certain steps not falling within his independent powers.[72] The problem is that the Committee's formulation, like the President's, contained no qualification that it was not intended to be binding. A statement that the United States *shall* take or not take certain steps in the international arena, when solemnly enshrined in law, may itself give rise to binding international undertakings. The establishment of such undertakings by Congress would naturally raise the gravest constitutional questions. As a Senate Judiciary Subcommittee pointed out, "To attempt to bind the United States to international obligations through the form of a joint resolution makes possible in principle what the Constitution and subsequent cases and commentary most certainly reject."[73] The *Restatement* underscores

---

binding; still, his statement was arguably no more equivocal than those that were held to give rise to legal obligations on the part of France in the *Nuclear Tests* cases and of Norway in *Eastern Greenland*.

[69] S.J. Res. 212, cl. 3, 97th Cong., 2d Sess. (1982), *reprinted in* Subcomm. on Separation of Powers of Senate Comm. on the Judiciary, 97th Cong., 2D Sess. Joint Resolution with Respect to Nuclear Arms Reductions: Report on S.J. Res. 212 at 7 (Comm. Print 1982) (hereinafter cited as Joint Resolution).

[70] This analysis assumes that both SALT I and SALT II are "existing agreements" within the meaning of the President's declaration, a proposition disputed by Senator Jesse Helms. *See* S. Rep. No. 493, 97th Cong., 2d Sess. 30 (1982) (additional views of Mr. Helms).

[71] *See Treaties and Executive Agreements*, *supra* note 20.

[72] *See generally supra* note 40 (discussing the power of Congress to limit the President's foreign-policy power in light of the concurring opinion of Justice Jackson in Youngstown Sheet & Tube Co. v. Sawyer, 343 U.S. 579 (1952).

[73] Joint Resolution, *supra* note 69, at 7. The Subcommittee quoted from the 1816 Senate Foreign Relations Committee report noted by the Supreme Court in *Curtiss-Wright*, 299 U.S. at 319:

> The President is the constitutional representative of the United States with regard to foreign nations. He manages our concerns with foreign nations and must necessarily be most competent to determine when, how, and upon what subjects negotiation may be urged with the greatest prospect of success. . . . 8 U.S. Senate, Reports, Committee on Foreign Relations, vol. 8, p. 24.

Joint Resolution, *supra* note 69, at 6.

this point: "Congress cannot itself conclude such an agreement; it can be concluded only by the President, who alone possesses the constitutional power to negotiate with other governments."[74]

Executive Agreements

Does the President have authority to make a *binding* international agreement without the consent of the Senate?[75] The *Restatement* says that the President may "make an international agreement dealing with any matter that falls within his independent powers under the Constitution,"[76] but this seems more truistic than helpful: What the President may do, he may agree to do. He may make an agreement to recognize a certain government, pardon an individual, or negotiate a treaty without the advice and consent of the Senate.

A recurring dispute concerns the extent of the President's power to enter into agreements *not* within the scope of his plenary power.[77] The Constitution provides that the President shall have power to make treaties with the advice and consent of the Senate.[78] But since the Constitution refers only to treaties, the constitutional basis for executive agreements is unclear.[79] The Constitution does not require that every international agreement be given the advice and consent of the Senate.[80] However, the obverse is clearly not true: Contrary to the State Department's assertion in 1975, the President does not have discretion to enter into any international agreement on his own authority, regardless of the gravity of the undertaking.[81] Stated in terms of the framework developed in Chapters 1 and 2, the President does not have an "initiating" power with respect to every conceivable international agreement, as is evident when the sources of constitutional power are examined.

[74] Restatement, § 303, Comment *e*.

[75] For the best recent work on this issue, particularly with respect to efforts within Congress to address the question by statute, *see* L. Johnson, The Making of International Agreements: Congress Confronts the Executive (1984).

[76] Restatement, § 303(4). The statement seems a truism: It is self-evident that the President can act within the scope of his independent powers. The debate has centered on the scope of those powers—where his end and those of Congress or the Senate begin. *Id.* § 303, Comments *h*, *i*; *see supra* note 20. In the case of arms control declarations, the ultimate issue may be an impoundment question: whether the President, as commander in chief, can refuse to spend certain funds Congress has directed him to spend. *See generally* L. Tribe, American Constitutional Law 193–98 (1978).

[77] *See generally* T. Franck & E. Weisband, Foreign Policy by Congress (1979); Bennet, *Congress in Foreign Policy: Who Needs It?* 59 Foreign Aff. 40 (1978).

[78] U.S. Const. art. II, § 2, cl. 2.

[79] *See* Restatement (Second) of the Foreign Relations Law of the United States, §§ 119–21 (1965).

[80] *Id.*

[81] Letter from Monroe Leigh to the Senate Office of Legislative Counsel (Oct. 6, 1975) (State Department Legal Adviser's Reply Concerning the Constitutionality of the Sinai Accords), *reprinted in* 1 Foreign Relations Law, *supra* note 10, at 304–5.

Constitutional Text

Nowhere does the text of the Constitution mention executive agreements or allude to any independent power on the part of the Chief Executive to make international agreements. It has been argued that the term *treaty* is used generically in the Constitution to encompass every form of international agreement; this, it is pointed out, is how the term was known to the Framers.[82] It must also be noted that the text of the Constitution indicates the Framers' awareness that another category of agreement might be entered into with foreign nations, a category not denominated "treaties": The Constitution prohibits states from entering into "compacts" with foreign governments without the consent of Congress.[83] As Professor Edgar Bodenheimer has pointed out, the Framers were acquainted with Vattel's distinction between *treaties* and *compacts* and seem to have used the terms intentionally to signify a requirement that *treaties* be used in the case of significant undertakings.[84]

Case Law

The Supreme Court has upheld the use of executive agreements to carry out what appears to be a plenary presidential power (specifically, recognition),[85] and it has also found certain agreements beyond the scope of a concurrent presidential "initiating" power. In *Valentine v. United States ex rel. Neidecker*,[86] the Court held that the President did not have the power, acting alone, to extradite an individual. Although the Court did not deal expressly with the issue, it seems clear that an executive agreement had been entered into and that the Court necessarily considered it invalid. Similarly, in *Seery v. United States*,[87] the United States Court of Claims declined to enforce a presidentially made claims-settlement agreement with Austria because it conflicted with prior federal law. "It would be incongruous," the court said, "if the Executive Department alone . . . could nullify the Act of Congress."[88]

Other agreements were within the President's initiating power. "Congress has not disapproved of the action taken here," the Supreme Court said in upholding the Iranian claims-settlement agreement in *Dames & Moore v. Regan*.[89] The Court thus found no need to consider arguments concerning the

[82] Staff of the Senate Comm. on Foreign Relations, *Treaties and Executive Agreements* (Comm. Print, 1944).

[83] U.S. Const. art. I, § 10, cl. 3.

[84] E. Bodenheimer, Jurisprudence § 71 at 339 (1974).

[85] United States v. Belmont, 301 U.S. 324 (1937).

[86] 299 U.S. 5 (1936).

[87] 127 F. Supp. 601 (Ct. Cl. 1955).

[88] *Id.* at 607.

[89] 453 U.S. 654, 687 (1981).

scope of the President's plenary powers.[90] The Carter Justice Department nonetheless concluded that Congress could by law override the agreement with a statute reviving claims the Executive had extinguished. "The authorities treat the power of Congress to enact statutes that supersede executive agreements and treaties for purposes of domestic law as a plenary one, not subject to exceptions based on the President's broad powers concerning foreign affairs."[91] The Department relied upon *La Abra Silver Mining Co. v. United States*:[92] "It has been adjudged that Congress by legislation, and so far as the people and authorities of the United States are concerned, could abrogate a treaty made between this country and another country which had been negotiated by the President and approved by the Senate."[93]

Two federal appeals courts have dealt with this issue of concurrent power, but not satisfactorily.[94] In *United States v. Guy Capps*,[95] the Fourth Circuit considered the validity of an agreement regarding the export of Canadian potatoes into the United States. The court concluded that the agreement was unlawful, but it is not altogether clear why. At certain points in the opinion, Judge Parker seems to suggest that Congress had effectively prohibited the agreement; he does not refer to Justice Jackson's *Steel Seizure* analysis, but appears to reason that the conclusion of the agreement fell within the zone of congressional disapproval. At other points, however, he seems to argue that Congress was silent, and that because Congress was silent, the President was without power to make the agreement. This rationale seems far too sweeping since it would view as invalid virtually all executive agreements, however trivial, not falling beyond the President's initiating powers.

Consumers Union v. Kissinger,[96] another appeals court decision, is occasionally cited as broad authority for executive agreement making. Indeed, it has been relied upon for the proposition that the President may disregard an act of Congress that restricts his power to make a certain agreement. Such claims rest upon a gross misreading of the opinion. The court clearly believed that the President, in negotiating the reduction of Japanese steel exports into the United States, had acted in the face of congressional silence. The "only

[90] *See generally* Note, *The Iranian Hostage Agreement Under International and United States Law,* 81 Colum. L. Rev. 822, 852 (1981).

[91] 4A Op. Office of the Legal Counsel, Department of Justice 289 (1980).

[92] 175 U.S. 423 (1899).

[93] *Id.*

[94] More frequently, cases such as this are dismissed on political question grounds. *See* Chapter 8. In *Dole v. Carter*, 569 F.2d 1109 (10th Cir. 1977), for example, another appeals court confronted the validity of President Carter's agreement to return the Crown of St. Stephen to the people of Hungary. Senator Robert Dole, the plaintiff, claimed that the agreement was a treaty requiring the advice and consent of the Senate and asked for an injunction preventing the Crown's return. The court found the dispute nonjusticiable.

[95] 204 F.2d 655 (4th Cir. 1953).

[96] 506 F.2d 136 (D.C. Cir. 1975).

question before us,'' the court held, ''is whether the actions of the Executive were a regulation of foreign commerce foreclosed to it generally by . . . the Constitution, and in particular the Trade Expansion Act of 1962. . . . To the extent that the District Court declared no such conflict to exist, we affirm its decision.''[97] ''Certainly Congress is not inhibited from enacting any legislation it desires to regulate by law the importation of steel,''[98] the court concluded, implying that the acts at issue were clearly subject to congressional control. The case has apparently been viewed by the Justice Department as involving recommendations ''which do not bind the United States and do not purport to have the force and effect of law.''[99]

Custom

Presidents have long claimed the power to make executive agreements, binding in international law, without the advice and consent of the Senate. John Adams asserted the authority to make such an agreement in 1799.[100] Literally thousands have been entered into by presidents,[101] and the trend has accelerated in recent years. In 1930, the United States concluded 25 treaties and only 9 executive agreements. In 1968, the United States concluded 16 treaties and 266 executive agreements, and by January 1, 1972, 947 treaties and 4,359 executive agreements were in force.[102]

Congress remained largely quiescent so long as the treaty mode represented the principal instrument. As executive agreements proliferated, however, congressional objection became more frequent. In 1969, the Senate agreed to the National Commitments Resolution, which warned presidents that the Senate intended to exercise its constitutional role and reserved the right to decline to implement presidential commitments.[103] In 1972, the Senate expressed its sense that a 1971 presidential agreement with Bahrain, which provided for the use of military facilities by the United States in Bahrain, should be submitted to the Senate as a treaty.[104] The next year, Congress enacted the War Powers Resolution, which prohibits the inference from any treaty, and presumably from any executive agreement, of authority to introduce the armed forces into

[97] *Id.* at 138.

[98] *Id.* at 143.

[99] 2 Opinions of the Office of the Legal Counsel 230 (1978).

[100] Lillich, *The Gravel Amendment to the Trade Reform Act of 1974: Congress Checkmates a Lump Sum Agreement*, 69 Am. J. Int'l L. 837, 844 (1975).

[101] L. Henkin, Foreign Affairs and the Constitution 173 (1972).

[102] Testimony of Senator Sam Ervin on S. 3475, *Congressional Oversight of Executive Agreements: Hearings Before the Subcommittee on Separation of Powers of the Committee on the Judiciary, United States Senate*, 92d Cong., 2d Sess., at 3 (1973).

[103] S. Res. 85, 91st Cong., 1st Sess. (1969).

[104] S. Res. 214, 92d Cong., 2d Sess. (1972).

hostilities absent specific implementing legislation.[105] During the next several years, legislation severely limiting presidential authority to make executive agreements was considered in both the House[106] and Senate.[107] As discussed in Chapter 4, the Senate finally adopted a procedure providing for consultation concerning the form of agreements.[108]

Intent of the Framers

The Framers intended to circumscribe presidential authority to act unilaterally in making international agreements. John Jay cautioned against delegation of the treaty-making power:

> The power of making treaties is an important one especially as it relates to war, peace, and commerce; and it should not be delegated but in such mode, and with such precautions, as will afford the highest security that it will be exercised by men the best qualified for the purpose, and in the manner most conducive to the public good.[109]

James Madison considered treaty making more a legislative function. "There are sufficient indications," he wrote, "that the power of treaties is regarded by the Constitution as materially different from mere executive power, and as having more affinity to the legislative than to the executive function."[110]

Even Hamilton, no admirer of legislative power, believed that the legislative branch had to be included in making international agreements:

> The power in question seems therefore to form a distinct department, and to belong, properly neither to the legislative nor to the executive. The qualities elsewhere detailed as indispensable in the management of foreign negotiations, point out the Executive as the most fair agent in those transactions; while the vast importance of the trust, and the operation of treaties as laws, plead strongly for the

[105] War Powers Resolution, § 8(a)(2), 87 Stat. 555, 50 U.S.C. § 1541–48 (1982).

[106] *See, e.g.*, H.R. 4438, 94th Cong., 1st Sess. (1975); *Congressional Review of International Agreements, Hearings Before the Subcommittee on International Security and Scientific Affairs of the Committee on International Relations, United States House of Representatives*, 94th Cong., 1st Sess. (1976).

[107] *See, e.g.*, S. 3830, 93d Cong., 2d Sess. (1974) (providing for the "legislative veto" of certain executive agreements); S. Res. 24, 95th Cong., 1st Sess. (1977) (providing for a point-of-order procedure to block measures funding certain executive agreements).

[108] S. Res. 536, 95th Cong., 2d Sess. (1978); S. Rep. No. 95-1171. For a discussion of the successful operation of this procedure, which has avoided disputes concerning executive agreements for over a decade, *see* S. Prt. 98-205, Comm. on Foreign Relations, 98th Cong., 2d. Sess., Treaties and Other International Agreements: The Role of the United States Senate (Study Prepared by the Congressional Research Service, Library of Congress) (Comm. Print., 1984) at 176–78.

[109] The Federalist No. 64, at 420 (Jay) (J. Cooke, ed. 1960).

[110] 6 J. Madison, Writings 138 (Hunt ed. 1910), ch. 2, note 12.

participation of the whole or a portion of the legislative body in the office of making them.[111]

He noted that although the King of England could make treaties by himself, this power was denied to the President: "In this respect, therefore, there is no comparison between the intended power of the President and the actual power of the British sovereign."[112] Hamilton apparently regarded the advice-and-consent power of the Senate as encompassing every international agreement:

> [F]rom the best opportunity of knowing the fact, I aver, that it was understood by all to be the intent of the provision to give the power the most ample latitude—to render it competent to all the stipulations which the exigencies of national affairs might require; competent to the making of treaties of alliance, treaties of commerce, treaties of peace, and every other species of convention usual among nations. . . . And it was emphatically for this reason that it was so carefully guarded; the cooperation of two-thirds of the Senate, with the President, being required to make any treaty whatever.[113]

In South Carolina, C. C. Pinckney warned of the danger of vesting in the President alone the power to make international agreements:

> Surely there is greater security in vesting this power as the present Constitution has vested it, than in any other body. Would the gentleman vest it in the President alone? If he would his assertion that the power we have granted was as dangerous as the power vested by Parliament in the proclamations of Henry VIII, might have been, perhaps, warranted. . . . [The Senate] joined with the President . . . form together a body in whom can be best and most safely vested the diplomatic power of the Union.[114]

Roger Sherman, a delegate to the Constitutional Convention, concluded that the Constitution required joint action by the Senate and the President with respect to "every transaction." The Senate and President, he said,

> [o]ught to act jointly in *every transaction* which respects the business of negotiation with foreign powers. . . . There is something more required than responsibility in conducting treaties. The Constitution contemplates the united wisdom of the President and Senate, in order to make treaties. . . . The more wisdom there is employed, the greater security there is that the public business will be well done.[115]

[111] The Federalist No. 75, at 505 (Hamilton) (J. Cook, ed., 1960).

[112] The Federalist No. 69, at 467–68 (Hamilton) (J. Cooke, ed., 1960).

[113] *Letters of Camillus*, 6A Hamilton, Works 183 (Lodge, ed. 1904).

[114] 4 Elliot, Jonathan, Debates in the Several State Conventions on the Adoption of the Federal Constitution 280–81 (Washington, 2d. ed. 1836).

[115] 1 Annals of Cong. 1085 (1789) (emphasis added).

Alexander Hamilton believed the treaty clause to be one of the "best digested and unexceptionable parts of the plan," in part because he considered it "utterly unsafe and improper to entrust that power to an elective magistrate of four years duration." He continued:

> The history of human conduct does not warrant that exalted opinion of human virtue which would make it wise in a nation to commit interests of so delicate and momentous a kind as those which concern its intercourse with the rest of the world to the sole disposal of a magistrate, created and circumstanced, as would be a president of the United States.[116]

Finally, James Monroe, who had participated in the Virginia Ratification Convention, submitted the 1817 "Rush-Bagot Agreement" to the Senate and inquired whether it was "such an arrangement as the executive is competent to enter into, by the powers vested in it by the Constitution, or is such a one as requires the advice and consent of the Senate. . . ."[117]

Functional Analysis

It is sensible to think that the President has sole power to enter into international agreements to carry out plenary powers—to negotiate and conclude cease-fires, recognition, pardons. But where no such power pertains, where the Senate has time to act, and where the agreement is one of unusual importance, arguments for an exclusive presidential prerogative are less persuasive. In those circumstances, the institutional attributes of the Senate[118] suggest that the decision-making process will benefit from its inclusion.

Effect of the Treaty on Treaties

The abuse of the executive-agreement power concerned members of the Senate Foreign Relations Committee in 1972 when the Committee considered the Vienna Convention on the Law of Treaties,[119] a treaty that states principles of international law concerning the making, observance, and validity of international agreements. The Convention permits nations to approach treaties with uniform assumptions, countenanced by the international community, about their significance.[120] Opponents of the Vienna Convention argued, then as now, that ratification of the treaty would further concentrate power in the hands of the Executive. For this and other reasons, the Committee failed to

[116] The Federalist No. 75 (Hamilton) (J. Cooke, ed. 1960) at 505.

[117] Quoted in Berger, *The President's Unilateral Termination of the Taiwan Treaty*, 75 Nw. U. L. Rev. 577 (1980).

[118] *See* Chapter 1.

[119] Vienna Convention, *supra* note 41.

[120] *See* Kearney & Dalton, *The Treaty on Treaties*, 64 Am. J. Int'l L. 495, 561 (1970).

recommend approval of the Vienna Convention. The Committee was particularly concerned about article 46, which limits a nation's ability to invoke the fact that a treaty was not properly ratified to excuse nonperformance of the treaty.[121] Article 46 of the Vienna Convention provides:

1. A State may not invoke the fact that its consent to be bound by a treaty has been expressed in violation of a provision of its internal law regarding competence to conclude treaties as invalidating its consent unless that violation was manifest and concerned a rule of its internal law of fundamental importance.
2. A violation is manifest if it would be objectively evident to any State conducting itself in the matter in accordance with normal practice and good faith.[122]

Article 46 thus touches a raw constitutional nerve—the extent of the President's authority to obligate the United States internationally, free from legislative restraint.[123] This issue has been at the core of the debate over the President's constitutional power to make executive agreements without the advice and consent of the Senate. In face of the uncertainty of the President's authority to make executive agreements, article 46 might be interpreted as defining the constitutional extent of this power. The President, it could be argued, should be accorded great deference, because United States treaties are the "supreme law of the land"[124] and only a "manifest" violation of domestic law would invalidate an executive agreement. Given the uncertain limits on executive agreements, courts might find it very difficult to conclude that a particular agreement was "manifestly" unconstitutional.[125] In effect, the President might be able to make international agreements completely free of Senate control.

In addition, article 46 cannot confidently be said merely to have codified existing international law. There are two polar viewpoints about the correct international law on this matter—the *constitutionalist* and the *internationalist*. According to the constitutionalists, a treaty concluded by a state's representatives is invalid if it exceeds their competence under the constitutional law of the state; the rationale of the rule is that no real consent has been given by the state concerned.[126] Internationalists, however, argue that although a treaty ob-

[121] A. Rovine, 1974 Digest of United States Practice in International Law 195 (1975).

[122] Vienna Convention, *supra* note 41, at art. 46.

[123] For a particularly thoughtful discussion of this issue, *see* Bishop, *Unconstitutional Treaties*, 42 Minn. L. Rev. 773 (1958).

[124] U.S. Const. art. VI, cl. 2.

[125] The Restatement recognizes, however, that this threshold is not so high as to be meaningless. "Some agreements," it provides, "such as the United Nations Charter or the North Atlantic Treaty, are of sufficient formality, dignity, and importance that, in the unlikely event that the President attempted to make such an agreement on his own authority, his lack of authority might be regarded as 'manifest.' " *Id.* at § 311, Comment *c*.

[126] Jacobs, *Innovation and Continuity in the Law of Treaties*, 33 Mod. L. Rev. 508, 510 (1970). Note that Jacobs, in stating the "constitutionalist" view, expressed no opinion as to its validity.

ligation may be invalid within a state because of failure to comply with constitutional requirements, the international obligation is unimpaired if it measures up to international-law requirements, because those requirements do not include any reference to internal law.[127]

The powerful tension between constitutionalism and internationalism, coupled with the paucity of international-law precedent,[128] has spawned diverse scholarly opinion. This diversity was reflected in the drafting of article 46. Ambassador Richard D. Kearney, who headed the United States delegation to the United Nations Conference on the Law of Treaties (the body that drafted the Convention), has described in some detail the numerous schools of thought presented at the Conference on this question and the long process of compromise that produced article 46.[129] As Kearney observed, "A variety of eminent scholars took very firm positions on the basis of rather sparse knowledge."[130] Between the two extremes were a variety of more moderate views, advanced by adherents who sought to introduce various elements of reasonableness into these exercises in pure theory.[131] The first Special Rapporteur of the Conference, Professor Brierly (an adherent to the constitutionalist view), concluded that "[i]n view of the division of opinion" on the matter, the Conference could "take up any one of" the positions.[132] Not surprisingly, the four Special Rapporteurs each took his own view of the proper rule, and the process of reconciling opposing views took fifteen years to complete.[133] The result was a compromise, article 46, directed not only at "upholding the stability of the international treaty structure" but also at "placing some domestic checks and balances upon the making of international commitments."[134]

See also J. Brierly, The Law of Nations 319–20 (6th ed. 1963); L. Oppenheim, International Law 887 (H. Lauterpacht ed., 8th ed. 1955).

[127] Kearney, *Internal Limitations on External Commitments—Article 46 of the Treaties Convention*, 4 Int'l Law. 1, 3 (1969). Professor Holloway quoted Sir Hersch Lauterpacht as placing Judge Anzilloti in this group. K. Holloway, Modern Trends in Treaty Law 131 n.32 (1967).

[128] *See* H. Blix, Treaty-making Power 375 (1960).

[129] Kearney, *supra* note 127, at 1.

[130] *Id.* at 5.

[131] *Id.* at 3. Among commentators who fall generally into this group are Lord McNair and Messrs. de Visscher, Fairman, Devaux, and von Szary. *See* K. Holloway, *supra* note 127, at 133 n.36. The moderates seem to have carried the day; as may be seen, the final text shows deference to clear constitutional provisions without holding international law hostage to the vagaries of constitutional interpretation. Perhaps the drafters of the Vienna Convention were motivated in part by the sort of concern raised by M. Cadieux of Canada, who pointed out that his "own country's constitution was so complex"—involving powers of the Crown (as represented by the Governor-General), of the Government of the Federal Parliament, and of the provinces—"that there were always some provisions it could invoke if it wished to elude its obligations. But the rule of law should be fostered and governments encouraged to act with prudence. . . ." Summary Records of the Fifteenth Session, 674th Meeting, [1963] 1 Y.B. Int'l. L. Comm'n 5, U.N. Doc. A/CN.4/Ser. A/1963.

[132] [1950] 2 Y.B. Int'l L. Comm'n 230, U.N. Doc. A/CN.4/Ser.A/1950.

[133] Kearney, *supra* note 127, at 5–6.

[134] *Id.* at 21.

It is because of this dual objective that article 46 creates a problem. The United States Constitution also places some domestic checks and balances upon making international commitments. The question of the legal effect of an ultra vires international agreement made by the President is thus common to two legal systems—international law and constitutional law. If article 46, which derives from international law, answers the question differently than does domestic law, then ratification of the Vienna Convention without reservation as to article 46 would, by definition, violate the Constitution.

But there is little evidence that the Constitution even addresses the question. The Constitution surely does not require the United States to "invoke the fact that its consent to be bound by a treaty has been expressed in violation of a provision of its internal law"[135] in situations not encompassed by article 46. The Constitution may require that the violation be "manifest," as required by article 46.[136] But it may require less—that the violation create only a "reasonable doubt" as to adherence. If the latter is correct, then an agreement negotiated in a way that makes it "reasonably doubtful" that the President was acting within his constitutional authority would be invalid as a matter of domestic law but would not be so "manifest" as to invalidate the agreement under article 46. Thus, article 46 may be formulated too broadly for United States constitutional purposes. But no one can say with certainty. As Hans Blix concluded, "It is obvious that the rule regulating the question is not a settled one."[137] Blix reviewed the constitutions (or practices) of eighty-five nations, seeking to identify those showing an intent that "certain unconstitutional features make treaties invalid internationally."[138] Only five are listed as "probables," and the United States is not among them.[139] The *Restatement* concluded simply, and accurately, that the international "case law" on the subject supports the rule "that a state is bound by apparent authority where lack of authority is not obvious to outside parties."[140]

It is thus difficult to argue that the standard set by article 46 is wrong as a constitutional matter. As a practical matter, the Vienna Convention's standard is surely far more sensible than puristic formulations that would advance either constitutionalism or internationalism at the other's expense. The *Restatement* is therefore reasonable in incorporating article 46 in section 311. However, because an enlargement of executive power by article 46 cannot be ruled out with certainty—just as the enlargement of Senate power cannot be ruled out—the Senate should confer its consent to the Convention upon the condition that

[135] Vienna Convention, *supra* note 41, at art. 46.

[136] *Id. See* Restatement, § 311, Comment *c*.

[137] H. Blix, *supra* note 128, at 392.

[138] *Id.* at 233–34.

[139] The five are Costa Rica, Denmark, Greece, Ireland, and Norway (only the latter two of which definitely manifest the intention). Lebanon is a possible addition to the list. *Id.* at 246.

[140] Restatement, § 311, Reporters' Note 4.

a "standstill" provision be applied to article 46: Article 46 may not be construed as conferring any authority upon the President that he would not have in its absence.[141]

That is all the Senate should do concerning article 46. Immediately after the Vienna Convention was transmitted to the Senate, the Foreign Relations Committee proposed to resolve the executive-agreements issue by attaching an "interpretation and understanding" to the resolution of ratification to the Convention that in effect would have made Senate (or congressional) approval of every agreement a requisite for avoiding invalidation of the agreement under article 46.[142] A similar proposal was advanced informally in 1977.[143] The Executive objected in both instances,[144] however, and the Convention as a consequence was not taken up by the Committee. Those who opposed Senate approval of the Convention in response to the Executive's rejection of the proposed condition were wrong. Insistence upon a condition that would effect a "solution," even a partial solution, would ultimately be construed by the Executive as attempting to take power away from the President and give it to the Senate (and perhaps the House of Representatives, depending upon the mechanism advanced).[145] The President need not proceed with the ratification of a treaty to which the Senate has attached conditions he finds unaccept-

[141] The same considerations apply with respect to article 18 of the Vienna Convention.

[142] Two different versions of this condition were considered by the Committee in 1972. The first provided that

> it is a rule of internal law of the United States of fundamental importance that no treaty (as defined by paragraph 1(a) of Article 2 of the Convention) is valid with respect to the United States, and the consent of the United States may not be given regarding any such treaty, unless the Senate of the United States has given its advice and consent to such treaty, or the terms of such treaty have been approved by law, as the case may be.

A. Rovine, *supra* note 121, at 195.

In view of opposition from the Department of State to this interpretation and understanding, the Committee reconsidered the Convention and discussed an alternative proposal. The alternative provided that "within the meaning of article 46 of the Convention, article II, section 2, of the United States Constitution . . . is a rule of internal law of the United States of fundamental importance." *Id.*

[143] Also labeled an "understanding and interpretation," the condition would have provided that article II, section 2, clause 2 of the United States Constitution is a "rule of its internal law of fundamental importance" within the meaning of paragraph 1 of article 46 of the Convention, and that a violation of such rule is "manifest" within the meaning of paragraph 2, article 46 of the Convention if the United States Senate by resolution so states.

[144] In 1974, the Department expressed concern about the possibility of confusion over use of the term *treaty*. *See* Letter from Marshall Wright, Assistant Secretary of State for Congressional Relations, to Pat Holt, Chief of Staff, Senate Foreign Relations Committee (Jan. 31, 1974), *reprinted in* A. Rovine, *supra* note 121, at 196–97. Similar concerns were voiced in 1977.

[145] One possibility discussed informally in 1977 was the attachment of a condition which would have given the Congress, by concurrent resolution, or the Senate, by simple resolution, the authority to say when a violation was "manifest" for purposes of article 46. The latter formulation would likely have proven as disagreeable to the House as to the Executive.

able,[146] and State Department officials left little doubt that the Vienna Convention would not be ratified if such a condition was attached.[147]

If the Senate is concerned about the circumvention of its treaty power, other less destructive remedies are available.[148] But in considering the Vienna Convention, the Senate should be content to ensure that it does not contribute to the erosion of the Senate's constitutional power. The "standstill" condition suggested above will achieve that objective, and both Democratic[149] and Republican[150] administrations have accepted such a condition. Continued inaction due to disagreement over a largely peripheral issue does nothing to

[146] *See, e.g.*, Restatement, § 314, Comments *a*, *b*; L. Henkin, *supra* note 101, at 136.

[147] The tone was effectively set in 1972, after the Committee, on Sept. 7, ordered reported a resolution of ratification to the Convention which incorporated the first alternative "understanding and interpretation" set forth *supra* note 121. In a letter to the Chairman, the Department objected as follows:

> Since the Convention applies not only to treaties but also to executive agreements, as those terms are used in our constitutional practice, the effect of the proposed interpretation and understanding would be very sweeping. Moreover, since the understanding and interpretation would become a part of our domestic law upon ratification of the treaty, it would substantially alter the present legal regime which applies to the conclusion of international agreements by the United States.

Letter from David M. Abshire, Assistant Secretary for Congressional Relations, to J. W. Fulbright, Chairman, Senate Foreign Relations Committee (Sept. 15, 1972) (on file with author).

[148] *See, e.g.*, S. Res. 24, 95th Cong., 1st Sess. (1977) ("Treaty Powers Resolution" sponsored by Senators Clark, Church, Kennedy, and Cranston). An earlier version, S. Res. 434, 94th Congress, 2d Sess. (1976), was described as follows by Senator Clark upon its introduction:

> It is a simple Senate resolution which, if agreed to, would cause a point of order to lie in the Senate against the consideration of any bill, joint resolution, or conference report which authorizes or appropriates funds to implement any agreement which the Senate by simple resolution finds to constitute a treaty. It is thus effective in that it rests on existing Senate powers—the rule-making power and the Senate's share of the legislative power. And it is unquestionably constitutional since it involves not the slightest invasion of executive power. It is patterned, in fact, after the House germaneness [*sic*] rule, which has taken on "extraterritoriality" all too familiar to Senators who have served on conference committees.

122 Cong. Rec. 10,966, 10,968 (1976).

[149] The Department of State, during the Carter Administration, indicated that "[w]hile the additional language might cause some comment or objection from foreign governments," it "would not object" to a Senate understanding and interpretation that the "provisions of the Convention do not give any international agreement of the United States, including particularly any international agreement other than a treaty, any standing, force, or effect under the Constitution of the United States or under international law that it would not have in the absence of the Convention." Letter from Arthur W. Rovine, Assistant Legal Adviser for Treaty Affairs, to Michael J. Glennon, Legal Counsel, Senate Foreign Relations Committee (May 2, 1977) (on file with author).

[150] During the Nixon Administration, the Department of State proposed a substitute statement for those considered by the Committee, *supra* note 142, which would have provided that "ratification of the Convention by the United States does not give any international agreement of the United States any internal standing under the Constitution of the United States that it would not have in the absence of the Convention." Letter from Marshall Wright, *supra* note 144, *reprinted in* A. Rovine, *supra* note 121, at 197.

advance the cause of constitutionalism, but it does thwart the advance of an international compact of signal importance in harmonizing international expectations, a compact that was accurately described as "a giant step for mankind toward a world in which the rule of law will be not a dream but a reality."[151]

Conclusion

If the Constitution were written today, the treaty clause might be written differently. We might reflect long and hard on whether senators representing 7 percent of the population—the seventeen least populous states—ought to be able to defeat a treaty. Perhaps approval by a majority of both houses, or of just the Senate, would be more sensible.[152] But that is not what the Constitution provides.

Professor Philip Kurland states the heart of the matter: "Should the Constitution really be read to mean that by calling an agreement an executive agreement rather than a treaty, the obligation to secure Senate approval is dissolved?"[153] The Ford[154] and Reagan[155] Administrations seemed to answer the question in the affirmative, having asserted unfettered discretion in the President to select the form of agreement. Professor Louis Henkin provides a persuasive answer to this assertion that "the President is constitutionally free to make any agreement on any matter involving our relations with another country."[156] He replies: "As a matter of constitutional construction . . . that view is unacceptable, for it would wholly remove the 'check' of Senate consent which the Framers struggled and compromised to write into the Constitution."[157]

Drawing the line is no easy task. A strong case can be made, however, that unless the treaty clause is to be rendered meaningless, agreements of exceptional national importance that do not "[deal] with [a] matter that falls within [the President's] independent powers under the Constitution," cannot be en-

[151] Kearney & Dalton, *supra* note 120, at 561.

[152] *See* B. Loeb, *Treaty Clause: Too much power in too few hands*, The Sacramento Bee, Feb. 28, 1988, at 5 (Forum Section).

[153] Kurland, *The Impotence of Reticence*, 1968 Duke L.J. 619, 626.

[154] *See* Memorandum of the Department of State Legal Adviser (Leigh), Oct. 6, 1975, and memorandum of the Senate Legislative Counsel (Glennon), Oct. 22, 1975, concerning constitutionality of the "Sinai accords," 14 I.L.M. 1593 (1975); 1 M. Glennon & T. Franck, United States Foreign Relations Law: Documents and Sources 295 (1980).

[155] *See* Crime of Genocide, Hearing Before the Comm. on Foreign Relations, U.S. Senate, 99TH Cong., 1st Sess. 178 (1985) (assertion of Dep'ts of State and Justice that President has constitutional power to conclude international agreements pursuant to "[t]he President's authority as Chief Executive to represent the nation in foreign affairs. . . .").

[156] L. Henkin, Foreign Affairs and the Constitution 179 (1972) (footnotes omitted).

[157] *Id.*

tered into by the President acting alone. Professor Edgar Bodenheimer has observed that the Framers were aware of the distinction in international law between treaties and compacts, and intended "as a general rule [to] leave executed agreements of a minor nature, transient interest, or short obligation, and not involving the imposition of substantial legal obligations of the United States, in the hands of the President, to be dealt with by means of an executive agreement."[158] The *Restatement* observes that "[s]ome agreements, such as the United Nations Charter or the North Atlantic Treaty, are of sufficient formality, dignity, and importance that, in the unlikely event that the President attempted to make such an agreement on his own authority, his lack of authority might be regarded as 'manifest.' "[159] The Senate Foreign Relations Committee was correct: "The Treaty Clause requires that, normally, significant international commitments be made with the concurrence of two-thirds of the Senate. Acting on the basis of his sole constitutional power, the President would be without the power to enter into such an agreement."[160] Insignificant agreements directed at acts falling outside the President's exclusive powers might be made by the President without Senate concurrence, but others should be seen as falling within the "negative implications" of the treaty clause—as prohibited, absent Senate advice and consent.

Conclusion

Critics of the American brand of constitutionalism argue that, at least in the realm of international agreement making, a unitary decisional authority would be more effective. One voice, they argue, can command respect; many voices generate confusion.

They are correct. The United States pays a price for its system, a price paid consciously but nonetheless a price.

On the other hand, critics of the international legal order contend that its rules hinder the ability of states, however enlightened, to structure their domestic legal systems as they deem best. The international order, they argue in particular, provides disincentives to the maintenance of a system of separate powers.

They too are correct. International law has no compulsory enforcement organs, at least none analogous to those of domestic legal systems. However, it does define norms of acceptable diplomatic conduct and in so doing, discourages the establishment of governmental structures that are more likely to transgress those norms through diplomatic maladroitness. Indeed, it could hardly do otherwise while remaining true to the objective of facilitating international intercourse with a juridical framework.

[158] E. Bodenheimer, Jurisprudence § 71 at 339 (1974).

[159] Restatement, § 311, Comment *c*.

[160] Exec. Rept. No. 95-12, 95th Cong., 2d Sess. (Panama Canal Treaties).

But both sets of critics are seriously wrong in assuming that neither system can achieve its ends without undercutting the other. The Constitution does not demand the abandonment of diplomacy any more than international law demands a surrender of sovereignty. Strengthening reciprocal confidence in the United States' relations with other nations depends in good part upon assuring other states that bargains with the United States will be binding. Because the Constitution prescribes a procedure for making such bargains, no such assurance is possible unless that procedure is honored.

While constitutional and international law do not always harmonize, they are thus, in another sense, mutually reinforcing. It is the task of both the diplomat and the constitutionalist to further that reinforcement. Neither can succeed by frustrating the work of the other.

Chapter Six

WAR-MAKING TREATIES

> The values of democracy are in large part the process of democracy—the way in which we pass laws, the way in which we administer justice, the way in which government deals with individuals. When the exigencies of foreign policy are thought to necessitate the suspension of these processes, repeatedly and over a long period of time, such a foreign policy is not only inefficient but utterly irrational and self-defeating.
>
> —J. William Fulbright[1]

IN THE EARLY DAYS of the Republic, perhaps because of the admonitions of respected Founders,[2] perhaps because the new nation had little military might to offer, perhaps because of its precarious geopolitical position, the United States avoided military alliances. As the nation celebrated its bicentennial, however, that practice had changed. Prompted by the advice of experts[3] and armed with the mightiest arsenal ever assembled, the United States found itself enmeshed in a vast network of mutual-security treaties. Seven such pacts now bind it militarily to twenty-five foreign states.

Considerable misunderstanding has arisen concerning the scope of the treaty obligations undertaken by the United States. They seem widely regarded as ironclad guarantees that the United States will automatically come to the defense of a treaty partner under armed attack. This confusion is exemplified by comments made during a debate in the House of Representatives on an amendment prohibiting the introduction of United States armed forces into combat in Nicaragua. One member, opposing the amendment, opined that "[u]nder the Rio Treaty . . . the United States is under a solemn obligation to the signatory states to come to their assistance in the event of an attack."[4] Another opposed the amendment because it denied "to our allies in Central

[1] J. W. Fulbright, The Crippled Giant 208 (1972).

[2] George Washington, in his famous "Farewell Address," urged the country to avoid entangling alliances. 1 J. Richardson, A Compilation of the Messages and Papers of the Presidents 221–23 (1896 ed.). "On the subject of treaties," Thomas Jefferson wrote, "our system is to have none with any nation, as far as can be avoided." 11 T. Jefferson, Writings 38–39 (Bergh ed. 1907).

[3] *See, e.g.*, Kennan ("X"), *The Sources of Soviet Conduct*, 25 Foreign Aff. 561 (1947).

[4] Cong. Rec. H5079 (daily ed. June 27, 1985) (statement of Rep. Kemp).

America any possibility of military assistance . . . under the Rio Treaty of 1947 in the event of an armed attack by Nicaragua against [its] neighbors.''[5]

Also misunderstood is the effect of the treaties upon the allocation of war-making power within the federal government. During the Nicaragua debate, the proposed prohibition expressly exempted any action taken ''in accordance with'' the Rio Treaty.[6] ''[O]bviously,'' the bill's sponsor explained, ''an armed attack against any American state would give authority for the President to act.''[7] One member echoed the views of many House colleagues when he referred to the United States' ''right to act under the full authority vested in the President by the Rio Treaty. . . .''[8] Presidents have also interpreted the security treaties as sources of authority to introduce United States armed forces into hostilities. The Johnson Administration, for example, claimed that the SEATO treaty committed the United States to defend South Vietnam and authorized the President to undertake independent military action toward that end.[9] President Nixon, in vetoing the War Powers Resolution,[10] claimed that it contained prohibitions ''against fulfilling our obligations under the NATO treaty as ratified by the Senate.''[11] President Reagan recently cited the ''serious threat of Communist aggression and subversion'' to Honduras, and told the country's visiting President that ''[t]here should be no doubt that we will fulfill our mutual defense obligation under the Rio Treaty.''[12] His implication seemed clear: The Treaty empowers the President to decide what steps, including the use of military force, should be taken to fulfill the United States' commitment.

These views are seriously mistaken. In mutual-security treaties to which the United States is a party, commitment is a myth. A 1979 report of the Senate Foreign Relations Committee correctly sums up the treaties:

> No mutual security treaty to which the United States currently is a party authorizes the President to introduce the armed forces into hostilities or requires the United States to do so, automatically, if another party to any such treaty is attacked. Each of the treaties provides that it will be carried out by the United States in accordance with its ''constitutional process'' or contains other languages to make clear that

[5] *Id.* at H5076 (statement of Rep. Livingston).

[6] *Id.* at H5063.

[7] *Id.* at H5067 (statement of Rep. Foley).

[8] *Id.* at H5093 (statement of Rep. Hunter).

[9] Memorandum of Leonard C. Meeker, Legal Adviser, Department of State, to the Senate Comm. on Foreign Relations (Mar. 8, 1966), *reprinted in* 54 Dep't St. Bull. 474, 480, 485 (1966). *But see U. S. Commitments to Foreign Powers: Hearings on S. Res. 151 Before the Senate Comm. on Foreign Relations*, 90th Cong., 1st Sess. 75 (1967) (statement of Nicholas deB. Katzenbach, Under Secretary of State, that the treaties ''cannot and do not spell out the precise action which the United States would take in a variety of contingencies. That is left for further decision by the President and the Congress. . . . [N]one of [the treaties] incur automatic response.'').

[10] Pub. L. No. 93-148, 87 Stat. 555 (codified at 50 U.S.C. §§ 1541–1548 [1976]).

[11] *Veto of the War Powers Resolution*, 9 Weekly Compilation Pres. Doc. 1285, 1287 (1973).

[12] N.Y. Times, May 22, 1985, at A5, col. 1.

> the United States' commitment is a qualified one—that the distribution of power within the United States Government is precisely what it would have been in the absence of the treaty, and that the United States reserves the right to determine for itself what military action, if any, is appropriate.[13]

This chapter elaborates that conclusion by exploring three key issues raised by those treaties.

First, can such a treaty constitutionally grant the President war-making power beyond what he would otherwise possess? The next part of this chapter reviews the constitutional text, case law, custom, and the Framers' intent in concluding that a treaty that did so would probably be unconstitutional.

Second, do the treaties confer any such authority upon the President? The answer depends upon the scope of the commitment: If the United States is viewed as having bound itself automatically to intervene if one of its treaty partners is attacked, it is reasonable to infer that the treaty confers such authority upon the President, for under such circumstances, any congressional role would be meaningless. Most frequently the specific presidential authority at issue is the authority to introduce the armed forces into hostilities, but the question also arises in connection with other exercises of presidential war-making power, such as the first use of ''tactical'' nuclear weapons. This chapter concludes that no treaty conferring additional war-making power upon the President is currently in force, a conclusion bolstered by the War Powers Resolution.

Third, if as a matter of law and fact the treaties cannot and do not represent binding military commitments, what do they represent? This chapter explores the treaties' meaning in light of the preceding conclusions.

Constitutionality

Text

The text of the Constitution empowers the President ''by and with the advice and consent of the Senate, to make treaties, provided two-thirds of the Senators present concur. . . .''[14] Yet it also grants to Congress the power ''[t]o declare war,''[15] ''[t]o raise and support armies . . . ,''[16] ''[t]o provide and maintain a navy,''[17] and ''[t]o make rules for the government and regulation of the land and naval forces. . . .''[18] Can these powers be exercised by the President and the Senate in making a treaty? Or are such powers reserved to

[13] S. Rep. No. 7, 96th Cong., 1st Sess. 31 (1979) (Taiwan Enabling Act).

[14] U.S. Const. art. II, § 2, cl. 2.

[15] *Id.* art I, § 8, cl. 11.

[16] *Id.* cl. 12.

[17] *Id.* cl. 13.

[18] *Id.* cl. 14.

Congress, to be exercised either through implementing legislation or a congressional agreement?

In oft-cited language, the Supreme Court seemed to uphold a treaty power of the broadest scope, extending to "any matter which is properly the subject of negotiation with a foreign country."[19] Frequently overlooked, however, is the Court's observation that the treaty power does *not* extend to "authorize what the Constitution forbids, or a change in the character of the government. . . ."[20] That a treaty must comply with the Constitution was reiterated—if it was ever seriously doubted—by Justice Black in *Reid v. Covert*, where a plurality of the Court reaffirmed that the treaty makers must "act in accordance with all the limitations imposed by the Constitution."[21]

The issue, then, is whether a treaty conferring war-making power on the President comports with the Constitution.[22] Because the President cannot confer such authority upon himself, the question does not arise with respect to executive agreements.[23]

Case Law: The Delegation Doctrine

The most pertinent cases are to be found under the heading of the "delegation doctrine." Since the founding of the Republic, prominent members of Congress have believed that the Constitution limits the authority of Congress to

[19] Geofroy v. Riggs, 133 U.S. 258, 267 (1890). *See also* Holden v. Joy, 84 U.S. (17 Wall) 211 (1872); Asakura v. Seattle, 265 U.S. 332 (1924).

[20] Geofroy v. Riggs, 133 U.S. 258, 267 (1890).

[21] 354 U.S. 1, 6 (1954).

[22] The question occasionally has been said to be whether mutual security treaties can be "self-executing." *See, e.g.*, S. Rep. No. 220, 93d Cong., 1st Sess. 26 (1973) (War Powers Resolution). To frame the issue in terms of self-execution, however, misplaces the emphasis. The question is not whether such a treaty could be enforced by the courts without implementing legislation; nonjusticiability obviously could prove an impediment to judicial enforcement. Rather, the issue is how power is allocated as between Congress and the treaty makers.

[23] In connection with Secretary of State Henry Kissinger's appearances before the Senate Foreign Relations Committee on Nov. 19, 1975, Senator Dick Clark submitted the following written question to the Department of State: "Does any executive agreement authorize the introduction of U.S. armed forces into hostilities, or into situations wherein imminent involvement in hostilities is clearly indicated by the circumstances?" The Department responded as follows:

> The answer is "no." Under our constitution, a President may not, by mere executive agreement, confer authority on himself in addition to authority granted by Congress or the Constitution. The existence of an executive agreement with another country does not create additional power. Similarly, no branch of the Government can enlarge its power at the expense of another branch simply by unilaterally asserting enlarged authority. The Supreme Court has limited the powers of the executive just as it has restricted its own authority and that of Congress. The President, for example, could not, solely under his own constitutional authority, validly conclude an executive agreement to extradite a criminal to a foreign nation. *See* Valentine v. U.S. ex rel. Neidecker, 299 U.S. 5 (1936). Also, neither an executive agreement, nor a treaty, may violate the Constitution. *See* Reid v. Covert, 354 U.S. 1, 5–6 (1957).

Letter from Robert J. McCloskey, Assistant Secretary of State for Congressional Relations, to Senator Dick Clark (Mar. 1, 1976) (on file with author).

transfer its war-making power to the Executive. In 1834, President Andrew Jackson requested statutory authorization for reprisals against France if France failed to satisfy claims arising out of attacks on United States shipping during the undeclared naval war between the two countries. The Senate Foreign Relations Committee, in a report apparently adhered to by Senator Henry Clay, recommended against Jackson's request:

> Congress ought to retain to itself the right of judging of the expediency of granting [letters of marque and reprisal] under all the circumstances existing at the time when they are proposed to be actually issued. The committee are not satisfied that Congress can, constitutionally, delegate this right. . . . Congress ought to reserve to itself the constitutional right, which it possesses, of judging of all the circumstances by which such refusal might be attended . . . and of deciding whether, in the actual posture of things as they exist, and looking to the condition of the United States, of France, and of Europe, the issuing of letters of marque and reprisal ought to be authorized, or any other measure adopted.[24]

In 1859, President James Buchanan asked for congressional approval to use land and naval forces to guarantee the neutrality of Colombia and to protect the lives and property of United States citizens in the area. Senator James William Seward answered as follows from the Senate floor:

> Could anything be more strange and preposterous than the idea of the President of the United States making hypothetical wars, conditional wars, without any designation of the nation against which war is to be declared; or the time, or place, or manner, or circumstance of the duration of it, the beginning or the end; and without limiting the number of nations with which war may be waged? No sir. When we pass this bill we do surrender the power of making war or of preserving peace, in each of the States named, into the hands of the President of the United States.[25]

The Supreme Court has long inveighed against the delegation of legislative power to the Executive. "[T]he general rule of law," Justice Story said in 1831, is "that a delegated authority cannot be delegated."[26] Sixty years later, the elder Justice Harlan reaffirmed "[t]hat Congress cannot delegate legislative power to the President. . . ."[27] This precept, he said, is "universally recognized as vital to the integrity and maintenance of the system of government ordained by the Constitution."[28]

Not until the New Deal, however, did the Court actually strike down an act of Congress as violative of the delegation doctrine. In *Panama Refining Co.*

[24] 7 J. Moore, Digest of International Law § 1095, at 127 (1906).

[25] Cong. Globe, 35th Cong., 2d Sess. 1120 (1859).

[26] Shankland v. Washington, 30 U.S. (5 Pet.) 390, 395 (1831).

[27] Field v. Clark, 143 U.S. 649, 692 (1892).

[28] *Id.*

v. Ryan,[29] the Court invalidated a provision of the National Industrial Recovery Act. Although the statute spelled out what action the President could take, it did not delineate the circumstances under which presidential action was permissible. Several months later, the Court struck down a second statutory provision. In *Schecter Poultry Corp. v. United States*,[30] it was the breadth of discretion conferred upon the President that raised problems. The President was given the authority to impose on the poultry industry virtually any regulation he deemed appropriate. "This," Justice Cardozo said in a concurring opinion, was "delegation running riot."[31]

The doctrine deriving from these cases, the "delegation doctrine," has been relied on by a number of authorities who view as unconstitutional any treaty automatically committing United States armed forces to hostilities. "[W]hat can't be done," the late Professor Alexander Bickel testified before the Senate Foreign Relations Committee, "is a generalized commitment. You, England, or France, are our pals, you are our friends, and any time you are in trouble we will help you. That can't be done."[32] "The attempt of Congress to transfer its power and responsibility to make war to the President," Professor Francis D. Wormuth wrote, "is constitutionally unauthorized and destroys the political system envisaged by the framers."[33]

THE DELEGATION DOCTRINE IN FOREIGN RELATIONS

Curtiss-Wright does *not* hold that the delegation doctrine has *no* application to international relations; rather, it does not have *equal* application. The distinction is of obvious importance and has often been overlooked.[34] Thus, the case could be restricted to its facts or at least not extended to "powers to go to war, or to use the armed forces."[35] But it was unnecessary to reach even that ques-

[29] 293 U.S. 388 (1935).

[30] 295 U.S. 495 (1935).

[31] *Id.* at 553 (Cardozo, J., concurring).

[32] War Powers Legislation: Hearings on S. 731, S.J. Res. 18 and S.J. Res. 59 Before the Senate Comm. on Foreign Relations, 92d Cong., 1st Sess. 565 (1979) (statement of Alexander M. Bickel, Professor of Law, Yale University).

[33] Wormuth, *The Vietnam War: The President vs. the Constitution*, in 2 The Vietnam War and International Law 799 (R. Falk ed. 1969). *See also* Lofgren, *War-Making Under the Constitution: The Original Understanding*, 81 Yale L.J. 672 (1972); Berger, *War-Making by a President*, 121 U. Pa. L. Rev. 29 (1972); Berger, *War, Foreign Affairs, and Executive Secrecy*, 72 Nw. U. L. Rev. 309 (1978); Casper, *Constitutional Constraints on the Conduct of Foreign and Defense Policy: A Nonjudicial Model*, 43 U. Chi. L. Rev. 463 (1976).

[34] *See, e.g.*, Patterson, *In re The United States v. Curtiss-Wright Corporation* (pts. 1 & 2), 22 Tex. L. Rev. 286 (1944); Quarles, *The Federal Government: As to Foreign Affairs, Are Its Powers Inherent as Distinguished from Delegated*? 32 Geo. L.J. 375 (1944).

[35] War Powers Legislation: Hearings on S. 731, S.J. Res. 18 and S.J. Res. 59 Before the Senate Comm. on Foreign Relations, 92d Cong., 1st Sess. 555 (1972) (statement of Alexander M. Bickel, Professor of Law, Yale University).

tion. As Professor Bickel suggested, the Court could have found simply that the standards encompassed in the law met delegation requirements.[36]

More important, the central policy reasons underpinning the delegation doctrine militate in favor of applying it to foreign-affairs matters. Justice Rehnquist has said that the delegation doctrine serves three important functions. "First, and most abstractly, it ensures to the extent consistent with orderly governmental administration that important choices of social policy are made by Congress, the branch of our government most responsive to the popular will."[37] It would be hard to imagine a "choice of social policy" more important than the choice to go to war, or the choice, once the armed forces are involved in hostilities, to use nuclear weapons. The responsiveness of Congress (as opposed to that of the Senate and the President) to the popular will apparently represented the precise reason that the Framers placed the decision to go to war in congressional hands.[38] A power allocated to one branch by the Constitution ought not be subject to reassignment to another branch by a vote of Congress, let alone the Senate. This is why the Constitution provides for amendments. There is no apparent reason why that should be less true of a power relating to foreign affairs.

"Second," Justice Rehnquist wrote, "the doctrine guarantees that, to the extent Congress finds it necessary to delegate authority, it provides the recipient of that authority with an intelligible principle to guide the exercise of the delegated discretion."[39] In this sense, the doctrine is not unlike other provisions of the Constitution directed at curbing the exercise of "naked preferences"—the dormant commerce, privileges-and-immunities, equal-protection, due-process, contract, and eminent-domain clauses.[40] The delegation decisions require that Congress "lay down the general policy and standards that animate the law, leaving the agency to refine those standards, [to] fill in the blanks, or [to] apply those standards to particular cases."[41] The exercise of arbitrary power is precluded. This concern seems particularly pertinent in foreign affairs. Given the broad presidential powers in the field, additional uncircumscribed discretion—discretion intended by the Framers to reside in the legislature—would write out of the Constitution any meaningful notion of separation of powers in the realm of foreign relations.

[36] "Whether this assumption was valid at the time," Bickel testified before the Senate Foreign Relations Committee, "is thoroughly questionable. . . . The [law] closely defined what the President was to do, and where he was to do it. . . . This was hardly delegation running riot. . . ." *Id.*

[37] Industrial Union Dep't v. American Petroleum Inst., 448 U.S. 607, 685 (1980) (Rehnquist, J., concurring).

[38] *See infra* notes 84–89 and accompanying text.

[39] *Industrial Union Dep't*, 448 U.S. at 685–86.

[40] *See* Sunstein, *Naked Preferences and the Constitution*, 84 Colum. L. Rev. 1689 (1984).

[41] *Industrial Union Dep't*, 448 U.S. at 675.

"Third, and derivative of the second," Rehnquist wrote, "the doctrine ensures that courts charged with reviewing the exercise of delegated legislative discretion will be able to test that exercise against ascertainable standards."[42] Because the courts have traditionally played a lesser role in foreign affairs, this consideration may be less relevant, although it clearly is not without some application.[43]

The reasons for exempting foreign-affairs powers from the operation of the delegation doctrine are thus less than compelling. The Court has backed steadily away from the exception suggested by *Curtiss-Wright*. The first major step was taken in 1952 with *Youngstown Sheet & Tube v. Sawyer*,[44] the famous *Steel Seizure Case*. President Truman justified the seizure on the ground that the continued operation of the steel mills was necessary for the successful continuation of the war effort in Korea and was therefore permitted under his powers as commander in chief. The Court rejected the argument and held that President Truman's action in effect represented an exercise of *legislative* authority. No examination was made of congressional enactments (such as defense authorization or appropriation acts) from which delegation might conceivably have been inferred. Nor was any reference made to powers that President Truman might have derived from the nation's "sovereignty" or from the "law of nations." Indeed, no reference was made to *Curtiss-Wright*.

Six years later, the Court moved further from Justice Sutherland's constitutional exegesis. In *Kent v. Dulles*,[45] the Court invalidated a passport revocation as beyond the statutory authority of the Secretary of State. If the "power is [to be] delegated," the Court said, "the standards must be adequate to pass scrutiny by the accepted tests."[46] In that case, as in the *Steel Seizure Case*, the Court indicated its willingness to invalidate acts of the Executive in foreign affairs.

CURRENT VIABILITY OF THE DELEGATION DOCTRINE

The invalidation of executive acts notwithstanding, no federal statute has been struck down through application of the delegation doctrine in fifty years.[47]

[42] *Id*. at 686.

[43] The "foreign affairs" cases decided by the Supreme Court are not so few as some might think. *See, e.g.*, M. Glennon & T. Franck, 5 United States Foreign Relations Law (1980) (setting forth cases).

[44] 343 U.S. 579 (1952).

[45] 357 U.S. 116 (1958).

[46] *Id*. at 129.

[47] The reasons are not hard to guess. The doctrine smacks of substantive due process, admitting of limited possibility for principled application and permitting statutory invalidation for reasons having less to do with the Constitution than with gastronomically derived notions of public policy. It is guilt by association: like substantive due process, it is remembered largely as a tool of jurid-

Although rumors of the doctrine's death have been frequently reported,[48] they are probably exaggerated. In the 1980 *Benzene Case*,[49] the plurality opinion relied upon the delegation doctrine in construing narrowly a federal statute conferring rule-making authority on the Secretary of Labor.[50] Justice Rehnquist, concurring, argued that the statute should have been invalidated through use of the doctrine.[51] He repeated the opinion the following term in the *Cotton Dust Case* and was joined by the Chief Justice.[52] On at least two occasions, Justice Brennan expressed a measure of approval for continued application of the doctrine.[53] It is one thing to use the doctrine as a canon of statutory construction and quite another to employ it as a criterion of validity; some justices willing to do the latter would doubtless agree on the doctrine's applicability in a given case. Nonetheless, it is not farfetched to believe that in the right case, for the right purpose, the doctrine could indeed command a majority of the current Supreme Court.[54]

However, in three recent passport cases—*Zemel v. Rusk*,[55] *Haig v. Agee*,[56] and *Wald v. Regan*[57]—the Court once again relied upon the *Curtiss-Wright* notion of generalized deference to the President. Chief Justice Warren noted in *Zemel* that "Congress—in giving the President authority over matters of foreign affairs—must of necessity paint with a brush broader than customarily it wields in domestic areas."[58] The Chief Justice reiterated, however, that *Curtiss-Wright* did "not mean that simply because a statute deals with foreign relations, it can grant the Executive totally unrestricted freedom of choice."[59]

---

ical reactionaries who sought to write Herbert Spencer's *Social Statics* into the Constitution. (That it has also received the approbation of judicial progressives has often escaped notice. *See, e.g.*, W. Douglas, Go East Young Man 217 (1974); Wright, *Beyond Discretionary Justice*, 81 Yale L.J. 575, 582–87 [1972].)

[48] *See, e.g.*, Eastlake v. Forest City Enterprises, Inc., 426 U.S. 668, 675 (1978) (Marshall, J., concurring). *See generally* Schwartz, *Of Administrators and Philosopher-Kings: The Republic, the Laws, and Delegations of Power*, 72 Nw. U. L. Rev. 443 (1978).

[49] Industrial Union Dep't v. Am. Petroleum Inst., 448 U.S. 607 (1980).

[50] *Id.*

[51] *Id.* at 687 (Rehnquist, J., concurring).

[52] American Textiles Mfrs. Inst. v. Donovan, 452 U.S. 490, 543 (1981) (Rehnquist, J., dissenting).

[53] California Bankers Ass'n v. Schultz, 416 U.S. 21, 91 (1974) (Brennan, J., dissenting); United States v. Robel, 389 U.S. 258, 272–73 (1967) (Brennan, J., concurring).

[54] *See* Note, *Rethinking the Nondelegation Doctrine*, 62 B.U. L. Rev. 257, 311–20 (1982) (suggesting that recent Supreme Court decisions indicate the doctrine's resurrection).

[55] 381 U.S. 1 (1964).

[56] 453 U.S. 280 (1981).

[57] 468 U.S. 222 (1984).

[58] 381 U.S. at 17.

[59] *Id.* Justice Black, dissenting, would have overturned the statute as an invalid delegation. *Id.* at 20–22.

The great deference shown by the Court to the independent constitutional powers of the President in foreign affairs heightens doubts about the continued viability of the delegation doctrine in foreign affairs. Nevertheless, delegating authority to the Executive to limit the international travel of private citizens is fundamentally different from conferring congressional war-making power on the President. If the magnitude of relevant social choices represents one criterion, then the policy considerations are manifestly incomparable: That an aspect of the foreign commerce power happens to be delegable says little or nothing about the delegability of central elements of the war power.

Whether there is a war-powers exception from the delegation doctrine is unclear. In *Dames & Moore v. Regan*,[60] the Iran claims-settlement agreement was upheld through the application of the analytical framework developed in the *Steel Seizure Case*.[61] The majority opinion made no reference to *Curtiss-Wright* or to any notion of presidential power deriving from sovereignty or the law of nations.

More important, perhaps, is the Court's 1983 opinion in *Immigration and Naturalization Service v. Chadha*.[62] In invalidating use of the "legislative veto," the Court mandated that Congress must adhere strictly to constitutionally required procedures for the enactment of legislation. "Convenience and efficiency"—apparently considerations foremost on Justice Sutherland's mind in upholding the broad delegation in *Curtiss-Wright*—were insufficient to save a statute "contrary to the Constitution." "Convenience and efficiency . . . are not the primary objectives—or the hallmarks—of democratic government."[63]

On the other hand, *Chadha* may be seen as reflecting the Supreme Court's indifference to the delegation doctrine. In some cases, the legislative veto was the only check on the unbridled exercise of presidential powers; its absence might be viewed in those instances as a standardless delegation of legislative power. Justice White's dissent noted that the majority opinion invalidated a number of "foreign affairs" vetos,[64] including those present in legislation concerning war powers[65] and arms exports.[66] A Court concerned about reju-

[60] 453 U.S. 654 (1981).

[61] 343 U.S. 579 (1952).

[62] 462 U.S. 919 (1983).

[63] *Id.* at 944.

[64] *Id.* at 967–68 (White, J., dissenting).

[65] *Id.* at 971 (White, J., dissenting). *See* War Powers Resolution, Pub. L. No. 93–148, 87 Stat. 555 (1973) (codified at 50 U.S.C. § 1541 [1976]).

[66] *Chadha*, 462 U.S. at 971 (White, J., dissenting). *See* International Security Assistance and Arms Export Control Act of 1976, Pub. L. No. 94–329, 90 Stat. 729 (codified at 22 U.S.C. § 2776(b)). *See* Chapter 3 on the legislative veto in the War Powers Resolution.

venating the delegation doctrine would seemingly go about the task differently.[67]

If the state of the delegation doctrine is confused as it applies to domestic affairs, it is thus thoroughly confused as it applies to foreign affairs. Yet one thing is clear: To whatever extent the doctrine has continued vitality, no persuasive reasons have been advanced to exempt from its application questions of war-making authority. And alive or not, the Framers' clear intent to include the House of Representatives in any decision to go to war would raise serious doubts about the validity of any treaty purporting to impose an "automatic" commitment on the United States to use armed force.

Custom

It is said that the United States has never been a party to such a treaty.[68] This appears to be correct; as indicated below, the United States is not currently a party to any such treaty[69] and evidently never has been.

On the other hand, presidents have argued on occasion that a treaty conferred discretionary authority to introduce the armed forces into hostilities to enforce the terms of that treaty. The position was not that such introduction was required but that it was permitted. Although not always articulated this way, the claim might have been that the Constitution required that the President "take care that the laws be faithfully executed"[70] and that treaties constitute law for purposes of the faithful-execution clause. Thus, in 1818, President Monroe placed some reliance upon a treaty with Spain when sending troops into Florida.[71] President Theodore Roosevelt's Secretary of War relied upon a provision of a 1904 treaty with Cuba (the infamous "Platt Amendment")[72] when Roosevelt dispatched the armed forces to that island in 1906.[73] And in 1966, the State Department relied in part upon the SEATO Treaty[74] as support for military involvement in South Vietnam.[75]

[67] It might also be pointed out that the most recent passport case, Regan v. Wald, 468 U.S. 222 (1984), was decided after *Chadha*. Had the Court in *Chadha* intended to resurrect the delegation doctrine, one might have expected it to evidence that intent in a case such as *Wald*, which could, one presumes, have fallen into line with Kent v. Dulles, 357 U.S. 116 (1958), rather than Zemel v. Rusk, 381 U.S. 1 (1964), and Haig v. Agee, 453 U.S. 280 (1981).

[68] L. Henkin, Foreign Affairs and the Constitution 160 (1972) ("no treaty has ever been designed to put the United States into a state of war without a declaration by Congress").

[69] *See* the discussion of the current treaties' text and history, *infra* this chapter.

[70] U.S. Const. art. II, § 3.

[71] 2 Messages and Papers of the Presidents 1789–1897, at 31–32 (J. Richardson ed. 1897).

[72] *See* Papers Relating to the Foreign Relations of the United States, Doc. 1, 58th Cong. 3d Sess. 244 (1905).

[73] W. H. Taft, Our Chief Magistrate and His Powers 87–88 (1916).

[74] *See supra* n. 9.

[75] 54 Dep't St. Bull. 474, 485 (1966).

As a constitutional matter, it is doubtful that the faithful-execution clause can serve as support for presidential introduction of the armed forces into hostilities to carry out treaties. Although a variety of interpretations are possible,[76] the Framers apparently intended to limit presidential enforcement power to laws resulting from legislative action.[77] Assuming *arguendo* a custom of reliance upon the clause for such purposes, such a construction has hardly gone unchallenged in Congress. Following President Wilson's reliance upon the clause in 1917 when ordering the arming of United States commercial shipping,[78] the Chairman of the Senate Foreign Relations Committee argued that Wilson's construction would rob the congressional war-making power of all meaning:

> I cannot consent that this clause confers, or was ever intended to confer, power upon the President to determine an issue between this Nation and some other sovereignty—an issue involving questions of international law—and to proceed to employ the Army and Navy to enforce his decision. A contrary view would clearly place the war making power in the hands of the President.[79]

Similar objections were voiced in Congress following executive reliance upon the SEATO Treaty during the Vietnam War.[80] Because a custom is without constitutional relevance unless, at a minimum, acquiesced in by the other branch and because acquiescence requires an absence of objection,[81] it is doubtful that any custom of executive reliance upon the faithful-execution clause to justify treaty enforcement has achieved constitutional legitimacy.

Finally, the terms of the treaties belie any intent to provide such authority. As noted below, each treaty qualifies the United States commitment with a reference to the parties' constitutional processes;[82] the effect is to leave the allocation of power as it would have been in the absence of the treaty.[83] It therefore seems doubtful that any constitutionally cognizable custom has developed that would permit an inference of presidential war-making power from either ''automatic'' commitments or the faithful-execution clause as applied to treaties.

[76] *See* Chapter 6.

[77] Madison referred to the President's power to execute ''the national laws.'' 1 Madison, The Constitutional Convention of 1787, at 52–53 (Hunt ed. 1908).

[78] 54 Cong. Rec. 4273 (1917).

[79] 54 Cong. Rec. 4884 (1917) (comments of Sen. Stone).

[80] *See e.g.*, U.S. Commitments to Foreign Powers: Hearings on S. Res. 151 Before the Senate Comm. on Foreign Relations, 90th Cong., 1st Sess. 205 (1967) (comments of Sens. Fulbright and Ervin).

[81] *See e.g.*, Myers v. United States, 272 U.S. 52, 163 (1926); United States v. Midwest Oil, 236 U.S. 458, 481 (1914).

[82] *See* the discussion of the current treaties' text and history, *infra* this chapter.

[83] *See infra* notes, 146, 157, 177, 180.

Intent of the Framers

''A treaty may not declare war,'' the Senate Foreign Relations Committee said in its report on the Panama Canal Treaties, ''because the unique legislative history of the declaration-of-war clause . . . clearly indicates that that power was intended to reside jointly in the House of Representatives and the Senate.''[84] The events the Committee referred to are recorded in Madison's notes of the Philadelphia convention. Alexander Hamilton submitted a plan that would have empowered the Executive ''to make war or peace, with the advice of the Senate.''[85] After the Committee of Detail recommended instead that the war power be given to Congress, Hamilton's ally, Charles Pinckney, again proposed that the power should reside in the Senate:

> Mr. Pinckney opposed the vesting [of] this power in the Legislature. Its proceedings were too slow. It would meet but once a year. The House of Representatives would be too numerous for such deliberations. The Senate would be the best depositary [*sic*], being more acquainted with foreign affairs, and most capable of proper resolutions. If the States are equally represented in the Senate, so as to give no advantage to large States, the power will notwithstanding be safe, as the small have their all at stake in such cases as well as the large States. It would be singular for one authority to make war, another peace.[86]

Sentiment opposing the Hamilton-Pinckney position was overwhelming. Oliver Elseworth and George Mason argued that the concurrence of both houses of Congress should be required to declare war because only the Senate's approval was required for peace treaties, and it should be easier to get out of war than into it. Mason further argued that the Senate was ''not so constructed as to be entitled to'' the war power.[87] Pierce Butler added that Pinckney's concerns about the institutional shortcomings of the House applied equally to the Senate.[88] Apparently Pinckney's proposal died for lack of a second. Speaking nine years later as a member of the House of Representatives, Madison pithily summarized his own objection to the view embodied in the defeated proposal: ''Congress, in case the President and Senate should enter into an alliance for war, would be nothing more than the mere heralds for proclaiming it.''[89] In

[84] S. Exec. Rep. No. 12, 95th Cong. 2d Sess. 65 (1978).

[85] 1 The Records of the Federal Convention of 1787, at 300 (M. Farrand rev. ed. 1937) (hereinafter cited as M. Farrand).

[86] 2 M. Farrand, *supra* note 85, at 318.

[87] *Id.* at 319.

[88] *Id.* at 318–19.

[89] 1 T. Benton, Abridgment of the Debates of Congress 650–51 (1857). It should be noted, however, that Madison also opposed including within the treaty power any act within the constitutional authority of Congress—a view that would leave virtually nothing on which the treaty power might operate and which has long since been rejected.

sum, then, it appears that the Framers explicitly decided not to confer upon the Senate the power to declare war.

United States Mutual-Security Treaties: Text and Legislative History

Owing perhaps to these vexing constitutional questions, the mutual-security treaties entered into by the United States at the conclusion of World War II made clear that no party was committed automatically to come to the defense of any other party. With regard to the United States, the legislative history on this point underscored the treaties' texts and also made clear that none of the treaties was intended to confer upon the President any war-making power that he would not have had in the treaties' absence. Legislative intent is always problematic;[90] nonetheless, an examination of the text and legislative history of those treaties is illuminating. Initially, however, it is worth looking briefly at the treaty that raised the issue for the first time during the postwar period—the United Nations Charter.[91]

The concerns took several forms.[92] One general concern was that the United States could not constitutionally place its armed forces at the disposal of an international organization such as the United Nations, which might cause those forces to be introduced into hostilities without presidential or congressional consent. A variation on that theme, which would recur in debates on mutual-security treaties, was that a treaty could not automatically commit United States armed forces to hostilities as the United Nations Charter arguably did when it required member states to make their forces available for use by the Security Council. This, it was said, could be done only with congressional concurrence.

At least with respect to the United Nations Charter, none of these concerns was justified. Members of the United Nations do agree to accept and carry out the decisions of the Security Council,[93] and measures involving the use of armed force may be undertaken by the Security Council.[94] But absent express agreement with a given member, the Security Council is authorized only to decide upon measures "not involving the use of armed force."[95] Moreover, the only forces available are forces of those members states that have entered into an agreement with the Security Council governing the use of those

[90] *See* Note, *Statutory Interpretation*, 43 Harv. L. Rev. 863 (1930), for the argument that it is unrealistic to talk about the collective intent of a legislative body, which is normally undiscoverable. For a response see Dickerson, *Statutory Interpretation: A Peek in the Mind and Will of a Legislature*, 60 Ind. L.J. 206 (1975).

[91] U.N. Charter, June 26, 1945, 59 Stat. 1031, T.S. No. 993, 3 Bevans 1153.

[92] *See* 91 Cong. Rec. 7118 (1945) (address by President Harry S. Truman).

[93] U.N. Charter art. 25.

[94] *Id*. art. 42.

[95] *Id*. art. 41.

forces.[96] The Charter requires that members enter into agreements with the Security Council to make their forces available to it,[97] but "on the initiative of the Security Council."[98] It also provides that such agreements "shall be subject to ratification by the signatory states in accordance with their respective constitutional processes."[99]

It was this last provision on which Senate debate centered. In testimony before the Senate Foreign Relations Committee, John Foster Dulles, who had been a member of the United States delegation at San Francisco, said that this provision was understood to contemplate the use of treaties.[100] On the Senate floor, several senators suggested that he misspoke; a treaty, they contended, would not be required.[101] Others disagreed.[102] The Chairman of the Senate Foreign Relations Committee, Senator Tom Connally, answered that it was premature to debate the question because the issue would be decided when such an agreement was actually concluded.[103] A message from President Truman, indicating that he would "ask the Congress for appropriate legislation to approve" any such agreement, caused some Senators to voice concern.[104] A statute governing United States involvement in the United Nations, the United Nations Participation Act,[105] was ultimately enacted requiring congressional approval of such an agreement.[106]

Finally, of course, the United States may exercise a veto against such action.[107] This was presented by administration spokesmen as a constitutional safeguard[108] and was so perceived by various senators.[109] It has been argued that the veto is inadequate because the United States representative may not be present when such a measure is voted on. This is true but irrelevant; the President might be unavailable to exercise his veto over certain legislation, but his absence could hardly imply a *constitutional* defect. Procedure can provide only opportunity; it cannot guarantee that an opportunity will be used.

These constitutional objections to the Charter thus appear without merit.

[96] *Id.* art. 43, para. 2.

[97] *Id.* art. 43, para. 1.

[98] *Id.* art. 43, para. 3.

[99] *Id.*

[100] The Charter of the United Nations: Hearings Before the Senate Comm. on Foreign Relations, 79th Cong., 1st Sess. 653 (1945).

[101] *See, e.g.*, 91 Cong. Rec. 8021 (remarks of Sen. Lucas) (1945); *id.* at 8022 (remarks of Sen. Fulbright).

[102] *See, e.g.*, *id.* at 8025 (remarks of Sen. Taft).

[103] *Id.* at 8029.

[104] *See, e.g.*, *id.* at 8185 (remarks of Sen. Donnell).

[105] 22 U.S.C. § 287 (1945).

[106] 22 U.S.C. § 287(a) (1945).

[107] U.N. Charter art. 27, para. 3.

[108] *The Charter of the United Nations: Hearings Before the Senate Comm. on Foreign Relations*, 79th Cong., 1st Sess. 298 (1945) (statement by Leo Pasvolsky, Special Assistant to the Secretary of State for International Organization and Security Affairs).

[109] *See., e.g.*, 91 Cong. Rec. 6876 (1945) (remarks of Sen. Connally).

They are usefully borne in mind, however, in assessing the arguments made in connection with the United States' mutual-security treaties, which are examined below in chronological order.

The Rio Treaty

The first mutual security treaty entered into by the United States after World War II was the Inter-American Treaty of Reciprocal Assistance,[110] the "Rio Treaty." Twenty-three Western Hemisphere nations are parties.[111]

When the Treaty was being negotiated, classified communications within the Department of State indicated an intent to "[s]pecify satisfactory procedures for reaching majority decisions in the consultations called for under the treaty that will not bind the United States without its consent."[112] It was recognized that "[a]greement in principle to the inclusion in the treaty of a provision for concrete action in event of armed attack does not make the difficult problem of wording such a provision much easier."[113] It was suggested that such a treaty would be "essentially political rather than military."[114]

The Treaty meets these specifications. The parties "agree that an armed attack by any State against an American State shall be considered as an attack against all the American States and, consequently, each one of the said Contracting Parties undertakes to assist in meeting the attack. . . ."[115] Unlike subsequent mutual-security treaties to which the United States became a party, this commitment is not qualified by language suggesting that it will be carried out in accordance with the "constitutional processes" of each party; the only reference to constitutional processes occurs in connection with the ratification provision.[116] The commitment is qualified by a provision stating that "each one of the Contracting Parties may determine the immediate measures which it may individually take in fulfillment of the obligation" referred to above.[117] Yet this applies only until the "Organ of Consultation" meets and "agree[s]

[110] Inter-American Treaty of Reciprocal Assistance, *opened for signature* Sept. 2, 1947, 62 Stat. 1681, T.I.A.S. No. 1838, 21 U.N.T.S. 77 (hereinafter cited as Rio Treaty).

[111] Current parties are Argentina, the Bahamas, Bolivia, Brazil, Chile, Colombia, Costa Rica, Cuba, the Dominican Republic, Ecuador, El Salvador, Guatemala, Haiti, Honduras, Mexico, Nicaragua, Panama, Paraguay, Peru, Trinidad and Tobago, the United States, Uruguay, and Venezuela. U.S. Dep't of State, Treaties in Force 229 (1985).

[112] Cable from the Assistant Secretary of State for American Republic Affairs (Braden) to the Under Secretary of State (Acheson), May 29, 1947 (Secret), *reprinted in* 8 U.S. Dep't of State, Foreign Relations of the United States 1 (1947).

[113] Memorandum by the Chief of the Division of Special Inter-American Affairs (Dreier), June 25, 1947 (Confidential), *reprinted in id.* at 5.

[114] Telegram from the Chargé in Ecuador (Shaw) to the Secretary of State, July 7, 1947 (Restricted), *reprinted in id.* at 12.

[115] Rio Treaty, *supra* note 120, art. 3, § 1.

[116] "This treaty . . . shall be ratified by the Signatory States as soon as possible in accordance with their respective constitutional processes." *Id.* art 23.

[117] *Id.* art. 3, § 2.

upon the measures of a collective character that should be taken."[118] Such decisions are taken by a vote of two-thirds of the parties.[119] All parties are bound to apply measures including recalling chiefs of diplomatic missions; breaking of diplomatic or consular relations; and interruption of economic relations or of rail, air, sea, postal, telegraphic, telephonic, or radio communications.[120] However, "no State shall be required to use armed force without its consent."[121]

This final provision set the tone for discussion of the constitutional ramifications that took place in the Senate, although the "escape clause" was downplayed in initial communications to the Senate Foreign Relations Committee. The report of Acting Secretary of State Robert A. Lovett to President Truman, which was transmitted to the Senate, stressed that each party to the Treaty would incur an *obligation*.[122]

In response to questions from the Senate Foreign Relations Committee, however, the State Department took a somewhat softer line. Assistant Secretary of State Norman Armour testified in executive session that, "[i]n the event of . . . attack, the parties to the treaty are bound to extend such immediate individual assistance to the attacked state as each party considers necessary. . . ."[123] He reiterated that the United States could not be required to use force without its consent.[124] The Senate Foreign Relations Committee con-

[118] *Id.*

[119] *Id.* art. 17.

[120] *Id.* arts. 20, 8.

[121] *Id.* art 20.

[122] [E]ach of the parties obligates itself to take affirmative action to assist in meeting an armed attack. This important provision converts the *right* of individual and collective self-defense, as recognized in the United Nations Charter, into an *obligation* under this treaty. The provision for immediate assistance is applicable to all cases of armed attack taking place within the territory of an American state. . . .

Letter of Acting Secretary of State to President Transmitting Rio Treaty, 17 Dep't St. Bull. 1189–90 (1947) (emphasis in original). This was transmitted to the Senate by President Truman. President's Message to Senate Transmitting Rio Treaty, *id.* at 1188.

[123] Inter-American Treaty of Reciprocal Assistance: Hearings Before the Senate Comm. on Foreign Relations (Historical Series), 80th Cong., 1st Sess. 126, 127 (1947) (statement of Norman Armour, Assistant Secretary of State).

[124] *Id.* at 129. Senator Connally asked General Matthew B. Ridgway, also representing the administration, about the scope of that discretion:

SENATOR CONNALLY [I]n the case of an attack by one American State against another . . . [w]hile the obligation to us is to immediately come to the assistance of the attackee, we have to choose our own measures for that purpose, is that right?

GENERAL RIDGWAY Yes, sir.

SENATOR CONNALLY In the case of an attack from without into the zone, we are obligated, are we not, to come to the assistance of the attacked State, and use arms?

GENERAL RIDGWAY No, the same obligation attaches, sir. We can choose the method by which we implement the obligation to assist in meeting that attack. We are not obligated to employ armed forces there, either.

Id.

cluded that in the event of an armed attack, "we would be called upon to extend immediate assistance to the state attacked."[125] But it added: "The character and amount of this assistance would be determined by our Government."[126] "In no case, however, would we be required to use our armed forces without our consent."[127]

On the Senate floor, the scope of the Treaty's obligation was further discussed. Senator Connally explained that "it is left to the discretion and wish of each of the nations to adopt such measures as it may approve in carrying out the obligation to assist the victim of the attack."[128] Senator Donnell was concerned with ambiguities in the Treaty's text and wondered whether a reservation might be appropriate to make clear that the United States would be under no obligation to use armed force.[129] Senators Vandenberg and Connally assured Senator Donnell that the Treaty was clear enough. "The total opinion remains with each individual signatory, without any limitation or instruction," Senator Vandenberg said.[130] "[A]ll through the treaty," Senator Connally said, "it is specific that even in the first instance each nation shall determine its own measures of meeting attack, which would mean that it would not have to adopt military action unless it so desired."[131] Senator Donnell then indicated that he was content to accept the Senator's views, and no reservation was offered.[132] Senator Millikin, who later cast the sole vote against the Treaty,[133] chided Senator Vandenberg for the apparent inconsistency in his position,[134] but the Senate appeared satisfied with the explanation. The Senate consented to ratification of the Treaty by a vote of 72 to 1.[135]

The NATO Treaty

The concern expressed during consideration of the Rio Treaty that the United States might be swept into war without deliberation was reflected in the draft-

[125] S. Exec. Rep. No. 11, 80th Cong., 1st Sess. 11 (1947), *reprinted in* 1947 U.S. Code Cong. & Ad. News.

[126] *Id.*

[127] *Id.*

[128] 93 Cong. Rec. 11,124 (1947).

[129] *Id.* at 11,128.

[130] *Id.*

[131] *Id.* at 11,129.

[132] *Id.*

[133] *Id.* at 11,137.

[134] The colloquy was as follows:

MR. MILLIKIN I suggest to the Senator that there is no point in having a cake if you do not eat it.

MR. VANDENBERG After you have eaten it, as I understand it, it has disappeared.

MR. MILLIKIN It has disappeared, but if you do not eat it what is the use of having it?

Id. at 11,131.

[135] *Id.* at 11,137.

ing of the NATO Treaty.[136] The reference to "constitutional processes" in the NATO Treaty is linked directly to the central commitment. The Treaty provides that "its provisions [shall be] carried out by the Parties in accordance with their respective constitution processes."[137] The principal provision referred to is undoubtedly that of article 5:

> The Parties agree that an armed attack against one or more of them in Europe or North America shall be considered an attack against them all; and consequently they agree that, if such an attack occurs, each of them, in exercise of the right of individual or collective self-defense, . . . will assist the Party or Parties so attacked by taking forthwith . . . such action *as it deems necessary*, including the use of armed force, to restore and maintain the security of the North Atlantic area.[138]

The terms make it clear that no nation is committed to introduce its armed forces into hostilities; it may do so if it deems such action necessary, but such introduction is not required. That this is the intended interpretation emerges from every level of consideration of the Treaty in the United States.

The day the text of the proposed NATO Treaty was made public, Secretary of State Dean Acheson addressed the nation. The Treaty, he said, "does not mean that the United States would be automatically at war if one of the nations covered by the pact is subjected to armed attack. Under our constitution, the Congress alone has the power to declare war."[139]

In his letter transmitting the treaty to President Truman, Secretary Acheson again emphasized that the United States would reserve the right to determine what action the Treaty required:

> The obligation upon each Party is to use its honest judgment as to the action it deems necessary to restore and maintain . . . security and accordingly to take such action as it deems necessary. Such action might not include the use of armed force depending upon the circumstances and gravity of the attack. . . . Each Party retains for itself the right of determination as to whether an armed attack has in fact occurred and what action it deems necessary to take. . . .
>
> This does not mean that the United States would automatically be at war if we or one of the other Parties to the Treaty were attacked. Under our Constitution, only the Congress can declare war. The United States would be obligated by the Treaty to take promptly the action which it deemed necessary to restore and main-

[136] North Atlantic Treaty, Apr. 4, 1949, 63 Stat. 2241, T.I.A.S. No. 1964, 34 U.N.T.S. 243 (hereinafter cited as NATO). Current parties to the treaty are Belgium, Canada, Denmark, France, the Federal Republic of Germany, Greece, Iceland, Italy, Luxembourg, the Netherlands, Norway, Portugal, Spain, Turkey, the United Kingdom, and the United States. U.S. Dep't of State, Treaties in Force 274 (1985).

[137] NATO, *supra* note 136, art. 11.

[138] *Id.* art. 5 (emphasis added).

[139] Address by Secretary of State Acheson delivered on Mar. 18, 1949, over the combined networks of the Columbia and Mutual Broadcasting Systems, 20 Dep't St. Bull. 384–88 (1949).

tain the security of the North Atlantic area. That decision as to what action was necessary would naturally be taken in accordance with our constitutional processes.[140]

This analysis was transmitted to the Senate by President Truman on April 12, 1949.[141]

Secretary Acheson reemphasized the limited scope of the NATO commitment on the first day of hearings before the Senate Foreign Relations Committee.[142] Senator Donnell, who had opposed the Rio Treaty, pressed Secretary Acheson on the scope of the United States obligation and the role of the President and Congress. In response, Secretary Acheson commented that the ''constitutional processes'' mentioned in the Treaty ''obviously mean that Congress is the body in charge of that constitutional procedure.''[143] In a response that would go directly to the power conferred by the Treaty upon the President to use nuclear weapons, Secretary Acheson said: ''Article 5 . . . does not enlarge, nor does it decrease, nor does it change in any way, the relative constitutional position of the President and the Congress.''[144]

These critically important qualifications were elaborated at some length in the State Foreign Relations Committee's report on the Treaty.[145] One passage is particularly pertinent:

[T]he Committee calls particular attention to the phrase ''such action as it deems appropriate.'' These words were included in article 5 to make absolutely clear that

140 20 Dep't St. Bull. 532, 534 (1949).

141 President's Message to Senate Transmitting North Atlantic Treaty, 20 Dep't St. Bull. 599 (1949).

142 North Atlantic Treaty: Hearings on Exec. L Before the Senate Comm. on Foreign Relations, 81st Cong., 1st Sess. 11 (1949) (statement of Dean Acheson, Secretary of State). Senator Connally questioned him about it.

THE CHAIRMAN Is there or is there not anything in the treaty that pledges us to an automatic declaration of war in any event?

SECRETARY ACHESON There is nothing in the treaty which has that effect, Senator.

THE CHAIRMAN Those matters still reside in the discretion and judgment of the Government and the Senate?

SECRETARY ACHESON That is true.

THE CHAIRMAN Even after the occurrence of events, we would still have that freedom, would we not?

SECRETARY ACHESON That is true.

Id. at 18. Senator Vandenberg asked the same questions and got the same answers:

SENATOR VANDENBERG Is there anything in the treaty which will lead automatically to a declaration of war on our part?

SECRETARY ACHESON No, sir.

SENATOR VANDENBERG The answer of course is unequivocally ''No.''

SECRETARY ACHESON Unequivocally ''No.''

Id. at 25.

143 *Id.* at 80.

144 *Id.*

145 S. Exec. Rep. No. 8, 81st Cong., 1st Sess. (1949).

> each party remains free to exercise its honest judgment in deciding upon the measures it will take to help restore and maintain the security of the North Atlantic area. . . . [W]hat we may do to carry out [the] commitment [of article 5] will depend upon our own independent decision in each particular instance reached in accordance with our own constitutional processes. . . .
>
> During the hearings substantially the following questions were repeatedly asked: In view of the provision in article 5 that an attack against one shall be considered an attack against all, would the United States be obligated to react to an attack on Paris or Copenhagen in the same way it would react to an attack on New York City? In such an event does the treaty give the President the power to take any action, without specific congressional authorization, which he could not take in the absence of the treaty?
>
> The answer to both these questions is "No." . . . In the event any party to the treaty were attacked the obligation of the United States Government would be to decide upon and take forthwith the measures it deemed appropriate to restore and maintain the security of the North Atlantic area. . . . Nothing in the treaty . . . increases or decreases the constitutional powers of either the President or the Congress or changes the relationship between them.[146]

These important limitations on the United States' commitment were reaffirmed on the Senate floor by Senator Connally, the Chairman of the Foreign Relations Committee, in explaining the Treaty to the Senate.[147] Senator Connally also addressed specifically the charge that the Treaty was an "automatic" commitment:

> While the treaty was being drafted rumors circulated about Washington that article 5 carried with it a commitment which would bind the United States automatically to go to war in the event of an armed attack. I challenge anyone to find such a commitment. . . . Not only must we ratify the treaty by constitutional processes, but it will be carried out under the provisions of the Constitution of the United States. The full authority of the Congress to declare war, with all the discretion that power implies, remains unimpaired.[148]

[146] *Id.* at 13–15. The Committee's report proceeded to address specifically what the term "constitutional processes" was meant to encompass:

> The Committee wishes to emphasize the fact that the protective clause . . . was placed in article 11 in order to leave no doubt that it applies not only to article 5, for example, but to every provision of the treaty. . . .
>
> The treaty in no way affects the basic division [sic] of authority between the President and the Congress as defined in the Constitution. . . . In particular, it does not increase, decrease, or change the power of the President as Commander in Chief of the armed forces or impair the full authority of Congress to declare war.

Id. at 18–19.

[147] "The treaty does not involve any commitment to go to war," he said, "nor does it change the relative authority of the President and the Congress with respect to the use of the armed forces." 95 Cong. Rec. 8812, 8814 (1949).

[148] *Id.* at 8815.

Senator Connally noted that this was understood by all the signatories to the Treaty, and included in the record a portion of a British white paper stating the understanding of the United Kingdom.[149] Senator Vandenberg affirmed the correctness of Senator Connally's interpretation at some length.[150]

Yet opposition arose, centering around the alleged vagueness of the Treaty's commitments and the possibility that it might draw the United States into foreign wars. Senator Jenner referred to "garbled diplomatic gibberish"[151] and charged that even supporters of the Treaty were divided over the "wisdom of clarifying beyond question of doubt the real nature of the military commitments contained in the weasel-worded clauses of this treaty."[152] He and Senator Donnell then engaged in an extended colloquy concerning what they saw as a "military alliance" that would "sabotage the United Nations" (and, conceivably, tie the United States to Communist governments that might become members of NATO).[153] European signatories, Senator Donnell argued, had proceeded under the belief that the United States would be pledged to go to war if one of them were attacked; he entered in the *Congressional Record* a statement to that effect by the Danish Foreign Minister.[154] Senator Watkins later complained that the Treaty "creates an obligation to defend our allies' territory in the event of an armed attack upon them,"[155] an obligation that he opposed.[156] He therefore proposed a reservation, worded as follows:

> The United States further understands and construes article 5 to the effect that in any particular case or event of armed attack on any other party or parties to the treaty, the Congress of the United States is not expressly, impliedly, or morally obligated or committed to declare war or authorize the employment of the military, air, or naval forces of the United States against the nation or nations making said attack, or to assist with its armed forces the nation or nations attacked, but shall have complete freedom in considering the circumstances of each case to act or refuse to act as the Congress in its discretion shall determine.[157]

Senator Connally described the reservation as a "complete repudiation of the treaty," under which the United States would have "no obligations."[158]

[149] *Id.*

[150] *Id.* at 8894–95.

[151] *Id.* at 9553.

[152] *Id.* at 9554. A Senator could be inconsistent or kid himself, Senator Jenner said, but "let him not delude the American people." *Id.*

[153] *Id.* at 9564.

[154] *Id.* at 9640.

[155] *Id.* at 9900.

[156] The historic and generally accepted American view is that only Congress sitting when the armed attack occurs has the power, when the attack is made in other than United States territory, to declare war and authorize the employment of the armed forces of the United States to repel such an attack. *Id.* at 9099.

[157] *Id.* at 9904.

[158] *Id.*

Senator Watkins responded by reading from a letter by Charles Evans Hughes to Senator Hale, wherein the late Justice wrote that article 10 of the treaty represented an "illusory engagement."[159] The argument had little effect, however; one senator proceeded to hail the treaty as "the logical next step in the development of the conception of the Monroe doctrine. . . ."[160] Senator Connally entered in the *Record* a letter from Secretary of State Dean Acheson opposing the reservation, which, the Secretary of State said, would "not only raise doubts as to our determination in the minds of those who might be considering aggression, but would certainly raise the gravest doubts in the minds of our partners in the pact. . . ."[161] The reservation was defeated, 87 to 8.[162] The Senate then consented to ratification of the Treaty by a vote of 82 to 13.[163]

Defeat of the reservation might be argued to represent a contrary will of the Senate, a belief that the Treaty did and should contain an "automatic" commitment to use armed force.[164] A better reading of the Senate's will, one more in keeping with the context in which the Watkins reservation was rejected, is that the reservation articulated a delicate but purposefully unexpressed element of the unanimous understanding of the signatories. Further, a spelling-out of that element would have undermined the political force of the treaty, thereby risking the possibility of renegotiation and throwing the solidarity of the alliance into jeopardy. Most senators seemed to believe, in short, that the element of noncommitment in the commitment was clear enough. And a consensus appeared to have been reached between the Executive and the Senate concerning the measure of specificity required to satisfy the demands of the Constitution as well as those of our putative allies.

ANZUS and the Philippines Treaty

The Mutual Defense Treaty Between the United States and the Republic of the Philippines[165] and the Security Treaty Between Australia, New Zealand, and the United States (ANZUS)[166] were next negotiated by the executive branch and

[159] *Id.* at 9907. The United States, Hughes' letter said, "should not enter into a guarantee which would expose us to the charge of bad faith or having defaulted in our obligation. . . . Democracies cannot promise war after the manner of monarchs." *Id.*

[160] *Id.* at 9911 (remarks of Sen. Smith).

[161] *Id.* at 9915.

[162] *Id.* at 9916.

[163] *Id.*

[164] Justice Jackson argued in Youngstown Sheet & Tube Co. v. Sawyer, 343 U.S. 579 (1952) that rejection of an amendment by the Senate that would have authorized the seizure of the steel mills effectively represented legislative *disapproval* of such an act. *Id.* at 634 (Jackson, J., concurring).

[165] Mutual Defense Treaty, Aug. 30, 1951, United States–Philippines, 3 U.S.T. 3947, T.I.A.S. No. 2529 (hereinafter cited as Philippines Treaty).

[166] Multilateral Security Treaty, Sept. 1, 1951, United States–Australia–New Zealand, 3 U.S.T. 3420, T.I.A.S. No. 2493 (hereinafter cited as ANZUS).

considered by the Senate on roughly the same schedule. The Senate concerns confronted during consideration of the Rio and NATO treaties were apparently taken as a given during the negotiation of these later treaties, so that Senate debate was far less protracted.

Nonetheless, United States negotiators occasionally tried to soft-pedal the significance of the "constitutional processes" language in explaining it to their foreign counterparts—in terms that would surely have raised alarm had they been used before the Senate. In a meeting with the foreign ministers of Australia and New Zealand, Ambassador Dulles was asked what was meant by "constitutional processes." In reply, he concluded that the phrase "did not . . . impose any serious limitation" on United States assistance to its allies.[167]

In intragovernmental communications, Dulles's emphasis shifted. In a top secret dispatch to General Douglas MacArthur, he candidly described the unfettered discretion the United States reserved for itself:

> While [the draft treaty] commits each party to take action (presumably go to war) it does not commit any nation to action in any particular part of the world. In other words, the United States can discharge its obligations by action against the common enemy in any way and in any area that it sees fit.[168]

Each party to the treaties, Dulles testified before the Senate Foreign Relations Committee, would have to decide what action was appropriate "in the light of the fact that there is recognition that it is a common danger, and that each will act in accordance with its constitutional processes to meet that danger."[169] The subject was not pursued, at least not nearly to the extent it had been during hearings on the NATO and Rio treaties. Perhaps Committee members knew the Administration's likely answers and expected to be satisfied with them. In any event, Dulles's statement was repeated in the Committee report[170] with the simple observation that "a whole range of defensive measures . . . might be appropriate depending upon the circumstances," and "any action in which the

[167] 6 U.S. Dep't of State, Foreign Relations of the United States 166 (1977). Ambassador Dulles's complete reply to the question, as recorded by a State Department official, was that

> the phrase was to be found in the United Nations Charter in article 43. It had been inserted there primarily to meet the sensibilities of Congress, which alone under our Constitution has the power to declare war. The phrase, which also appears in the North Atlantic Treaty, makes clear that the President does not have this power. . . . [W]hile it is quite true that under our Constitution only Congress can *declare* war, the question of *making* war is a different matter. War can be made by others, leaving us little choice. Congress has declared war in only one of the wars in which the U.S. has been engaged. In every other case Congress has found that a state of war already existed. Only in the unlikely event that the U.S. started a war would the phrase have any relevance. It did not in fact therefore impose any serious limitation.

Id.

[168] *Id.* at 177.

[169] Japanese Peace Treaty and Other Treaties Relating to Security in the Pacific, Hearings Before the Senate Comm. on Foreign Relations, 82d Cong., 2d Sess. 62 (1952).

[170] S. Exec. Rep. No. 2, 82d Cong., 2d Sess. (1952).

United States joined would have to be taken in accordance with our constitutional processes.''[171]

Discussion of the issue on the Senate floor was equally cursory; a number of other issues had now captured the attention of opponents of the treaties. Each treaty was approved overwhelmingly. The issue of ''automatic commitments'' apparently had had its day. Yet three more security treaties currently in force remained to be approved by the Senate.

The South Korea Treaty

Like the Philippines and ANZUS treaties (and unlike the NATO and Rio pacts), the Mutual Defense Treaty Between the United States and the Republic of Korea[172] has no language indicating that an attack on one party will be regarded as an attack on the other. Otherwise, although somewhat more succinct—the entire text of the treaty is less than two pages—material obligations of the treaty parallel those of the other mutual-security treaties. Each party recognizes that an attack on the other in the Pacific area ''would be dangerous to its own peace and safety and declares that it would act to meet the common danger in accordance with its constitutional processes.''[173] This means, Secretary of State John Foster Dulles said in his letter of transmittal to the President, that ''[a]n armed attack by [*sic*] either party does not obligate the other to come to its assistance.''[174] President Eisenhower transmitted this report to the Senate on January 11, 1954.[175]

This was not the commitment that the Koreans sought. President Singman Rhee of South Korea had asked President Eisenhower for a security pact under which ''[t]he United States will agree to come to our military aid and assistance immediately without any consultation or conference with any nation or nations, if and when an enemy nation or nations resume aggressive activities against the Korean Peninsula.''[176] The commitment they got, as Secretary of State Dulles explained to the Senate Foreign Relations Committee, was a bit different. Asked by Senator George about what assistance the United States would be obligated to give if South Korea was attacked, the Secretary of State said:

[171] *Id.*

[172] Mutual Defense Treaty, Oct. 1, 1953, United States–Republic of Korea, 5 U.S.T. 2368, T.I.A.S. No. 3097.

[173] *Id.* art. III.

[174] Secretary of State's Letter to President Transmitting Mutual Defense Treaty with Korea, 30 Dep't St. Bull. 132 (1954).

[175] *Id.* at 131.

[176] Letter from President Singman Rhee to President Dwight D. Eisenhower (May 30, 1953), *reprinted in* A Mutual Defense Treaty Between the United States of America and the Republic of Korea: Hearings on Exec. A Before the Senate Comm. on Foreign Relations, 83d Cong., 2d Sess. 57 (1954).

> It would be wholly within the determination of the United States. The other party to the treaty would have no right to make any specific demand upon us and say that we were obligated by the treaty to do any particular thing. The choice of means is entirely ours.[177]

In fact, Dulles went further and explained that the textual difference between operative provisions of the Korean and NATO treaties derived from his personal effort to avoid the constitutional controversy on ratification of the NATO Treaty by making it abundantly clear that no "automatic commitment" was implied.[178] In the Senate Foreign Relations Committee's report, this was described as the "Monroe Doctrine" formula because, the Committee said, its origins traced to the Monroe Doctrine. "It has the additional advantage of never having been challenged throughout our history, from the constitutional standpoint, as altering the balance of power between the President and Congress."[179]

On the Senate floor, a thoroughly confused discussion occurred. Several senators addressed the issue whether the term "constitutional processes" required congressional participation under all circumstances.[180] There was no agreement. All apparently did agree, however, that the United States would not be required to come to the defense of South Korea if it was attacked and that in this sense the Treaty, in the words of Senator Smith of New Jersey, did "not go beyond the general type of commitment which we have made in our other Pacific-area security treaties."[181] The Treaty was approved 81 to 6.[182]

[177] *Id.* at 17 (statement of John Foster Dulles, Secretary of State).

[178] "I, myself, invented this new formula," he testified, "at the time when I was negotiating the security treaties with Australia, New Zealand, and the Philippines. . . ." *Id.* at 7. The purpose there, he said, had been the same, although from a standpoint of actual practice, the difference is "perhaps more academic than it is practical." *Id.* at 29.

[179] S. Exec. Rep. No. 1, 83d Cong., 2d Sess (1954).

[180] Senator Wiley, Chairman of the Foreign Relations Committee, was asked by Senator Stennis about the extent of the commitment and the role of Congress in its implementation:

> MR. STENNIS [A]re we committing ourselves now, in agreeing to this treaty, to go to war if Korea is attacked, without any declaration by the Congress?
>
> MR. WILEY In my opinion, very definitely the answer is no. . . [W]e will do that which we think is advisable.
>
> MR. STENNIS Who is "we"? Is that the President, or is it the Congress?
>
> MR. WILEY It is the Congress and the President who have to determine that question. . . . [I]f an overt act is committed by an aggressor upon an ally, it then rests with the constituted authority, to wit, the Congress, to decide whether or not we shall regard such aggression as a basis for going to war. . . .
>
> [T]here is nothing in the treaty which would change, delimit or add to the powers of the President of the United States.

100 Cong. Rec. 785 (1954).

[181] *Id.* at 794.

[182] *Id.* at 819.

The SEATO Treaty

The Southeast Asia Collective Defense Treaty,[183] like other Pacific-area treaties ratified over the previous thirty years, omits any indication that an attack on one party is to be regarded as an attack on all. Its operative commitment provides that "[e]ach party recognizes that aggression by means of armed attack in the treaty area against any of the Parties . . . would endanger its own peace and safety, and agrees that it will in that event act to meet the common danger in accordance with its constitutional processes."[184] This, Secretary of State Dulles reported to President Eisenhower, "leaves to the judgment of each country the type of action to be taken in the event an armed attack occurs. There is, of course, a wide range of defensive measures which might be appropriate depending upon the circumstances."[185] The report was transmitted to the Senate.[186]

In executive-session hearings before the Senate Foreign Relations Committee, Secretary Dulles explained why the Pacific-area treaties did not contain the provision in the NATO and Rio treaties that an attack on one was to be regarded as an attack on all. That language, Secretary Dulles said, had created "doubts and uncertainties" concerning the treaties' "constitutional effect." Those uncertainties had been resolved in both the NATO and Rio treaties, he said, but in negotiating the treaties with Australia, New Zealand, and the Philippines, "it seemed to me more prudent to use the language which had been used by President Monroe. . . ." That language, he testified, "commends itself perhaps to a general acceptance by the Senate."[187] Secretary Dulles went on to describe the effect of the Treaty's obligatory provisions:

> Well, Article IV, paragraph 2, contemplates that if that situation arises or threatens, that we should consult together immediately in order to agree on measures which should be taken. That is an obligation for consultation. It is not an obligation for action.[188]

Secretary Dulles described the linguistic evolution of the treaties again in open session. The NATO Treaty, he said, raised the question whether the Pres-

183 Southeast Asia Collective Defense Treaty and Protocol, Sept. 8, 1954, 6 U.S.T. 81, T.I.A.S. No. 3170, 209 U.N.T.S. 28 (hereinafter cited as SEATO Treaty). Current parties are Australia, France, New Zealand, the Philippines, Thailand, the United Kingdom, and the United States. U.S. Dep't of State, Treaties in Force 229 (1985).

184 SEATO Treaty, *supra* note 183, art. IV.

185 Secretary of State's Letter to President Transmitting Southeast Asia Collective Defense Treaty and Protocol, 31 Dep't St. Bull. 820, 821 (1954).

186 President's Message to Senate Transmitting Southeast Asia Collective Defense Treaty and Protocol, *id.* at 819.

187 Southeast Asia Collective Defense Treaty: Hearings Before Executive Session of Senate Comm. on Foreign Relations, 83d Cong., 1st Sess. 1,4 (1955) (statement of John Foster Dulles, Secretary of State).

188 *Id.* at 25.

ident had the same power in the event of an attack on Norway that he would have in the event of an attack on New York City. Dulles recalled that he had been a member of the Senate at the time and had participated in the debate. The new formula was devised for the ANZUS, Philippine, and Korean treaties to avoid reopening the constitutional debate.[189] He reiterated, however, that the "difference practically is not that great. . . ."[190] He was thus careful to avoid intimating that the NATO Treaty contained an "automatic" commitment.

Testifying after Dulles, former Representative Hamilton Fish recommended to the Committee that it modify the Treaty to make it clear that the term *constitutional processes* was understood to require a declaration of war before the armed forces could be used to carry out United States obligations under the Treaty.[191] The Committee discussed the question in executive session and concluded that presidential powers were—or could be—broader than Fish had suggested; the consensus was that the Treaty should simply make clear that it neither contracted nor expanded the President's powers.

Senator George, the Committee Chairman, acted as floor manager of the Treaty in the Senate. He explained that the NATO-Rio reference had been dropped because of the "constitutional controversy" it provoked. Instead, the Treaty used the formula of the Monroe Doctrine, which, he said, left "no doubt that the constitutional powers of the Congress and the President are exactly where they stood before. [The Treaty] has no effect whatsoever on the thorny question of whether, how, and under what circumstances the President might involve the United States in warfare without the approval of Congress."[192] No significant discussion of the issue occurred, and on February 1, 1955, the SEATO Treaty was approved by a vote of 82 to 1.[193]

The Japan Treaty

The Treaty of Mutual Cooperation and Security Between the United States and Japan[194] sets forth an obligation virtually identical to the other Pacific-area mutual-security treaties: "Each Party recognizes that an armed attack against either Party . . . would be dangerous to its own peace and safety and declares that it would act to meet the common danger in accordance with its constitutional provisions and processes."[195] By 1960, the year this treaty was signed,

[189] *Id.* at 21.

[190] *Id.* at 29.

[191] Southeast Asia Collective Defense Treaty: Hearings Before Senate Comm. on Foreign Relations, 84th Cong., 1st Sess. 50 (1955) (statement of Hamilton Fish, President, American Political Action Committee).

[192] 101 Cong. Rec. 1049, 1051 (1955).

[193] *Id.* at 1060.

[194] Treaty of Mutual Cooperation and Security Between the United States and Japan, Jan. 19, 1960, 11 U.S.T. 1632, T.I.A.S. No. 4509.

[195] *Id.* art. V.

the Senate had apparently come to so firm an understanding of the meaning of such language that the issue was virtually ignored.[196]

The War Powers Resolution

The War Powers Resolution[197] addresses the issue in section 8(a)(2):

> [a]uthority to introduce United States Armed Forces into hostilities or into situations wherein involvement in hostilities is clearly indicated by the circumstances shall not be inferred . . . from any treaty heretofore or hereafter ratified unless such treaty is implemented by legislation specifically authorizing the introduction of United States Armed Forces into hostilities or into such situations and stating that it is intended to constitute specific statutory authorization within the meaning of this joint resolution.[198]

The proscription against inferring such authority from a treaty "heretofore" ratified seems clear enough. Because none of those treaties is implemented by legislation meeting the two conditions specified in section 8(a)(2)—specific authorization and express reference to the War Powers Resolution—the Resolution seems to say that no authority to introduce armed forces into hostilities may be inferred from any treaty.

Yet a subsequent provision appears contradictory. Section 8(d)(1) provides that "[n]othing in this joint resolution . . . is intended to alter the . . . provisions of existing treaties."[199] If an "existing treaty"—presumably one in force at the time of the enactment of the Resolution—*did* permit such an inference of authority, how is that authority affected by the War Powers Resolution? Does the Resolution, as one commentator put it, talk "out of both sides of its mouth"?[200]

[196] Compare the questioning of Secretary of State Christian Herter by the Senate Foreign Relations Committee with that of other Secretaries of State testifying on previous treaties. Treaty of Mutual Cooperation and Security with Japan: Hearings Before the Senate Comm. on Foreign Relations, 86th Cong., 2nd Sess. 1 (1960) (statement of Christian Herter, Secretary of State). Also, this was a "replacement" treaty with Japan; at Japan's request, the treaty was revised, although the commitment provisions remained the same. Testifying on the scope of those provisions in 1952, Senator Brewster asked John Foster Dulles what United States obligations would be "if Russian Troops did move down from the islands into Japan?" He replied, "We have no obligation." *The Japanese Peace Treaty and Other Treaties Relating to Security in the Pacific: Hearings Before the Senate Comm. on Foreign Relations*, 82d Cong., 2d Sess. 117–27 (1952) (statement of John Foster Dulles, personal representative of President on Japanese Treaty).

[197] Pub. L. No. 93-148, 87 Stat. 555 (codified at 50 U.S.C. §§ 1541–1548) (1976) (hereinafter cited as War Powers Resolution).

[198] *Id.* § 8(a)(2).

[199] *Id.* § 8(d)(1).

[200] A Review of the Operation and Effectiveness of the War Powers Resolution: Hearings Before the Senate Comm. on Foreign Relations, 95th Cong., 1st Sess. 76 (1977) (statement of Monroe Leigh).

The provision originated in the Senate version of the Resolution,[201] which provided that ''[n]o treaty in force at the time of the enactment of this Act shall be construed as specific statutory authorization for, or a specific exemption permitting, the introduction of the Armed Forces of the United States into hostilities. . . .''[202]

In its report, the Senate Foreign Relations Committee explained its understanding of ''existing'' treaty commitments:

> Treaties are not self-executing. They do not contain authority . . . to go to war. Thus, by requiring statutory action, . . . the War Powers Resolution would perform the important function of defining that elusive and controversial phrase—''constitutional processes''—which is contained in our security treaties.[203]

The conference report[204] set forth section 8 as it reads in the Resolution; the joint statement of the managers (appended thereto and explaining the meaning of the conference report) says merely that the Conference Committee ''agreed to [the] adoption of modified Senate language defining specific statutory authorization, and defining the phrase 'introduction of United States Armed Forces' as used in the joint resolution.''[205] No explanation is given of the meaning of the cryptic indication of an intent not to alter the provisions of existing treaties.

Given this background, what is to be made of section 8? Conflicting interpretations are possible, but the most reasonable is that the section was intended to make clear that no treaty may serve as a source of authority for the introduction of the armed forces into hostilities. This limitation should be construed as applying to all treaties, ratified before and after enactment of the War Powers Resolution. To construe the provision as exempting ''existing'' mutual-security treaties would be to create a confused two-tier system of security treaties. Such a result would be without support in the legislative history and completely at odds with the oft-repeated belief that no treaty in force at the time of the debate on the Resolution committed, or could commit, the United States automatically to introduce its armed forces into hostilities. The apparently inconsistent reference of section 8(d)(1) to the ''provisions'' of ''existing'' treaties can in fact be read as a straightforward (if infelicitous) attempt to state the congressional understanding that no existing treaty *is* altered by the War Powers Resolution because no existing treaty *does* provide the au-

[201] S. 440, 93d Cong., 1st Sess., 119 Cong. Rec. 25, 119–20 (1973).

[202] *Id.* § 3(4).

[203] S. Rep. No. 220, 93d Cong., 1st Sess. 26 (1973). The Committee said further that the war powers of Congress are vested in both Houses of Congress and not in the Senate (and President) alone. A decision to make war must be a national decision. Consequently, to be a truly national decision, and, most importantly, to be consonant with the Constitution, it must be a decision involving the President and both Houses of Congress. *Id.*

[204] H. Rep. No. 547, 93d Cong., 1st Sess (1973).

[205] *Id.*

thority that the Resolution rules out. This is, in fact, how the treaties were construed by both the Ford[206] and Carter[207] administrations.

CONCLUSION

As Senator Stennis said during the confused debate on the Treaty with South Korea, it is important to "keep our eye on the ball."[208] The issue is *not* what procedures are implied or required by the term *constitutional processes*; whether congressional approval is required before the President can introduce the armed forces into hostilities is an issue dealt with in Chapter 3. Rather, the issue here is whether mutual-security treaties can and do serve as a supplementary source of authority on which the President can rely to introduce United States armed forces into hostilities.

Part of the confusion has derived from a focus on the word *constitutional* to the virtual exclusion of the word *process*. *Process* suggests deliberation; it implies *procedure* leading to *choice*.[209] In one sense, the question of whether

[206] In connection with Secretary of State Henry Kissinger's appearances before the Senate Foreign Relations Committee on Nov. 19, 1975, Senator Dick Clark submitted a question asking whether "any *treaty* authorize[s] the introduction of U.S. armed forces into hostilities? . . ." The Administration replied: "[T]he answer is 'no.' Treaties of the United States which express defense commitments to other nations commit the United States to act only in accordance with its constitutional processes. Such treaties do not confer authority which would not otherwise be available through the constitutional process of the United States." Letter from Robert J. McCloskey, Assistant Secretary of State, to Sen. Dick Clark (Mar. 1, 1976) (on file with author.)

[207] In response to a letter from Senator George McGovern to Secretary of State Cyrus Vance, the Administration replied:

> [A]lthough our mutual security agreements entail a legal obligation to respond to an armed attack on another party, the nature and scope of that response is left to the discretion of the responding party. . . . Accordingly, such treaties do not confer "Authority to introduce United States Armed Forces into hostilities" within the meaning of Section 8(a)(1) of the War Powers Resolution.

Letter from Douglas J. Bennet, Jr., Assistant Secretary for Congressional Relations, to Sen. George McGovern (June 2, 1977) (on file with author).

[208] 100 Cong. Rec. 779, 789 (1954).

[209] This is illustrated by the Senate Foreign Relations Committee's use of the term in another, similar context. As submitted to the Senate, the Panama Canal Treaty, Treaty on the Panama Canal, Sept. 7, 1977, United States–Panama, U.S.T., T.I.A.S. No. 10,030, originally provided that "[t]he Parties *shall conclude* an agreement" concerning the exchange of prisoners. *Id.* art. IX(11). The Committee recommended (and the Senate later accepted, 124 Cong. Rec. 10,541 (1978) an understanding which provided that any such agreement "shall be concluded in accordance with the constitutional processes of both parties." S. Exec. Rep. No. 12, 95th Cong., 1st Sess. 6 (1978). The Committee indicated its intent to require that the agreement take the form of a treaty. One additional purpose of the understanding, the Committee said, was to clarify the substance of the international commitment undertaken by the United States:

> As paragraph 11 has been drafted, it could be construed as requiring the United States to enter into a prisoner exchange agreement, and would thereby place the United States in violation of this treaty should the United States elect not to do so. Obviously, the authority of the

Congress should *choose* to act is academic, or at least in certain situations it can be. Those are circumstances in which the President clearly possesses independent constitutional authority to introduce the armed forces into hostilities. There, the extent to which a mutual-security treaty does or does not provide such authority need not be reached. Where units of the United States armed forces are stationed where they have a legal right to be and are subject to an armed attack, for example, it is irrelevant that a treaty might also provide support for the use of armed force. The President could find it useful for domestic political purposes to cite the attack upon a treaty ally as further justification for using armed force. But as a constitutional matter, it is clear that under such circumstances, the Constitution provides all the authority the President requires.

On the other hand, the issue is far from academic where no colorable source of authority exists other than a mutual-security treaty. One respected commentator has suggested that the question is not a serious one because the United States can simply "refuse to honor"[210] such a commitment, which is "no different from other treaty undertakings. . . ."[211] Congress and the President do have it within their power, acting together, to disregard international obligations of the United States; the point is a useful reminder that when the political branches join in the breach, there is no corresponding domestic rule.[212]

But that, of course, assumes the very point at issue: Are the United States' mutual-security treaties really *obligations*? On this question, domestic contract law may offer some wisdom. No one would argue that the parallels are exact; the Vienna Convention on the Law of Treaties[213] is not article 2 of the

---

> Senate to advise and consent to a treaty is meaningless if it is required to be given; the authority to disapprove is implied if our "constitutional processes" are to be upheld.

Id. at 11. The Committee also recommended use of the term *constitutional processes* in an amendment to a companion treaty, the so-called *Neutrality Treaty*. Treaty Concerning the Permanent Neutrality and Operation of the Panama Canal, Sept. 7, 1977, United States–Panama, U.S.T., T.I.A.S. No. 10,029. In language illuminating the meaning of the phrase in the mutual security treaties, the Committee explained its intent:

> The effect of this language is to make clear that the treaty does not obligate the United States to introduce its armed forces into hostilities or authorize the President to do so. It thus places the Neutrality Treaty, in terms of the "automaticity" of the United States' international commitment, in the same category as mutual security treaties to which the United States is a party. All such treaties implicitly reserve to the United States a right of choice in each individual situation to act, militarily, as it deems appropriate under the circumstances. Any treaty which did not do so would, in the Committee's opinion, unconstitutionally divest the House of Representatives of its share of the warmaking power and would, unconstitutionally, delegate to the President the power to place the United States at war.

S. Exec. Rep. No. 12, 95th Cong., 1st Sess. 74 (1978).

[210] L. Henkin, Foreign Affairs and the Constitution 192–93 (1972).

[211] *Id.* at 192.

[212] Where the President acts alone, however, his action does raise constitutional problems. *See generally* Chapter 7.

[213] Vienna Convention on the Law of Treaties, May 23, 1969, U.N. Doc. A/Conf. 39/11/Add. 2, 8 I.L.M. 697.

Uniform Commercial Code.[214] It contains no provision dealing with such concepts as "illusory obligation," "moral obligation," or the requirements of a "meeting of the minds" and "mutuality of obligation." Yet these are subjects that have long occupied the attention of respected English and United States jurists, and international law does derive, at least in part, from "the general principles of law recognized by civilized nations. . . ."[215] Although domestic contract rules do not apply, the policy considerations underpinning those rules may at least provide a useful perspective.

An *illusory promise* is an expression cloaked in promissory terms, which, upon closer examination, reveals that the promisor has committed himself to nothing.[216] Illusory promises make for illusory contracts, and illusory contracts are void. The illusion lies in a retained option of nonperformance: if performance of a promise is entirely within the discretion of the promisor, the promise is illusory.[217]

Closely related are requirements of *certainty*. A contract does not exist unless its terms are reasonably certain.[218] Uncertainty as to incidental or collateral matters is seldom fatal to the existence of a contract. But if the essential terms are so uncertain that there is no basis for deciding whether the agreement has been broken, there is no contract and no legal obligation.[219]

The courts enforce legal obligations, not moral ones. In rare instances, a moral obligation may be transformed into a legal obligation, but these are almost exclusively situations involving past consideration or preexisting benefit.[220] A moral obligation, it has been said, is not worth the paper on which it is not written.

The reasons for these rules are familiar. Specificity is necessary to determine whether the parties truly intended to form a contract. It is also essential for determining the existence of a breach. An appropriate remedy cannot be forged unless the court can determine what promise was violated.[221]

Under domestic contract rules, the United States' mutual-security treaties would be fatally defective. In debates on the treaties' ratification, members of the Senate repeated over and over that the United States was committing itself

[214] *Compare* article 19(c) precluding reservations incompatible with the object and purpose of a treaty.

[215] Statute of the International Court of Justice, art. 38, para. 1(c), 59 Stat. 1055, T.S. No. 993, 3 Bevans 1153.

[216] J. Calamari & J. Perillo, Contracts §§ 4–17 (2d ed. 1977).

[217] *Id.* In fact, the "promise" is merely a statement of intention to pursue whatever course of conduct the "promisor" may choose to pursue. Restatement (Second) Contracts § 2, Comment *e* (1982). The classic example is a promise to buy as much as the promisor may choose; there is no promise, and no contract. *Id.* § 77, Illustration 1.

[218] Restatement (Second) Contracts § 33 (1982).

[219] *Id.* Comment *a*.

[220] J. Calamari & J. Perillo, Contracts § 5-2 (2d ed. 1977).

[221] Restatement (Second) Contracts, § 33, Comment *b* (1982).

only to do what it deemed appropriate. The United States, in its sole discretion, retained the option to do nothing. The treaties say nothing about what the United States must do if another party is attacked. They say nothing about when the United States must do it. They say nothing about how long the United States must do it. They say nothing about what the United States will *take into account* in determining what it will do. The treaties say nothing, in short, about any of the myriads of factors essential to deciding whether the United States has honored or abandoned its treaty commitment.

But so what? No domestic tribunal will ever sit in judgment of the United States' action in responding or failing to respond to an armed attack on a treaty partner. No court will ever be confronted with the problem of "fashioning relief" for an aggrieved party. And the formality, the solemnity, with which these commitments were entered into leaves little ground for doubting the intent of any state to become a party.

Why, then, should anyone care that the "obligations" are vague to the point of meaninglessness? The reason is clear: *because no one will know, in circumstances that leave room for reasonable dispute, whether this nation has lived up to its commitments*. The treaties leave the war-making powers of each branch precisely where those powers would have been in the treaties' absence, and therefore no one can know what the treaties bind those branches to do.

The cost, or potential cost, of the treaties' indeterminate language is manifest. Credibility is the currency of diplomacy. Vaguely worded undertakings may generate initial good will; the peoples of those nations bound to the United States in mutual-security pacts may have felt a measure of consanguinity with this country as a consequence of our seeming public-spiritedness. It was not, after all, every nation that sent its representatives flying about the postwar globe signing up treaty partners.

Yet what will happen to the United States' credibility if it exercises the choice *not* to go to war that it has so clearly reserved for itself under the treaties? What price will be paid by this country in the long term if it appears to act in bad faith, even though its act is one that is legally sanctioned? Are not the expectations of our treaty partners, in short, drastically different from those of those who would take comfort in, to use Senator Jenner's term,[222] the "weasel words" of the treaties?

One response is that their expectations are irrelevant. All that they might reasonably base their expectations upon, the argument might go, is the text of the treaty they have ratified. That is, after all, the purpose of having reduced the understanding to writing—to evidence what the parties *actually* agreed upon as well as what they did not.

But four-cornered, sharp-penciled United States legalism is likely to win little in the battle for the hearts of the officials of a country under siege. Actual

[222] *See supra* text accompanying note 167.

expectations of foreign diplomats, not the expectations of the reasonably prudent United States law professor, are the touchstone of whether the United States, through inaction or too little action, would suffer an unacceptable loss of credibility.

On that, our knowledge is scant. No country-by-country study has been conducted of the understanding of the treaties in foreign ministries. Nor has there been any systematic review of what those views may be today. What is known is largely anecdotal, consisting primarily of foreign newspaper accounts entered in the *Congressional Record* at the time of the ratification debates[223] and occasional foreign reaction to official discussion of the scope of United States commitments.[224]

In the absence of hard evidence, it is reasonable to view most diplomatic personnel of our treaty partners as moderately sophisticated realists who share the conclusion of a study conducted fifteen years ago at the Hebrew University of Jerusalem. The study assessed the permissible scope of a United States security guarantee that might emerge from a Middle East peace settlement. It reviewed the form required by the Constitution; the breadth of authority that such a guarantee might confer upon the President to "redeem" the United States pledge; and who could constitutionally "renege on, or terminate," such a commitment. The conclusion:

> [E]ven treaties must be viewed as mere policy statements. They reflect valid—indeed solemnly accepted—policy of the moment of their adoption, but their future implementation will be dependent on the shape of *future* policy. . . . No American treaty incorporating a defense commitment has failed—if only by its very vagueness and by its specific allusion to "constitutional processes"—to leave all future U.S. options entirely open. . . . The formality of the guarantee will most certainly not be the decisive factor in the crunch; as in the past, the execution or non-execution of the guarantee will be determined primarily by the perceived real interests of the guaranteeing power at the "moment of truth."[225]

The "perceived real interests" of the United States at the "moment of truth" are—and are probably seen to be—extensions of the reasons that motivate the United States to conclude security arrangements at the outset. Like other world powers, we doubtless explain our purposes differently to ourselves than those purposes would be explained by an "outside observer." Under Secretary of State Nicholas Katzenbach, for example, told the Senate For-

[223] 95 Cong. Rec. 9443, 9640 (1949).

[224] Murata, *Japan's Defense Delusion*, Japan Times, Dec. 30, 1977, at 14 (describing Japan's "assumption" that "the U.S. WILL come to Japan's aid AUTOMATICALLY when Japan is attacked" and discussing the "blind spot" in Japanese thinking about the security arrangement) (emphasis in original).

[225] M. Pomerance, American Guarantees to Israel and the Law of American Foreign Relations 30–31 (No. 9, Dec. 1974) (emphasis in original) (footnotes omitted).

eign Relations Committee that the "basic objective of our foreign policy is the security of the United States and the preservation of our freedoms,"[226] which probably also explains the perceived interest in entering into the mutual-security treaties. Others, less involved in policy-making than in its analysis, are perhaps more detached. Robert Osgood has suggested, for example, that alliances are made because they "are the most binding obligations [states] can make to stabilize the configurations of power that affect their vital interests."[227]

It is possible that the reasons the United States (or any nation, for that matter) enters hostilities proceed from the same general rationale for an alliance. And it is possible that the multifarious means to carry out that objective elude the efforts of the most skillful diplomat to reduce them to writing in a mutual-security treaty.

It should not be surprising, therefore, that a country like Israel should view with skepticism the value of a mutual-security relationship with the United States. For the same reasons, it should not be unexpected that treaty partners view mutual-security pacts as providing little security for themselves, apart from a generalized confluence of interests that may encourage United States intervention at the "moment of truth."

All of this suggests that the hole does not subsume the doughnut, that notwithstanding their gaping escape clauses, such treaties have important benefits for both sides that should not be overlooked. If their commitments are not absolute, they at least provide some reassurance that the parties do not stand alone in facing what could otherwise be overwhelming opposing forces. It may be a fair question whether congealed opposition is a cause or effect of our mutual-security treaties; the Warsaw Pact may see itself as having the same defensive purposes as NATO and may also derive some measure of cohesion from NATO's existence.

Be that as it may, NATO's symbolic value has tangible consequences, military and nonmilitary. It provides a congenial framework where important planning can take place if its parties should ever elect to employ armed force collectively. The appearance and reality of military unity may deter Warsaw Pact aggression. It may also deter foreign-policy gyrations by NATO members; when a party begins to act inconsistently with the objectives of the alliance, the alliance's cooperative framework and diplomatic channels can provide useful leverage for the application of diplomatic pressure by other parties. (This is probably more true in the case of an alliance composed of parties of vastly disparate power like the Rio alliance.) A military alliance seems, in

[226] *U.S. Commitments to Foreign Powers: Hearings on S. Res. 151 Before the Senate Comm. on Foreign Relations*, 90th Cong., 1st Sess. (1967).

[227] R. Osgood, Alliances and American Foreign Policy 19–20 (1968).

short, to provide the international analogue to a ''neighborhood''; bonds develop that conduce generally to the protection of multiple interests.

However great those benefits, they cannot mask the ultimate juridical unreality of the notion of commitment. If it means anything in this context, *commitment* means that under *some* circumstances, armed force will be required. Yet the treaties—all of them—in their express terms and equally in their legislative history are clear that under *no* circumstances is any party required to take any military action. With regard to the United States, this qualification carries an important corollary: None of the treaties confers any war-making power on the President that he or she would not have had in its absence. This means that he is given no additional power by any treaty to introduce the armed forces into hostilities, and it also means that once the forces are involved in hostilities, he is given no additional power to carry out any otherwise unauthorized military operation.

The dilemma confronting United States treaty negotiators was a real one. The prime purpose of the mutual-security pacts was to deter aggression. Deterrence is effective, in international relations as in domestic criminal justice, only to the extent that it is swift and sure. Yet the negotiators were also compelled to ensure the pacts' consistency with the deliberative decision-making processes of the democracies they sought to preserve. Speed and certainty are not the hallmarks of democratic procedure, particularly of the decision to use armed force. The evolution of Anglo-American constitutionalism is in no small part a history of the decline of the war-making power as a ''prerogative'' power, a history of its transfer to legislative authorities. To disregard that evolution—at least in the United States—would have ensured the rejection of the pacts. An initial flirtation with ''automatic'' commitments, reflected in the ambiguous language of the Rio and NATO treaties, was thus quickly ended when those treaties were taken up by the Senate.

So the negotiators wrote into the treaties the fullest measure of commitment that their domestic legal and political systems would allow—zero. They rejected swift and sure deterrence in favor of the right to decide: to weigh the facts of each incident, to judge whether an armed attack actually occurred, to assess whether the attack was provoked, to determine whether a military response is the most propitious, to consider all the factors that go into an evaluation of which action is most appropriate. The United States promised that it will in good faith consider such assistance as it deems appropriate if another party is attacked. But that is all it promised.

In mutual-security treaties to which the United States is a party, the notion of commitment is a myth. To pretend otherwise is to undermine the very constitutional processes that the treaties were intended to preserve.

Chapter Seven

INTERNATIONAL LAW AS OUR LAW

The most effectual restraint is an upright judiciary.
—Chief Justice John Marshall[1]

ON MARCH 25, 1898, the forty-three-foot sloop *Paquete Habana* sailed under the Spanish flag from Havana harbor and made its way along the Cuban coast to the western end of the island, stopping there to fish.[2] Her three-man crew had no knowledge of the war between Spain and the United States or of the American blockade of Cuba.[3] On April 25, 1898, while the *Paquete* was returning to Havana with a cargo of fresh fish, the United States gunboat *Castine* captured the *Paquete Habana*.[4] The *Castine* brought the *Paquete Habana* to Key West; despite claims interposed by her master, owner, and crew, a decree of condemnation was issued, and she was sold.[5] On appeal, the Supreme Court, following a lengthy review of customary international law, concluded that "it is an established rule of international law . . . that coast fishing vessels . . . are exempt from capture as prize of war."[6] In words that have made *The Paquete Habana* the leading case concerning the incorporation of international law into United States domestic law, the Court stated:

> International law is part of our law, and must be ascertained and administered by the courts of justice of appropriate jurisdiction, as often as questions of right depending upon it are duly presented for their determination. For this purpose, where there is no treaty, and no controlling executive or legislative act or judicial decision, resort must be had to the customs and usages of civilized nations.[7]

The Court therefore reversed the decree and ordered that the proceeds of the sale be restored to the claimants, with damages.[8]

Reflecting on the general question of the incorporation of international law

[1] *Quoted in* L. Baker, John Marshall: A Life in the Law 338 (1974).

[2] The Paquete Habana, 175 U.S. 677, 678–79 (1900).

[3] *Id.* at 678.

[4] *Id.* at 679.

[5] *Id.* Under international law, when a hostile vessel is captured in time of war, a judicial decree of condemnation normally is required to ensure that the capture is legal and to transfer title to the captor. The Nassau, 71 U.S. (4 Wall.) 634, 641 (1866).

[6] The Paquete Habana, 175 U.S. at 708.

[7] *Id.* at 700. For a discussion of *The Paquete Habana*, see *infra*, notes 102–114 and accompanying text.

[8] *Id.* at 714.

into United States domestic law, one judge recently wrote that the issue "cries out for clarification by the Supreme Court."[9] This chapter addresses a central aspect of that problem: As a matter of domestic law, is the President prohibited from violating principles of customary international law?[10] Because many international obligations undertaken by the United States are set forth in international agreements, the question arises most frequently with respect to the principle of customary international law known as *pacta sunt servanda*: Every international agreement is binding upon the parties to it and must be performed by them in good faith.[11] Yet the issue can also arise in connection with other customary norms, such as those that prohibit the acts of aggression directed at the government of Nicaragua.[12]

There is no dearth of literature concerning the relationship of international law to United States domestic law.[13] But in the absence of subsequent clarification by the Court, *The Paquete Habana* has continued to generate extensive disagreement as to whether the President may violate international law. The *Restatement* observes that "[t]here is authority that the President, acting within his constitutional authority, may have the power under the Constitution to act in ways that constitute violations of international law by the United States."[14] One group of commentators has agreed, viewing *The Paquete Habana* merely as imposing a curb on local military commanders who exceed the authority granted them by the President.[15] Another commentator, however, has read the case to stand for the proposition that "the President of the United States is . . . bound by international law, which is part of the supreme law of the land under article VI."[16] Another commentator has concluded that "adher-

[9] Tel-Oren v. Libyan Arab Republic, 726 F.2d 774, 775 (D.C. Cir. 1984) (Edwards, J., concurring).

[10] The extent to which a treaty imposes a domestic legal obligation upon the President, apart from the obligation imposed by norms of customary international law, is discussed in Chapter 4.

[11] This principle is codified in article 26 of the Vienna Convention on the Law of Treaties, which provides that "[e]very treaty in force is binding upon the parties to it and must be performed by them in good faith." U.N. Conf. on the Law of Treaties, U.N. Doc. A/Conf.39/27 (May 23, 1969). For a discussion of the customary norm, see W. Bishop, International Law, Cases and Materials 133 (3d ed. 1962). An excellent overview of the place of treaties in United States law is set forth in a succinct essay by Professor John Jackson, *United States*, *in* F. Jacobs & S. Roberts, The Effect of Treaties in Domestic Law (1987).

[12] Military and Paramilitary Activities in and against Nicaragua (Nicaragua v. United States of America), Merits, 1986 I.C.J. Rep. 14 (Judgment of June 27).

[13] *See, e.g.*, B. Ziegler, The International Law of John Marshall (1939); P. Wright, The Enforcement of International Law Through Municipal Law in the United States (1915); C. Picciotto, The Relation of International Law to the Law of England and of the United States of America (1915); Willoughby, *The Legal Nature of International Law*, 2 Am. J. Intl. L. 365 (1908); Scott, *The Legal Nature of International Law*, 1 Am. J. Intl. L. 856 (1907).

[14] Restatement § 115, Reporters' Note 3.

[15] L. Henkin, R. Pugh, O. Schachter, & H. Smit, International Law 120 (1980).

[16] Paust, *Is the President Bound by the Supreme Law of the Land?—Foreign Affairs and National Security Reexamined*, 9 Hastings Const. L.Q. 719, 727 (1982). *See also id.* at 728 n.24

ence to international law'' is ''a matter of Constitutional necessity. . . . [T]his is the way the Constitution ought to be authoritatively construed.''[17] Still another has argued for complete presidential discretion in international-law violation.[18]

This chapter considers the issue of presidential power to act in violation of international law, applying the framework for constitutional analysis developed in Chapters 1 and 2. It draws these conclusions:

1. When Congress approves of a presidential act violative of customary international law, that act is constitutionally permissible.
2. When Congress disapproves of such a presidential act, the act is not constitutionally permissible. No such act will fall within the President's plenary powers because Congress is granted exclusive power to define and punish offenses against the laws of nations.[19] The scope of the President's plenary powers therefore does not embrace the authority to violate customary international law.[20]
3. When the President acts in the face of congressional silence, federal common law governs the controversy. Because federal common law includes certain norms of customary international law,[21] presidential violation of those norms is unconstitutional.[22]

(''In *The Paquete Habana* . . . the Supreme Court actually avoided an executive action involving use of our armed forces in time of war precisely because it was violative of international law.''); *id.* at 731 n.39 (''In *The Paquete Habana*, the President clearly had direct constitutional authority to act in time of war, but his specific actions . . . were found to be violative of the law of the land and were therefore voided.'').

[17] Falk, *International Law and the United States Role in Viet Nam: A Response to Professor Moore*, 76 Yale L.J. 1095, 1150 (1967). For a similar argument *see* Lobel, *The Limits of Constitutional Powers: Conflicts Between Foreign Policy and International Law*, 71 Va. L. Rev. 1071 (1985).

[18] Charney, *The Power of the Executive Branch of the United States Government to Violate Customary International Law*, 80 Am. J. Intl. L. 913 (1986). The question generated a lengthy debate in the pages of the American Journal of International Law; for follow-up commentary, *see* Glennon, *Can the President Do No Wrong*? 80 Am. J. Intl. L. 923 (1986); Henkin, *The President and International Law*, 80 Am. J. Intl. L. 930 (1986); Kirgis, *Federal Statutes, Executive Orders and ''Self-Executing Custom,''* 81 Am. J. Intl. L. 375 (1980); D'Amato, *The President and International Law: The Missing Dimension*, 81 Am. J. Intl. L. 375 (1980); Paust, *The President* Is *Bound by International Law*, 81 Am. J. Intl. L. 377 (1980); Sweeney, letter, 81 Am. J. Intl. L. 637 (1980). *See also* Paust, *Rediscovering the Relationship Between Congressional Power and International Law: Exceptions to the Last-in-Time Rule and the Primacy of Custom*, 28 Va. J. Intl. L. 393 (1988); Weisburd, *The Executive Branch and International Law*, 41 Vand. L. Rev. 1205 (1988) (hereinafter ''Weisburd''); Riesenfeld, *The Powers of Congress and the President in International Relations: Revisited*, 75 Cal. L. Rev. 405 (1987).

[19] U.S. Const. art. I, § 8, cl. 10.

[20] *See* Chapter 8.

[21] The Paquete Habana, 175 U.S. 677, 700 (1900).

[22] The President's action, in other words, is unconstitutional until authorized by Congress; it is ''contingently'' constitutional.

In developing this analysis, I consider the power of the federal courts to incorporate international law into federal common law binding upon the Executive. I conclude that federal common law invalidates presidential acts in violation of international law until Congress, by statute, supersedes the federal common-law rule. The chapter suggests that by relying on federal common law, courts can decide cases without drawing permanent constitutional lines, a practice that comports with past decisions and with the proper institutional role of the federal judiciary in our constitutional system.

Presidential Power to Violate Customary International Law

Statutory Approval

Because there is no provision of the Constitution and no constitutional doctrine holding that the political branches, acting together, may not breach international rules, the President, acting with congressional support, is not constitutionally bound to respect international law. Chief Justice Marshall affirmed this view in a series of decisions.

Initially, in deciding *Murray v. The Charming Betsy*,[23] Marshall wrote that "an act of Congress ought never to be construed to violate the law of nations if any other possible construction remains."[24] Marshall indicated, however, that if the courts cannot construe congressional action to comply with international law, they nevertheless must enforce the action.[25] Later, in *Brown v. United States*,[26] the Chief Justice, in dictum, stated that the President and Congress, acting together, may violate customary international law.[27] Marshall reaffirmed this position a year later in deciding *The Nereide*;[28] he had no doubt that customary international norms would govern ownership of a seized vessel in the event of congressional silence.[29] If Congress had enacted another rule, however, that rule would control.[30] In 1848, the Court further explained its rationale for rejecting international law as an "absolute" constitutional constraint on the exercise of legislative power when it stated in *Waring v. Clarke*

[23] 6 U.S. (2 Cranch) 64 (1804).

[24] *Id.* at 118.

[25] *Id.* at 119. Marshall's only requirement was that such an intent be "plainly expressed." *Id.*

[26] 12 U.S. (8 Cranch) 110 (1814).

[27] Marshall stated that "usage is a guide which the sovereign follows or abandons at his will." *Id.* at 128.

[28] 13 U.S. (9 Cranch) 388 (1815).

[29] *Id.* at 422.

[30] Marshall wrote, "If it be the will of the government to apply to Spain any rule respecting captures which Spain is supposed to apply to us, the government will manifest that will by passing an act for the purpose. Till such an act be passed, the Court is bound by the law of nations which is a part of the law of the land." *Id.* at 423.

that "[i]t would be a denial to Congress of all legislation upon the subject."[31] By the time of *The Paquete Habana*,[32] the Court had established clear precedent that "resort [could] be had to the customs and usages of civilized nations" only "where there is . . . no controlling . . . legislative act."[33]

The principle that statutes prevail over inconsistent customary international law developed simultaneously with correlative principles concerning the relationship between statutes and treaties. In the 1870 *Cherokee Tobacco Case*,[34] the Court confronted a conflict between an 1866 treaty with the Cherokees and an 1868 revenue statute. "Undoubtedly," the Court said, "one or the other must yield. The repugnancy is clear and they cannot stand together. . . . The effect of treaties and acts of Congress, when in conflict, is not settled by the Constitution. But the question is not involved in any doubt as to its proper solution. A treaty may supersede a prior act of Congress, and an act of Congress may supersede a prior treaty."[35] Fourteen years later, the doctrine was reaffirmed in the *Head Money Cases*[36] when a conflict arose between another revenue statute and a treaty. The Court said that to the extent the provisions of any law "may be found to be in conflict with any treaty with a foreign nation, they must prevail in all judicial courts of this country. . . . [T]he Constitution gives [treaties] no superiority over an act of Congress in this respect, which may be repealed or modified by an act of a later date."[37] Similarly, the *Chinese Exclusion Case*[38] held that an 1888 law limiting Chinese immigration prevailed against an 1868 treaty with China. In *Whitney v. Robertson*,[39] the Court succinctly summarized the doctrine:

> By the Constitution, a treaty is placed on the same footing, and made of like obligation, with an act of legislation. . . . When [treaty and statute] relate to the same subject, the courts will always endeavor to construe them so as to give effect to both, if that can be done without violating the language of either; but, if the two are inconsistent, the one last in date will control the other: provided, always, the treaty on the subject is self-executing.[40]

[31] *Waring*, 46 U.S. (5 How.) 441, 457 (1847). Justice Wynne continued, "It would make, for all time to come, without an amendment to the Constitution, that unalterable by any legislation of ours, which can at any time be changed by the Parliament of England,—a limitation which never could have been meant. . . ." *Id.*

[32] 175 U.S. 677 (1900).

[33] *Id.* at 700. The Court stated some years later, "There is no mystic over-law to which even the United States must bow." The Western Maid, 257 U.S. 419, 432 (1922).

[34] 78 U.S. (11 Wall.) 616 (1870).

[35] *Id.* at 620–21.

[36] 112 U.S. 580 (1884).

[37] *Id.* at 597, 598–99.

[38] 130 U.S. 581 (1889).

[39] 124 U.S. 190 (1888).

[40] *Id.* at 194. Because only self-executing treaties are law of the land, Foster & Elam v. Neilson,

Although this so-called last-in-time doctrine pertains to the relationship between statutes and treaties rather than statutes and customary norms, its relevance to customary norms is manifest. When a treaty is violated, customary international law is also violated, since customary international law requires that treaties be carried out in good faith. Thus, just as the President and Congress, acting together, can violate a prior treaty, so may they violate a preexisting customary norm. This conclusion makes sense: Since the supremacy clause[41] makes treaties the law of the land and says nothing about customary law, it would be unreasonable to construe the Constitution as elevating customary law *above* treaty law in its ability to withstand a subsequent inconsistent statute.

Note that the last-in-time doctrine relates only to United States domestic law; that a statute breaches a treaty or customary international norm has no effect on the continuing validity of the norm, for no nation may unilaterally dispense with its international obligations.[42]

Note also that although the Court in the *Cherokee Tobacco Case* regarded the matter as "not settled by the Constitution," by the time of *Whitney v. Robertson*, it felt sanguine in announcing that the priority was assigned "[b]y the Constitution." In one sense, this later statement is correct; as Charles Evans Hughes said, the Constitution means what the judges say it means.[43] In another sense, however, the Court's earlier statement is probably closer to the mark: The last-in-time doctrine is, like other canons of construction, judge-made, designed to find legislative intent where it is unclear. The Court might have formulated a different rule, making treaties superior to inconsistent statutes so long as the treaties remain in effect internationally. And at some point it might rethink the doctrine to give more domestic weight to the nation's international obligations.

Meanwhile, the doctrine remains robust,[44] and the federal courts have even suggested that the President may not disregard a decision to violate international law, once made by Congress.[45] In 1966, for example, the UN Security Council adopted a resolution requiring that all UN members impose a trade embargo upon Southern Rhodesia.[46] In 1971, Congress enacted the so-called Byrd Amendment,[47] intended to "detach this country from the UN boycott of Southern Rhodesia in blatant disregard of our treaty undertakings."[48] In *Diggs*

---

27 U.S. (2 Pet.) 253 (1829), the issue does not arise with respect to non-self-executing treaties not yet implemented by legislation.

[41] U.S. Const. art. VI, § 2.

[42] Restatement § 115, Comment *b* and § 311(3).

[43] Speech at Elmira, N.Y., May 3, 1907.

[44] *See* Restatement § 115(a).

[45] Diggs v. Shultz, 470 F.2d 461, 466 (D.C. Cir. 1972).

[46] Security Council Resolution 232 (1966).

[47] 22 U.S.C. 287c (1982).

[48] *Diggs*, 470 F.2d at 466.

v. Shultz, the plaintiffs asserted that Congress did not intend to force the President to violate the UN resolution but to give him the option to do so.[49] The court, however, openly rejected the plaintiffs' argument and found that Congress intended to violate the treaties.[50] The court held that Congress could denounce international treaties and that the other branches of government could not prevent it.[51] Although the court did not extend its analysis to customary international law, the treaty violation necessarily placed the United States in violation of the customary norm of *pacta sunt servanda*.[52]

Similarly, in 1988, it was alleged that congressionally approved assistance to the Nicarguan Contras violated the United Nations Charter, since the Charter[53] required compliance with a decision of the International Court of Justice ordering a halt to such aid.[54] The court, however, held the treaty obligation legally subordinate to the subsequent congressional authorization.[55] This time the court did extend its analysis to customary international law, ruling that "no enactment of Congress can be challenged on the ground that it violates customary international law."[56]

Perhaps the most noted recent application of these principles came in connection with the statute relating to the PLO Mission to the United Nations in New York. The United States had in 1947 entered into an agreement with the UN providing that "[t]he federal authorities . . . of the United States shall not impose any impediments to transit to or from the headquarters district of . . . other persons invited to the headquarters district by the United Nations. . . ."[57] Nonetheless, Congress enacted the Anti-Terrorism Act of 1987, prohibiting the establishment or maintenance of "an office, headquarters, premises, or other facilities or establishments within the jurisdiction of the United

[49] *Id*. at 465.

[50] *Id*. at 466. "[N]o amount of statutory interpretation now can make the Byrd Amendment other than what it was as presented to the Congress, namely, a measure which would make—and was intended to make—the United States a certain treaty violator." *Id*.

[51] "Under our constitutional scheme Congress can denounce treaties if it sees fit to do so, and there is nothing the other branches of government can do about it. We consider that this is precisely what Congress has done in this case. . . ." *Id*. at 466–67.

[52] For a statement of this norm, see *supra* text accompanying note 10.

[53] Article 94 provides that "[e]ach Member of the United Nations undertakes to comply with the decision of the International Court of Justice in any case to which it is a party."

[54] In Nicaragua v. United States of America, 1986 I.C.J. 14, Merits (1986), the International Court of Justice concluded that the United States is under a "duty immediately to cease and to refrain from all such acts as may constitute breaches of the foregoing legal obligations," *id*. at 149, including acts relating to the "training, equipping, financing, and supplying [of] the *contra* forces." *Id*. at 146.

[55] Committee of U.S. Citizens in Nicaragua v. Reagan, 859 F.2d 929, 937 (D.C. Cir. 1988).

[56] *Id*. at 939. The court expressly declined to extend that holding to peremptory norms, however, *id*. at 940, holding that none was there at issue. *Id*.

[57] Agreement between the United Nations and the United States of America regarding the Headquarters of the United Nations, June 26, 1947, 11 U.N.T.S. 11, T.I.A.S. 1676.

States at the behest of, or with funds provided by the Palestine Liberation Organization. . . ."[58] On March 11, 1988, the United States Attorney General advised the Permanent Observer of the PLO to the UN that "maintaining the PLO Observer Mission . . . will be unlawful."[59] A Justice Department official explained that the Anti-Terrorism Act had "superseded the requirements of the UN Headquarters Agreement to the extent that those requirements are inconsistent with that statute. . . . The statute's mandate governs, and we have no choice but to enforce it."[60]

It was argued that the President had power to decline to enforce the law because the precedents according primacy to statutes in conflict with subsequent treaties do not involve treaties that impose host obligations with respect to an international organization. The application of the last-in-time doctrine, it was contended, can and should be narrowed to exclude such treaties; to do so would serve the cause of world order.[61]

None of the last-in-time treaty opinions of the Court indicates that the Court had in mind only treaties not involving host obligations. The opinions indicate that the Court intended the rule to apply to all treaties, without exception. It is correct that none of the fact situations before the Court in any of those cases raised issues involving host obligations. But so what? None of the fact situations, for that matter, involved arms-control treaties, treaties granting most-favored-nation status, or extradition treaties. Are these classes of treaties also to be deemed exempt from the operation of the last-in-time doctrine? A precedent cannot be factitiously narrowed by cramming its facts into a thimble when the judge who *found* those facts chose a bucket. The power to find facts, to state broadly or narrowly the circumstances in which the announced rule applies, is integral to the common law. To claim the discretion to refind those facts in every rereading of a case is to render the law infinitely elastic and ultimately meaningless. The precedents yield a stark reality: No court has ever upheld the authority of the executive branch to violate a statute on the ground of its breaching a treaty obligation or denied the authority of Congress to enact legislation that violates such an obligation.

The Anti-Terrorism Act is a silly law. But there is nothing in the Constitution, as Holmes wrote, that prevents the United States from going to hell in a handbasket. It is not within the constitutional power of the President to disregard a law because it is bad.[62] The Constitution does not denominate the Pres-

[58] Foreign Relations Appropriations Act for 1988 and 1989, Pub. L. No. 100-204, §§ 1001–5, 101 Stat. 1331 at 1406; 22 U.S.C. §§ 5201–3.

[59] Applicability of the Obligation to Arbitrate under § 21 of the United Nations Headquarters Agreement of 26 June 1947, 1988 I.C.J. 12 (slip op.).

[60] *Id.* at 13.

[61] Reisman, *Take It to Court*, N.Y. Times, Mar. 16, 1988, at 16.

[62] Whether the President can disregard a statute because he believes it to be *unconstitutional* is another question, as noted in Chapter 3 in connection with the War Powers Resolution. The Anti-

ident as quality-control chief, with power to pick and choose among the good, the bad, and the silly. It makes him Chief Executive, and it requires that he "take care that the laws be faithfully executed."[63] It carves no exception for laws he deems violative of international law.

A more subtle effort to circumvent the operation of the last-in-time doctrine in such circumstances is the proposal of one commentator[64] that the cases be read "less regressive[ly]"[65] by requiring that disputes arising out of a conflict between a treaty and a subsequent inconsistent statute be regarded as nonjusticiable. It has been persuasively shown, however, that such an interpretation of the cases is implausible and that the two readings would still yield similar consequences.[66]

Terrorism Act does raise serious constitutional questions. The Justice Department defended it in court against a First Amendment challenge, replying that "[t]he political branches . . . may use their extraordinarily broad foreign affairs powers to forbid individuals from speaking as the personification of the PLO." Memorandum of Points and Authorities in Support of Defendant's Motion to Dismiss, Mendelsohn v. Meese, 88-CIV-2005 (ELP) at 41–42. "[E]ven to the extent the Anti-Terrorism Act might be thought to affect plaintiffs' first amendment rights, the Act is permissible because it furthers a *bona fide* foreign policy objective." *Id.* at 46. Under this rationale, the office of every domestic organization that advocates on behalf of foreign principals could also be closed. The offices of the American–Israel Public Affairs Committee, for example, might be closed as a method of registering governmental disapproval of Israel's handling of the crisis on the West Bank. The Constitution has never been construed to permit the government to regulate speech based exclusively on a citizen's association with a foreign principal. *See* Lamont v. Postmaster General, 381 U.S. 301 (1965). The PLO office was operated entirely by United States citizens and permanent residents, whose conduct had hitherto been completely lawful.

The federal district court in Mendelsohn v. Meese, 695 F. Supp. 1474 (S.D.N.Y. 1988), disagreed with the government that no first amendment interests were implicated in the application of the Anti-Terrorism Act to the PLO. *Id.* at 9. Accordingly, while reading the Act as permitting the establishment and maintenance of an office, the court upheld the prohibitions related to spending and receiving money. *Id.* at 23. The court reasoned that "[i]t would make no sense to allow American citizens to invoke their constitutional rights in an effort to act as official representatives of foreign powers upon which the political branches have placed limits." *Id.* at 13–14.

There are several problems with this approach. First, the PLO is not a "foreign power"; it is an organization, on a different footing for constitutional purposes than a foreign government. Second, as the court itself recognized, "[t]hree speaking plaintiffs explicitly deny acting in any sort of official capacity at all." *Id.* at 14. Third, the case law does not support holding certain speech protected by the first amendment when made on the speaker's own behalf but unprotected when made on another's behalf. In First Nat'l Bank of Boston v. Belloti, 435 U.S. 765 (1978), the Supreme Court struck down a state law prohibiting corporate advocacy; speech protected by the Constitution, the Court held, does not become unprotected merely because made on behalf of a corporation. The Supreme Court focused on the constitutional interests of the audience in hearing the speech, interests that derived from the substance of the speech rather than the identity of the speaker.

[63] U.S. Const. art. II, § 3.

[64] Westen, *The Place of Foreign Treaties in the Courts of the United States: A Reply to Professor Henkin*, 101 Harv. L. Rev. 511 (1987).

[65] *Id.* at 512.

[66] Henkin, *Lexical Priority or "Political Question: A Response*, 101 Harv. L. Rev. 524 (1987).

The PLO litigation did not result in a finding that the UN Headquarters Agreement and Anti-Terrorism Act conflicted. A federal district court, on June 29, 1988, found no "clear legislative intent that Congress was directing the Attorney General, the State Department, or this Court to act in contravention of the Headquarters Agreement."[67] The court acknowledged "that Congress *has the power* to enact statutes abrogating proper treaties or international obligations entered into by the United States," but concluded that because that power was not "clearly and unequivocally exercised" in that case, the court was under a duty to interpret the Anti-Terrorism Act "in a manner consonant with existing treaty obligations."[68]

Congress may therefore enact statutes that place the United States in violation of conventional and customary rules of international law.[69] When Congress has approved of a presidential violation of international law, the only question is whether the national government as a whole possesses the power to act in violation of international law. A series of judicial decisions make it clear that an otherwise constitutional[70] act of Congress may place the United States in violation of a rule of international law. However, when Congress has disapproved of the presidential action, the issue arises whether the President's initiative is within his exclusive power.

Statutory Disapproval

What if the President's violation of customary international law falls within the scope of his plenary constitutional powers?[71] Would not an exercise of such a power prevail against any contrary assertion of authority? Suppose that under the facts of *The Paquete Habana*,[72] the President had ordered the seizure of coastal fishing vessels[73] and that that act lay within his plenary power as commander in chief; would his act not be legal?

[67] United States v. Palestine Liberation Organization, 695 F. Supp. 1456 (S.D.N.Y., 1988).

[68] *Id.* at 15–16 (emphasis added).

[69] Chief Justice Marshall had taken this position earlier in Brown v. United States, 12 U.S. (8 Cranch) 110, 128 (1814) with respect to customary international law. Such a rule, in Marshall's words, "cannot be disregarded by him without obloquy, yet it may be disregarded." *Id.*

[70] For the suggestion that the breadth of protection afforded by the first amendment is a function of customary international law, *see* Finzer v. Barry, 798 F.2d 1450 (D.C.Cir. 1986). The court there upheld a District of Columbia statute limiting the display of signs and demonstrations before foreign embassies. The law of nations, it found, "demands security for the persons and respect for the dignity and peace of foreign emissaries. . . ." *Id.* at 1458.

[71] "[T]he President," Professor Henkin has written, "may *exercise his constitutional powers in foreign affairs* without regard to international law." Henkin, *The Constitution and United States Sovereignty: A Century of Chinese Exclusion and Its Progeny*, 100 Harv. L. Rev. 853, 882 (1987) (emphasis added).

[72] 175 U.S. 667 (1900).

[73] In fact, in *The Paquete Habana*, 175 U.S. 667 (1900), the President ordered that international law be honored. The issue in that case was not whether the President could violate custom-

The answer is that the question is tautological. As the question is posed, it answers itself: The exercise of a plenary power is *by definition* not susceptible of abridgment. The decision to recognize the People's Republic of China, the decision to pardon Richard Nixon, or the decision to land on the beaches of Normandy rather than Calais—these are all acts that fell within the President's sole constitutional powers. But what does that mean?

Although the term *plenary* is used frequently in the abstract, as discussed in Chapter 1, it has relevance only in a specific context. *Plenary power* refers to the power of the President to act, *even if Congress prohibits that act*. Put another way, the exercise of a plenary presidential power precludes Congress from acting.

However, we know from the constitutional text that the President is possessed of no plenary power to violate international law. Article I, section 8, clause 10 explicitly confers upon Congress power to define and punish offenses against the law of nations. In clear terms, Congress is directly empowered to prohibit international law violations. It simply cannot be, therefore, that the Constitution gives the President plenary power to violate international law. An act of Congress that prohibits him from doing so will prevail.

Stated meaningfully, the question is: *Do* the President's plenary powers permit him to violate a norm of customary international law? Because the power to prohibit an international-law violation is lodged in Congress, the answer clearly is no. The President has no more power to violate international law in the face of a congressional prohibition than he or she has power to coin money or to regulate interstate commerce or to exercise any other power set forth in article I, section 8 of the Constitution in the face of a congressional prohibition.

Plenary, in short, does not mean "unlimited." A plenary power ends where a power of Congress begins. Because the power of Congress includes the power to prohibit any, or all, offenses against international law, if Congress does so, its law binds the President. The President therefore could not have plenary power to seize coastal fishing vessels in violation of customary international law.

Statutory Silence

The real issue is not whether the President can cause the United States to violate international law in the face of a statutory prohibition but whether he can do so in the face of congressional silence. As discussed in Chapter 2, when Congress remains silent, two possibilities exist: (1) the act may fall within the political branches' concurrent powers, one that the President can perform until

ary international law, but whether the military commander ordered to carry out the naval blockade of Cuba had acted in accordance with the President's order, which incorporated international law by reference.

Congress prohibits it; or (2) the act may fall within Congress's plenary powers, one that the President cannot perform without congressional approval.

The starting point for analyzing a presidential act violative of international law carried out in the face of congressional silence is necessarily a traditional inquiry into the text of the Constitution, case law, custom, and the Framers' intent.

THE CONSTITUTIONAL TEXT

As is true with many inquiries, the text of the Constitution does not disclose a dispositive answer. A variety of conflicting interpretations of constitutional language emerge.

The Offenses Clause. The Constitution expressly refers to international law only once: Congress may "define and punish . . . Offenses against the Law of Nations."[74] Under one reading, the offenses clause might mean that international law is not part of domestic law. The clause might require Congress to act affirmatively before any part of international law becomes part of federal law, leaving undefined and unpunished "unincorporated" offenses. On the other hand, the offenses clause might carve out an exception from an otherwise fully incorporated body of international law. Under this reading, all noncriminal provisions of international law would be part of federal law, but criminal provisions would be included only to the extent defined by Congress.[75] The offenses clause lends itself to additional interpretations. Until fairly recently, international law almost exclusively related to the rights and obligations of nations, not of individuals engaged in foreign affairs.[76] Accordingly, the offenses clause might grant Congress the power to control the conduct of federal officials who act on behalf of the United States.[77] Under a similar theory, the offenses clause might permit Congress to prohibit any individual American—private citizen or governmental official—from doing anything that would place the United States in violation of its obligations to other nations.

The Faithful-Execution Clause. The word *law* appears in the Constitution with some frequency, and several such instances might encompass international law. The requirement that the President "take Care that the Laws be

[74] U.S. Const. art. I, § 8, cl. 10 ("To define and punish Piracies and Felonies committed on the high Seas, and Offenses against the Law of Nations").

[75] Whether statutory incorporation requires both definition and punishment also is unclear. Arguably, Congress might elect to define something in the nature of a civil offense without imposing criminal punishment.

[76] *See generally* J. G. Starke, An Introduction to International Law 53–65 (5th ed. 1963) (discussing the subjects of international law).

[77] Statutes thoroughly regulate the conduct of federal agents, but often the statutes do not make violations a criminal offense or do not proscribe any other penalty.

faithfully executed''[78] might compel him to observe the precepts of international law. In this instance, Congress might wish to ''define'' offenses against the law of nations without ''punishing'' them, to identify those customary international norms by which the President shall be bound. A second, less rigorous interpretation of the provision would emphasize presidential authority rather than obligation. The clause might confer independent power upon the President to enforce international law, without regard to congressional inaction.

The Supremacy Clause. The supremacy clause declares that the Constitution, ''Laws of the United States which shall be made in Pursuance thereof,'' and treaties shall be the supreme law of the land.[79] Although the clause does not expressly apply to all international law, the reference to treaties alone apparently confers domestic supremacy only upon treaty obligations, leaving nontreaty obligations unincorporated. Moreover, since *made* refers to the act of legislating, international law would not qualify as law of the United States unless affirmatively ''defined'' by Congress. Thus, because the language of the Constitution is ambiguous as to the status of international law, reference to the intent of the Framers might resolve the ambiguities.

CASE LAW

Case law and derivative constitutional doctrine, on the other hand, provide strong authority that the President lacks power to violate international law. Courts have held consistently that ''[i]nternational law is part of our law,''[80] and as recently as 1983, the Supreme Court cited *The Paquete Habana* for that ''frequently reiterated'' statement.[81] Yet only one court has confronted directly the issue whether the President, acting alone, may place the United States in violation of international law.[82] The two cases most frequently relied upon in commentary discussing the question are *Brown v. United States*[83] and

[78] U.S. Const. art. II, § 3.

[79] U.S. Const. art. VI, § 2. The supremacy clause states,

> The Constitution, and the laws of the United States which shall be made in Pursuance thereof; and all treaties made, or which shall be made, under the Authority of the United States, shall be the Supreme Law of the Land; and the judges in every State shall be bound thereby, anything in the Constitution or Laws of any State to the contrary notwithstanding.

Id.

[80] The Paquete Habana, 175 U.S. 677, 700 (1900). Many other cases reiterate the doctrine. *See, e.g.*, First Nat'l City Bank v. Banco Nacional de Cuba, 406 U.S. 759, 763 (1972); Skiriotes v. Florida, 313 U.S. 69, 72–73 (1941); United States v. Howard-Arias, 679 F.2d 363, 371 (4th Cir. 1982).

[81] First Nat'l City Bank v. Banco Para El Comercio, 462 U.S. 611, 623 (1983).

[82] *See* Garcia-Mir v. Meese, 788 F.2d 1446 (11th Cir.), *cert. denied*, 107 S. Ct. 289 (1986). It is hard to see how either Tag v. Rogers, 267 F.2d 664 (D.C. Cir. 1959), *cert. denied*, 362 U.S. 904 (1960), or The Over the Top, 5 F.2d 838 (D. Conn. 1925), constitutes authority for the view that the President has the power to disregard a rule of international law.

[83] 12 U.S. (8 Cranch) 110 (1814).

The Paquete Habana.[84] Given their importance, an examination of each is appropriate.

Brown v. United States. During the War of 1812, the federal government seized certain property located in the United States that belonged to British nationals.[85] The plaintiff claimed that the seizure was illegal.[86] Chief Justice Marshall, writing for the majority, held that the government could not seize the plaintiff's property.[87] The President, he reasoned, lacked independent constitutional power to effect such seizures and therefore could proceed only with congressional authorization.[88] Because the declaration of war did not constitute such authorization and the only further legislation Congress had enacted did not bear upon the subject, the President did not have the necessary authorization.[89]

Professor Henkin has read *Brown* as supporting a presidential power to act in violation of international law.[90] It would appear, however, that the principal question was not whether the President may violate international law but whether his duty to "take Care that the Laws be faithfully executed"[91] gives him an affirmative power to "execute" the law of nations to expand his power—a question the Court answered in the negative. To the extent that the Court addressed the President's authority to violate international law, the Court intimated that the President lacks the constitutional power to violate international law.

Justice Story, sitting as a circuit judge, wrote the lower-court opinion in *Brown*.[92] Marshall responded to Story's circuit opinion at the end of his opinion.[93] Story, Marshall explained, had rested his judgment in favor of the United States on the theory that the President, in seizing alien property, was merely "executing" the law of nations, which allowed such seizure incident to the declaration of war.[94] Marshall replied that international law was not a source of presidential authority unless Congress expressly incorporated it by statute.[95] Marshall thus declined to accept Story's view that international law

[84] 175 U.S. 677 (1900).

[85] 12 U.S. (8 Cranch) at 121–22.

[86] *Id*. at 123.

[87] *Id*. at 129.

[88] *Id*. at 128–29.

[89] *Id*. at 129.

[90] L. Henkin, Foreign Affairs and the Constitution 460 n.61 (1972).

[91] U.S. Const. art. II, § 3.

[92] Justice Story's circuit court opinion is set forth in his dissent, 12 U.S. (8 Cranch) at 129–47 (Story, J., dissenting).

[93] *Id*. at 128–29.

[94] *Id*. at 128.

[95] *See* L. Henkin, *supra* note 90, at 460 n.61. In this context Marshall made his oft-quoted response, relied upon by Professor Henkin:

> It is urged that, in executing the laws of war, the executive may seize and the Courts condemn all property which, according to the modern law of nations, is subject to confiscation. . . .

expanded executive power. The Constitution, Marshall wrote, did not authorize the President to seize such property. Because of the potentially far-reaching consequences of such acts (here, the possibility of reprisals against American property located in the belligerent state), Marshall believed that Congress must authorize acts that violate international law.[96]

Far from suggesting that the President, acting alone, may disregard international law,[97] therefore, Marshall strongly implied that the President can do so only with congressional authorization.[98] It was "fundamental" to his thinking that if Congress was silent, the courts must enforce international law:

> If there is any fundamental concept of Marshall's that is especially noteworthy and outstanding, it is that . . . those rules of conduct which have been so generally consented to by the civilized countries of the world must be deemed the law of the world, and if the political department of the United States had not manifested any views with reference to them at all, it was to be the duty of the courts to follow those generally accepted rules as laws in all cases that came before them for judicial determination; for until the political department does act, "the Court is bound by the law of nations which is part of the law of the land."[99]

> This argument must assume for its basis the position that modern [international] usage constitutes a rule which acts directly upon the thing itself by its own force, and not through the sovereign power. This position is not allowed. This usage is a guide which the sovereign follows or abandons at his will. The rule, like all other precepts of morality, of humanity, and even of wisdom, is addressed to the judgment of the sovereign; and although it cannot be disregarded by him without obloquy, yet it may be disregarded.

12 U.S. (8 Cranch) at 128.

[96] The rule which we apply to the property of our enemy will be applied by him to the property of our citizens. Like all other questions of policy, it is proper for the consideration of a department which can modify it at will; and for the consideration of a department which can pursue only the law as it is written. It is proper for the consideration of the legislature, not of the executive or the judiciary.

12 U.S. (8 Cranch) at 128–29.

[97] A rule that the declaration of war, "by its own operation . . . vest[s] the property of the enemy in the government," would violate international law. *Id.* at 123.

[98] Justice Story clearly concurred in this opinion. *See* 12 U.S. (8 Cranch) at 149, 153–54 (Story, J., dissenting). Justice Story replied that Marshall misunderstood the reasoning of his circuit court opinion, to which he continued to adhere. Story claimed that he had not argued that international law can be carried out by the President under the faithful execution clause. Story had argued only, he maintained, that the declaration of war can be so executed, and that it, not the state of war recognized by international law, empowered the President to seize British property. In the conduct of hostilities, Story believed, international law becomes relevant as a limitation on presidential discretion. "[B]y what rule . . . must he be governed? I think the only rational answer is by the law of nations as applied to a state of war." *Id.* at 149. The President, Story continued, "cannot lawfully transcend the rules of warfare established among civilized nations. He cannot lawfully exercise powers or authorize proceedings which the civilized world repudiates and disclaims." *Id.* at 153. "The modern usage of nations is . . . a limitation [on his] discretion." *Id.* at 154.

[99] B. Ziegler, The International Law of John Marshall 30 (1939) (quoting Schooner Exchange v. M'Faddon, 7 Cranch 116, 137 (1812)).

Yet Marshall's remark that the United States Attorney who brought the libel suit "acted from his own impressions of what appertained to his duty" rather than under the direct order of the President weakened the force of this precedent.[100] This same distinction was made by the Court eighty-five years later in *The Paquete Habana*,[101] when the constitutionality of acts of lower-level executive-branch officials was again challenged as violative of international law.

The Paquete Habana. Just as commentators have erroneously relied upon *Brown* as authority for the proposition that the President may violate international law, authorities have mistakenly cited *The Paquete Habana*[102] in support of the reverse proposition that the President is bound by international law.[103] A close reading of *The Paquete Habana* reveals that the Court invalidated acts of lower-level executive officials, not those of the President, because the acts violated the President's orders.[104]

Justice Gray, writing for the majority, suggested that the seizure of the *Paquete Habana* contravened the order of the President.[105] On April 22, 1898, three days before the seizure, "the President issued a proclamation declaring that the United States had instituted and would maintain" a blockade of Cuba "in pursuance of the . . . law of nations applicable to such cases."[106] The President repeated this statement on April 26.[107] Nonetheless, on April 28, the Secretary of the Navy received a communication from the commander of the American squadron, Admiral Sampson, requesting authority to take Cuban fishermen as prisoners because they might be liable for military service in the Spanish Navy.[108] The Secretary's response was equivocal,[109] but the Supreme Court construed it as a denial of the request and therefore consonant with the acts of the President limiting United States military activities to those permitted by international law.[110]

The Paquete Habana, therefore, does not consider whether the President is bound by international law. The Court clearly distinguished between the Pres-

[100] *Id.* at 122.

[101] 175 U.S. 677 (1900).

[102] *Id.*

[103] *See, e.g.*, Paust, *supra* note 16, at 731 n.39.

[104] *See* The Paquete Habana, 175 U.S. 677, 712–13 (1900).

[105] *Id.* at 712.

[106] *Id.*

[107] *Id.*

[108] *Id.* at 712–13. The Court took this request as an acknowledgment by Admiral Sampson that he lacked the authority to arrest peaceable coast fishermen. *Id.* at 713.

[109] The Secretary "guardedly answered: 'Spanish fishing vessels attempting to violate blockade are subject, with crew, to capture, and any such vessel or crew considered likely to aid the enemy may be detained.' " *Id.* at 713.

[110] "[T]he necessary implication and evident intent of the response of the Navy Department were that Spanish coast fishing vessels and their crews should not be interfered with, so long as they neither attempted to violate the blockade, nor were considered likely to aid the enemy." *Id.*

ident and the lower-level military officials who effected the seizure in violation of his proclamation, which incorporated international law.[111] As to the Court's apparent willingness to except a personal order of the President from the constraints of international law,[112] the observation is dictum since no personal order was given to violate international law. Moreover, the Court's reference to a ''controlling'' executive act[113] does not explain what *kind* of presidential act controls—for example, whether the President may act alone or whether Congress must authorize the act. Obviously some presidential acts are *not* ''controlling''; otherwise, the word would be surplusage. *The Paquete Habana* thus leaves open the question whether the President, acting alone, may violate international law.[114]

CUSTOM

As stated in Chapter 2, the intent of the Framers is normally not dispositive in constitutional analysis. More important is constitutional custom. Custom provides little support for the proposition that the President possesses plenary power to violate international law; among other things, the executive branch invariably claims that questionable presidential actions comply with international law.

INTENT OF THE FRAMERS

The intent of the Framers as a source of constitutional power was discussed in Chapter 1; it might suffice now to recall Justice Jackson's observation that their intent must frequently ''be divined from materials almost as enigmatic as the dreams Joseph was called upon to interpret for Pharaoh.''[115] Unhappily, the comment applies all too accurately to the materials discussing the constitutional provisions discussed above.

[111] *See supra* text at note 100.

[112] ''This rule of international law is one which prize courts, administering the law of nations, are bound to take judicial notice of, and to give effect to, in the absence of any treaty *or other public act* of their own government in relation to the matter.'' The Paquete Habana, 175 U.S. 677, 708 (1900) (emphasis added).

[113] *Id.* at 700.

[114] The dissenters believed that the President could abandon international law. They also misinterpreted Justice Marshall's remark in *Brown v. United States* that ''usage is a guide which the sovereign follows or abandons at his will.'' The Paquete Habana, 175 U.S. at 715 (Fuller, J., dissenting) (citing Brown v. United States, 12 U.S. (8 Cranch) 110, 128 (1814)). *See also supra* text accompanying note 5. On the other hand, the Court's use of the word *controlling* with reference to an ''executive act,'' 175 U.S. at 700, suggests that not every executive act qualifies as a ''public act'' and may be subject to the application of customary international law. Professor may be subject to the application of customary international law. Professor Henkin defines *controlling* acts similarly to ''legislative acts.'' *See* Henkin, *International Law as Law in the United States*, 82 Mich. L. Rev. 1555, 1564 n.3 (1984).

[115] Youngstown Sheet & Tube Co. v. Sawyer, 343 U.S. 579, 634 (1952) (Jackson, J., concurring).

The Offenses Clause. The provision authorizing Congress to "define and punish offenses against the Law of Nations"[116] apparently relates to the Continental Congress's concern that foreign powers view the American revolutionary government as dependable and law-abiding. On a number of occasions, the Continental Congress affirmed its intent to comply with international law.[117] The Articles of Confederation, however, contained no reference to international law, and many viewed the absence of legislative authority to punish offenses against international law as a major defect of the Articles. Hamilton and Madison feared that the Articles would permit reckless citizens and states to entangle the United States in conflicts with foreign nations.[118] In addition, the Framers were concerned with a need for uniformity in the international rules applied by state courts[119] and with fairness to criminal defendants, who otherwise could be confronted with undefined offenses of "loose signification."[120]

Other Framers agreed on the need for specificity concerning offenses under international law. On the day the principal discussion of the offenses clause took place, the draft read, "To define & punish piracies and felonies on the high seas, and punish offenses against the law of nations."[121] Gouverneur Morris moved to strike out "punish" in the second clause "so as to let these be *definable* as well as punishable."[122] Edmund Wilson responded that "[t]o pretend to *define* the law of nations which depended on the authority of all the Civilized Nations of the World, would have a look of arrogance that would make us ridiculous."[123] Morris replied that the "word *define* is proper when applied to *offenses* in this case; the law of [nations] being often too vague and deficient to be a rule."[124] His amendment was passed by a vote of 6 to 5, and the offenses clause took its present form.

[116] U.S. Const. art. I, § 8, cl. 10.

[117] *See, e.g.*, 19 Journals of the Continental Congress 315, 361 (1912); 20 *id.* at 762; 21 *id.* at 1136–37, 1158.

[118] "[F]or want of authority [to punish international offenses]," Hamilton said, "the faith of the United States may be broken, their reputation sullied, and their peace interrupted by the negligence or misconception of any particular state." 1 A. Hamilton, The Works of Alexander Hamilton 295 (Long ed. 1971); 5 Debates in the Several State Conventions on the Adoption of the Federal Constitution 543 (J. Elliot 2d ed. 1866) (hereinafter cited as Elliot). Madison too feared that "any indiscreet member [might] embroil the Confederacy with foreign nations." The Federalist No. 42, at 272 (J. Madison) (Bicentennial ed. 1976).

[119] The Federalist No. 42, (Madison), at 272. The concept of felonies on the high seas, Madison wrote, "is not precisely the same in any two of the States; and varies in each with every revision of its criminal laws." *Id.*

[120] *Id.* This would constitute, Madison wrote, a "dishonorable and illegitimate guide." *Id.*

[121] 2 Records of the Federal Convention of 1787, at 614 (Farrand ed. 1911) (hereinafter cited as Farrand).

[122] *Id.* (emphasis in original).

[123] *Id.* at 615 (emphasis in original).

[124] *Id.* (emphasis in original).

The Faithful-Execution Clause. The requirement that the President "take Care that the laws be faithfully executed"[125] was apparently based upon the 1777 New York Constitution,[126] although several other colonial constitutions contained similar provisions.[127] Earlier drafts of the United States Constitution referred to the President's responsibility "to attend to the Execution of the Laws of the U.S."[128] and, later, to "take care that the laws of the United States be duly and faithfully executed."[129] There is no meaningful record of why the Framers left out all reference to the United States in the final version of the faithful-execution clause. However, there is evidence that the Framers believed that the clause, taken together with applicable principles of international law, could circumscribe presidential discretion. The conclusion seems to be one on which Hamilton and Madison agreed, although disagreeing on the reasons. Hamilton wrote in *Pacificus* that under the clause, the President was bound by the Clause not to violate international neutrality rules by "giving a cause of war to foreign powers":

> The Executive is charged with the execution of all laws, the laws of Nations as well as the Municipal law, which recognizes and adopts those laws. It is consequently bound, by faithfully executing the laws of neutrality, when that is the state of the nation, to avoid giving a cause of war to foreign powers.[130]

Madison, in *Helvidius*, also conceived of executive power as limited by "internal and external" law:

> That the executive is bound faithfully to execute the laws of neutrality, whilst those laws continue unaltered by the competent authority, is true; but not for the reason here given, to wit, to avoid giving cause of war to foreign powers. It is bound to the faithful execution of these as of all other laws, internal and external, by the nature of its trust and the sanction of its oath. . . .[131]

The Supremacy Clause. The word *supreme* may appear unqualified, but in the evolved lexicon of American constitutionalists, some supreme laws of the land are more supreme than others. The Constitution is the most supreme law, prevailing over all treaties, federal and state statutes, and principles of federal and state common law. Next come federal statutes and treaties, which are of

[125] U.S. Const. art. II, § 3.

[126] B. Poore, The Federal and State Constitutions, Colonial Charters and Other Organic Laws of the United States 1335 (2d ed. 1878) ("That it shall be the duty of the governor . . . to take care that the laws are faithfully executed to the best of his ability.").

[127] *See id.* at 1521, 1528, 1545, 1863, 1871 (setting forth parallel provisions of Pennsylvania and Vermont constitutions).

[128] 2 Farrand, *supra* note 121, at 158.

[129] *Id.* at 171.

[130] H. Syrett, ed., 15 The Papers of Alexander Hamilton 38 (1961–79).

[131] 2 Writings of James Madison 107 (G. Hunt ed. 1906).

equal status domestically,[132] then federal common law,[133] and finally state statutory and common law.[134] This hierarchy is generally accepted today, but in 1789, it was hardly manifest. The supremacy clause itself gives no hint of any hierarchy; even the Constitution is given no primacy. It is not surprising, therefore, that the hierarchical position of international law is somewhat obscure.

Yet the concept of ''supreme law of the land'' traces to the Magna Carta[135] and was familiar to the colonists and the Framers. For example, the colonial charters made English statutory and common law the supreme law of the colonies.[136] In structuring the Constitution, however, the Framers devoted their attention to the notion of supremacy primarily in the context of federal-state relations.[137] Only because Madison complained at the Convention that the ''files of Congress contain complaints, already, from almost every nation with which treaties have been formed,''[138] the Convention made treaties binding upon the states. Thus, by textually conferring supremacy upon treaties in particular rather than upon international law in general, the Framers met the problem at which the offenses clause was also directed—restoring foreign confidence in the new Nation.[139]

Judicial Authority in the Face of Congressional Silence

Congressional silence in this context raises issues concerning not only the scope of presidential power but also the role the Judiciary should play in determining the scope of presidential power. The role of the courts in this ''zone of twilight'' is in many ways analogous to the role played by Congress when

[132] The Chinese Exclusion Case, 130 U.S. 581, 604–05 (1889); Head Money Cases, 112 U.S. 580, 598–99 (1884). *See generally* L. Henkin, Foreign Affairs and the Constitution 163–64 (1972).

[133] For a discussion of federal common law, see *infra* text at notes 163–212.

[134] J. Nowak, R. Rotunda & J. Young, Constitutional Law (2d ed. 1983).

[135] W. McKechnie, Magna Carta, A Commentary on the Greater Charter of King John 375 (2d ed. 1914) (''No freeman shall be taken or [and] imprisoned or disseised or exited or in any way destroyed nor will we go upon him or send upon him except by lawful judgment of his peers or by the law of the land.'').

[136] D. Hutchison, The Foundations of the Constitution 241 (1975).

[137] 2 W. Crosskey, Politics and the Constitution in the History of the United States 763–64 (1953).

[138] 5 Elliot, *supra* note 118, at 207.

[139] Professor Henkin views the omission of customary international law from the text of the supremacy clause as insignificant for purposes of this issue, arguing that the clause was intended to ensure federal supremacy as against the states. Henkin believes that the framers viewed customary international law as ''supreme'' over federal as well as state law and binding upon both federal and state courts. *See* Henkin, *International Law as Law in the United States*, 82 Mich. L. Rev. 1555, 1566 (1984).

it restricts the exercise of presidential power. Disapproval of a presidential act in violation of international law, whether that disapproval takes the form of a statute or a rule of common law, precludes the President from acting until he or she receives statutory authorization. As developed below, because customary international law is part of federal common law and the courts require the Executive to obey federal common law, the courts can require the President to obey customary international law.

As a preliminary matter, it might be observed that the Supreme Court has sought to avoid prescribing absolute rules of conduct for the political branches. The Court has made a particular effort, when upholding or striking down an act of the President, to do so without laying down an inflexible constitutional rule that might straitjacket the Executive or aggrandize presidential power. Instead, the Court has attempted to find that Congress has assented to or prohibited the act.[140]

The courts thus draw ''soft'' constitutional lines by holding that certain presidential acts are constitutional or unconstitutional only in a conditional sense. Normally, the President must procure statutory authorization or the removal of a statutory prohibition to satisfy the condition. When the President fails to fulfill the condition, his act is contingently unconstitutional. This was true, for example, in the *Steel Seizure Case*,[141] where President Truman's failure to obtain congressional authorization rendered his seizure of the steel mills unconstitutional. The President's independent constitutional powers were insufficient to sustain the action, but the invalidity of the act was remediable; all the Chief Executive needed was legislative approval.[142]

Although the Court has not identified explicitly the element of conditionality as such, the idea of contingent unconstitutionality has long pervaded the Court's approach to the question of presidential power. In *Little v. Barreme*,[143] discussed in Chapter 1, Chief Justice Marshall held illegal the seizure of a Danish ship during the undeclared naval war with France.[144] Marshall suggested that in the absence of an effective statutory prohibition, the President might have the constitutional power to seize the vessel. Given the existence of a statutory bar, however, its capture was invalid.[145] In *Brown v. United States*,[146] discussed above,[147] Marshall held that the Executive's seizure of the property of British subjects during the War of 1812 was invalid in the absence

[140] *See, e.g.*, Brown v. United States, 12 U.S. (8 Cranch) 110, 115 (1814); Little v. Barreme, 6 U.S. (2 Cranch) 170, 177–78 (1804).

[141] 343 U.S. 579 (1952).

[142] *Id.* at 586.

[143] 6 U.S. (2 Cranch) 170 (1804).

[144] *Id.* at 178.

[145] *Id.*

[146] 12 U.S. (8 Cranch) 110 (1814).

[147] *See supra* text accompanying notes 85–101.

of statutory authorization.[148] In both cases, the Court recognized that the President's act might be constitutional under certain circumstances but concluded that the requisite condition, congressional authorization, had not been fulfilled. On the other hand, in *Dames & Moore v. Regan*,[149] the Court held that since the condition of statutory authorization had been fulfilled before the Executive entered into the Claims-Settlement Agreement with Iran, the Agreement was contingently constitutional.[150]

The Court's adoption of the theory of contingency, in *Dames & Moore* outlined by Justice Jackson in the *Steel Seizure Case*, thus came as no surprise.[151] Reliance upon notions of contingency has provided the Court with a happy medium: It may settle the important cases,[152] leaving the system flexible enough to adapt to unforeseeable future crises.

Although it normally looks to the legislative posture to determine whether the constitutional condition has been fulfilled, on occasion the Court has referred to the posture of the federal judiciary itself. Justice Brandeis wrote in *Erie Railroad Co. v. Tompkins*[153] that "[t]here is no federal general common law,"[154] but pockets of *specific* federal common law have survived.[155] The Court has applied federal common law in a variety of cases, including those involving disputes between states[156] and those raising questions concerning admiralty,[157] labor relations,[158] and federal negotiable instruments.[159] Although rules of federal common law are not legislation, they represent legislation by another name, for in substance if not in form, they perform the same

[148] *Brown*, 12 U.S. at 129.

[149] 453 U.S. 654 (1981).

[150] *Id.* at 688.

[151] *Id.* at 669.

[152] The Court thus lives up to the lofty task set out for it by Chief Justice Marshall in Marbury v. Madison, 5 U.S. (1 Cranch) 137, 177 (1803) ("It is emphatically the province and duty of the judicial department to say what the law is.").

[153] 304 U.S. 64 (1938).

[154] *Id.* at 78.

[155] *See* Friendly, *In Praise of Erie—And of the New Federal Common Law*, 39 N.Y.U. L. Rev. 383, 406 (1964).

[156] On the same day the Court decided *Erie*, Justice Brandeis held, in another case, that the apportionment of the water of interstate commerce "is a question of 'federal common law.' " Hinderlinder v. La Plata River & Cherry Creek Ditch Co. 304 U.S. 92, 110 (1938) (federal question presented by dispute between private litigants over rights to stream water diverted pursuant to interstate compact).

[157] *See, e.g.*, Moragne v. States Marine Lines, Inc., 398 U.S. 375 (1970) (federal maritime law affords cause of action for wrongful death within state territorial waters).

[158] *See, e.g.*, Textile Workers Union v. Lincoln Mills, 353 U.S. 448, 451 (1957) (federal labor law and policy mandates that federal courts enforce agreements to arbitrate grievance disputes made in return for no-strike agreement).

[159] *See, e.g.*, Clearfield Trust Co. v. United States, 318 U.S. 363, 366–67 (1943) (desirability of uniformity makes federal law appropriate when United States disburses funds or pays debts).

function of creating public rights and obligations.[160] The one real difference is that federal common law is interstitial: The federal courts legislate at the sufferance of Congress by filling statutory gaps, and their legislative handiwork stands only so long as Congress permits it.

Legislative acquiescence is perhaps the most plausible contemporary rationale for judicial legislation, although hardly the only one.[161] Substantive rulemaking power has been found to flow from a jurisdictional grant.[162] Although the constitutional justification for the practice of judicial lawmaking remains unclear, judicial "legislation" has been part of the federal system since the beginning, and the process dovetails with the concept of contingent constitutionality. Judge-made rules today are effectively interchangeable with statutes for the purpose of assessing the scope of presidential power. A judicial negative to a presidential initiative, interposed not as a constitutional requirement but as an exercise in judicial lawmaking, has the same effect as a congressional negative.

Customary International Law as Federal Common Law

THE CONSTITUTIONAL TEXT

Article III provides that the judicial power shall extend to cases "arising under . . . the Laws of the United States."[163] However, the text does not indicate whether the phrase "Laws of the United States" includes federal common law.

The supremacy clause provides that laws of the United States "made in pursuance" of the Constitution shall be the supreme law of the land.[164] The word *made* could include only the act of legislating, but a more reasonable interpretation would encompass judicial acts as well; judges also "make" law, a power implied in jurisdictional grants. The Supreme Court's original jurisdiction, for example, extends to "all Cases affecting Ambassadors, other public Ministers, and Consuls."[165] If it is not within the power of Congress to alter the scope of the Court's original jurisdiction through legislative action,[166]

[160] *See, e.g.*, INS v. Chadha, 462 U.S. 919 (1984) (provision of Immigration and Naturalization Act authorizing one house of Congress, by resolution, to invalidate decision of executive branch to allow particular deportable alien to stay in United States is unconstitutional).

[161] *See infra* text at notes 213–218.

[162] *See* Textile Workers Union v. Lincoln Mills, 353 U.S. 448 (1957). It is clear that cases arising under customary international law are "Cases . . . arising under the Laws of the United States. . . ." Restatement § 111, Comment *e*.

[163] U.S. Const. art. III, § 2.

[164] U.S. Const. art. VI, § 2.

[165] U.S. Const. art. III, § 2.

[166] Marbury v. Madison, 5 U.S. (1 Cranch) 137 (1803).

it should not be possible for Congress to do so through legislative inaction. In other words, congressional failure to enact a statutory grant of original jurisdiction does not render the Court powerless to hear cases falling within the *constitutional* jurisdictional grant. The possibility of adjudicating a controversy in the absence of any congressional action implies an absence of any statutorily prescribed rule of decision. Under such circumstances, the Court therefore must "make" its own substantive rule—a rule that is appropriately regarded as the law of the land.

The Constitution suggests no reason why an inference of substantive rule making power should arise only with respect to constitutional grants of original jurisdiction. The general judicial power extends, for example, to "all Cases of admiralty and maritime Jurisdiction."[167] That constitutional grant should permit the courts to fashion their own substantive rules for deciding admiralty and maritime cases, at least until Congress develops different ones.[168] In such cases, as well as in cases involving ambassadorial immunity or the legality of privateers' seizures, the courts adhere to that body of law that has historically been applied and is conceptually suited to such questions—namely, customary international law. This approach is all the more plausible since early American common-law judges regularly relied upon natural law and English common law, both of which were once linked closely to international law.[169]

THE ENGLISH HERITAGE

As the Framers met in Philadelphia to draft the Constitution, they worked against the backdrop of an American common-law system that had borrowed heavily from that of the English. The English system viewed the common law as embracing principles of natural and international law. Therefore, English and American judges of the eighteenth century typically conceived of their work as including the application of natural law.[170] In *Dr. Bonham's Case*, for

[167] U.S. Const. art. III, § 2.

[168] *See generally* Note, *From Judicial Grant to Legislative Power: The Admiralty Clause in the Nineteenth Century*, 67 Harv. L. Rev. 1214 (1954).

[169] J. G. Starke, *supra* note 76, at 20–22; S. W. Verzul, International Law in Historical Perspective 3–8 (1968); Holdsworth, *The Relation of English Law to International Law*, 26 Minn. L. Rev. 141 (1942).

[170] Chief Justice Marshall regarded "resort to the great principles of reason and justice" appropriate for determining principles of international law. Bentzon v. Boyle, 13 U.S. (9 Cranch) 191, 198 (1815). Justice Story believed that "every doctrine . . . that might fairly be deduced by correct reasoning from the nature of moral obligations, may theoretically be said to exist in the law of nations." United States v. The Schooner *La Jeune Eugenie*, 26 F. Cas. 846 (C.C.D. Mass. 1822) (No. 15,551). And in 1814 the Supreme Court said simply that the "law of nations . . . may be stated to be the law of nature, rendered applicable to political societies." The Views, 12 U.S. (8 Cranch) 297 (1814). The "law of nations," the Court continued, "is a law founded on natural practice. . . ." *Id. See generally* Corwin, *The "Higher Law" Background of American Constitutional Law*, 42 Harv. L. Rev. 149 (1928); Holdsworth, *supra* note 169, at 141; Sprout,

example, Lord Coke wrote that "when an Act of Parliament is against common right and reason, or repugnant, or impossible to be performed, the common law will contrul [*sic*] it, and adjudge such Act to be void."[171] The United States Supreme Court adopted similar principles, evidenced by the classic statement of Justice Chase in *Calder v. Bull*: "An Act of the Legislature (for I cannot call it a *law*), contrary to the great first *principles* of the *social compact*, cannot be considered a *rightful exercise of legislative authority*."[172]

Although early commentators on the sources of international law included a number of postivists who saw its origins in man-made customs and conventions,[173] the weight of scholarly opinion at the time of the nation's founding regarded international law as deriving from principles of natural law.[174] These writings reveal the profound influence of Roman law on the development of international law. Rome promulgated a law of nations that has been interpreted as little different from natural law in its emphasis on universal principles of justice and equity.[175] Emerich de Vattel wrote in 1758 that "the Law of Nations is in its origin merely the Law of Nature applied to Nations."[176]

Given the interwoven fabric of English common law, natural law, and customary international law, English judges before the American Revolution held international law to be part of the law of England. In 1736, Lord Talbot held that "the law of nations in its full extent was part of the law of England."[177] Thirty years later came the famous case of *Triquet v. Bath*,[178] in which Lord Mansfield adjudicated the diplomatic immunity of a domestic servant by relying upon international law. The court held that "this privilege of foreign ministers and their domestic servants depends upon the law of nations."[179]

Theories as to the Applicability of International Law in the Federal Courts of the United States, 26 Am. J. Int'l L. 280 (1932).

[171] 77 Eng. Rep. 646, 652 (1610).

[172] 3 U.S. (3 Dall.) 386, 388 (1798) (emphasis in original).

[173] Cornelius Van Bynkershock, a Dutch judge, was perhaps the prime exponent of the positivist view in the eighteenth century. *See* C. Bynkershock, Quaestionum Juris Publici (1737); C. Bynkershock, De Domino Maris (1702).

[174] *See* H. Maine, International Law 37 (1885).

[175] *See* Nussbaum, *The Significance of Roman Law in the History of International Law*, 100 U. Pa. L. Rev. 678, 682–87 (1952).

[176] E. De Vattel, The Law of Nations 4 (C. Fenwick trans. 1916) (emphasis in original). Samuel Pufendorf argued similarly that principles of the law of nations derived from nature. S. Pufendorf, De Jure Naturae et Gentium (1672). Hugo Grotius, the "Father of International Law," despite efforts to secularize the subject, nonetheless made occasional reference to "natural law among all nations." H. Grotius, 1 De Jure Belli et Pacis 16 (Whewell ed. 1853). Henry Maine thus concluded that "[t]he grandest function of the law of nature was discharged in giving birth to modern international law." H. Maine, *supra* note 174, at 37.

[177] Barbuit's Case, Talbot 281 (1736).

[178] 3 Burr. 1478, 97 Eng. Rep. 936 (K.B. 1764).

[179] *Id.* at 1480, 97 Eng. Rep. at 937. William Blackstone, who represented the plaintiff in the case, reiterated Lord Mansfield's principle in his Commentaries. *See* 4 W. Blackstone, Commentaries on the Laws of England 68 (1926). *See also* 1 *id.* at 1–2.

After the American Revolution but before the Constitution took effect, English common law became part of the law of the states, and some states considered themselves bound to apply the law of nations as their own law.[180] In Pennsylvania in 1784, when an individual was indicted for assault upon a French diplomat, Chief Justice McKean instructed the jury that the case, while one of "first impression in the *United States*, . . . must be determined on the principles of the law of nations, which form a part of the municipal laws of *Pennsylvania*."[181] He continued: "[T]he law of Nations, in its full extent, is part of the law of this state. . . ."[182]

CASE LAW

Although the courts have only recently described customary international law as federal common law, the courts have always considered the law of nations to be part of the law of the United States. As early as *The Nereide*, Marshall asserted that while an act of Congress could violate international law, "till such an act be passed the Court is bound by the law of nations, which is part of the law of the land."[183] The Supreme Court did not refer to federal common law in either *Brown v. United States*[184] or *The Paquete Habana*.[185] Perhaps this is because the term is relatively new. Whatever the vocabulary, the courts have long assumed that they may apply norms of customary international law as domestic law.[186]

Professor Henkin has argued that customary international law is not properly thought of as common law.[187] An earlier draft of the revision of the *Restatement* saw no trouble in denominating customary international law as federal common law:

> International law was part of the common law of England and as such of the American colonies. With independence, it became part of the law of the thirteen states. When the United States came into existence, international law became part of the common law also for the courts of the United States wherever courts applied common law.[188]

[180] *See generally* Kent, 1 Commentaries on American Law 1–2 (1926).

[181] Respublica v. de Longchamps, 1 U.S. (1 Dall.) 111, 114 (1874) (emphasis in original). "This law," the Chief Justice continued, "is to be collected from the *practice* of different Nations, and the *authority* of *writers*." *Id.* at 116 (emphasis in original).

[182] *Id.* at 116. *See also* Steinmetz v. Currie, 1 Dal. 270 (Sup. St. of Penn., 1788) ("The honor and justice of the state are . . . interested . . . that the decision should be conformable to the general mercantile law of nations, lest a deviation should be imputed to our ignorance or disrespect of what is right and proper.").

[183] 9 Cranch 388, 423 (1815).

[184] 12 U.S. (8 Cranch) 110 (1814).

[185] 175 U.S. 677 (1900).

[186] *See, e.g.*, Filartiga v. Pena-Irala, 630 F.2d 876 (2d Cir. 1980).

[187] Henkin, *The Constitution and United States Sovereignty: A Century of Chinese Exclusion and Its Progeny*, 100 Harv. L. Rev. 853 (1987).

[188] Restatement § 40 (Tent. Draft No. 1, 1980).

This reference to "common law" was dropped, however, and the *Restatement* indicates that customary international law is "like" federal common law.[189] Professor Henkin has said elsewhere that he views customary international law as *sui generis* for domestic purposes.[190]

The rationale for a fundamental new[191] category is far from convincing. *Common law* has long been viewed as comprising judge-made law, as embracing all law save statutes and constitutions. Professor Martha Field has defined it to include "any rule of federal law created by a court (usually but not invariably a federal court) when the substance of that rule is not clearly suggested by federal enactments—constitutional or congressional."[192] Predictability in the law is better advanced by retaining basic categories we already have and burnishing existing rules rather than creating new categories to which indeterminate rules apply. The justification for a new category appears to turn primarily on the argument that a judge who applies a customary international-law norm "finds" rather than "makes" law, a distinction that seems tenuous. In *Erie R.R. v. Tomkins*,[193] the Supreme Court seems to have rejected the proffered distinction, which had been relied upon by the judiciary in the era of *Swift v. Tyson*[194] to justify broad lawmaking power by the courts. Applying it, a judge who selects Rawls as a rule of decisional authority (or Posner or Ely or George Gallup, for that matter) is supposedly engaged in a more restrained exercise than one who selects Brownlie. One needn't be a legal realist (or whatever they are called today) to see that that distinction understates the breadth of discretion inherent in judicial decision making. Moreover, if it is indeed correct that judges applying customary international-law rules are somehow "less free to follow their own bent,"[195] that would suggest that a judge should feel even less restraint in applying such a rule to the Executive; he or she is not, after all, creating a new rule out of whole cloth but applying a known rule in circumstances where its application was foreseeable.

However it is denominated, therefore—whether customary international law is called federal common law or something else—the policy considerations raised by its domestic incorporation are the same. So is the history of

[189] Restatement § 111, Comment *d*.

[190] *See Authority of the Executive to Interpret, Articulate, or Violate Customary International Law* 80 Am. Soc'y Int'l L. Proc. (1986). Deposition of Louis Henkin, Fernandez-Rogue v. Smith, Civil Action No. C81-1084A, June 13, 1985.

[191] As Professor Henkin himself notes, commentators from Blackstone and Hamilton through Jessup and Bork have all thought of international law as common law. Henkin, *The Constitution and United States Sovereignty: A Century of Chinese Exclusion and Its Progeny*, 100 Harv. L. Rev. 875, n. 95 (1987).

[192] Field, *Sources of Law: The Scope of Federal Common Law*, 99 Harv. L. Rev. 883, 897, n.64 (1986).

[193] 304 U.S. 64, 79–80 (1938).

[194] 16 Pet. 1 (U.S. 1842).

[195] L. Henkin, Foreign Affairs and the Constitution 217 (1972).

that process: many times since *Erie*[196] federal courts have applied their own rules, not statutes, to acts of the Executive. Those rules have been accorded the same legal weight as acts of Congress. ''All constitutional acts of power,'' John Jay wrote, ''whether in the executive or the judicial department, have as much legal validity and obligation as if they proceeded from the legislature.''[197] The Supreme Court has agreed. ''[F]ederal courts have an extensive responsibility of fashioning substantive rules of law. . . . These rules are as fully 'laws' of the United States as if they had been enacted by Congress.''[198] Indeed, it would be difficult theoretically *not* to view court-made rules as supreme. As Professor Henkin has put it, ''In principle, any authority exercised by the courts under their own constitutional authority ought to be equal to the authority of Congress or of the treaty-makers, and their 'enactments' entitled to equal weight. . . .''[199]

INTENT OF THE FRAMERS

The Framers intended the federal courts to apply customary international law ''to all Cases of admiralty and maritime Jurisdiction.''[200] Hamilton wrote, apparently without exaggeration, that no one had ''shown a disposition to deny the national judiciary the cognizance of maritime causes. These so generally affect the rights of foreigners, that they fall within the considerations which are relative to the public peace.''[201] Thus, Chief Justice Marshall could later conclude that ''[a] case in admiralty does not, in fact, arise under the Constitution or laws of the United States . . . and the law, admiralty and maritime, as it has existed for ages, is applied by our Courts to the cases as they arise.''[202] Secretary of State John Marshall confronted firsthand the consequences of international-law violations—impressed American seamen, captured American ships, and confiscated American cargo. He gathered evidence and sent it to the American minister in London, Rufus King, hoping that King could proceed in the British courts. It was in this connection that he wrote King: ''The

[196] Erie Railroad Co. v. Tompkins, 304 U.S. 64 (1938).

[197] The Federalist No. 64 (Jay).

[198] Romero v. International Terminal Operating Co., 358 U.S. 354, 393 (1959).

[199] Henkin, *International Law as Law in the United States*, 82 Mich. L. Rev. 1555, 1563 (1984).

[200] U.S. Const. art. III, § 2, cl. 3.

[201] The Federalist No. 80, at 519 (A. Hamilton) (Bicentennial ed. 1976). *See also* G. Gilmore & C. Black, The Law of Admiralty 45 (1975) (''At the time of the adoption of the Constitution, it probably seemed 'self-evident' that there already was in existence a corpus of maritime law . . . which certainly needed no express or implied legislative action on the part of any one nation to make it valid''); 1 J. Wilson, Works 375 (J. Wilson ed. 1804) (statement of Justice Wilson that the law applied in maritime cases is ''not the law of a particular country, but the general law of nations'').

[202] American Ins. Co. v. Canter, 26 U.S. 1 (1 Pet.) 511, 545–46 (1818).

most effectual restraint is an upright judiciary.''[203] Little wonder that Marshall should call international law "a law which contributes more to the happiness of the human race than all the statues which will come from the hands of the sculptor, or all the paintings that were ever placed on canvas.''[204]

The Framers also intended the federal courts to apply customary international law in appropriate nonmaritime cases, believing that such application was necessary to maintain international harmony.[205] The fragile new nation was thought to have an important interest in the maintenance of world order; the harassment and capture of neutral shipping during the Revolutionary War (and later the Napoleonic Wars) "struck deeply at the commercial interests of the United States,''[206] a maritime nation heavily dependent upon respect for international law. The Constitutional Convention unanimously resolved "[t]hat the jurisdiction of the national Judiciary shall extend to cases arising under laws passed by the general Legislature, and to such other questions as involve the National peace and harmony.''[207] John Jay, writing in *The Federalist*, thus extolled "[t]he wisdom of the Convention'' for committing questions concerning "treaties and articles of treaties, as well as the law of nations,'' to the federal courts.[208] James Wilson, lecturing on law from 1790 through 1792, underscored the English connection:

> In that country, from which the common law has been brought, the law of nations has always been most respectfully and attentively adopted and regarded by the municipal tribunals, in all matters, concerning which it is proper to have recourse to that rule of decision. The law of nations, in its full extent, is part of the law of England.[209]

"The law of nations,'' he concluded, "will still be applicable, as before the national constitution was established, to controversies in all those different enumerated cases [set forth in article III of the Constitution].''[210]

The courts' authority to apply international law thus derived from English common law, incorporated into the law of the United States.[211] Alexander

[203] L. Baker, John Marshall: A Life in the Law 338 (1974). Marshall's frustration in dealing with the partial, dishonest courts of the Vice Admiralty gave impetus to his campaign, as Chief Justice, to establish an independent American judiciary. *Id.* at 338–39.

[204] L. Baker, John Marshall: A Life in the Law 554 (1974).

[205] *See generally* Dickinson, *The Law of Nations as Part of the National Law of the United States*, 101 U. Pa. L. Rev. 26, 38 (1952).

[206] B. Ziegler, The International Law of John Marshall 12 (1939).

[207] Farrand, *supra* note 121, at 39.

[208] The Federalist No. 3, at 15 (J. Jay) (Bicentennial ed. 1976).

[209] 1 J. Wilson, Works 374 (1804).

[210] *Id.* at 379.

[211] James Wilson observed: "In that country, from which the common law has been brought, the law of nations has always been most respectively and attentively adopted and regarded by the municipal tribunals, in all matters concerning which it is proper to have recourse to that rule of

Hamilton best summed up the intent of the Framers concerning this step-by-step process of incorporation. He declared that the United States was "a party to" the law of nations since the country did not dissent from its rules upon independence.[212] That the law of nations is part of the law of the United States, he concluded, is "indubitable."

Probable Constitutional Rationale

The Supreme Court has not presented a rationale for the power of the federal courts to create their own substantive rules of decision. In the absence of an explanation, legal commentators have been left to speculate. At least two plausible jurisdictions exist for the common-law power of the federal judiciary.

JURISDICTIONAL GRANTS

The jurisdictional rationale presupposes that federal common law after *Erie* binds state courts as well as federal courts. The Supreme Court has claimed jurisdiction over cases in which state courts refuse to apply federal common law. If the Court has jurisdiction, that jurisdiction must derive from article III. Since the jurisdiction does not arise under the Constitution or any treaty, it must arise under the "laws of the United States." "Laws" in article III, therefore, relates not only to federal statutes but also to federal common law. Thus, the federal courts possess the power to make substantive rules of law coextensive with this jurisdictional grant.[213]

CONGRESSIONAL ACQUIESCENCE

A second justification for lawmaking by the federal courts is that Congress has consistently consented to the exercise of that judicial power. Just as courts are on notice of laws enacted by the legislative branch, the legislative branch is on notice of common-law decisions issued by the courts.[214] The Judiciary may infer Congress's consent from its knowledge of and acquiescence in lawmaking by federal judges. The courts therefore comply with the Constitution's most fundamental precept—that laws be made by the elected representatives of the people. When Congress chooses not to legislate and the federal interest is sufficiently strong with respect to a particular controversy, a judge-made rule is not only permissible but vital to the smooth functioning of a modern federal government. Judge Friendly praised this justification on functional grounds: "One of the beauties of [federal common law]," he wrote, "is that

---

decision. The law of nations in its full extent, is a part of the law of England." J. Wilson, *supra* note 201, at 374.

[212] A. Hamilton, *supra* note 118, at 436.

[213] For a fuller discussion of the reasoning leading to this conclusion, see Note, *Federal Common Law and Article III: A Jurisdictional Approach to Erie*, 74 Yale L.J. 325 (1964).

[214] For cases so holding, *see* 2 Sutherland Statutory Construction § 38.03 (D. Sands ed. 1973).

it permits overworked federal legislators . . . so easily to transfer a part of their load to federal judges, who have time for reflection and freedom from fear as to tenure and are ready, even eager, to resume their historic lawmaking function—with Congress always able to set matters right if they go too far off the desired beam.''[215]

The acquiescence rationale, like the jurisdictional rationale, has engendered criticism.[216] Yet the rationale's emphasis on the tentativeness of judge-made rules also has attracted support, particularly from jurists inclined to defer to legislative authority. Justice Rehnquist, for example, recently defended federal common law on the theory that it is ''subject to the paramount authority of the Congress.''[217]

Whatever rationale seems most reasonable, the conclusion is the same: The power of federal courts as *lawmakers* is broad indeed. For Professor Field, the only limit on the federal courts' power to create common law is the requirement that the creation be based ultimately on ''a federal enactment, constitutional or statutory, that it interprets as authorizing the federal common law rule.''[218]

FEDERAL COMMON LAW AND THE EXECUTIVE

The Supreme Court has held that the actions of the executive branch are subject to the rules of federal common law. In *Clearfield Trust v. United States*,[219] for example, the Court held that federal common law controlled the ''duties of the United States'' toward commercial paper issued by the government.[220] Federal courts have also applied their own substantive rules to executive officials in cases involving choice-of-law questions with respect to government contracts,[221] the effect of a federal lien,[222] federal tort liability,[223] and immunity.[224] The line of federal common-law cases dealing directly with executive

[215] Friendly, *supra* note 155, at 419 (citation omitted).

[216] *See, e.g.*, H.L.A. Hart, The Concept of Law (1961).

[217] City of Milwaukee v. Illinois, 451 U.S. 304, 313–14 (1981) (citations omitted). Justice Rehnquist also stated that federal common law ''applies in the absence of an applicable Act of Congress,'' and is no longer needed ''when Congress addresses a question previously governed by a decision [that] rested on federal common law.'' *Id.*

[218] Field, *Sources of Law: The Scope of Federal Common Law*, 99 Harv. L. Rev. 833, 887–88 (1986).

[219] 318 U.S. 363 (1943).

[220] *Id.*

[221] *See, e.g.*, United States v. Seckinger, 397 U.S. 203 (1970); Wissner v. Wissner, 338 U.S. 655 (1950).

[222] *See, e.g.*, United States v. Kimbell Foods, Inc., 440 U.S. 715 (1979); United States v. Brosnan, 363 U.S. 237 (1960).

[223] *See, e.g.*, United States v. Standard Oil Co., 332 U.S. 301 (1947).

[224] *See, e.g.*, Barr v. Matteo, 360 U.S. 564 (1959). The Supreme Court has held that federal officials are not immune from acts knowingly committed in violation of constitutional rights. *See*

activities in the realm of foreign relations, however, provides the greatest insights.

FROM JUDICIAL DEFERENCE TO INDEPENDENCE

In deciding the seminal case of *Banco Nacional de Cuba v. Sabbatino*,[225] the Court stated that it "did not have rules like the act-of-state doctrine in mind when it decided *Erie Railroad Co. v. Tompkins*."[226] A close reading of *Sabbatino* and related cases suggests that the act-of-state doctrine was not the only common-law foreign-relations rule that the Court did not have in mind when it decided *Erie*. In formulating such rules, the Court abandoned its earlier posture of extreme deference toward executive "legislation" in the foreign-relations realm.

Sabbatino Revisited. The Supreme Court applied the act-of-state doctrine in *Sabbatino* to allow recovery by the Cuban government of the proceeds of a sale of sugar.[227] Although the defendant alleged that the Cuban government's title was defective because the sugar had been confiscated in violation of international law, the Court held that the act-of-state doctrine applied even with respect to acts that violate international law.[228]

In analyzing the issue, the Court was not engaged in the process of discovering a precept of customary international law to be incorporated in United States domestic law.[229] To the contrary, Justice Harlan ingenuously acknowledged that international law did not require application of the act-of-state doctrine.[230] Moreover, Harlan noted that international law did not forbid use of the doctrine, "even if it is claimed that the act of state in question violated international law."[231] International law, the Court concluded, permits a na-

---

Butz v. Economou, 438 U.S. 478 (1978). The Court has extended this principle to senior presidential aides. *See* Harlow v. Fitzgerald, 457 U.S. 800 (1982).

[225] 376 U.S. 398 (1964).

[226] *Id.* at 425. Commentators have construed this statement to imply that all questions of foreign relations law are issues of federal common law. *See* Henkin, *The Foreign Affairs Power of the Federal Courts: Sabbatino*, 64 Colum. L. Rev. 805, 817–19 (1964).

[227] *Sabbatino*, 376 U.S. at 437. The act-of-state doctrine encompasses the principle that the courts of one country will not sit in judgment of the acts of the government of another state within its own territory.

[228] *Id.* at 427–37.

[229] The Court, for example, previously incorporated rules of international law relating to confiscation of enemy property located on land, *see* Brown v. United States, 12 U.S. (8 Cranch) 110 (1814), and coastal fishing vessels, *see* The Paquete Habana, 175 U.S. 667, 711 (1900).

[230] *Sabbatino*, 376 U.S. at 421–22. An individual's usual method seeking relief, Justice Harlan observed, is to "repair to the executive authorities of his own state to persuade them to champion his claim in diplomacy. . . ." *Id.* at 423.

[231] *Id.* at 422.

tion's sovereign discretion to decide how it will respond within its own territory to a perceived foreign wrong.[232]

Justice Harlan's acknowledgment that although the act-of-state doctrine has "'constitutional' underpinnings," it is not compelled by the Constitution underscores the importance of *Sabbatino*.[233] In *Banco Nacional de Cuba v. Farr*,[234] a rerun of *Sabbatino* following the enactment by Congress of the second Hickenlooper Amendment,[235] a federal court held that the Constitution did not mandate the act-of-state doctrine. The Court of Appeals for the Second Circuit upheld the congressional legislation and decided against the Cuban government.[236] Thus, the act-of-state doctrine, at least for "supremacy" purposes, falls squarely into the same category of federal common law as customary international law. Both are interstitial and give way to subsequent inconsistent acts of Congress. Yet both are nonetheless promulgated pursuant to the constitutional authority of the courts and are therefore the supreme law of the land.

However, much in *Sabbatino* suggests that the Judiciary owes some deference to the President concerning the conduct of foreign policy. The Court emphasized that judicial activism "in the task of passing on the validity of foreign acts of state may hinder rather than further this country's pursuit of goals both for itself and for the community of nations as a whole."[237] Further expressions of concern about the possibility of conflict between the Judicial and the Executive and embarrassment of the Executive in its dealings with other countries pervade the Court's opinion.[238]

Yet eight years later, the Court made clear that the result favored by the Executive in act-of-state cases is not ineluctably mandated. In *First National City Bank v. Banco Nacional de Cuba*,[239] six Justices rejected the so-called Bernstein exception, under which the Court could not apply the act-of-state doctrine when the executive branch expressly represents to the Court that its application would not advance the foreign-policy interests of the United States. Under the Bernstein exception, Justice Douglas wrote, "the Court becomes a mere errand boy for the Executive Branch which may choose to pick some people's chestnuts from the fire, but not others.' "[240] Justice Powell wrote that he "would be uncomfortable with a doctrine which would require the judiciary to receive the Executive's permission before invoking its juris-

[232] *Id.* at 423.

[233] *Sabbatino*, 376 U.S. at 427.

[234] 383 F.2d 166 (2d Cir. 1967), *cert. denied*, 390 U.S. 956 (1968).

[235] 22 U.S.C. § 2370(e)(2) (1982). The second "Hickenlooper Amendment" was intended to limit the act-of-state doctrine's application to cases not involving a violation of international law.

[236] *Farr*, 383 F.2d at 168.

[237] *Sabbatino*, 376 U.S. at 423.

[238] *See, e.g., id.* at 430, 432, 433, 436.

[239] 406 U.S. 759 (1972).

[240] *Id.* at 773 (Douglas, J., concurring) (footnotes omitted).

diction."[241] The Bernstein exception, Justices Brennan, Stewart, Marshall, and Blackmun believed, "would require us to abdicate our judicial responsibility."[242] The real meaning of *Sabbatino*, the Court stated, was that "the validity of a foreign act of state in certain circumstances is a 'political question' not cognizable in our courts."[243] Even when the Executive's conduct of foreign affairs would be impaired, the *Sabbatino* Court had not regarded deference to the Executive as automatically required.[244] Thus, the Court carefully qualified the self-imposed restraint in *Sabbatino*. Indeed, it expressly emphasized its continued willingness to apply agreed-upon principles of international law.[245]

That willingness makes sense. The act-of-state doctrine, mandated neither by the Constitution nor by international law, is a rule created by the federal courts. To the extent that a distinction exists between law that the courts "make" and law they "find"—such as international law—the case for judicial activism seems greater in the latter category: The courts are less open to the charge of capriciousness when the source of decisional authority is a preexisting body of law.

Recognition and Sovereign Immunity. The trend in recent foreign-relations cases, particularly those relating to recognition and sovereign immunity, indicates that the courts will consider questions of international law and may decide them against executive policy. Upon the advent of the New Deal, the Supreme Court initially extended its newly found self-restraint to recognition and sovereign immunity. Extreme deference to the Executive became the rule. In *United States v. Pink*,[246] for example, the Court held that executive recog-

[241] *Id*. (Powell, J., concurring). Justice Powell further observed that "[s]uch a notion, in the name of the doctrine of separation of powers, seems to me to conflict with that very doctrine." *Id*.

[242] *Id*. at 778 (Brennan, J., dissenting).

[243] *Id*. at 787–88 (footnote omitted). "Only one and not necessarily the most important of those circumstances concerned the possible impairment of the Executive's conduct of foreign affairs." *Id*.

[244] *Id*. at 788. The Court stated:

> It should be apparent that the greater the degree of codification or consensus concerning a particular area of international law, the more appropriate it is for the judiciary to render decisions regarding it, since the courts can then focus on the application of an agreed principle to circumstances of fact rather than on the sensitive task of establishing a principle not inconsistent with the national interest or with international justice.

Id.

[245] *Sabbatino*, 376 U.S. at 428. The Court found "areas of international law in which consensus as to standards is greater and which do not represent a battleground for conflicting ideologies. This decision in no way intimates that the courts of this country are broadly foreclosed from considering questions of international law."

[246] 315 U.S. 203 (1942).

nition of the Soviet Union was "final and conclusive in the courts."[247] A year later, in *Ex parte Peru*,[248] the Court held that certification by the State Department that a certain vessel should be immune from libel imposed a "duty" on the courts to release the vessel.[249] The Court reiterated that duty two years later in *Republic of Mexico v. Hoffman*.[250] Thus, at the conclusion of World War II, the courts appeared unwilling, at least in recognition and sovereign-immunity cases, to substitute their judgment for that of the Executive. The Supreme Court did not address whether that same measure of deference would obtain, even if the Executive's action violated international law.[251]

Commentators harshly criticized the Court for having forsaken its independence. One respected scholar asked, after *Hoffman*, whether the Court had "abdicated one of its functions."[252] Another opined that the Court, confused, had elevated nonembarrassment of the Executive to the dignity of a doctrine.[253]

The Court soon returned to the role of independent arbiter in *Zschernig v. Miller*[254] where the Court addressed the constitutionality of an Oregon statute

[247] *Id.* at 230.

[248] 318 U.S. 578 (1943).

[249] *Id.* at 589.

[250] 324 U.S. 30 (1945).

[251] Little in the case law supports the notion that policy made by the Executive is binding on the courts "regardless of what international law might say about it." L. Henkin, *supra* note 90, at 59. None of the cases relied upon involved a violation of international law, and the cases contain nothing indicating that the Judiciary must remain indifferent to a violation. *See, e.g.*, Berizzi Bros. Co. v. S.S. Pesaro, 271 U.S. 562 (1926); *Ex parte* Muir, 254 U.S. 522 (1921); Victory Transport, Inc. v. Comisaria General de Abastecimientos y Transportes, 336 F.2d 354 (2d Cir. 1964), *cert. denied*, 381 U.S. 934 (1965). To the contrary, the decisions imply that the Executive's claim of compliance with international law justified judicial deference.

[252] Jessup, *Has the Supreme Court Abdicated One of Its Functions?*, 40 Am. J. Int'l L. 168 (1946):

> In cases involving sovereign immunity, it used to be assumed that the only question which the political branch of government was called upon to decide was the status of the government or its agents. The trend of the United States decisions, culminating in the *Hoffman* case, would now make it appear that the State Department must also determine the basic legal principle governing the immunity.

Id. at 169 (citations omitted).

[253] Dickinson, *supra* note 205, at 450:

> There is even less excuse for loose talk concerning judicial reluctance to embarrass a coordinate governmental service. In the American constitutional system as the founders so clearly anticipated, the embarrassments of relationship among coordinate departments are a toughness in the lubricant which keeps the tripartite distribution of the principal powers in balance.

See also Note, *Judicial Deference to the State Department on International Legal Issues*, 97 U. Pa. L. Rev. 79, 92 (1948) (arguing that the "judicial branch should not be forced to vary with every changing wind of foreign policy").

[254] 389 U.S. 429 (1968). That this is not an international-law case (and, as the context of this discussion makes clear, I do not suggest otherwise; *contra see* Weisburd, *supra* note 18 at 1264) and that the Executive "was not arguing that the Oregon statute should stand" (again, I have never contended otherwise; *contra see id.*) does not alter the clear implication of the opinion that

denying inheritance to an East German because he failed to establish a reciprocal right of inheritance for Americans under East German law.[255] The State Department had advised that the statute had ''little effect on the foreign relations and policy of this country,''[256] yet the Court declined the Executive's invitation to let the statute stand. The Court held the Oregon law invalid as an illicit effort to interfere with foreign policy, the control of which was vested in the federal government.[257] ''In the result,'' Professor Henkin observed, ''the Court disregarded the State Department's stated view and substituted its own judgment on issues of foreign policy.''[258]

Four years later, the Court reaffirmed its return to its traditional role in *First National City Bank v. Banco Nacional de Cuba*;[259] the Court declined to require lower-court deference to a State Department determination that the United States could disregard the act-of-state doctrine.[260] Six Justices rejected the notion that judicial deference to the Executive was required.[261] Moreover, the Court never referred to its earlier seemingly inconsistent opinions. The Court has thus come full circle, from the position of virtual adjunct of the State Department to the current posture of independent adjudicator.

WHICH NORMS APPLY

Although international law forms part of United States law, not *all* norms of customary international law are necessarily part of federal common law. Some authorities have interpreted English cases decided since 1876 as holding that ''customary international law is part of the law of England *only in so far* as the rules have been clearly adopted and made part of the law of England by legislation, judicial decision, or established usage.''[262] From a strict jurisprudential standpoint, the same rule applies to the United States. Although the

---

the Court will exercise the role of independent arbiter in foreign-relations cases and will not automatically defer to the wishes of the Executive.

[255] *Id.*

[256] Memorandum for the United States at 5, Zschernig v. Miller, 389 U.S. 429 (1968).

[257] 389 U.S. at 432.

[258] L. Henkin, *supra* note 93, at 62.

[259] 406 U.S. 759 (1972).

[260] 406 U.S. at 762.

[261] *Id.* at 773 (Douglas, J., concurring); *id.* (Powell, J., concurring); *id.* at 779 (Brennan, J., dissenting) (joined by Stewart, Marshall, and Blackmun, JJ.). Again, contrary to the suggestion of one commentator, there is no suggestion here that ''the [Court's] determination was a matter of . . . international law.'' Weisburd, *supra* note 18, at 1265. Indeed, I have explicitly noted in the text that the Court in act-of-state cases is *not* ''engaged in the process of discovering a precept of international law.'' *See supra* text at note 226. The point is simply that six members of the Supreme Court flatly rejected the reflexive judicial deference to the Executive in foreign-affairs matters for which such commentators argue. (The decision in act-of-state cases is not, incidentally, reached as a ''matter of constitutional law,'' Weisburd, *supra* note 18 at 1265; *see* Sabbatino, 375 U.S. at 427. The matter is one of federal common law.)

[262] I. Brownlie, Principles of Public International Law 46 (1979) (emphasis in original).

courts often have repeated that international law is part of our law, *all* of international law has never been before any court in a single case. All that has been before the court was a specific norm of international law that the court elected to employ as the rule of decision. In each case, the statement that "international law is part of our law" was thus arguably dictum; the most that each court could have held was that the specific norm upon which it relied is a part of our law.

The preceding argument, though correct as a mechanical application of the common-law technique, overstates the role of courts in identifying law. As Ronald Dworkin[263] and H.L.A. Hart[264] have demonstrated, law exists prior to its judicial promulgation. Yet the argument properly emphasizes that the process of making and applying international law is an ongoing one that does not lead inescapably to the application of every customary international norm as a domestic rule of decision. A norm cannot become part of our law if the United States rejects it during its process of formation, because no state can be bound by a principle of customary international law to which it has not consented.[265] Nor should a norm be domestically incorporated that does not square with the one overriding prerequisite developed by the courts of this country in the course of applying international law domestically—the requirement that the norm be widely accepted and clearly defined.[266] The *Sabbatino* Court capsulized that requirement, declaring that "the greater the degree of codification or consensus concerning a particular area of international law, the more appropriate it is for the judiciary to render decisions regarding it."[267]

Although the Court has not developed a hard-and-fast test for the degree of consensus that must exist before a norm becomes domestic law, the Court in *The Paquete Habana* required that the international norm be "a settled rule of international law [by] the general assent of civilized nations."[268] In *Filartiga v. Pena-Irala*,[269] the Court of Appeals for the Second Circuit applied this

[263] *See* R. Dworkin, Taking Rights Seriously 81–130 (1978). Brownlie himself acknowledges that the distinction makes little practical difference. I. Brownlie, *supra* note 262, at 46 n.3. There is, he argues, something in the nature of a "presumption" of incorporation. *Id.*

[264] H. Hart, The Concept of Law 98 (1961).

[265] *See* Restatement § 102, Comment *d.* While a norm is in its embryonic stage, it seems sensible to hold that either the President, acting alone, or the Congress, by statute, may except the United States from its application (in the event the norm should develop to a level of applicability). The Congress should be seen as having such power because such authority follows a fortiori from its authority to place the United States in violation of a norm that has matured to applicability; the President should be seen as having such power because in the absence of a fully applicable norm, nothing yet exists to constrain him.

[266] Banco Nacional de Cuba v. Sabbatino, 376 U.S. 398, 422 (1964).

[267] *Id.* at 428. The "specificity" precept is a corollary of the separation-of-powers doctrine. The Court may not impose on the political branches rules of uncertain breadth or application because it would work a reallocation of the constitutional distribution of powers.

[268] 175 U.S. 677, 694 (1900).

[269] 630 F.2d 876 (2d Cir. 1980).

"stringent" standard, holding that the prohibition against torture represented such a rule.[270] At a minimum, therefore, the Court should apply every peremptory norm of international law, because those norms involve a clear consensus in the international community.[271]

The Court might also apply other customary norms that represent settled rules of fundamental importance to the international order. One such norm is the principle of *pacta sunt servanda*, the notion that a treaty is binding upon its parties and must be performed in good faith.[272] The norm's incorporation in the Vienna Convention on the Law of Treaties indicates that *pacta sunt servanda* is a settled rule of international law.[273] Scholarly commentary[274] and logic also demonstrate the rule's fundamental importance. A treaty disavowing the norm of *pacta sunt servanda* would represent a "logical conundrum" because its "validity would appear to depend on the very norm which it purports to abolish."[275] *Pacta sunt servanda* is therefore appropriately applied by the federal courts as a rule of federal common law and in the absence of congressional authorization, constrains the power of the Executive to violate or abrogate treaties to which the United States is a party.[276]

Another norm appropriately applied by the courts is the principle of *proportionality*, which requires that force used in self-defense be proportionate to the provocation necessitating its use.[277] Although the principle may produce uncertainty in some conflicts, in many conflicts, as Professor Oscar Schachter has noted, it has practical applications.[278] The mining of Nicaragua's harbors by the United States in February and March of

[270] *Id.* at 881.

[271] Widely regarded as outlawed under this principle of *jus cogens* are acts such as genocide, slavery, piracy, armed aggression, and war crimes. *See* Whiteman, Jus Cogens, in *International Law, with a Projected List*, 7 Ga. J. Int'l Comp. L. 609, 625–26 (1977).

[272] Vienna Convention on the Law of Treaties, May 23, 1969, U.N. Doc. A/Conf. 39/27, *reprinted in* 8 I.L.M. 679 (1969), at art. 26.

[273] *Id.*

[274] *See, e.g.*, D. Anzilotti, I Corso di Diritto Internazionale 43 (3d ed. 1928); J. Brierly, The Law of Nations 331 (6th ed. 1963); J. Sztucki, Jus Cogens and the Vienna Convention on the Law of Treaties 79 (1974); Note, *Nuclear* Jus Cogens, 13 Cornell Int'l L.J. 63, 75 (1980).

[275] I. Sinclair, The Vienna Convention on the Law of Treaties 121 (1973).

[276] *See* Chapter 4.

[277] The classic statement of the requirement has "met with general acceptance." J. Brierly, *supra* 274, at 405. *See also* Higgins, *The Legal Limits to the Use of Force by Sovereign States, United Nations Practice*, 37 British Y.B. of Int'l L. 301–02 (1961); Schwarzenberger, *The Fundamental Principles of International Law*, 87 Hague Recueil 332–33 (1955, I); Waldock, *The Use of Force in International Law*, 81 Hague Recueil 496–98 (1952, II). Secretary of State Daniel Webster, during the 1837 *Caroline* case, said that the action taken must involve "nothing unreasonable or excessive, since the act justified by the necessity of self-defense must be limited by that necessity and kept within it." *Id.* at 406.

[278] O. Schachter, General Course in Public International Law, Academy of International Law, Offprint from the Collected Courses, vol. 178 (1982-V) at 155.

1984, for example, violated international law.[279] Acting without congressional concurrence, the President's authority was limited by federal common law, including the principle of proportionality. Similarly, the courts might note that abduction of a criminal defendant in a foreign country without the consent of the government would represent a violation of international law.[280] Professor Henkin earlier suggested that certain international human-rights norms also limit the President's power domestically.[281] He supported the incorporation of those norms because such principles "are essentially for the benefit of individuals, principally a State's own inhabitants,"[282] and because "[t]hey do not directly implicate the State's foreign relations" and thus do not circumscribe the President's foreign-affairs powers.[283]

Professor Henkin's rationale for favoring international human-rights norms over other customary international norms is that the imposition of international human-rights norms by the courts would not interfere with the President's foreign-affairs powers. The President's plenary foreign-affairs powers, however, do *not* embrace the authority, acting alone, to place the United States in breach of customary international law.[284] Professor Henkin provides no persuasive authority to the contrary[285] and seems necessarily to accept key elements of the argument he rejects. Moreover, the rationale proceeds from a proffered distinction between the rights of states versus the rights of individuals that

[279] Military and Paramilitary Activities in and against Nicaragua (Nicaragua v. United States of America), 1986 I.C.J. 14, Merits (1986).

[280] *See Extraterritorial Apprehension by the Federal Bureau of Investigation*, 48 Op. of Office of Legal Counsel, Dept. of Justice 543 (1980).

[281] Henkin, *International Law as Law in the United States*, 82 Mich. L. Rev. 1555, 1569 n.44 (1984). In this article, Professor Henkin reiterated his (apparently earlier) belief that the President is constitutionally empowered to make decisions, without congressional concurrence, that disregard international law. *Id.* at 1569. *Compare* Henkin, *The Constitution and United States Sovereignty: A Century of Chinese Exclusion and Its Progeny*, 100 Harv. L. Rev. 853 (1987).

[282] *Id.*

[283] *Id.*

[284] *See* Chapter 4 text at notes 199–215.

[285] Neither Tag v. Rogers, 267 F.2d 664 (D.C. Cir. 1959), *cert. denied*, 362 U.S. 904 (1960), nor The Over the Top, 5 F.2d 838 (D. Conn. 1925), the two cases cited by Professor Henkin, supports this conclusion. Statutory authorization existed in each case. In *Tag*, a German citizen claimed a trust fund left to him by an American relative, claiming that the Trading with the Enemy Act, under which his rights to the funds had vested with the Attorney General, was invalid. *Tag*, 267 F.2d at 665–66. The Act, he claimed, conflicted with customary international law, as well as with a 1923 treaty with Germany. *Id.* at 666. The Court held that the Act superseded international law under the last-in-time doctrine. *Id.* at 668. The Court did not discuss the President's power, acting without congressional consent, to violate international law. *Id.* at 665–69. Similarly, the question did not arise in *The Over the Top*, a case in which a libel action by the government, based upon the sale of liquor nineteen miles off-shore to an agent of the Internal Revenue Service, was dismissed because the sale violated neither the Tariff Act of 1922 nor a 1922 treaty with Great Britain. The Over the Top, 5 F.2d at 839–46.

appears factitious in this context. As stated in the next chapter, the state is merely an aggregate of individuals; it makes little sense to say that the "beneficiary" of the principle of proportionality is Nicaragua rather than a Nicaraguan peasant who has been denied medicine because his country's harbors have been mined. Nor did Professor Henkin explain why it should matter constitutionally that the norm in question is "primarily for the benefit of individuals." In all, Professor Henkin's comments concerning human-rights norms seemed to raise more questions than they answered; as noted below, his views have modified, and he now seems less committed to a position that the President can disregard international norms without limit.[286]

TO WHOM THE NORMS APPLY

Although the terms *president*, *executive*, and *executive branch* seem interchangeable, the Court on occasion has distinguished between the President and lower-level executive officials.[287] The issue might arise in four situations:

1. *The President directs executive officials not to carry out an act violative of customary international law, but, contrary to his order, they proceed to do so.* Under such circumstances,[288] the violation of international law is irrelevant. Under long-standing principles of administrative law, violation of the presidential directive renders the act ultra vires,[289] and the courts need not reach constitutional issues.
2. *The President issues no directive, and, in the face of presidential silence, executive officials carry out an act violative of customary international law.* This appears to have been the situation in *Brown v. United States*.[290] Under such circumstances, the Court should invalidate the act unless Congress enacts a statute authorizing it.
3. *The President directs executive officials to carry out an act violative of customary international law, and in accordance with his directive, they proceed to do so.* Here the courts can require the executive official to comply with his legal obligations, even though the President has ordered otherwise. In *Marbury v. Madison*,[291] Chief Justice Marshall stated that the Court could direct the Secretary of State to deliver a judicial commission, notwithstanding President Jefferson's order to the contrary, since the right to the commission had vested and the act of delivery was ministerial.[292] Likewise, in *Kendall v. United States ex rel.*

[286] *See* Henkin, *The Constitution and United States Sovereignty: A Century of Chinese Exclusion and Its Progeny*, 100 Harv. L. Rev. 853 (1987).

[287] This distinction occurred in both *Brown* and *The Paquete Habana*.

[288] These appear to have been the circumstances of *The Paquete Habana*.

[289] *See generally* B. Schwartz, Administrative Law Casebook 87 (1983).

[290] 12 U.S. (8 Cranch) 110, 111–20 (1814).

[291] Marbury v. Madison, 5 U.S. (1 Cranch) 137 (1803).

[292] *Id.* at 158. President Jefferson personally gave the order not to deliver the commission. L. Baker, John Marshall: A Life in the Law 413 (1974).

Stokes,[293] notwithstanding orders to the contrary by President Andrew Jackson, the Court directed the Postmaster General to pay certain debts incurred by the United States for mail delivery.[294] The Supreme Court expressed alarm at the suggestion that "every officer in every branch is under the exclusive direction of the President."[295] In the *Steel Seizure Case*,[296] the Court prohibited the Secretary of Commerce from carrying out the directive of President Truman to seize and run the steel mills.[297] Although the challenged action in each of these cases allegedly violated the Constitution, federal common-law rules also apply to executive officials. The courts therefore have the power to impose appropriate rules of customary international law on executive officials and to enforce their compliance.[298]

4. *The President himself carries out an act violative of international law, with no involvement by any other executive official*. The President in modern times conducts few executive functions without the aid of lower officials. In several cases, however, the courts have ordered the President to perform certain acts personally. Chief Justice Marshall, sitting as a circuit judge in the trial of Aaron Burr, issued a subpoena directing President Jefferson to appear and give testimony.[299] Similarly, in *United States v. Nixon,*[300] the Court ordered President Nixon to turn over certain tape recordings to the Special Prosecutor.[301] On the other hand, in *Mississippi v. Johnson*[302] the Court held that it lacked jurisdiction to enjoin President Andrew Johnson from carrying out allegedly unconstitutional Reconstruction

[293] 37 U.S. (12 Pet.) 524 (1838).

[294] *Id.* at 610–11.

[295] *Id.* at 609.

[296] Youngstown Sheet & Tube Co. v. Sawyer, 343 U.S. 579 (1952).

[297] *Id.* at 589.

[298] It has been asserted that executive officials acting in violation of customary international law should be seen as cloaked in something "like" immunity. Charney, *The Power of the Executive Branch of the United States Government to Violate Customary International Law*, 80 Am. J. Int'l L. 913, 919 (1986). Yet recognition that no plenary power inheres in the Executive to breach customary international law also removes any rationale for giving subordinates immunity. The relevance of immunity law is unclear to begin with, inasmuch as immunity attaches only in circumstances that would otherwise give rise to personal liability, something not at issue here; the question of immunity arises in a different factual context and triggers different policy questions. (Certain immunity cases, however, do illustrate the point made above that court-made rules have been applied to executive officials. *See, e.g.*, Barr v. Matteo, 360 U.S. 464 (1959).) The central point is, however, that the Chief Executive cannot give what he does not have: *no one* in the executive branch has the authority to breach customary international law in the absence of congressional authorization. As indicated above, *The Paquete Habana*, 175 U.S. 667 (1900) provides no support for exempting the President.

[299] United States v. Burr, 25 F. Cas. 30 (C.C. Va. 1807) (No. 14,692). Jefferson, however, ignored the command of the Court. L. Baker, *supra* note 292, at 485.

[300] United States v. Nixon, 418 U.S. 683 (1974).

[301] *Id.* at 714.

[302] 71 U.S. (4 Wall.) 475 (1866).

> statutes, and in *Nixon v. Fitzgerald*,[303] the Court accorded President Nixon tort immunity more extensive than that enjoyed by his aides, granting him "absolute immunity from damages liability predicated on his official acts."[304]

Whatever the validity of the distinction between the President and his subordinates in such cases, there seems little reason to draw such a distinction in the event of an international-law violation. First, the distinction has its roots in antiquated notions of sovereign immunity—the idea that the king can do no wrong.[305] Second, the embarrassment to the federal government would be no greater when the President is a defendant in a case involving international-law violations than it was in *United States v. Nixon*.[306] Third, the policy considerations underlying the separation-of-powers doctrine are virtually the same, regardless of the identity of the defendant. It would have made little difference in the *Steel Seizure Case*,[307] if the defendant had been President Truman or in *Goldwater v. Carter*[308] if the defendant had been Secretary of State Cyrus Vance. Indeed, the Court in *Goldwater* expressed no concern whatever about the identity of the defendant. The real issue is not whose name appears in the case caption but whether, notwithstanding the identity of the defendant, the substantive outcome upholds or undermines the constitutional responsibilities and institutional capabilities of the three branches of the federal government.

Functional Capabilities and Constitutional Responsibilities

The President

The conclusions suggested by constitutional text, case law, custom, and Framers' intent are corroborated by a consideration of the three branches' functional attrubutes. Viewed functionally, permitting unilateral executive violation of international law would yield little benefit. International law already makes sufficient allowance for a state to act swiftly to meet an emergency. In addition to the right to take necessary and proportionate countermeasures in response to an international-law violation, noted above,[309] a state has the right to use armed force in individual and collective self-defense.[310] It is therefore difficult to hypothesize exigent circumstances that would require presidential action before Congress could act. Rather, the more typical situation in which a vio-

[303] 457 U.S. 749 (1982).

[304] *Id.* at 749.

[305] For a discussion of the origins of sovereign immunity, *see* E. Henderson, Foundations of English Administrative Law (1974).

[306] 418 U.S. 683 (1974).

[307] 343 U.S. 579 (1952).

[308] Goldwater v. Carter, 444 U.S. 996 (1979).

[309] *See supra* text at note 36.

[310] *See* United Nations Charter, art. 51.

lation might be desirable is one that permits the collective, deliberative reflection of a legislative body.

It is hard to see how the distribution of authority I have outlined could have any appreciable effect on the exercise of legitimate executive ''flexibility.'' An Executive indifferent to international law or unable to make a persuasive case for its violation could of course face constraints. But that is as it should be. Flexibility is not the only value that the Constitution seeks to uphold; flexibility, like convenience and efficiency, does not eclipse other important constitutional values.[311] To seek efficiency alone in foreign-policy-making would always lead to exclusion of the courts and Congress.[312] Even more vital to the Framers' scheme was the value of *process*, the notion that *how* a decision is made can be as important as its substance. If it is imperative that the United States violate customary international law, then the President should have no difficulty persuading Congress to authorize that violation. If he or she cannot, then the United States should continue to honor international law.

One critic of this approach, although acknowledging that the presidential power at issue is not plenary, seems nevertheless to believe that it is only under executive direction that the United States participates in the process by which customary norms are changed.[313] This is not so. The courts, Congress, and the Executive all partake in the process of customary law formation and transformation; a norm of customary international law reflects the acts of all three branches.[314] *The Paquete Habana*,[315] in its time, surely constituted evidence of customary law concerning the seizure of coastal fishing vessels. Congressional legislation concerning human rights, enacted in the 1970s, surely contributed to the development of human-rights norms, such as the customary prohibition against prolonged arbitrary detention.

This does not mean that the President can *never* act alone. The Executive might, for example, indicate its dissent while a customary rule is being developed. That nascent rule, should it develop into a customary norm, would then have no application to acts of the United States, either internationally or domestically.[316] This measure of discretion is permitted because at the time the

[311] *See* INS v. Chadha, 462 U.S. 919 (1983).

[312] As Justice Douglas said, ''The President can act more quickly than Congress. The President with the armed forces at his disposal can move with force as well as speed. All executive power—from the reign of ancient kings to the rule of modern dictators—has the outward appearance of efficiency.'' Youngstown Sheet & Tube Co. v. Sawyer, 343 U.S. 579, 629 (1952) (Douglas, J., concurring).

[313] Charney, *The Power of the Executive Branch of the United States Government to Violate Customary International Law*, 80 Am. J. Intl. L. 913 (1986).

[314] *See* art. 38(1) of the Statue of the International Court of Justice, June 26, 1945, 59 Stat. 1055, T.S. No. 993, providing that the Court in resolving international law disputes shall apply ''general principles of law recognized by civilized nations'' as well as ''judicial decisions . . . of the various nations.''

[315] 175 U.S. 667 (1900).

[316] Restatement § 102, Comment *d*.

Executive objects, the rule is not yet part of customary international law and a fortiori not yet part of federal common law, thus lacking wide acceptance and perhaps even clear definition.

There is little reason to believe, therefore, that the modest limitations imposed by this approach would handicap United States participation in international-law formation or any other diplomatic arena. The urgent need today is that international law and international institutions be strengthened, not further eroded. In this task, federal courts have a role to play; not *the* role—Congress has the last word—but *a* role. Acting without congressional consent, it is not within the President's constitutional power to breach a clearly defined and widely accepted norm of customary international law. It is within the constitutional power of the courts to order that violation stopped.

This conclusion comports fully with the Chief Executive's constitutional role. The rule does not permit interference with the plenary authority of the President. The scope of the courts' power to preclude presidential violation of customary international law is no broader than the scope of Congress's power to do so. On the other hand, if Congress can act, as it clearly can under the offenses clause,[317] there is no constitutional reason that the courts cannot act; in applying customary international law as federal common law, the judiciary also plays its constitutional role as lawmaker in Congress's stead.[318] And its rules are equally binding. "All constitutional acts of power," John Jay wrote, "whether in the executive or the judicial department, have as much legal validity and obligation as if they proceeded from the legislature."[319]

The Court in *Sabbatino* recognized that some international-law issues "touch much more sharply on national nerves than do others."[320] The Court's concern about embarrassing the Executive in foreign affairs[321] led the *Sabbatino* Court to suggest that "the less important the implications of an issue are for our foreign relations, the weaker the justification for exclusivity in the political branches."[322] The Court's language suggests that it will be more willing to apply international law to the Chief Executive when it makes little difference. A more restrained interpretation of the opinion, however, would note that the Court referred to the "political branches," not merely to the Executive, indicating that the Court recognized the heightened propriety of abstention when both Congress and the Executive have undertaken a full-fledged national commitment. Under such circumstances, international law poses no

[317] *See supra* notes 70–73 and accompanying text.

[318] Professor Henkin has acknowledged that "[i]n principle, any authority exercised by the courts under their own constitutional authority ought to be equal to the authority of Congress . . . and their 'enactments' entitled to equal weight." Henkin, *International Law*, *supra* note 199, at 1563.

[319] The Federalist No. 64 (Jay).

[320] Banco Nacional de Cuba v. Sabbatino, 376 U.S. 398 (1964).

[321] *Id*. at 433.

[322] *Id*. at 428.

domestic legal constraint;[323] heightened judicial deference is appropriate because the courts necessarily have the last word. When Congress has joined forces with the Executive, the only hurdle placed in their path is an *absolute* constitutional one—a bar that neither political branch can overcome.[324]

The Congress

The case for judicial deference is weaker when the Judiciary is not the final arbiter; this occurs when the President breaches customary international law without congressional authorization.[325] If the Court finds a legislatively unauthorized executive act violative of international law, the President can always appeal to Congress for statutory approval. If Congress grants authorization, the Court acts in the same procedural role as when it interprets a statute. The Court prefers statutory to constitutional construction as a means of disposing of cases because that practice manifests greater deference to a coordinate branch of government.

For the same reason, the justification for deference is weaker when the President, acting alone, violates international law and the Court requires him to stop. If Congress does not honor the President's request for statutory authorization, the Executive should lose. Violation of international law may cause the nation to incur serious costs, tangible and intangible. The international "obloquy" alluded to by Chief Justice Marshall[326] represents one level of cost: A nation seen as a lawbreaker is treated like a lawbreaker. Moreover, its precedent can be invoked against it. Abu Abbas, the mastermind of the *Achille Lauro* hijacking in 1985, asserted that the United States had no standing to blame Palestinians for terrorism. "They are the ones," he asserted, "who support dictatorial regimes in Latin America and violate . . . international laws."[327] As Senator J. William Fulbright has pointed out, governmental law violation is self-defeating:

> Because the law is by its very nature a buttress of the status quo, it is rational for revolutionaries to try to overthrow it and for conservatives to uphold it. It is not rational for conservatives to play fast and loose with the law in a seizure of anti-revolutionary zeal. When they do, it is rather like the defenders of a besieged fort firing their artillery through the protecting walls instead of over them: They may blow up some of the attackers on the other side, but in the process they are making a nice opening through which the enemy can pour into the fort in their next attack.[328]

[323] *See supra* notes 140–162 and accompanying text.

[324] *Id.*

[325] *See supra* text accompanying notes 23–70.

[326] *See* Brown v. United States, 12 U.S. (8 Cranch) 110, 128 (1814).

[327] The Sacramento Bee, Feb. 17, 1987, at A5.

[328] J. Fulbright, The Arrogance of Power 92–93 (1966).

The United States may choose to join the ranks of the lawless in a given situation, but if it does, the decision should be made by the elected representatives of the people. The international community may also impose economic and diplomatic sanctions upon lawbreakers. Those sanctions can be severe, including monetary damages,[329] trade embargoes,[330] prohibitions against arms sales,[331] diplomatic relations and recognition,[332] and financial and other economic assistance.[333] The decision to risk such sanctions can have a sweeping impact on the life of the entire nation. In addition, the decision can implicate directly the powers of Congress, including the appropriations power,[334] the power to regulate commerce with foreign nations,[335] and the power to declare war.[336] Congressional consent should precede such steps.[337]

[329] The Wimbleton Great Britain v. Germany, 1923 P.C.I.S., Ser. A., No. 1, at 31, 32 (Judgment of Aug. 17); The Lusitania (United States v. Germany), Reports: A.J., C/III (1924), p. 177; Witenberg, vol. 1, p. 18; Kiesselbach, p. 174. Reports: A.J. XVIII (1924), p. 361: Witenberg, vol. 1, p. 22; Kiesselbach, p. 186; Case Concerning the factory at Chorzow (Germany v. Poland) 1928 P.C.I.J., ser. A., No. 17, at 31, 46–48 (Judgment of Sept. 13); The Corfu Channel Case [United Kingdom v. Albania], 1949 I.C.J. 249 (Judgment of Dec. 15).

[330] S.C. Res. 418, 32 U.N. Scor, Resolutions and Decisions of the Security Council 5–6 U.N. Doc. S/INF/32 (1977) (mandatory arms embargo against South Africa); S.C. Res. 232, 21 U.N. Scor., Resolutions and Decisions of the Security Council 7–9, U.N. Doc. S/INF/21/Rev. 1 (1966) (trade sanctions against Rhodesia imposed during the Rhodesian revolt from British colonial rule); 19 Harv. Int'l L.J. 887, 896 n.44 (1978); (Res. 1, Ninth Meeting of Consultation of Ministers of Foreign Affairs, Washington, D.C., U.S.A., July 21–26, 1964, Final Act, OAS Off. Rec. OEA/Ser. D/III 15 (English), at 3 (1964) (trade embargo against Cuba imposed as a reaction to Cuba's policy of ''exporting revolution'' to other countries).

[331] Res. 1, Sixth Meeting of Consultation of Ministers of Foreign Affairs, San Jose, Costa Rica, August 16–21, 1960, Final Act, OAS Off. Rec. OEC/SER. C/II 6 (English), at 8 (1960) (OAS imposed sanctions against the Dominican Republic when the Trujillo regime controlled the government); S.C. Res. 232, 21 U.N. Scor, Resolutions and Decisions of the Security Council 7–9, U.N. Doc. S/INF/21/Rev. (1966) (prohibition of arms sales to Southern Rhodesia); S.C. Res. 181, 18 U.N. Scor, Resolutions and Decisions of the Security Council (1963) (prohibition against trading in materials and equipment for manufacture and maintenance in arms and ammunition in South Africa; S.C. Res. 418, 32 U.N. Scor (2046th mtg) at 1, U.N. Doc. S/RES/418 (prov. ed. 1977) (mandatory arms embargo against South Africa).

[332] Res. 1, Sixth Meeting of Consultation of Ministers of Foreign Affairs, San Jose, Costa Rica, August 16–21, 1960 Final Act, OAS Off. Rec. OEA/SER. C/III 6 (English), at 8 (1960) (OAS ordered breaking of diplomatic relations with the Trujillo regime in the Dominican Republic); Res. 1, Ninth Meeting of Consultation of Ministers of Foreign Affairs, Washington, D.C. U.S.A., July 21–26, 1964, Final Act, OAS Off. Rec. OEA/SER. D/III 15 (English), at 3 (1964) (OAS ordered the withholding of diplomatic recognition of the Castro regime in Cuba).

[333] S.C. Res. 232, 21 U.N. Scor, Resolutions and Decisions of the Security Council 7–9, U.N. Doc. S/INF/21/Rev. 1 (1966).

[334] U.S. Const. art. I, § 8, cl. 1.

[335] U.S. Const. art. I, § 8, cl. 3.

[336] U.S. Const. art. I, § 8, cl. 11.

[337] *See* Youngstown Sheet & Tube v. Sawyer, 343 U.S. 579, 630 (1952) (Douglas, J., concurring) (arguing that the ''taking'' of the nation's steel mills would require just compensation, thus requiring an appropriation—an act within the exclusive power of Congress).

The Supreme Court

The Supreme Court has long adjudicated disputes involving assertions of executive power. What is not commonly known is that the early Court regularly visited disputes involving international law and foreign relations—more often, in fact, than it did constitutional controversies: ''Between 1801 and the time of Marshall's death in 1835, there were 1,215 cases decided. Of these there were 62 involving constitutional questions, and 195 involving questions of international law or in some way affecting international relations.''[338]

In the model cast in this chapter, the Court participates in the resolution of controversies concerning the legality of presidential acts under international law, but its decisions are not determinative. The Court decides in the first instance whether the President's act is permissible, but that decision is not final because Congress may displace that rule of federal common law with a statutory rule of its own. The Court's role is consistent with the Court's proclivity for deference to the political branches on matters of foreign policy, though the role also comports with the Court's duty ''to say what the law is.''[339] Additionally, the Court need not engage in the credibility-impairing task of ''finding'' legislative intent when its existence is doubtful. Instead, the Court's reliance upon international law bolsters the credibility of the legal system.

Initial judicial decision making does not, however, resolve the problem of embarrassment to the Executive. The Court's decision may still have ''implications for our foreign relations.''[340] But the United States is a member of the community of nations and is subject to international law. A nation that violates international law *should* be embarrassed. If the fact of a violation has ''implications for the foreign relations'' of the offending country, then the international system is working as it should.

Yet in *Sabbatino*,[341] the Supreme Court rejected the argument that United States courts can ''make a significant contribution to the growth of international law, a contribution whose importance . . . would be magnified by the relative paucity of decisional law by international bodies.''[342] The Court's reasoning does not extend beyond *Sabbatino*, for two reasons.

First, the application of the act-of-state doctrine is not compelled by international law.[343] Perhaps international rules concerning act-of-state questions should be codified by convention or left to evolve on their own.[344] But this is

[338] B. Ziegler, The International Law of John Marshall 13 (1939).

[339] Marbury v. Madison, 5 U.S. (1 Cranch) 137, 177 (1803).

[340] Banco Nacional de Cuba v. Sabbatino, 376 U.S. 398, 427–28 (1964).

[341] 376 U.S. 398 (1964).

[342] *Id*. at 434.

[343] *Id*. at 427.

[344] The Court in *Sabbatino* said that ''given the fluidity of present world conditions, the effec-

not a practical alternative for all of customary international law. Barring the few areas where codification has been possible,[345] the "patchwork" approach of adjudication has been the only available method of incorporating international law. Moreover, the "fluidity of present world conditions" makes all the more imperative judicial involvement in the establishment of a stable and international juridical framework.

Second, the *Sabbatino* Court doubted the "sanguine presupposition that the decisions of the courts [of the United States] would be accepted as disinterested expressions of sound legal principle by those adhering to widely different ideologies."[346] Again, however, that rejoinder was made in a very different context. The Court questioned the ability of the judiciary of "the world's major capital exporting country and principal exponent of the free enterprise system" to play the role of impartial expositor of expropriations laws.[347] That concern is inapposite with respect to customary international law, which has been applied by the Court since the earliest days of the Republic, sometimes supporting and sometimes opposing executive interests.

The judicial role outlined here would not entail a radical departure from existing institutional roles or relationships. The notion of contingent constitutionality provides the Supreme Court with a doctrinally traditional medium for overturning some acts falling within the "zone of twilight" but upholding other acts in that category.[348]

As to concern about "straitjacketing" the Executive, it might simply be said that the customary international norms of federal common law are not a suicide pact, any more than is the Constitution. If they ever became one, it is within the power of Congress to change them. Moreover, the costs of circumscribing executive discretion must be weighed against the costs inherent in judicial indifference to executive international-law violations. Violations may on occasion benefit the nation, but violations undercut the international legal

---

tiveness of such a patchwork approach toward the formulation of an acceptable body of law concerning state responsibility for expropriations is, to say the least, highly conjectural." *Id.* at 434.

[345] In 1947, the United Nations General Assembly created the International Law Commission to promote codification of customary international law. Although the Commission produced draft conventions that served as the basis for several of the most important conventions negotiated under the auspices of the United Nations, the Commission no longer plays a central role in the international lawmaking process. One reason apparently lies in the inconsequential topics it has selected for codification. "Today the areas of economic and technological development, environmental protection, violence control and human rights . . . occupy the minds and imaginations of the world. They certainly are felt to be more important than the status of the diplomatic pouch." El Baradei, Franck & Trachtenberg, *The International Law Commission: The Need for a New Direction*, in Policy and Efficacy Studies No. 1, Project of the Unitar Research Department, United Nations Institute for Training and Research 34 (1981).

[346] *Sabbatino*, 376 U.S. at 434–35.

[347] *Id.*

[348] Youngstown Sheet & Tube Co. v. Sawyer, 343 U.S. 579, 637 (1952) (Jackson, J., concurring).

system and ultimately cost each of its members.[349] The task of weighing systemic costs against benefits is a formidable one, requiring prudence no less than prescience. The Court's institutional capabilities are well suited to this task, for whatever its shortcomings as a foreign-policy decision maker, the judiciary is as capable as the President to assess the systemic costs of a violation of international law. It is, after all, a *legal* system that is at stake. It does not seem farfetched to think that judges may have something to contribute to the task of preserving that system.

A Case Study: Garcia-Mir v. Meese

Many of the considerations outlined in this chapter came together for the first time in 1986. In *Garcia-Mir v. Meese*,[350] undocumented Cuban refugees who had come to the United States in the Mariel boatlift were detained indefinitely by the federal government. No statutory authority permitted the detention.[351] The federal district court found that the determination of the Attorney General

[349] The new ''realists'' of the Right seem inattentive to the costs incurred through international law violations, and to the national interest of the United States in the maintenance of world order. One conservative commentator, for example, has inveighed against adherence to international law when United States ''national interest'' requires another course:

> Who seriously declaims on the virtues of ''international law'' among a ''world community of nations'' as a relevant solution to American foreign policy problems? . . . Our State Department is still committed to this outlook, but everyone else now talks about our ''national interest.'' It is the conception of our ''national interest'' that sets the terms for all our debates on foreign policy.

Kristol, *Don't Count Out Conservatism*, N.Y. Times Sunday Magazine, June 14, 1987, at 53. *See also* Weisburd, *The Executive Branch and International Law*, 41 Vand. L. Rev. 1205, 1269 (''Arguments certainly can be made that adherence to customary international law is in the interests of the United States, but the courts focus on the interests of the United States.'').

Professor Louis Henkin has given a forthright answer to such soft-headedness:

> It seems to set up a dichotomy between law observance and national interest, to treat their concurrence as coincidental and their opposition as common. [I]t see[s] immediate tangible advantage—the gain from a violation—as the only national interest. It does not seem to consider that the law of nations may be in the interest of all nations, as the law of an enlightened society is in the interest of all its citizens. It does not see national interest in law observance—in order and stability, in reliable expectations, in confidence and credit, in the support of other nations and peoples, in friendly relations, in living up to a nation's aspirations and self-image, in satisfying the ''morality'' of its own officials of its own citizens. It tends to discount the national interest in avoiding other, immediate, ''concrete'' responses to violation. The issue of law observance . . . is never a clear choice between legal obligation and national interest; a nation that observes law, even when it ''hurts,'' is not sacrificing national interest to law; it is choosing between competing national interests; when it commits a violation it is also sacrificing one national interest to another.

L. Henkin, How Nations Behave 331 (2d ed. 1979). *See also* Henkin, *International Law and National Interest*, 25 Colum. J. Intl. L. 1 (1986).

[350] 788 F.2d 1446 (11th Cir.), *cert. denied*, 107 S. Ct. 289 (1986).

[351] 788 F.2d at 1454.

that they should be detained was binding on the federal courts,[352] even though it violated customary international law.[353] The Court of Appeals for the Eleventh Circuit affirmed,[354] not reaching the question whether the detention violated international law and holding merely that "the executive acts here evident constitute a sufficient basis for affirming the trial court's finding that international law does not control."[355]

The district court was correct in concluding that international law was violated. Because the norm prohibiting prolonged arbitrary detention is clearly defined and widely accepted, however, it should have found the norm to be binding on the President. As the Senate Foreign Relations Committee said in its report on interpretation of the ABM Treaty, "In the absence of statutory authorization, . . . the President is bound by . . . rules of customary international law [that are] clearly defined and widely accepted."[356]

In concluding that the President was not bound to follow international law, both courts relied heavily upon the reference in *The Paquete Habana* to "controlling executive acts." Neither, however, analyzed precisely *which* executive acts are controlling. Neither, for example, entertained the possibility that only statutorily authorized executive acts control. Nor did either consider carefully the question of *who* in the executive branch is constitutionally empowered to carry out a "controlling" executive act. Rather, both seemed to assume that *any* act of *any* executive official will do—which effectively robs the term *controlling* of any substantive content, for in the view of these courts, *all* executive acts apparently are controlling.

Professor Henkin has criticized these opinions in an article in which he dissociates himself from the "extreme dualist position" seemingly espoused in his earlier work:[357]

> [T]he argument that the President unilaterally may order acts that clearly derogate from . . . basic principles of customary international law requires taking a step deeper into dualism than this nation has ever taken. It is one thing to treat international and domestic law as equal in our jurisprudential hierarchy; it is quite another to say that customary international law or treaty not only can be super-

[352] Fernadez-Roque v. Smith, 622 F. Supp. 887, 908 (N.D. Ga. 1985).

[353] *Id.*

[354] Garcia-Mir v. Meese, 788 F.2d 1446 (11th Cir.), *cert. denied*, 107 S. Ct. 289 (1986).

[355] *Id.* at 1455.

[356] Rept. No. 100-164 at 54–55 (1987).

[357] Henkin, *The Constitution and United States Sovereignty: A Century of Chinese Exclusion and Its Progeny*, 100 Harv. L. Rev. 853, 882 (1987) (hereinafter "Chinese Exclusion") (referring, inter alia, to his remark in Foreign Affairs and the Constitution 221–22 (1972), that "the Constitution does not forbid the President . . . to violate international law, and the courts will give effect to acts within the constitutional powers of the political branches without regard to international law.").

seded by later law adopted by those having legislative power but also can be violated by executive fiat.[358]

Henkin, now, would thus disallow presidential derogation from customary international norms, except where "an act of the President having legislative effect, supervenes and is inconsistent with the principle of international law. . . ."[359] "[T]he President may derogate from principles of international law only where he is acting within his constitutional powers."[360] Examples of instances in which the President may have some lawmaking power include certain executive agreements and executive orders, such as those upheld in *United States v. Pink*[361] and *United States v. Belmont*;[362] presidential "suggestions" that the courts deny sovereign or diplomatic immunity; presidential voiding of a treaty voidable by the United States; and presidential termination of a treaty in accordance with its terms.[363]

For the reasons discussed in Chapters 1 and 2, it is critical to distinguish between plenary and concurrent presidential powers. Some of the acts on Professor Henkin's list, such as the making of executive agreements to carry out the recognition power, would fall within the President's plenary powers; others, such as treaty termination, admit of the possibility of presidential initiation but are subject to congressional control; they would thus fall with his concurrent powers. For the reasons given earlier in this chapter, it seems improper to regard the President's plenary powers as encompassing acts that would place the United States in violation of international law; the power to limit international-law violation is expressly assigned to Congress in the text of the Constitution.[364] If no *plenary* presidential power extends so far, a fortiori no concurrent power does. Accordingly, the President's constitutional powers in foreign affairs, plenary or concurrent, do not permit him to disregard international law.

In practice, few instances will arise in which Professor Henkin's approach will yield different results from that suggested by this chapter. It is difficult to hypothesize circumstances in which the "lawmaking" powers of the President might be used in a manner that would transgress an applicable international-law norm. Ordinarily there is no conflict. One example, however, may be the Reagan Administration's recognition of Eric Arturuo Delvalle as President of the Republic of Panama. If the act violated international law as has been al-

[358] *Id*. at 883.
[359] *Id*. at 885.
[360] *Id*. at 884.
[361] 315 U.S. 203 (1942).
[362] 301 U.S. 324 (1937).
[363] Chinese Exclusion, *supra* note 357 at 879–80 (1987).
[364] U.S. Const. art. I, § 8, cl. 10.

leged,[365] under the approach outlined in this chapter, the act of recognition would lie beyond the President's constitutional power. On the other hand, under Professor Henkin's former "extreme dualist" approach, it apparently would not, for he would seemingly consider recognition to be a plenary presidential power that may be exercised without regard to international law.

The Delvalle recognition is also useful in examining the practicality of another aspect of the "extreme dualist" approach—the suggestion that the breadth of the President's constitutional power may be assessed by referring to the relationship of the act in question to some foreign country. "[T]he courts may not enjoin the President from taking an action in relation to another country, ordinarily outside the United States, on the ground that the action violates international law . . . ,"[366] the position asserts. But an "international obligation of the United States designed for the benefit of private persons in the United States and incorporated and operative as law in the United States" may thus be the subject of a judicial order.

Is this dichotomy practicable? To test it, let us ask into which of these two categories two acts would fall. What of the Delvalle recognition? Recognition of a foreign government surely is an "action in relation to another country." Yet are its effects felt "outside the United States" or within? The principal practical effects of nonrecognition occur domestically: The unrecognized regime is denied access to courts in the United States, denied entitlement to own property, denied effect to its acts applicable beyond its territory.[367] Or suppose the President determines to "violate a diplomat's immunity."[368] Are the effects of that act felt outside the United States or within? In the end, efforts to measure presidential foreign-affairs powers through reference to the locus of its effects seem doomed to failure, for the standard seems to rely upon a distinction of little utility.

If the direct practical differences between the two approaches are few, the theoretical differences nonetheless seem important. Professor Henkin has written, for example, that the *Garcia-Mir* courts "failed to attend to [the] essential qualification that the President may derogate from international law only when he is acting within his constitutional powers."[369] It appears that, to

[365] A state, it is pointed out, is required to treat as the government of another state a regime that is in effective control of that state. Restatement § 203. When a state recognizes a regime as the successor government while the previously recognized regime is still in control, that constitutes unlawful interference in the internal affairs of the other state. *Id.*, Comment *g*. Memorandum of law in support of Defendant Air Panama Internacional, S.A.'s motion to dissolve temporary restraining orders and for a temporary restraining order and preliminary injunction, Republic of Panama v. Air Panama Internacional, S.A., et al., No. 88-0435-CIV-Hoeveler (S.D. Florida, 1988).

[366] Chinese Exclusion, *supra* note 357, at 882 (1987).

[367] Restatement § 205.

[368] Chinese Exclusion, *supra* note 357, at 879–80 (1987).

[369] *Id*. at 884 (1987).

the contrary, both courts believed that the President was acting precisely within his constitutional powers. That is why they declined to invalidate his act. Both concluded, as noted above, that the President acted without statutory authority. On what basis other than the Constitution could his act have been upheld?

By carving out an exception for acts "within the President's constitutional powers," the extreme dualist approach thus creates a gaping hole. For it implicitly conceives of any otherwise constitutional act of the President, performed within the zone of twilight, as permissible. The approach "requires taking a step deeper in dualism than this nation has ever taken"—that is, until *Garcia-Mir v. Meese*. Far better had the courts minded the teaching of W. W. Willoughby:

> All orders of the President, or of the Secretary of War issued under his authority, . . . must, . . . if issued by virtue of his constitutional authority, be in accordance with the generally accepted principles of international law and custom. Where this is not done, they will not justify the acts of subordinates acting under them.[370]

Conclusion

Whatever rationale most persuasively supports the power of the federal courts, federal common law, and thus customary international law is the supreme law of the land. The same tripartite framework applied by the Court in analyzing presidential power in light of federal statutory law should apply when presidential power is analyzed in light of federal common law. Customary international law is relevant only regarding acts performed in the "zone of twilight" when Congress has not acted. In zones 1 and 3 of the Jackson-Rehnquist framework, when Congress has spoken, federal common law does not exist, and customary international law has no bearing on the constitutionality of that act.

When Congress is silent, customary international law serves as a provisional "stand-in" for statutory law for purposes of the Jackson-Rehnquist framework. International law narrows the zone of twilight to lessen the uncertainty that attaches when the legality of executive action in the international arena is at issue. Presidential violation of customary international law represents violation of federal common law, and the courts have not hesitated to strike down such action. On the other hand, when the President acts in accord with customary international law and in a statutory vacuum, there is no reason to invalidate his act.

Federal common law and the norms of customary international law subsumed within it substitute for federal statutory law in assessing the constitu-

[370] W. Willoughby, 3 The Constitutional Law of the United States § 1031 at 1566 (2d ed. 1929) (footnotes omitted).

tionality of presidential acts in the absence of an express congressional will. A clearly defined and widely agreed-upon norm of customary international law represents a provisional constitutional rule, one that can be reversed with the consent of Congress. When Congress declines to concur in the President's violation, however, the courts can and should proceed to halt it.

Chapter Eight

NATIONAL SECURITY: CONGRESSIONAL OVERSIGHT AND JUDICIAL REVIEW

Experience should teach us to be most on our guard to protect liberty when the Government's purposes are beneficent. Men born to freedom are naturally alert to repel invasion of their liberty by evil-minded rulers. The greatest dangers to liberty lurk in insidious encroachment by men of zeal, well-meaning but without understanding.
—Justice Louis Brandeis[1]

The Mandate of National Security

The garbled vocabulary of professional national-security aficionados too often obscures the truth that national security consists of no more than the safety and well-being of individuals composing the state. In the United States, the law places the individual above the state; its guarantees of individual liberty are not considered interests to be balanced against those of the state. We do not weigh the ''good of the state'' against the good of any individual, for the scales would invariably tilt toward the good of the collective entity. Rather we compare one individual interest against another individual interest, or one group interest against another group interest—thereby avoiding a jury-rigged result.

Yet this impartial calculus is quickly forgotten against a backdrop of geopolitical games where, on boards in policymakers' minds, one anthropomorphic state befriends another, betrays another, or bedevils another. The point is too quickly lost that the ''state'' is no more than a mental construct, an aggregate of individual interests, and that United States foreign policy is conducted for the purpose of preserving the primacy of the individual over the state.[2]

That primacy is enshrined in what we refer to as the rule of law. It is the

[1] Olmstead v. United States, 277 U.S. 438, 479 (1928) (Brandeis, J., dissenting).

[2] As the Supreme Court said in United States v. Robel, 389 U.S. 258, 264 (1967):

[T]his concept of ''national defense'' cannot be deemed an end in itself, justifying any exercise of legislative power designed to promote such a goal. Implicit in the term ''national defense'' is the notion of defending those values and ideals which set this Nation apart. . . . It would be ironic indeed if, in the name of national defense, we would sanction the subversion of one of those liberties . . . which makes the defense of the Nation worthwhile.

rule of law that lends legitimacy to efforts to protect the national security. To abandon the rule of law is thus to forsake the ultimate right to rule to which government can lay claim. In formulating a policy, the question in each instance must therefore be whether the tools of diplomacy, all intended to strengthen the nation's security, will subordinate, or be subordinated to, the processes provided by the Constitution to maintain the rule of law. The issue is "whether, in defending our institutions, we sacrifice the values which make the defense worthwhile. . . ."[3]

Nowhere is the willingness to sacrifice those values more evident than in the comments of defenders of the Iran-Contra policies such as Congressman Henry Hyde. Hyde, a member of the House Select Committee to Investigate Covert Arms Transactions with Iran, openly questioned the propriety of holding hearings on the matter.[4] Indeed, he challenged the propriety of creating the Committee on which he served.[5] The real reason for doing so, "to be simple, accurate, and blunt," he revealed, was that "there are Members of the House and Senate who do not believe that communism in Central America is a grave threat to peace and freedom. . . ."[6]

Now it may be that some members of Congress fail to share Hyde's insight into the magnitude of the Communist peril. But is it not possible that others differ not about ends but about *means*? Is it not possible that others are not willing to sacrifice the rule of law in this country to impose rulers (perhaps under law, perhaps not)[7] on another country?

Rather than defending a manifest transgression of the law, the rule of law would be better served by acknowledging the transgression and arguing from necessity rather than legality. Arthur Schlesinger has wisely written that while the Framers did not rule out the possibility that "crisis might require the executive to act outside the Constitution," neither did they intend to confer constitutional legitimacy on such acts, believing that the "legal order would be better preserved if departures from it were frankly identified as such than if they were anointed with a factitious legality and thereby enabled to serve as constitutional precedents for future action."[8] It is doubtless true, as Jefferson opined after leaving the Presidency, that the "laws of self-preservation, of saving our country when in danger, are of a higher obligation" than a "strict

[3] Remarks of Professor Thomas Emerson at the First Symposium of the Allard K. Lowenstein International Human Rights Law Project, Yale Law School (Apr. 10, 1982).

[4] S. Rept. 100-216, 100th Cong., 1st Sess. at 668 (1987) (Iran-Contra committees).

[5] *Id.*

[6] *Id.*

[7] "Terrorism is in itself acts of violence or threats of violence perpetrated in such a way as to cause some kind of political outcome absent what one would consider to be a declaration of war." Testimony of Oliver North, 100-7 Iran-Contra Investigation: Joint Hearings Before the House Select Committee to Investigate Covert Arms Transactions with Iran and the Senate Select Committee on Secret Military Assistance to Iran and the Nicaraguan Opposition, 100th Cong., 1st Sess. (part I) 211 (1987).

[8] A. Schlesinger, The Imperial Presidency 8 (1973).

observance of the written laws.''[9] Yet it must be hastily noted that only once in American history has a President confronted a crisis that made such a rationale for overt law violation plausible. Upon the Rebel attack on Fort Sumter, President Lincoln suspended the writ of habeas corpus, asking, ''Are all the laws, *but one*, to go unexecuted, and the government itself go into pieces, lest that one be violated?''[10] Legal institutions, Jefferson and Lincoln knew, are not shock-resistant; they must be nurtured and enriched with a respect deriving from constant vigilance, lest cracks grow and fractures multiply.

With recent events demonstrating ever more starkly the law's fragility, the task confronting the constitutionalist is plain: to fortify a decision-making structure directed at minimizing the risk of myopically self-destructive policies.[11] This means, among other things, more aggressive congressional oversight, particularly of intelligence activities, and more active judicial review.

Aggressive Congressional Oversight

In 1968, Louis Heren wrote that ''[t]he modern American presidency can be compared with the British monarchy as it existed for a century or more after the signing of Magna Carta in 1215. . . .'' He continued: ''Indeed, it can be said that the main difference between the modern American President and a medieval monarch is that there has been a steady increase rather than a diminution of his power. In comparative historical terms the United States has been moving steadily backwards.''[12] The Senate Foreign Relations Committee, a year later, was equally bleak: ''It is no longer accurate to characterize our government, in matters of foreign relations, as one of separated powers checked and balanced against each other.''[13]

The reasons for continuing tendencies toward governmental disequilibrium have been fully detailed by Arthur Schlesinger in his landmark 1974 work, *The Imperial Presidency*. Some are cultural, some historical, some structural. None can question, however, Professor Philip Kurland's bluntly stated conclusion that Congress has simply lacked ''the guts to stand up to its responsibilities.''[14] Those responsibilities are clear; in the realm of national security, as in the domain of foreign affairs generally, the President shares responsibility

[9] *Id.* at 24–25.

[10] S. Levinson, *The Specious Morality of the Law*, Harper's, May 1977, at 36.

[11] One of the best works generally on this matter is Professor Raoul Berger's book Executive Privilege: A Constitutional Myth (1973).

[12] L. Heren, The New American Commonwealth 8–9 (1968). *Compare* Dames & Moore v. Regan, 453 U.S. 654, 662 (1981) (''The example of such unlimited power that must have most impressed the forefathers was the prerogative exercised by George III, and the description of its evils in the Declaration of Independence, leads me to doubt that they were creating their new Executive in his image.'').

[13] S. Rept. No. 129, 91st Cong., 1st Sess. 7 (1969) (National Commitments Resolution).

[14] Kurland, *The Impotence of Reticence*, 1968 Duke L.J. 619.

with Congress. The United States Court of Appeals for the D.C. Circuit put it well:

> While the Constitution assigns to the President a number of powers relating to national security, including the function of commander in chief and the power to make treaties and appoint Ambassadors, it confers upon Congress other powers equally inseparable from the national security, such as the powers to declare war, raise and support armed forces and, in the case of the Senate, consent to treaties and the appointment of Ambassadors.[15]

If and when it musters the will to fulfill its constitutionally assigned tasks, it will find no shortage of tools available to get the job done, beginning with its time-honored power over the purse.

The Power over the Purse

The ultimate weapon available to a Congress unhappy with an executive activity is to cut off the funds,[16] an action often taken in recent years with respect to a variety of executive foreign-policy initiatives, from termination of the United States military involvement in Indochina[17] to banning aid to guerrillas in Angola,[18] and cutting off military aid to Turkey, Chile, and Argentina.[19] This is the constitutional tool Congress used in enacting the so-called Boland Amendments, statutory restrictions that limited the availability of appropriated funds to the Contras.[20] Corwin regarded the power over the purse as "the most important single curb in the Constitution on Presidential power."[21] Its history and scope reveal his view to be no exaggeration.

The Constitution flatly prohibits statutorily unauthorized expenditures by the President. Article I, section 9, clause 7 confers on Congress exclusive power over the purse. It provides that "no money shall be drawn from the treasury, but in consequence of appropriations made by law." The only prohibitions in the text of the Constitution against the use of the appropriations power to curtail the activities of another branch are the requirements that the Justices of the Supreme Court and the President receive a compensation that may not be diminished.[22] Had the Framers intended further limitations on the appropriations power, they would have included them. Indeed, in the case of military matters, they went to the other extreme. In addition to the power to appropriate funds—and to refuse to do so—they gave Congress the power to

[15] U.S. v. A.T.& T. Co., 567 F.2d 121, 128 (D.C. Cir. 1977).

[16] *See generally* L. Fisher, Presidential Spending Power (1975).

[17] *See infra* note 43.

[18] *See* Congressional Quarterly, Powers of Congress 82 (2d ed. 1982).

[19] *Id.* at 80.

[20] *See* Chapter 1.

[21] E. Corwin, The Constitution and What It Means Today 101 (13th ed., 1975).

[22] U.S. Const. art. II, § 1, cl. 6; art. III, § 1.

"raise and support Armies"[23] and to "provide and maintain a Navy"[24]—and to refuse to do so.

Its historical background reveals why the appropriations clause conferred such broad power upon Congress.[25] The provision was framed against the backdrop of 150 years of struggle between the king and Parliament for control over the purse, often centering on military matters. In 1624, the House of Commons for the first time conditioned a grant of funds to the king. The Subsidy Act of that year prohibited the use of any military monies, except for financing the navy, aiding the Dutch, and defending England and Ireland.[26] Two years later, Charles I attempted to wage war without popular support, but Parliament promptly denied him funds to conduct it.[27]

By the 1670s, parliamentary control over the purse was firmly established. Charles II insisted that the stationing of troops in Flanders was a prerogative of the Crown. Parliament, however, saw it differently. It enacted the Supply Act of 1678,[28] requiring that funds granted be used to disband the Flanders forces.[29]

Meeting in Philadelphia in 1787, the Framers were well aware of the tradition of parliamentary power over the purse and its use to check unwanted military operations. "The purse and the sword must not be in the same hands," George Mason said.[30] Madison considered it "particularly dangerous to give the keys of the treasury, and the command of the army, into the same hands."[31] He regarded the power over the purse as "the most complete and effectual weapon with which any Constitution can arm the immediate representatives of the people. . . ."[32] Accordingly, the Framers chose, in the words of Jefferson, to transfer the war power "from the executive to the legislative body, from those who are to spend to those who are to pay."[33]

Early practice comported with a broad reading of the appropriations clause. Presidents Jefferson and Jackson, when requesting congressional instructions for the proper course in the face of threatened aggression by Spain and marauding by South American pirates, recognized that control of the "means" necessary to carry out any military effort lies exclusively with Congress.[34] The Nixon Administration recognized the supremacy of Congress's power over the purse even as it asserted broad power under the commander-in-chief clause to

[23] *Id.*, art. I, § 8, cl. 12.

[24] *Id.*, art. I, § 8, cl. 13.

[25] *See generally* R. Berger, Executive Privilege: A Constitutional Myth 125–27 (1974).

[26] J. Kenyon, The Stuart Constitution 58 (1966).

[27] F. Dietz, English Public Finance 1558–1641 (2d ed. 1964).

[28] 30 Car. II. c. 1 (1678).

[29] *See generally* W. Abbot, *The Long Parliament of Charles II*, 21 Eng. Hist. Rev. 254 (1906).

[30] M. Farrand, 1 The Records of the Federal Convention of 1787, at 144 (1937).

[31] The Federalist No. 26 (Madison).

[32] M. Farrand, 2 The Records of the Federal Convention of 1787, at 81 (1937).

[33] 15 The Papers of Thomas Jefferson 397 (J. Boyd, ed. 1958).

[34] *See* Chapter 3.

prosecute the war in Vietnam.[35] Indeed, it conceded that Congress could use the power over the purse to control troop-*deployment* decisions.[36]

Accordingly, the Supreme Court has never held unconstitutional any use of the appropriations power as an unconstitutional encroachment on executive power.[37] The use of the appropriations power that the Court has invalidated[38] exceeded a constitutional limitation on the power of Congress—the prohibition against bills of attainder.[39] The Court has, in fact, upheld a statutory denial of funds even to certain persons who had received presidential pardons.[40] "Congress alone controls the raising of revenues and their appropriations," Justice Robert Jackson wrote in the *Steel Seizure Case* in 1952.[41] Only it "may

[35] The following exchange took place between Senator Frank Church and Secretary of State William Rogers when the latter testified before the Senate Foreign Relations Committee on May 14, 1971:

SENATOR CHURCH If the Congress were to decide to limit the funds for the purpose of effecting a withdrawal of our forces from Indochina and such defensive action as may be needed to protect them against imminent danger in the event that became necessary, as they withdrew, do you think that that falls within the constitutional power of the Congress to determine how public money is spent, or do you think that that would be an interference with the President's inherent powers as Commander in Chief?

SECRETARY ROGERS Here again, I would want to see the language, of course, but I fully recognize the power of the Congress to appropriate funds, and we do respect the wishes of Congress. For example, Congress included some restrictions on the use of ground troops in that area, and we have observed those restrictions. So we are not at odds with the Congress.

Hearings on War Powers Legislation Before the Senate Comm. on Foreign Relations, 92d Cong., 1st Sess. 508 (1971). *Accord* testimony of Hon. Gerald R. Ford, The War Power After 200 Years: Congress and The President at a Constitutional Impasse: Hearings Before the Special Subcomm. on War Powers, Comm. on Foreign Relations, U.S. Senate, 100th Cong., 2d Sess. 162–63 (1989); testimony of Hon. Brent Scowcroft, *id.* at 120, 125–26.

[36] CHAIRMAN FULBRIGHT Do you question the constitutionality of the right of Congress to bring back the troops from Europe? Do you think it is going beyond our constitutional power?

SECRETARY ROGERS Well, no. As I understand Senator Mansfield's resolution, it refers to appropriation of funds, and that is, of course, within the constitutional powers of the Congress.

THE CHAIRMAN It is clearly within our powers.

War Powers Legislation: Hearings Before the Comm. on Foreign Relations, U. S. Senate, 92d Cong., 1st Sess. 504 (1971).

[37] Congressional Research Service, U.S. Library of Congress, The Constitution of the United States of America: Analysis and Interpretation, S. Doc. No. 82, 92d Cong., 2d Sess. 1597–1619 (1973) (setting forth a summary of all acts of Congress held unconstitutional in whole or in part).

[38] United States v. Lovett, 328 U.S. 303 (1946). Although substantive limitations included in appropriations acts have on occasion been struck down, those limitations have not actually purported to deny funds and thus cannot be viewed as an exercise of the appropriations power. *See, e.g.*, United States v. Klein, 13 Wall. 128 (1872).

[39] U.S. Const. art I, § 9, cl. 3.

[40] "The pardon cannot [authorize payment to the claimant] merely because the [law] says that it shall not have such effect. It was entirely within the competency of Congress to declare that the claims mentioned in the [law] should not be paid till the further order of Congress." Hart v. United States, 118 U.S. 62, 67 (1885). The law did not take away anything the pardon could confer, the Court said, because a pardon ipso facto could not have the effect of authorizing a payment. *Id.*

[41] Youngstown Sheet & Tube v. Sawyer, 343 U.S. 579, 643 (Jackson, J., concurring).

determine in what manner and by what means they shall be spent for military and naval procurement.''[42]

Congress thus relied upon its sole power over the purse to end the Vietnam War. Beginning in 1973, seven statutory funding limitations, worded much like the Boland Amendment, prohibited the use of any appropriated funds for military or paramilitary operations in, over, or off the shores of North Vietnam, South Vietnam, Cambodia, and Laos.[43] Though strongly objecting on policy grounds, the Nixon Administration never challenged the constitutional power of Congress to cut off funds for the war. Similarly, in 1975, when President Ford sent in the Marines to rescue the container ship *Mayaguez* from the Cambodian military, his Administration never argued that those funding limitations were unconstitutional, only that they were inapplicable. On May 7, just prior to the *Mayaguez* incident, the State Department legal adviser Monroe Leigh testified before a subcommittee of the House International Relations Committee that the statutory funding prohibitions did not apply to the evacuations because ''there was . . . a very substantial legislative history that it was not the intent of Congress in the funds limitation statutes to curtail. . . [the] exercise of presidential authority [to evacuate Americans].''[44] (In fact, the legislative history of the funding prohibitions was as unsupportive[45] as it

[42] *Id.* at 644.

[43] Section 30 of the Foreign Assistance Act of 1973 was typical, except in referring to ''military or paramilitary operations'' rather than ''combat activities'' or ''involvement . . . in hostilities.'' Section 30 provides: ''No funds authorized or appropriated under this or any other law may be expended to finance military or paramilitary operation by the United States in or over Vietnam, Laos, or Cambodia.'' 87 Stat. 732. The other provisions were: Department of Defense Appropriation Act, 1975 Pub. L. No. 93-437, Section 839, 1974 U.S. Code Cong. & Adm. News 1400 (1974); Department of Defense Appropriations Act, 1974 Section 741, 87 Stat. 1045; Department of Defense Appropriation Authorization Act, 1974, Section 806, 87 Stat. 615 (1973); Department of State Appropriations Authorization Act of 1973 Section 123, 87 Stat. 454; Joint Resolution of July 1, 1973, Pub. L. No. 93-52, Section 108, 87 Stat. 134; Second Supplemental Appropriations Act, 1973 Section 307, 87 Stat. 129.

[44] *Hearings on Compliance with the War Powers Resolution Before the Subcomm. on International Security and Scientific Affairs of the House Comm. on International Relations*, 94th Cong., 1st Sess. 90–91 (1975) (hereinafter cited as Hearings) at 16–17. At the June 4 session of the hearings, Leigh extended his opinion to the *Mayaguez* incident. *Id.* at 88–89.

In addition, Leigh—speaking for himself, not the Administration—questioned the constitutional authority of the Congress to circumscribe by means of funding prohibitions the President's supposed authority as commander in chief to order such operations as the evacuations and the rescue of the *Mayaguez* crew. *See infra* text accompanying notes 103–16.

[45] Leigh offered only two items in support of his reference to a ''very substantial'' legislative history indicating the inapplicability of the funding prohibitions to the evacuations and the *Mayaguez* incident. *See* Hearings, *supra* note 44, at 27, 31. Each item relates to only one of the several prohibitions. One is a statement by Congressman Joseph Addabbo that seems to imply that the prohibition in question, Joint Resolution of July 1, 1973, Pub. L. No. 93-52, Section 108, 87 Stat. 134, was not intended to prohibit the President from exercising any of his commander-in-chief powers. 119 Cong. Rec. 21,313 (1973). There is no evidence that other members of Congress shared Addabbo's view. Representative Jonathan Bingham, for one, disagreed. Responding to Leigh's interpretation of the legislative history, he said:

was irrelevant.[46]) Speaking not for the Administration but for himself, Mr. Leigh did attempt to argue that Congress may not constitutionally employ funding prohibitions to restrict the President in what he believes to be a constitutional use of armed force. Such prohibitions, Mr. Leigh testified, are "conditions subsequent." In order to cut off funds for a specific activity, Mr. Leigh argued, Congress must wait for the President to "use up all the moneys appropriated."[47]

> Well, I would suggest to you that those provision were put into the law to curtail what President Nixon at the time said was his authority as Commander in Chief to protect and safeguard the evacuation of American troops which was the reason he gave, for example, for going into Cambodia. If your interpretation is correct, then that statutory limitation had no effect.

Hearings, *supra* note 44, at 17.

The other item is an exchange of remarks that Leigh claims occurred during testimony given "in executive session . . . before the Senate Foreign Relations Committee: on Aug. 3, 1973, by Admiral Moorer, then Chairman of the Joint Chiefs of Staff. *Id.* at 31. In fact, the Admiral did not testify before the Committee on that date. He did meet unofficially with congressional leaders at that time, but the transcript of that proceeding remained classified as of Sept. 15, 1975. Thus the remarks, whatever their content, were heard by no more than a handful of the members of Congress who voted on the funding prohibition in question and are not part of its legislative history.

It is worth noting, in addition, that President Ford sought statutory authority for the Vietnam evacuation because of the existence of the funding prohibitions. Leigh's contends that "the President thought he had adequate constitutional power despite the funds limitation provisions to take out Americans. . . ." Hearings, *supra* note 44, at 26, but not to take out foreign nationals. *Id.* at 25. If this was the President's thought, he certainly did not reveal it in his request that Congress "clarify" the funding prohibitions. Clarification was sought for evacuation of Americans as well as South Vietnamese. *See* 33 Cong. Q. Weekly Report 730 (1975); note 39 *supra* and accompanying text.

[46] "One of the most common of insights about the process of communication," says Sutherland, "was given classic expression by the Supreme Court . . . in the declaration that 'the meaning of the statute must, in the first instance, be sought in the language in which the act is framed, and if that is plain, . . . the sole function of the courts is to enforce it according to its terms.' [Caminetti v. United States, 242 U.S. 470 (1917).]" 2a C. Sands, Statutes and Statutory Construction § 46.01 (4th ed. 1973).

Expressing that insight from the layman's viewpoint, Representative Stephen Solarz remarked, in commenting on Leigh's theory, that "one of the disadvantages of not being a lawyer [is that] you tend to think language means what it appears to mean. . . ." Hearings, *supra* note 44, at 28.

[47] MR. SOLARZ Do you believe that in a situation where the President would commit American troops into combat pursuant to what he believed was his inherent constitutional authority that the Congress, if it determined that it did not want the troops there—would the Congress have the authority, in your judgment, to pass a law cutting off funding for the troops and thereby in effect requiring the President to withdraw them?

MR. LEIGH Again, I make the distinction as between the condition subsequent in an appropriation not yet completely spent and new appropriations.

MR. SOLARZ I have to confess that without a legal background—

MR. LEIGH If he has used up all the money appropriated and then Congress refuses to provide any more, I think the Congress has effectively stopped the President from continuing the military action. I don't know how he can go on. If, on the other hand, he still had moneys that were unexpended, he could continue to spend those until such time as there was a court challenge and the court found that he was acting illegally.

Precisely what type of appropriation Mr. Leigh meant by "all the moneys appropriated" is not clear. Whether he meant the entire defense budget, something less, or something more, must be guessed but is not important, for the clear implication of his remarks is that the President can use for one purpose funds that were designated for another until those funds are exhausted, notwithstanding a law prohibiting that use.

It is hard to see why this argument does not rob the appropriations clause of all meaning, for followed to its logical conclusion, Mr. Leigh's argument would deprive Congress of the power to specify the purpose for which funds are appropriated. The principle is long established that Congress has the exclusive power to specify how appropriated moneys shall be spent.[48] The only difference between an appropriation for a specified object (a "line item") and an express prohibition against the use of funds for a certain activity is a semantic one, the positive language of the one contrasting with the negative language of the other. Every appropriations act thus contains "conditions subsequent," in the sense that each specifies the purposes for which funds are appropriated—and, by implication, not appropriated. Transfer authority to take funds from one appropriations account and place them in another is a statutorily granted privilege, not a constitutional right.

Given the flimsiness of such arguments, it is not surprising that leaders of the Reagan Administration (before the Iran-Contra affair clarified official thinking on the issue) had no reservations in recognizing an unqualified power of Congress to restrict executive spending. The Secretary of Defense[49] and President Reagan himself[50] acknowledged absolute congressional authority to deny funding for unwanted executive activities.

It seemed late in the game, therefore, for the Reagan Administration to suggest, after the Iran-Contra affair came to light, that Congress lacked power

---

Hearings on Compliance with the War Powers Resolution Before the Subcomm. on International Security and Scientific Affairs of the House Comm. on International Relations, 94th Cong., 1st Sess. 92 (1975). The funding prohibitions are not, of course, *conditions subsequent* under any accepted legal definition of that term.

[48] Professor Raoul Berger, reviewing the history of the clause, quotes Hallam in noting that, after 1665,

> it became "an undisputed principle" that moneys "granted by Parliament, are only to be expended for particular objects specified by itself. . . ." The Framers were quite familiar with parliamentary practice; and we may be sure that in reposing in Congress the power of raising revenues and of making and reviewing appropriations for support of the armies, they conferred the concomitant right to "specify" the "particular objects upon which its appropriations are to be expended."

Berger, *War-Making Power of the President*, 121 U. Pa. L. Rev. 29, 78–79 (1972).

[49] "Who can doubt that we cannot literally do anything—we can't send a soldier anywhere, we can't spend a dime or a nickel or a shilling—that is not approved by our Congress?" Remarks by Hon. Caspar W. Weinberger at the Oxford Union Debate, London, England (News Release, Office of Assistant Sec. of Defense [Pub. Aff.], Feb. 27, 1984), at 5.

[50] "The President of the United States cannot spend a nickel. Only Congress can authorize the spending of money." N.Y. Times, Oct. 22, 1987, at 8.

to deny funds for aid to the Contras.[51] If the Reagan Administration wished to challenge 350 years of parliamentary and constitutional tradition, the time to do so was when the Boland Amendment was enacted. The President has a constitutional duty to take care that the laws be faithfully executed. Normally that duty attaches until a law is struck down by the courts. If the President believed that he was not bound to respect the Boland Amendment, he should have said so when it was presented for his signature. Instead, his spokesmen said that the Administration would honor the Amendment, including its implicit prohibition against asking third countries to aid the Contras.

The argument has been made that this prohibition interfered with a plenary presidential power to communicate with foreign governments and heads of state.[52] With narrow exceptions, however, this presidential power does not embrace the power to formulate policy, but rather to communicate policy made by others.[53] Moreover, set against the power is Congress's plenary power over the purse. How extensive is that power? Let us suppose, for purposes of argument, that the congressional appropriations power is no broader in scope than any other substantive power of Congress, that Congress cannot do anything in the exercise of that power that it could not otherwise accomplish through an exercise of the war power or the treaty power or its power over foreign commerce or under the necessary-and-proper clause. Let us, in effect, read the power over the purse out of the Constitution as a separate source of constitutional power, which is precisely what the minority report of the Iran-Contra committees strains to do.[54] (Professor Henkin has

[51] N.Y. Times, May 15, 1987, at A13.

[52] Oliver North revealed to the Iran-Contra committees that he did not consider the Boland Amendments constitutional:

> MR. VAN CLEVE . . . [I]f Congress told the President he could not ask for financial assistance for the Contras, there would be serious doubt about whether Congress had exceeded its constitutional power, correct?
>
> MR. NORTH You are asking for my opinion, I think there is no doubt. If the Congress had passed such a measure, it would clearly, in my opinion, be unconstitutional.

Testimony of Oliver North, 100-7 Iran-Contra Investigation: Joint Hearings Before the House Select Committee to Investigate Covert Arms Transactions with Iran and the Senate Select Committee on Secret Military Assistance to Iran and the Nicaraguan Opposition, 100th Cong., 1st Sess. (part I) 207 (1987).

The secret was well kept beforehand, however:

> MR. LIMAN Did you or any member of your staff ever tell Congress that you already were free to and were engaging in the solicitation of lethal aid at the time you asked Congress for permission to do restricted solicitation of humanitarian aid?
>
> MR. NORTH No. . . .

Id. at 272.

[53] *See* the discussion of United States v. Curtiss-Wright, 299 U.S. 304 (1936) in Chapter 1.

[54] S. Rep. No. 100-216 & H. Rept. 100-433, 100th Cong., 1st Sess. 476 (1987) ("[The] basic [constitutional] rules apply to appropriations as much as to any other kinds of laws."). If Congress's appropriations powers have no greater reach than its substantive legislative powers set forth in article I, § 8 of the Constitution, then the power over the purse is of course rendered

at times seemed close to construing the appropriations clause in the same way.[55])

Could Congress constitutionally enact the Boland Amendment pursuant to its legislative powers? Could it, without reference to federal expenditures, prohibit the President from asking the Sultan of Brunei to contribute money to the Contras?

Because Congress in exercising those substantive powers can decide that the United States government will not support certain belligerents, Congress seemingly could prohibit the use of official governmental offices, salaries, and

---

surplusage, for Congress in controlling executive activities might as well exercise one of those legislative powers rather than cut off funds.

[55] ''Where the President has independent constitutional authority to act,'' he has written, ''Congress is constitutionally bound to implement his actions, notably by appropriating the necessary funds.'' Letter from Louis Henkin to Hon. Louis Stokes, *reprinted in* H.R. 1013, H.R. 1371, and Other Proposals Which Address the Issue of Affording Prior Notice of Covert Actions to the Congress, Hearings Before the Subcomm. on Legislation, Perm. Select Comm. on Intelligence, U.S. House of Representatives, 100th Cong., 1st Sess. 220 (1987) (hereinafter ''Notice Hearings''). He continues: ''Where the President's authority to act is not exclusive but is subject to regulation by Congress, Congress may prohibit or limit the Presidents directly by legislation, or indirectly by denying him funds or imposing conditions on the use of funds appropriated.'' *Id.* at 220–21. Under this analysis, ''direct'' versus ''indirect'' checks are in reality identical; the distinction between the two is reduced to the verbal form with which they are enacted (''no funds authorized to be appropriated may be used for . . .'' versus ''the President may not carry out . . .'').

This analysis thus seems to recognize no substantive distinction between the breadth of the appropriations power and other legislative powers. If a substantive distinction is to be found, the appropriations power must be different in scope from congressional powers to legislate, and that distinction must reflect the plenary character of the appropriations power.

Does this mean that Congress could deny funds to negotiate a certain treaty during the negotiation of the Panama Canal Treaties? Rep. Gene Snyder offered an amendment to the fiscal-year 1976 State Department appropriation bill prohibiting the use of funds for negotiating ''the surrender or relinquishment of any United States rights in the Panama Canal Zone.'' It passed the House by a vote of 246 to 164 but was dropped in conference. *See* C. Crabb & P. Holt, Invitation to Struggle: Congress, the President, and Foreign Policy 70–71 (1980); U.S. Dept. of State, 1975 Digest of International Law 436–38 (A. Rovine, ed.). Is this not an instance in which plenary presidential and plenary congressional powers collide? If so, on what principled basis can we choose one over the other?

The courts have given us little guidance as to how such a conflict ought be resolved, and Congress seems in fact never to have used its appropriations power to limit an exclusive power of the President. If the line must be drawn, however, it would seem to make sense that Congress could not use its appropriations power to disable another branch from operating; Congress could not, for example, deny funds to the courts to pay criminal defense lawyers or deny funds to the President to pay his core staff. Congress cannot work fundamental structural changes in our form of government through the exercise of its power over the purse. Appropriations restrictions directed at *programs* rather than *structure*, however, seem to be on a different constitutional footing. If formulated as a clash between unreconcilable plenary powers, the question is unanswerable; to be meaningful, the question is *which* power is truly plenary. Unless the congressional appropriations and legislative powers are coextensive, the appropriations power is not plenary. *See generally* Stith, *Congress' Power of the Purse*, 97 Yale L.J. 1343 (1988).

services to support the Contras. The activity in question—solicitation of foreign governments and private individuals—is within the power of Congress to restrict. Historically, Congress has done precisely that in one of the oldest laws on the books: the Neutrality Act of 1794.[56] The Act is in many ways broader than the Boland Amendment; it prohibits organizing within the United States any military expedition against a foreign government, including raising money for such an expedition. In one of the earliest prosecutions under the Neutrality Act, *United States v. Smith*, it was established that the President and the entire executive branch were within the scope of its application. In that case, a Colonel Smith was indicted for "setting on foot" an expedition to liberate Venezuela from the rule of Spain. Colonel Smith, at his trial, claimed that the expedition had been approved, not only by Secretary of State Madison but by President Jefferson personally. To prove this, he sought at his trial to compel testimony from Madison. The court denied the request, holding that that evidence would be irrelevant: "The President of the United States cannot control the [Neutrality Act], nor dispense with its execution, and still less can he authorize a person to do what the law forbids."[57] The court continued:

> [T]he Constitution . . . explicitly directs that [the President] shall "take care that the laws be faithfully executed." This instrument, which measures out the powers and defines the duties of the President, does not vest in him any authority to set on foot a military expedition against a nation with which the United States are at peace. . . . [I]t is the exclusive province of Congress to change a state of peace into a state of war.[58]

In nearly forty convictions over nearly two hundred years, no court has ever suggested that the Neutrality Act is unconstitutional because it applies to the President personally.

It has also been suggested that "mere advocacy" from the President is at issue. In fact, in all likelihood, much more took place. Probably an implicit agreement was made: In return for the contribution to the Contras, certain favors would be extended. Even in the absence of an actual agreement, however, it is frivolous to suggest that this is "protected speech" by the President. One cannot claim first-amendment protection in soliciting *X* to give money to *Y* to burn down *Z*'s house. The "speech" at issue is part of a scheme, part of a criminal conspiracy, that the first amendment has never been thought to protect. Could the President advocate a contribution by the Sultan of Brunei to the GOP National Committee, in violation of the federal election laws? Of

[56] 18 U.S.C. §§ 959, 960, 961. For a thorough review of the history, interpretation, and application of the Act *see* Lobel, *The Rise and Decline of the Neutrality Act: Sovereignty and Congressional War Powers in United States Foreign Policy*, 24 Harv. Int'l. L.J. 1 (1983).

[57] United States v. Smith, 27 F. Cas.1233 (C.C.D.N.Y.) (No. 16, 342) 1806.

[58] *Id*. at 1230.

course not: Election contributions are within the power of Congress to control. Similarly, foreign commerce and war are within the power of Congress to control, which is why the Neutrality Act in *United States v. Smith* was held applicable to the President.

These conclusions are fortified by supposing that Oliver North and CIA Director William Casey had been successful in setting up "the enterprise," the "off-the-shelf" entity funded by nongovernmental sources that they hoped would be able to engage in covert operations free from constitutional and statutory limitations. Could not Congress prohibit the President from soliciting contributions for it? If not, what becomes of separated power, of the idea of limited government, of the rule of law? Professor Laurence Tribe put it well:

> Stripped of its technical camouflage, the [argument] ultimately reduces to the claim that this President, being somehow outside the government, is above the law. . . . Our whole constitutional system—not to mention common sense—rebels at any such notion. . . . Congress's control over the purse would be rendered a nullity if the President's pocket could conceal a slush fund dedicated to purposes and projects prohibited by the laws of the United States.[59]

No one has yet explained how the President could expend funds for Contra support in the face of an express statutory prohibition. "While Congress cannot deprive the President of the command of the army or navy," Justice Jackson wrote, "only Congress can give him an army or navy to command."[60] Only Congress, one might add, can give him the means to assist those who act in the army or navy's place. Corwin wisely summed up matters as follows: "The President can always veto Congressional measures intended to curb him directly, and his veto will be effective nine times out of ten. But a President cannot do much very long without funds, and these Congress can withhold from him simply by inaction."[61]

To appropriate public funds responsibly or to restrict their use requires information. It is to the process by which Congress gets information from the Executive that we now turn. Because information concerning intelligence activities has seemed at once the most tightly held and yet the most critical, the process of getting that information is most usefully examined.

The Process of Getting Information

The central activity of congressional oversight is the process by which a congressional committee obtains information concerning a matter within that committee's jurisdiction. If the truth indeed makes us free, we must confront

[59] Tribe, "Reagan Ignites a Constitutional Crisis," N.Y. Times, May 20, 1987, at A31.

[60] Youngstown Sheet & Tube v. Sawyer, 343 U.S. 579, 643 (1952) (Jackson, J., concurring).

[61] E. Corwin, The Constitution and What It Means Today 134 (H. Chase & C. Ducat, eds., 14th ed. 1978).

the unvarnished bad tidings: With respect to intelligence activities, the truth is that congressional oversight of intelligence activities hasn't worked, and it hasn't worked largely because congressional oversight committees haven't regularly obtained the information they need. After Attorney General Edwin Meese announced (following a report by a Lebanese newspaper)[62] that the Reagan Administration had sold arms to the Ayatollah to support the Contras,[63] the Chairman of the Senate Select Committee on Intelligence, David Durenberger, was asked by Dan Rather why his Committee had never found out about it. Senator Durenberger took umbrage; the system worked, he replied—''The alarm went off!'' That is rather like claiming that a burglary alarm worked because a burglar, after loading the TV and stereo into a getaway van, went back inside to trigger the siren. There is a familiar saying in the law: *res ipsa loquitur*, ''the thing speaks for itself.'' When a patient is operated on for a second time and the surgeon discovers a sponge, the thing speaks for itself: no further proof is required to establish negligence. When a president succeeds in selling arms (illegally) to a terrorist state to use the proceeds (again illegally) to support an insurgency and when Congress finds out about it months afterwards only because the President chooses to announce it, then, I suggest, the thing speaks for itself. A sponge has been discovered within the body politic.[64]

Rather than demonstrating that congressional intelligence oversight is ineffectual,[65] therefore, our discussion is more usefully directed at *why* it has been ineffectual—why the oversight committees have encountered often insurmountable obstacles in getting the comprehensive and meaningful information needed to do their jobs properly, and what might be done about it.

If one central lesson emerges from the experience of the oversight committees, it is that the classic constitutional tools that the textbooks tell us are available to the two branches—the subpoena power, the appointment power, the power over the purse, executive privilege, and the rest—are, in practice, largely irrelevant to the daily give and take of congressional intelligence oversight, for the real battles are fought in a practical arena in which the executive agencies maintain a significant advantage.

It would normally take a bureaucrat of impoverished imagination to recommend a claim of executive privilege in response to a congressional request

[62] Testimony of Oliver North, 100-7 Iran-Contra Investigation: Joint Hearings Before the House Select Committee to Investigate Covert Arms Transactions with Iran and the Senate Select Committee on Secret Military Assistance to Iran and the Nicaraguan Opposition, 100th Cong., 1st Sess. (part I) 249 (1987).

[63] N.Y. Times, Nov. 26, 1986, at A1.

[64] Following the mining of Managua's harbors, the N.Y. Times put it this way: ''Thanks to Mr. Casey's clumsiness, the watchdogs can now claim that they were misled when in fact they were asleep or dreaming.'' N.Y. Times, Apr. 11, 1984, at A30.

[65] *See generally* Bentley, *Keeping Secrets: The Church Committee, Covert Action, and Nicaragua*, 25 Col J. Trans. L. 601 (1987).

for information. Readily available is a plethora of means for accomplishing the same result, without a messy public confrontation. Here are some of the most effective tools at the Executive's disposal.

DELAY

Committees and subcommittees come and go, as do their chairmen and staff members, but the executive bureaucracy grinds on forever. Accordingly, its first principle in dealing with an unwanted congres ·onal investigation is *delay, delay, and delay again*. How is it done? Let us count only some of the ways: vacations, work overload, personnel transfers, meetings, sickness, marriage, divorce. The list of excuses is endless, but the consequence is always the same: the clock ticks ever closer to the inevitable date on which the subcommittee is abolished, a new chairman takes over, or the chief counsel returns to a law firm. Delays of months are not uncommon for many document requests. If Congress's power of the purse is the ultimate constitutional weapon, delay is the great equalizer, because many minor triumphs turn out to be Pyrrhic victories when weighed against the time they cost.[66]

THE "MOU"

Before any executive agency agrees to give any comprehensive information to a congressional committee investigating an intelligence matter, it has become customary to require the committee to enter into a memorandum of understanding, or MOU, setting forth the conditions under which classified information will be provided. In negotiating this contract, a principal point of contention is likely to be the procedure for public disclosure. The executive agencies can be counted on to push for the final say as to what information the committee will make public, whereas the committee, if it has any respect for separation-of-powers principles, will resist. Although this and other terms are in a sense negotiable, the starting point is implicit: no MOU, no information. Possession, as a CIA official once reminded me, is nine-tenths of the law. The result, therefore, is that the MOU will likely establish a fairly complex procedure under which both the committee and the executive agency participate in deciding what to make public. In theory, this satisfies separation-of-powers requirements, but in practice it gives the Executive veto power over the outcome of a congressional investigation. By eventually refusing to participate in the preparation of a "sanitized" unclassified version of the committee's re-

[66] The mining of Nicaraguan harbors reveals an especially adroit use of this technique. The first public report about the mining was made Jan. 3, 1984, when a report was broadcast by Managua radio. The CIA role was not discussed in detail with the Senate Select Committee on Intelligence until Apr. 2, 1984, and, because of cumbersome internal procedures, some members (such as Sen. Moynihan) did not learn about it until Apr. 6, 1984—four days *after* voting on legislation to provide an additional $21 million in aid to the Contras. N.Y. Times, Apr. 16, 1984, at A1, A8.

port, the agency can effectively prevent release of any documented study which criticizes its activities. Undocumented, a report will be nearly useless.

SENATE RESOLUTION 400

This Resolution, passed by the second session of the Ninety-fourth Congress in 1976, established the Senate Select Committee on Intelligence (SSCI). The executive branch has repeatedly argued that creation of the SSCI has limited the right of other committees to see classified intelligence information because the Senate has now centralized the intelligence-oversight functions in the new Committee. This is an erroneous interpretation. Whatever the merits of the argument for consolidation, the Senate, in establishing the SSCI, made clear beyond question that it did not intend to confer upon it exclusive jurisdiction over intelligence matters. Section 3(c) of Resolution 400 provides that "[n]othing in this resolution shall be construed as prohibiting or otherwise restricting the authority of any other committee to study and review any intelligence activity to the extent that such activity directly affects a matter otherwise within the jurisdiction of such committee." Nonetheless, the setting up of the SSCI has been used by certain executive agencies as a pretext for denying key information to other committees with jurisdiction over the subject. It must be admitted that in making this argument, they have found no lack of sympathy among the SSCI's senior staff. Congress, like any fragmented power, is very open to "divide-and-conquer" tactics.

THE "THIRD AGENCY RULE"

The so-called Third Agency Rule is a National Security Council directive, adhered to by all elements of the intelligence community, that prohibits one agency from disseminating material originating in another agency without the consent of the originating agency. For example, information possessed by the FBI that it has received from the CIA will not be made available to Congress without the consent of the CIA. Such a rule may provide some assurance within the executive branch that sensitive intelligence information will not be passed around haphazardly, but its invocation in response to a congressional committee frequently delays and obstructs.

CLASSIFICATION

Normally, congressional committees have available a variety of sources of outside expertise (think tanks, lobbies, university and law school faculties) they are accustomed to call upon when their own staffs lack knowledge or experience. For a committee investigating an intelligence matter, however, those sources are generally not available; the questions about which expert opinion is needed often are so entangled with classified information that they cannot be addressed to persons lacking security clearance. Thus, it may be impossible to solicit expert legal opinion without to some extent revealing the underlying facts, which are classified. As a consequence, some important public-policy questions relating to intelligence are not weighed and debated in a public forum; even when they are discussed in a private governmental forum, expert opinion—particularly expert opinion likely to be critical of official policy—is not available. This is true with respect to basic questions such as whether a procedure is typical; whether alternatives exist for accomplishing the same objective; whether an activity raises legal issues; and, the most fundamental question, whether a course of action is wise public policy. The upshot is that certain aspects of intelligence activity may be largely insulated from meaningful review.

THE "SOURCES-AND-METHODS" CLAUSE

Section 102(c)(3) of the National Security Act of 1947[67] provides that the "Director of Central Intelligence shall be responsible for protecting intelligence sources and methods from unauthorized disclosure." The terms *source* and *method* are not defined by the Act, and in the absence of any definition, their elasticity and subjectiveness can be exploited by agency officials looking for some statutory provision to justify nondisclosure to the Congress. With minimal creativity, it can be argued that virtually any intelligence information relates to intelligence "sources and methods." It is conveniently overlooked by the agencies that this refers only to *unauthorized* disclosure, which should make the stricture inapplicable to a congressional committee exercising its lawful responsibilities.

These are some of the reasons (and there are many others) why a skillful bureaucrat seldom issues a flat refusal to a congressional request for information. It is possible to achieve the same result while maintaining the appearance of cooperation.

There are also factors intrinsic to the legislative process that make effective inquiry difficult. Senators are notoriously busy people who cannot possibly focus on the day-to-day details of an investigation. This makes it more difficult for staff to call upon them for assistance very frequently, and it also makes it more difficult for them to help effectively. The more information involved, the more time it takes to learn and remember how the pages fit together and to appreciate the gaps that must be filled.

Congressional staff work is sometimes inexcusably sloppy. Although the CIA did delay fully informing the Senate Select Committee on Intelligence about the mining of Nicaragua's harbors,[68] the Committee had been informed several weeks earlier, but the reference had not been sufficiently highlighted

[67] 50 U.S.C. § 403(c)(3).

[68] *See supra* note 65.

for the Committee, having occurred only in "a single sentence of 27 words," according to the Committee's Vice Chairman, Senator Moynihan.[69]

Finally, for a staff member who intends someday to move, or return, to the executive branch, making waves at the State Department, CIA, or Pentagon may not be the best career strategy.

Thus far, I have been discussing impediments to effective congressional inquiry into intelligence matters. I do not mean to imply that faced with these obstacles, a committee is helpless. A letter or telephone call from the chairman to the agency head can get results, and the threat of a press release or press conference detailing noncooperation may get even better results. Agency personnel can sometimes be convinced that a coincidence of interests exists between the objectives of their employer and the committee. Divide and conquer is a two-way street; interagency and intra-agency rivalries can sometimes be played upon. Although their own operations are invariably presented (to use Adlai Stevenson's formulation) as shining temples of administrative purity and political probity, it often requires little effort to elicit from executive officials accounts of chronic bungling and outright iniquity. And if all else fails, a determined staff member can simply make it clear that he is not going to go away, hoping that agency officials will produce a given document simply to get the matter resolved.

But the "big guns"—the power over the purse, the confirmation power, the subpoena power—can seldom be wheeled out. Generally, these are of use only in response to an absolute executive refusal to cooperate in a specific material way, not in a war of attrition waged by officials wise enough not to present a large stationary target. Moreover, politicians are conditioned by their craft to make friends, not to seek enemies, so confrontation is extremely distasteful to most members of Congress. When Oliver North's lawyer, Brendan Sullivan, interrupted Senator Daniel Inouye during the latter's closing statement, many wondered (not for the first time) who was running the hearings.[70]

This brings us to the most serious impediment to rigorous congressional oversight of intelligence matters: The congressional investigatory process is too vulnerable to pressures from the public. Witness the widespread belief in Congress that intelligence reform has been drained of all political capital, that we have entered an era of pernicious foreign threats, or at least widespread public perception of such threats, in which any criticism of the United States intelligence establishment is made at one's political peril. A *Time* magazine essay appearing toward the end of the Carter Administration illustrated the

[69] N.Y. Times, Apr. 16, 1984, at A8.

[70] It is entirely appropriate that a congressional committee permit a witness to be advised by counsel, although the Constitution does not require it. It seems less appropriate, however, for counsel to be permitted to interrupt at will or to serve as a public-relations adviser on matters that clearly do not implicate the witness's constitutional rights.

mood. "This is a troubled world," it declared. "Threatening forces continue to challenge us. . . . In the past, the [CIA] engaged in some practices that are not acceptable in America, but those days are behind us. The CIA has reformed." *Time* concluded that the "oversight committees should be reduced to the two current Select Committees on Intelligence, which, as a matter of fact, have done their job fairly seriously."[71]

It could be that the CIA really had then "reformed," only to become unreformed a few years later. It may also be true that the congressional intelligence committees had taken their job fairly seriously. But how did *Time* know? On the basis of what information could *Time* have been so sure that institutions almost entirely removed from public scrutiny have reformed and will stay reformed? I suspect that *Time* succumbed to the proclivity identified by the astronomer Carl Sagan to mistake absence of *evidence* for evidence of *absence*. It is an error shared by much of the public and many in Congress.

The sensitivity, or vulnerability, of Congress to every change in the political climate poses the principal obstacle to effective legislative oversight. To a large extent, legislative action and inaction should reflect the popular will. But this is likely to mean that legislative committees responsible for intelligence oversight will normally be only as vigorous as the popular will allows. In practical terms, this means that in periods of relative public indifference, a subpoena will simply not be issued by the committee when the Executive refuses to reveal a significant document; no press conference will be called, no letter will be sent by the chairman to the head of the recalcitrant agency, no telephone call will be made.

In the end, no structural safeguards can ensure the integrity of governmental processes. "Liberty," Judge Learned Hand said, "lies in the hearts of men and women; when it dies there, no constitution, no law, no court can save it."[72] It may be that the public temper is all that can really be counted upon to prevent the abuse of power. "Democracy," as William James said, "is still upon its trial. The civic genius of our people is its only bulwark, and neither laws nor monuments . . . can save us from degeneration if the inner mystery is lost. That mystery . . . consists of nothing but . . . common habits . . . carried into public life. . . . One of them is the habit of . . . fierce and merciless resentment toward every man or set of men who break the public peace."[73]

There is no substitute for a vigilant body politic, and in its absence any purely legislative oversight mechanism is but a stopgap. In the end, the American people must depend not upon Congress, not upon the courts, but upon

[71] Apr. 30, 1979, p. 95.

[72] L. Hand, *The Spirit of Liberty*, in The Spirit of Liberty 189–190 (3d ed. 1960).

[73] William James, "Memories and Studies," 1911.

themselves. For these legal institutions derive their strength from the spirit of respect for law and truth reflected by individual citizens.[74] Archibald Cox put it well:

> If constitutionalism and the rule of law are to protect our liberties in hard cases, public support for court decrees must be strong enough to compel compliance even from an unwilling president who is carrying on an otherwise popular but unlawful program, such as a military expedition held to violate the War Powers Act or the conduct of unconstitutional intelligence activities in the United States.[75]

In and of itself, therefore, congressional oversight by *any* committee is not sufficient, and arguments about which committee is best suited to do the job miss the mark. An effective oversight structure must include at least two additional elements: (1) a statutory framework placing clear limits upon the foreign and domestic operations of our intelligence community and (2) an oversight mechanism that is, to the maximum extent, *removed* from the political process.

Strengthening Statutory Controls

The need for meaningful intelligence charters was widely discussed in the mid-1970s, when serious abuses by the FBI and the CIA were investigated by the Pike and Church committees.[76] The latter reported that in carrying out the program code-named COINTELPRO,[77] the FBI infiltrated and harassed numerous civil-rights, peace, and social-action groups. The FBI engaged in blanket wiretaps, mail openings, and break-ins; it initiated counterdemonstrations, dis-

[74] Barbara Tuchman's penetrating insights on America in the latter days of the Reagan Administration remain unsurpassed:

> [H]ateful though it is to say it, falsehood and false dealing have become so much a part of American life that we almost take them for granted. . . .
>
> A peculiar vacuum exists in American public opinion: not ''where's the beef?'' but where's the *outrage*? . . . [W]here's the outrage over the disclosures of misconduct and incompetence in Government by public officials of the highest rank? . . .
>
> If the American people do not grow angry when their sons' lives are sacrificed to official negligence, or when statutes are casually violated by the caretakers of the nation's security, one cannot expect any change to a steadier Government that commands more respect. Anger when anger is due is necessary for self respect and for the respect of our nation by others.

Tuchman, *A Nation in Decline?* N.Y. Times Sunday Magazine, Sept. 20, 1987, at 142, 143.

[75] Cox, *Storm Over the Supreme Court*, in The Evolving Constitution: Essays on the Bill of Rights and the U.S. Supreme Court 14 (N. Dorsen, ed. 1987).

[76] For an excellent inside account of the investigation of the Church Committee *see* L. Johnson, A Season of Inquiry (1985).

[77] Senate Select Comm. to Study Governmental Operations with Respect to Intelligence Activities, Foreign and Military Intelligence: Final Report (Book II), S. Rep. No. 755, 94th Cong., 2d Sess. 10 (1976) (hereinafter Final Report).

rupted tours and peaceful meetings, sent anonymous "poison-pen" letters to discredit leaders, stimulate factional disputes, and intimidate contributors. The CIA, in OPERATION CHAOS, carried out extensive activities within the United States with some of the same objectives.[78] The Church Committee concluded that "Congress has failed to provide the necessary statutory guidelines to ensure that intelligence agencies carry out their necessary missions in accord with constitutional processes."[79]

Little has changed. No charters were enacted,[80] and both agencies continue to operate under the flimsiest of statutory limitations. The cost of congressional lethargy soon became evident. As Erwin Griswold, a member of the Rockefeller Commission, and Ernest Gellhorn, its senior counsel, wrote: "The agonizing details that have surfaced in the Iran-Contra hearings could have been lifted from the transcript of hearings about the CIA activity 12 years ago."[81] The CIA was at the center of the Reagan Administration's sale of arms to Iran and diversion of profits to the Contras. The FBI conducted extensive surveillance of hundreds of American citizens and groups opposed to the Administration's policies in Central America.[82] If we are truly a government of laws, then laws limiting these agencies' discretion, and not merely words of good will uttered by executive officials at closed congressional hearings, are absolutely essential. Domestically, the charters must (among other things) prohibit investigations flowing from the exercise of constitutionally protected rights; prohibit efforts to disrupt or discredit constitutionally protected activities; impose a high standard for initiating the investigation of such groups, including a tightening of warrant requirements with respect to wiretapping, bugging, infiltration, and mail openings; and impose criminal penalties on executive personnel who violate those and other prohibitions.[83]

With respect to intelligence activities conducted abroad, the law must distinguish between intelligence collection and covert operations. Intelligence

[78] *Id.* at 99–104.

[79] *Id.* at 425, Book I.

[80] It was not until Feb. 8, 1980, that the drafting process was completed and legislation introduced. *See* S. 2284, 94th Cong., 2d Sess. (1980). As Professor Koh has pointed out, the proposed 263-page charter was trimmed down to two pages—which relied largely upon a presidential willingness to issue and enforce effective executive orders governing the intelligence community. "In the Reagan years, this choice of informality proved costly." Koh, *Why the President (Almost) Always Wins in Foreign Affairs: Lessons of the Iran-Contra Affair*, 97 Yale L.J. 1255, 1271 (1988).

[81] N.Y. Times, July 21, 1987, at A2.

[82] N.Y. Times, Jan. 28, 1988, at 1.

[83] *See* H.R. 3665, 100th Cong., 1st Sess. (1988) (providing for criminal penalties for executive officers and employees who "order or engage in the planning of, preparation for, initiation or conduct of any intelligence activity which violates any statute or Executive Order in force or international agreements to which the United States is a party").

collection carried out overtly may not call for special rules concerning matters such as justification, scope, or standards of review. Restrictions on covert intelligence gathering, however, particularly activities involving sensitive methods that may violate the laws of the target nation, must be tighter; the possibility of discovery presents the possibility of reprisals against the United States and its citizens. Finally, the most rigorous limitations must be placed on covert operations. The Church Committee, after "serious consideration of the option of proposing a total ban on all forms of covert activity," favored covert operations only in "extraordinary circumstances involving grave threats to United States national security."[84] Given the plain record of abuse, it is time to enact this standard into law. In addition, the law should explicitly prohibit a variety of covert operations, including assassination of foreign officials,[85] creation of epidemics,[86] torture,[87] and other acts incompatible with core values of American society. Those limitations must be painstakingly drafted to avoid implicitly or inadvertently conferring authority upon the intelligence establishment to conduct unacceptable activities.

The constitutionality of such restrictions would rest on essentially the same framework applicable to other executive activities, including the war power and executive agreements. The restrictions would place the President's power at its lowest ebb, and analysis would then shift from congressional intent to the issue of plenary presidential power. The case for the constitutionality of restraints on intelligence operations is strengthened by the fact that Congress, not the President, created the CIA and assigned its functions and responsibilities. "Congress therefore holds the power to decide that the President cannot use the resources and facilities of the CIA to carry out covert operations."[88] As the Supreme Court said in *Stark v. Wickard*, "When Congress passes an Act empowering administrative agencies to carry on governmental activities, the power of those agencies is circumscribed by the authority granted."[89] Even the minority report of the Iran-Contra committees acknowledged the constitutionality of a statute that would "set rules for [the] use" of funds Congress makes available to the intelligence community.[90]

One mode of analysis unlikely to command future judicial support is that of the federal district court in *American Foreign Service Association (AFSA) v.*

[84] Final Report, *supra* note 77, at 446, 448.

[85] The executive order issued by President Carter on Jan. 26, 1978, 12036, did so in § 134.

[86] *Id.*, § 135(a)(4).

[87] *Id.* § 135(a)(5).

[88] Note, *The Central Intelligence Agency: Present Authority and Proposed Legislative Change*, 62 Va. L. Rev. 332, 373 (1976).

[89] 312 U.S. 288, 309 (1944).

[90] "[E]ven though a contingency fund [for intelligence activities] is an essential tool for foreign policy, there is nothing in the Constitution requiring Congress to set one up. Once Congress makes the decision to establish such a fund, it may as a quid pro quo set rules for its use." S. Rept. 100-216 & H. Rept. 100-433, 100th Cong., 1st Sess. 476 (1987) (Iran-contra affair) (minority report).

Garfinkel.[91] At issue was the constitutionality of a law proscribing the use of appropriated funds to implement or enforce certain nondisclosure agreements, those that prohibited the employees (and former employees) party to the agreements from disclosing information that was not actually classified but merely "classifiable."[92] Following the Supreme Court's conclusional decision in *Snepp v. United States*[93] upholding the validity of such agreements against a first amendment challenge (dismissed in a footnote, without even having heard argument on the issue),[94] their use proliferated. Over 3 million present and former federal employees, of the executive as well as Congress, are parties to such agreements.[95] In response, Congress enacted the law. In striking it down, the district court engaged in no analysis of the breadth of Congress's power over the purse. Instead, it relied upon *United States v. Curtiss-Wright*,[96] a case that dealt with a presidential act carried out *pursuant to* statute, not at odds with statutory authority, and the concurring opinion of Justice Stewart in *New York Times v. United States*,[97] a case dealing with presidential authority in the face of congressional silence where Stewart nonetheless acknowledged that "[u]ndoubtedly Congress has the power to enact specific and appropriate criminal laws to protect government property and preserve government secrets."[98] Two other cases are thrown into the opinion without regard to relevance.[99] The lower court's *ipse dixit* opinion took no note whatever of the

[91] 688 F. Supp. 685 (D.D.C. 1988), *vacated and remanded as partially moot*, 109 S. Ct. 1693 (1989).

[92] Pub. L. 100-202, § 630 (1987).

[93] 444 U.S. 507 (1980).

[94] *See* Franck & Eisen, *Balancing National Security and Free Speech*, 14 N.Y.U. J. Int'l L. & Pol. 339 (1982).

[95] General Accounting Office Testimony, *Hearing on Congress and the Administration's Secrecy Pledges Before Subcom. on Legislation and National Security of House Comm. on Gov't Operations*, 99th Cong., 2d Sess. 3–4 (Aug. 10, 1988).

[96] 299 U.S. 304 (1936).

[97] 403 U.S. 713 (1971).

[98] *Id.* at 729–30.

[99] Department of the Navy v. Eagan, 108 S. Ct. 818 (1988), raised the issue whether the statutory structure permitted administrative review of the merits of a security-clearance denial underlying an employee's removal. The "statute's 'express language' along with 'the structure of the statutory scheme, its objectives, its legislative history, and the nature of the administrative action involved' " all militated against such review. *Id.* at 825 (quoting Block v. Community Nutrition Institute, 467 U.S. 340, 345 (1984)). Congress thus *agreed*, rather than disagreed, with the Executive's position. Indeed, in an important passage unnoted by the *AFSA* court, the Supreme Court in this case pointed out that deference to the Executive in military and national-security affairs is only appropriate "*unless Congress specifically has provided otherwise*." *Id.* (emphasis added). In § 630, Congress specifically provided otherwise.

The second case, *United States v. American Telephone and Telegraph Co.*, 551 F.2d 384 (1976), seems to be cited by the *AFSA* district court as authority that the role of Congress in this realm is limited to protecting its own access to classified information, rather than "intruding upon the President's oversight of national security information. . . ." In fact, the case said nothing of cases in which Congress and the Executive disagreed, such as *Youngstown Sheet & Tube Co. v. Sawyer*[100] and *Little v. Barreme*.[101]

A similar constitutional issue was posed by legislation that would have required the President to notify the two intelligence committees of covert operations (beyond mere intelligence gathering) within forty-eight hours after their initiation.[102] The framework under which such a requirement is analyzed is, again, no different from that applicable to questions of the war power, executive agreements, or other foreign-relations matters. That framework, elaborating Justice Jackson's *Steel Seizure* approach, is set forth in Chapters 1 and 2 of this book. Justice Jackson's concurring opinion in that case, as Professor William Van Alstyne put it, "remains the single most reliable utterance in this field."[103] "Accordingly," he concluded,

> to the extent Congress desires clarity, certainty, and reliability in highly problematic areas of executive direction of foreign intelligence activity, it is both appropriate and essential that Congress should say so, by law, as concretely as it can agree to do. The current proposals appear to recognize such a need.[104]

Nonpolitical Oversight Authority

A politically insulated supervisory process raises Plato's dilemma: Who will guard the guardians? Congressional oversight alone will not suffice. As currently structured, it doesn't work. Neither can the mechanism be placed within the intelligence establishment. In-house review boards, inspectors general, and general counsels vested with oversight functions do not have the necessary independence. Agencies with a demonstrated propensity for transgressing boundaries cannot be counted on to police themselves, to insure that abuses are investigated and statutory guidelines respected. To a lesser extent, the same difficulty arises with the placement of oversight elements elsewhere in the executive branch. They still report to the same authority—the White House—that is ultimately responsible for the activities. In short, if the logic

---

the sort. While it did present "nerve-center constitutional questions," *id.* at 394, the court expressly declined to resolve those issues, *id.* at 393, urging the parties to pursue an out-of-court settlement. No statute was struck down; no executive act flouting the will of Congress was upheld.

[100] 343 U.S. 579 (1952).

[101] 6 U.S. (2 Cranch) 170 (1804).

[102] *See* H.R. 1013, 100th Cong., 1st Sess. (1987); S. 1721, 100th Cong., 1st Sess. (1987). The legislation was shelved by House Speaker Jim Wright in 1989 at the opening of the new Congress as "an opening gesture of good faith." Wright said he wanted to smooth out relations with the White House. N.Y. Times, Feb. 1, 1989, at A8.

[103] H.R. 1013, H.R. 1371, and Other Proposals Which Address the Issue of Affording Prior Notice of Covert Actions to the Congress: Hearings Before the Subcomm. on Legislation of the Permanent Select Comm. on Intelligence, U.S. House of Representatives, 100th Cong., 1st Sess. 212 (1987).

[104] *Id.*

of nonpolitical oversight is accepted, it would appear that the process cannot be placed squarely in either political branch.

I have reservations about the creation of entities, such as special prosecutors, that fall in the interstices between the two branches. The principal difficulty is that they are not accountable. But in these unique circumstances, the creation of such a body is warranted, for without such a body, unaccountability is likely to persist on a far more massive scale—namely, in the unrestrained exercise of power by the intelligence establishment. It may well persist in any event; various independent regulatory agencies have proven anything but immune to the pressures of co-optation. Yet our experience with the Federal Reserve Board and the General Accounting Office (GAO) has been largely favorable, and an independent intelligence oversight organization could be based on the GAO model. I do not propose the establishment of a "super National Security Council" to approve individual covert operations or to perform other functions properly in the executive branch. I suggest that the oversight process would be strengthened by the establishment of an independent body with statutory access to all intelligence information, capable of insisting upon strict compliance with every applicable statute and executive order (possibly through prosecution) and able to function continuously, whatever the political climate.[105]

"Consultation" and "Centralized" Congressional Oversight

This is not meant to suggest that if such an entity was established, the congressional intelligence committees should be abolished. Nor should they be combined into a joint committee, as recommended by the Tower Commission.[106] The new joint committee, the Commission recommended, should be "patterned after the Joint Committee on Atomic Energy that existed until the mid-1970s."[107] The reason—the only reason—given by the Commission for cutting congressional oversight by 50 percent is increased secrecy: "[T]he number of Members and staff involved in reviewing covert activities is large; it provides cause for concern and a convenient excuse for Presidents to avoid Congressional consultation."[108]

[105] As discussed in Chapter 2, the constitutionality of the independent counsel law was upheld in Morrison v. Olson, 108 S. Ct. 2597 (1988).

[106] It was also proposed by Oliver North. Testimony of Oliver North, 100-7 Iran-Contra Investigation: Joint Hearings Before the House Select Committee to Investigate Covert Arms Transactions with Iran and the Senate Select Committee on Secret Military Assistance to Iran and the Nicaraguan Opposition, 100th Cong., 1st Sess. (part I) 182 (1987).

[107] Report of the President's Special Review Board [Tower Commission] at 98 (N.Y. Times ed., 1987).

[108] *Id.*

This is a non-solution to an illusory problem. As two commentators pointed out,

> [t]he Tower report clearly shows. . . that the administration resisted the congressional oversight process at every stage of the Iran-contra operation. It is thus difficult to understand the commission's recommendation, which would effectively diminish the oversight role of Congress.[109]

Concern about the large number of members of Congress overlooks the even larger number of executive (often foreign) officials also involved. For "security" reasons, President Carter declined to consult Congress concerning the Iran rescue mission; his counsel, Lloyd Cutler, challenged the constitutionality of the consultation provision:

> Where the President has inherent constitutional authority to conduct a rescue operation dependent on surprise and reasonable ground to believe that proper consultation would unreasonably endanger the success of the operation and the safety of those to be rescued—this would raise grave issues as to the constitutionality of Section 3.[110]

What Cutler neglected to mention (as later pointed out by the individual serving at the time as Assistant Secretary of State for Congressional Relations) is that apparently up to two thousand military personnel received a briefing on some aspect of the rescue operation, including up to one hundred nonmilitary personnel, and that upwards of seventy-five individuals might normally be involved in the planning of that sort of operation. This does not include foreign officials, who might have numbered up to one hundred. "It hardly seems justifiable in the context of these combined numbers to exclude 18 Members of Congress who have a clear constitutional mandate."[111]

Moreover, the major historical failing of legislative oversight in all policy areas has been "co-optation," the succumbing of legislators to the blandishments of executive officials.[112] Top officials in the executive branch are lobbyists of great skill who often succeed in cultivating their overseers to the point where little meaningful review of executive programs is carried out. The Senator who presided over the Select Committee on Intelligence while it snored through the Iran-Contra affair, David Durenberger, afterward opposed measures to improve congressional oversight of the CIA. "That's not what

[109] Halperin & Whiting, *A Joint Intelligence Committee?* Wash. Post, May 20, 1987, at A 19.

[110] The War Powers Resolution: A Special Study of the Committee on Foreign Affairs, U.S. House of Representatives 243 (committee print, 1982).

[111] War Powers, Libya, and State-Sponsored Terrorism: Hearings Before the Subcom. on Arms Control, Intl. Security and Science of the Comm. on Foreign Affairs, U.S. House of Representatives, 99th Cong., 2d Sess. 67–68 (1986) (testimony of J. Brian Atwood).

[112] *See generally* Johnson & Glennon, *Combining House, Senate intelligence Committees a Simple-minded Idea*, Atlanta Cons't., Oct. 21, 1987.

oversight is all about,'' he said. ''The purpose is to help intelligence, not to have an audit team sitting on the back of the [CIA] operations department.''[113]

One prominent example of co-optation at work was the panel seemingly regarded as a paradigm of investigative probity by the Tower Commission, the former Joint Committee on Atomic Energy. The Joint Committee no longer exists because it was widely believed in Congress that the Joint Committee and its staff had been co-opted. Intended as a watchdog of weapons-production facilities and the nuclear power industry, it became—through a long process of courtship and favors—a lapdog, unable to make the independent judgments critical for effective oversight.[114]

Co-optation becomes all the easier when intelligence bureaucrats can direct their largess at only one legislative committee. Pulling the wool over the eyes of two is still possible, as recent events demonstrate, but harder. Wisely, both the Senate and House intelligence committees are governed by a unique rule among oversight panels: They rotate their members on a staggered basis, bringing in fresh personnel every two years. (While this helps fend off co-optation, an added measure would be to prohibit staff members from working in the intelligence community after leaving the committee staff.)

The use of two committees makes sense for other reasons. Here is one way to assure that each chamber of Congress has an opportunity to state its views to the intelligence agencies, without mixing them with the sometimes different views of the other chamber. Further, each chamber has distinct constitutional authority that depends upon separation, such as the power of the Senate to confirm the CIA Director and the prerogative of the House to initiate funding proposals.

As for leaks, the record shows that the two committees have kept secrets. Every study on security leaks has concluded that most leaks come from the executive branch, where hundreds of people are privy to top secrets. Further, the two panels have elaborate security measures to guard the secrets entrusted to them, procedures borrowed from the CIA and FBI. Now and then, a leak may have come from one of the committees, but none has been remotely as damaging to the nation as the loss of information from the executive branch in the series of notorious spy cases of the 1980s involving the Walker family, CIA defectors, and poor security at the United States Embassy in Moscow. Finally,

[113] Wash. Post (weekly ed.), *supra* note 109, at 31.

[114] The Chairman and Vice Chairman of the Senate Intelligence Committee apparently saw co-optation as a less serious problem. They wrote, in opposing the idea of a joint committee, that

> [t]he intelligence community would . . . lose an important advocate of its interests in the House and Senate by combining the committees. The Senate committee can, and often does, promote the interests and budgetary needs of the intelligence agencies in Senate deliberations. The same is true in the House. A joint committee would not have the influence in either chamber to protect legitimate intelligence programs.

Boren & Cohen, *Keep Two Intelligence Committees*, N.Y. Times, Aug. 17, 1987, at 19.

it should be remembered that a joint committee is no panacea against leaks. Joint committees, including that on atomic energy, have leaked in the past; no system can preclude all leaks.

Rather than cut by half the congressional resources devoted to intelligence oversight, we might more profitably consider how to identify and correct the shortcomings in the present procedures, and ask where oversight resources should be located institutionally. It might make sense, for example, to reconsider the existence of the two committees *as committees* rather than subcommittees of the foreign-affairs committees of the two houses. Intelligence is a subset of foreign-relations information; it simply is secret information about policy that would otherwise fall within the jurisdiction of the foreign-affairs committees. The foreign-policy expertise and background of the members and staff of those committees suggest at least a possibility that adding intelligence oversight to their jurisdictional portfolios would allow *secret* foreign-policy information to be placed in the broader foreign-policy perspective it requires.

But it would make little sense to combine the House and Senate operations. However inconvenient and redundant the mandate of bicameralism, it at least holds the promise, like other bicameral institutions, that when one engine sputters, the other will continue to run. What is needed is a system that prevents both from sputtering simultaneously. Statutory reform will help. But most important will be the attitudes of legislative overseers: an improved capacity to be skeptical, to question, to persevere, to do their jobs as guardians of the guardians.

A similar recurrent and equally ill-conceived proposal concerns the establishment of a single joint "consultative" committee, apparently intended to speak for Congress in time of national-security emergencies.[115] The Carter Administration, for example, proposed setting up a "crisis consultative committee," consisting of the leadership of each house.[116] The proposed committee would have served as the consultative entity of Congress under the War Powers Resolution.[117] A similar suggestion was made recently by Senators Byrd, Nunn, Warner, and Mitchell in proposing to amend the Resolution;[118] their "permanent consultative group" would also have been composed of sixteen congressional leaders.[119]

[115] *See also* the similar proposal for the creation of a congressional committee to regulate the first use of nuclear weapons, Stone, *Presidential First Use Is Unlawful*, 56 For. Pol'y 94 (1984), which would surely run afoul of the Supreme Court's proscription against legislative vetoes. *See* INS v. Chadha, 462 U.S. 919 (1983).

[116] Letter from Douglas J. Bennet, Assistant Secretary for Congressional Relations, to John Sparkman, Chairman, Senate Foreign Relations Committee (Aug. 2, 1977), *reprinted in* A Review of the Operation and Effectiveness of the War Powers Resolution: Hearings Before the Committee on Foreign Relations, United States Senate, 95th Cong., 1st Sess., 199 (1975).

[117] *Id.* at 202.

[118] S.J. Res. 323, 100th Cong., 2d Sess (1988), discussed in Chapter 3.

[119] *Id.* § 1.

These and other proposals overvalue legislative-executive consultation. Recalling senators' complaints that they were not informed of the scheme to mine Nicaraguan harbors, Justice Hans A. Linde asked, "Why should we sleep better if Senator Moynihan and Senator Goldwater, or their successors, have been let in on the secret? . . . A great constitutional issue is reduced to the right to serve as a test sample."[120] It is not surprising that the "compromise" suggested by Secretary of State Baker concerning compliance with the War Powers Resolution was an "informal" system of consultation, with the Executive not "conceding it as a requirement," coupled with an unabashed acknowledgment that the Executive would challenge the constitutionality of the Resolution.[121]

Many of the same problems discussed in connection with a joint intelligence-oversight committee would afflict a single consultative committee. In addition, such a committee could be vulnerable to processes of psychological distortion that bend both facts and analysis. These problems can prove debilitating to groups charged with decision making in the cloistered, high-security environment necessitated by the sensitive subject matter.[122] One is "irrational consistency," the tendency of decision makers to ground conclusions upon previously formed images of reality, resulting in cognitive dissonance that causes a selective processing of information to conform to those presuppositions.[123] Another is "defensive avoidance," an effort of decision makers to reduce the stress that derives from uncertainty by unconsciously exaggerating the attractiveness of one or more options, thus denying responsibility for making the wrong choice.[124] A third is "groupthink," phenomena of group dynamics that chill a full discussion of all alternatives open to highly cohesive groups constrained by unarticulated premises of loyalty and consistency.[125]

Two measures can be taken to counteract these phenomena; the principal

[120] Linde, *A Republic . . . If You can Keep It*, The Seventh Biennial Biddle Lecure, Harvard Law School, Oct. 17, 1988 (on file with author). He continued:

> Consultation has a price. Leaders who have had their say may be coopted, if not to assent, at least to silence. When their colleagues and the public are deceived, they share in the deception. . . . And the executive can deflect criticism in Congress by pointing to its consultation with a few members who cannot speak for others and whose undisclosed views the executive need not accept.

Id.

[121] N.Y. Times, Feb. 1, 1989, at A8.

[122] *See generally* Smith, *Congressional Authorization of Nuclear First Use: Problems of Implementation*, in First Use of Nuclear Weapons: Under the Constitution, Who Decides? 169 (P. Raven-Hansen, ed. 1987).

[123] *See* R. Jervis, Perception and Misperception in International Politics 145–146 (1976); R. Lebow, Between Peace and War: The Nature of International Crisis 104 (1981).

[124] R. Lebow, *id.* at 105, 107–108; *see also* I. Janis & L. Mann, Decision-Making: A Psychological Analysis of Conflict, Choice and Commitment 46 (1977).

[125] *See generally* I. Janis, Groupthink: Psychological Studies of Policy Decisions and Fiascoes (1982 ed.)

proposals recently on the table fail to incorporate them. First, access to information must be continuous and complete. Members of the consultative group ought not have a sense of having "walked in off the street" to be confronted by monumental questions never before contemplated. To an extent, that is the nature of a crisis; key aspects are by definition unforeseen. Yet the agencies that deal with national-security crises normally engage in much "contingency planning" where options are drawn up in advance for the various scenarios most likely to arise. To approach a crisis with full perspective, a decision maker must be knee-deep in the relevant stream of information and analysis prior to the outbreak of the crisis. The consultative groups proposed by the Carter Administration and the Byrd-Nunn bill are ad hoc entities with no continuing role, making a bolt-out-of-the blue, where's-my-pen atmosphere all the more likely. Moreover, given the historical disinclination of the executive branch to share information with Congress,[126] it would seem unduly optimistic to think that such a group would ever have access to all the information necessary to make a balanced, informed judgment in a crisis.

Second, a highly qualified professional staff can diminish the effects of psychological distortion, but only under certain conditions. They too must have complete and continuous access to all pertinent information. They must be present at all meetings to analyze and answer arguments of executive experts. They must be able to travel instantly to trouble spots, sometimes under unsafe conditions.[127] Most important, they must be skeptics, doubters, unbelievers—persons of independent judgment who are willing to say no, able to acknowledge uncertainty, and able to resist pressures for consensus. Other proposals advanced thus far do not provide for a continuously serving staff but rather would draw upon existing committee staffs (some of which have become highly politicized) for an unstructured, free-floating, amorphous group of advisers whose role, presence, and ability would be uncertain.

Justice Jackson was doubtless correct when he said that "[t]he chief restraint upon those who command the physical forces of the country, in the future as in the past, must be their responsibility to the political judgments of their contemporaries and to the moral judgments of history."[128] But the difficulty in making such judgments regarding intelligence matters is that the public domain is almost entirely devoid of facts upon which those judgments

[126] Francis O. Wilcox wrote in 1971 about the long resistance of the executive branch "to give Congress access to its policy-planning documents at an early enough stage to be significant. . . . The result is virtually to deny Congress effective access to the policy-making process until it has been completed." F. Wilcox, Congress, the Executive and Foreign Policy 48–49 (1971).

[127] During the evacuation of South Vietnam following the collapse of the Thieu government, the on-site investigations of two members of the professional staff of the Senate Foreign Relations Committee, Richard Moose and Charles Meissner, proved invaluable in assessing executive testimony concerning the number of refugees expected and American capabilities for their removal.

[128] Korematsu v. United States, 323 U.S. 214 (1944) (Jackson, J., dissenting).

might be based.[129] That is why the test of effective intelligence oversight can be whether it plays in Pocatello. The agencies to be overseen do not regulate truck widths or set train schedules; they can radically and permanently alter the political and legal contours of our society. Their activities require the closest possible scrutiny, a scrutiny that cannot depend upon whether vigilance happens to be in vogue in a particular year.

The Role of the Courts

The unreliability of congressional oversight, the proclivity of clandestine executive agencies for law violation, and the traditional responsibility of the courts as the last guardians of the Constitution all point to the propriety of an active role for the Judiciary in ensuring governmental compliance with the law of the land. Courts should not be deterred by "talismanic incantation[s]"[130] of "national security" ritualistically uttered by the Executive to ward off judicial review. "No nation," Livingston wrote, "has ever yet found any inconvenience from too close inspection into the conduct of its officers; but many have been brought to ruin and reduced to slavery, by suffering gradual imposition and abuses, which were imperceptible, only because the means to publicity had not been secured."[131]

Chief Justice Rehnquist, writing for an eight-member majority in the 1988 case *Webster v. Doe*,[132] took the right approach. The Court there held that the Judiciary is not precluded from hearing a constitutional challenge to the dismissal of a CIA employee, even though the Executive had repeatedly claimed that sensitive national-security information would be compromised.[133] The decision signifies, wisely, that the Court will not accord automatic deference to the Executive in cases touching on national security. The *Harvard Law Review* put it well: "To allow the executive to usurp the judiciary's role as arbiter of conflicts between legitimate security interests and individual rights—the inevitable consequence of the government's . . . argument in *Webster*—would be to remove all external guarantees that the rule of law governs the national security apparatus of the United States."[134]

I have argued in Chapter 3 for the inclusion of provisions in the War Powers Resolution facilitating judicial review. Even in the absence of such statutory

[129] Edward Livingston put it well: "No nation has ever found any inconvenience from too close an inspection into the conduct of its officers, but many have been brought to ruin, and reduced to slavery, by suffering gradual impositions and abuses, which are imperceptible, only because the means of publicity had not been secured." Reynolds v. United States, 192 F.2d 987, 995 (3d Cir. 1951).

[130] United States v. Robel, 389 U.S. 258, 263 (1967).

[131] E. Livingston, Criminal Jurisprudence 15 (1873).

[132] 108 S. Ct. 2047 (1988).

[133] *See* Note, *The Supreme Court—Leading Cases*, 102 Harv. L. Rev. 143, 337 n.52 (1988).

[134] *Id.* at 339.

directives, however, the courts should not decline to resolve disputes between Congress and the President, and they should be lenient in permitting members of Congress to litigate such controversies. This means, specifically, that courts should be loath to find that a dispute presents a "political question," that they should limit application of the doctrine of remedial discretion, and that they should apply a broad standard for determining whether a plaintiff has "standing" to sue.

Political Questions

As noted in Chapter 3, the district court in *Lowry v. Reagan*[135] dismissed a challenge by 110 members of Congress to President Reagan's violation of the War Powers Resolution in the Persian Gulf. It grounded the dismissal on two doctrines: political question and remedial discretion.

The "now-classic catalogue of conditions to which the political question doctrine applies," as the *Lowry* court put it,[136] was set forth by the Supreme Court in *Baker v. Carr* :

> Prominent on the surface of any case held to involve a political question is found a textually demonstrable constitutional commitment of the issue to a coordinate political department; or a lack of judicially discoverable and manageable standards for resolving it; or the impossibility of deciding without an initial policy determination of a kind clearly for non-judicial discretion; or the impossibility of a court's undertaking independent resolution without expressing lack of respect due coordinate branches of government; or an unusual need for unquestioning adherence to a political decision already made; or the potentiality of embarrassment from multifarious pronouncements by various departments on one question.[137]

A dispute falling within one or more of these categories is regarded as "nonjusticiable," or inappropriate for resolution by the courts. Such a controversy will thus be left for the political branches to resolve. The district court in *Lowry* found that judicial decision of the dispute would have risked "the potentiality of embarrassment [that would result] from multifarious pronouncements by various departments on one question. . . . [T]he volatile situation in the Persian Gulf demands, in the words of *Baker v. Carr*, a 'single-voiced statement of the Government's views. . . .' "[138]

A variety of rationales have been advanced in support of the political-question doctrine. First, constitutional requirements aside, the Court must be free to exercise prudence to decline to hear cases that might undermine its legiti-

[135] 676 F. Supp. 333 (D.D.C. 1987).

[136] *Id*. at 339.

[137] Baker v. Carr, 369 U.S. 186 (1962).

[138] 676 F.Supp. at 340 (1987) (footnotes omitted).

macy.[139] The courts simply lack the institutional capacity to handle certain matters. One hears this argument with particular force in the realm of foreign affairs. Professor Franck has argued, for example, that "[t]he courts should not . . . be put in the position of actually stopping a war, a politically loaded task."[140] Second, certain decisions are indeed committed by the Constitution to the political branches rather than to the courts.[141] Third, decision by the courts blocks the majoritarian resolution of a dispute; the answer arrived at by democratically constituted branches normally should be respected. Fourth, there are uncharted reaches of legal terrain, areas where no rules exist; here, especially, majoritarian processes should be left to work their will, even if that will is that there be *no* law.[142] Fifth, judicial resolution of hot controversies merely encourages legislative buck-passing; the judiciary should encourage congressional responsibility by declining to "bite the bullet" for Congress. Finally, as Dean Choper has argued, in separation-of-powers disputes especially, there is little room for Supreme Court intervention:

> Each branch—legislative and executive—has tremendous incentives jealously to guard its constitutional boundaries and assigned prerogatives against invasion by the other. If either branch perceives a constitutional violation of this kind, not only will it be encouraged to respond vigorously but each department possesses an impressive arsenal of weapons to demand observance of constitutional dictates by the other.[143]

Dean Choper thus concludes that "the federal judiciary should not decide constitutional questions concerning whether executive action (or inaction) violates the respective powers of Congress or whether legislative action (or inaction) transgresses the realm of the President. . . ."[144] His theory would seem to suggest that the courts should not have decided cases such as *Youngstown Sheet & Tube v. Sawyer*[145] and *United States v. Nixon*.[146] And he too believes that "the federal courts should hold that the ultimate issue of the President's inherent constitutional power to lead the nation into a war is nonjusticiable. . . ."[147]

In modern American society, these justifications for judicial abstention

[139] *See* A. Bickel, The Least Dangerous Branch (1962).

[140] *See* Franck, *After the Fall: The New Procedural Framework for Congressional Control Over the War Power*, 71 Am. J. Intl. L. 605, 640 (1977). *See also* J. Choper, Judicial Review and the National Political Process 295–97 (1980).

[141] Wechsler, *Toward Neutral Principles of Constitutional Law*, 73 Harv. L. Rev. 1, 7 (1959).

[142] *See, e.g.*, Field, *The Doctrine of Political Questions in the Federal Courts*, 8 Minn. L. Rev. 485 (1924) ("Where no rule exists the courts are powerless to act." *Id.* at 511.)

[143] J. Choper, Judicial Review and the National Political Process 263 (1980).

[144] *Id.* at 263.

[145] 343 U.S. 579 (1952).

[146] 418 U.S. 683 (1973).

[147] J. Choper, Judicial Review and the National Political Process 295 (1980).

seem increasingly to be calls for judicial abdication.[148] The courts have a core responsibility under the Constitution to resolve disputes. "It is emphatically the province and duty of the judicial department," Chief Justice Marshall wrote in *Marbury v. Madison*, "to say what the law is."[149] The political-question doctrine does not square with this fundamental tenet of our form of government; it is "at odds with our commitment to constitutional and limited government, to the rule of law monitored and enforced by judicial review."[150] Many of the arguments for the political-question doctrine are thus upon close inspection, unveiled as bare attacks upon the very idea of judicial review.

Few today could seriously believe that the Court places itself at risk by deciding a controversial case. It may have been true, before widespread public acceptance of judicial review, that an overzealous Judiciary might have gotten "too far out in front" to continue to act as final legal arbiter. But that day has long passed. When President Nixon's Treasury Secretary, John Connally, implied that the President might disregard an illicit decision of the Supreme Court, the public outcry only hastened Nixon's downfall. There is no modern justification for use of the doctrine "as a means of escape for fearful judges unwilling to address challenges to governmental usurpation of authority in foreign affairs."[151]

Dean Choper places heavy reliance upon the argument that disputes between Congress and the President involve no genuine claims of abridgment of personal liberty.[152] Should the courts decline to find that one branch has encroached upon the power of the other because "the 'liberty' claims are merely derivative"?[153] I think not. The Constitution protects individual liberty not merely through the direct safeguards of the Bill of Rights but also through indirect protections inherent in the separation of powers. As the Supreme Court affirmed recently, "The Framers recognized that, in the long term, structural protections against abuse of power were critical to preserving liberty."[154] Even assuming that the substance of individual and separation claims can be neatly distinguished—a proposition that the *Steel Seizure Case* must surely call into question—there seems little ground for believing that the two should be subject to different rules of judicial review. Whatever the liberty

[148] Two seminal pieces have inspired much of the scholarly reconsideration of the political question doctrine. *See* Henkin, *Is There a Political Question Doctrine*, 85 Yale L.J. 597 (1976); Tigar, *Judicial Power, the Political Question Doctrine, and Foreign Relations*, 17 UCLA L. Rev.1135 (1970).

[149] 5 U.S. (1 Cranch) 137, 176 (1803).

[150] Henkin, *Lexical Priority or 'Political Question': A Response*, 101 Harv. L. Rev. 524, 529 (1987).

[151] *Id.* at 530.

[152] J. Choper, Judicial Review and the National Political Process 296 (1980).

[153] *Id.* at 273.

[154] Bowsher v. Synar, 106 S. Ct. 3181, 3191 (1986).

claims Marbury made, it is worth remembering that *Marbury v. Madison*[155] was at its most enduring level, a dispute about the locus of governmental decision-making authority.

Concern about the courts' "lack of capacity" also seems misplaced. This concern animated the district court's dismissal of an earlier suit, in *Crockett v. Reagan*,[156] that challenged noncompliance with the War Powers Resolution in El Salvador, just as it did the appellate court's dismissal of *Lowry*.[157] The district court in *Crockett* reasoned that "[t]he question here belongs to the category characterized by a lack of judicially discoverable and manageable standards for resolution."[158] The court of appeals in *Lowry* wrote that decision on the merits would have required an assessment of the stability of the Gulf cease-fire; "an inquiry of this sort is beyond the judicial competence."[159]

Apprehensions about judicial fact-finding incapacities are doctrinally misdirected. It is clear from the Supreme Court's discussion in *Baker* that the Court meant to foreclose the judicial resolution of disputes characterized by indeterminate legal standards, not fact-finding difficulties. The "lack of criteria by which a court could determine which form of government was republican,"[160] was the reason that a political question was presented in *Luther v. Borden*.[161] The Supreme Court did not suggest that judicial abstention was required by any proof problem presented by the facts of the case. Yet it is for the latter reason, the proof problem, that the *Crockett* court dismissed the plaintiff's complaint. "[T]he Court no doubt would be presented conflicting evidence. . . . The Court lacks the resources and expertise (which are accessible to the Congress) to resolve disputed questions of fact concerning the military situation in El Salvador."[162] Such questions of fact can be addressed as they always are, through the use of interrogatories, depositions, testimony, and all the other means of gathering evidence. It may or may not be correct that the plaintiffs would succeed in establishing their claim by a preponderance of the evidence; the opportunity to meet that burden is one that the law accords them. The problem is addressed not by the political-question doctrine but by the law of evidence.

As for claims that the courts' legitimacy is undermined by venturing into the political thicket (by, say, stopping a war), it must be remembered that *not* stopping an illegal war can also be a "politically loaded task." It is not self-

[155] 1 Cranch 137 (U.S. 1803).

[156] Crockett v. Reagan, 720 F.2d 1355 (D.C. Cir. 1983), *aff'g* 558 F. Supp. 893 (1982).

[157] *See also* Chaser Shipping Corp. v. United States, 649 F. Supp. 736 (S.D.N.Y. 1986) (dismissing damages action in connection with mining of Nicaraguan harbors as political question).

[158] *Crockett*, 558 F. Supp. at 898. The court was referring to the formulation of the Supreme Court in Baker v. Carr, 369 U.S. 186 (1962).

[159] *See* Appendix A.

[160] 369 U.S. at 222.

[161] 48 U.S. (7 How.) 1 (1849).

[162] *Crockett*, 558 F. Supp. at 898.

evident that public respect for the courts would be enhanced if the courts sat idly by in the face of a manifest constitutional violation—if a President ordered an invasion of Mexico to rectify Mexican election irregularities. Why is judicial *in*action in the face of controversy necessarily more prudent than judicial *action*? Some compelling reason needs to be advanced why the courts should take on the "political load" that they inevitably would through *passivity* in permitting a manifest constitutional violation to continue. Professor Martin Redish put it well: "The moral cost of such a result, both to society in general and to the Supreme Court in particular, far outweighs whatever benefits are thought to derive from the judicial abdication of judicial review."[163]

It does not do to say that such decisions are allocated constitutionally to Congress or the President. The political-question doctrine, the Supreme Court has reminded us, is "one of 'political questions,' not one of 'political cases.' The courts cannot reject as 'no law suit' a bona fide controversy as to whether some action denominated 'political' exceeds constitutional authority."[164] In disputes between Congress and the President, the question is not whether one of the political branches has the authority in question but *which* branch has that authority. In *Goldwater v. Carter*,[165] for example, Justice Brennan correctly pointed out in dissent that although the courts would have been precluded from reviewing the President's decision *if* the Constitution had committed that decision to the President, the nub of the case was *whether* the President had that authority. "[T]he doctrine does not pertain when a court is faced with the *antecedent* question whether a particular branch has been constitutionally designated as the repository of political decisionmaking power. The issue of decisionmaking authority must be resolved as a matter of constitutional law, not political question. . . ."[166]

It must be admitted that in some cases, judicial resolution of certain disputes can encourage legislative forbearance. Courts inevitably make political decisions.[167] Why should a member of Congress cast a controversial vote if a judge will probably decide the issue in any event?[168] In other cases, however, the likely intervention of the courts might actually *induce* Congress to act, on the notion that a clear statement of legislative intent might serve to narrow the courts' latitude in subsequent litigation or actually forestall judicial intervention. Moreover, the argument equates legislative forbearance with legislative

[163] Redish, *Judicial Review and the 'Political Question*,' 79 Nw. U. L. Rev. 1031, 1060 (1984–85).

[164] *Baker*, 369 U.S. at 217.

[165] 444 U.S. 997 (1979).

[166] *Id.* at 1007 (Brennan, J., dissenting) (citations omitted) (emphasis in original).

[167] *See generally* L. Fisher, Constitutional Dialogues (1988).

[168] Sen. Alan J. Dixon responded to arguments concerning the constitutionality of certain legislation with the observation that "it is for the courts, not the Senate" to dispose of the issue. 130 Cong. Rec. S5297-305 (daily ed. May 3, 1984) (quoted in L. Fisher, *supra* note 167, at 167).

irresponsibility, presupposing the preferability of legislation to adjudication. Why the courts should abstain from deciding disputes constitutionally within their jurisdiction is not explained.

Finally, the argument that Congress has enough arrows in its legislative quiver to respond successfully to executive illegality is unpersuasive. For five decades, the Executive responded successfully to the putative illegality of the legislative veto simply by disregarding those it constitutionally contested, but that success did not discourage the Supreme Court from reaching the merits in *INS v. Chadha*.[169] Further, the argument underestimates practical problems that frequently render Congress's textbook tools too unwieldy.[170] Dean Choper himself acknowledges that the tactics he describes to control executive usurpation of power—refusal to appropriate funds, to enact laws, to confirm appointments, and impeachment—"may reasonably be viewed as both unseemly and unreasonable."[171] Further, if this argument were correct, there would be no case law on separation-of-powers controversies; in disputes from *Little v. Barreme*[172] through the *Steel Seizure Case*,[173] Congress would have been left to fend for itself.

In rare circumstances, it may turn out that the question is one on which there is no law.[174] If the courts encounter a juridical vacuum, if no primary or secondary source of constitutional power is available to resolve the dispute, then the Court is justified in resorting to tertiary sources of constitutional power.[175] In *Goldwater v. Carter*, for example, the Court could have reached the merits and found that although constitutional text and constitutional custom were not dispositive, functional and institutional considerations indicated that the matter fell within the President's concurrent initiating power as well as the concurrent power of Congress to act (or react) if it chose to do so.

Thus the purported merits of judicial abstention in foreign-affairs decision-making disputes shrink under scrutiny. And the drawbacks, frequently brushed aside by those who inveigh against "judicial activism," are substantial. Arguments against the judicial resolution of such disputes are often, in reality, thinly disguised pleas for executive hegemony,[176] for the Executive

[169] 462 U.S. 919 (1983).

[170] *See supra* text at notes 66–68.

[171] J. Choper, Judicial Review and the National Political Process 286 (1980).

[172] 6 U.S. (2 Cranch) 170, 179 (1804).

[173] Youngstown Sheet & Tube v. Sawyer, 343 U.S. 579 (1952).

[174] "[T]he Supreme Court has never been at a loss to decipher roughly workable standards for the vaguest of constitutional provisions when it so desires." Redish, *Judicial Review and the 'Political Question,'* 79 Nw. U. L. Rev. 1031, 1060 (1984–85).

[175] This idea is elaborated in Chapter 2.

[176] Dean Choper, while not directly addressing the "validity of the presidentially ordered military activities" in Vietnam, J. Choper, Judicial Review and the National Political Process 295 (1980), seems to accept the argument that presidents since the time of Jefferson have sent troops abroad on their own authority over a hundred times and that those incidents represent constitu-

almost always wins if the courts sit on the sidelines. The reason is manifest: The Executive can move quickly—by introducing troops, making an international agreement, mining harbors, transferring arms—and Congress, if and when it finds out, is faced with a fait accompli. During the Vietnam War, the state of Massachusetts put the argument cogently (if unsuccessfully) to the United States Supreme Court:

> [I]f the President takes the nation into war without Congressional authorization, the practical situation will [lead] [m]any legislators, for a variety of reasons . . . not [to] vote for legislation which would cut off the use in the war of defense appropriations. Even if a majority of legislators could be amassed, the President could veto the bill and thus raise the burden much higher to the 2/3rds majority level.[177]

To permit the Executive to proceed unencumbered by judicial review would work a radical reallocation of constitutional power. If the Court declines to intervene when a fundamental threat to the separation of powers is posed by the Executive, the Executive, not the Judiciary, becomes the ultimate arbiter of the meaning of the Constitution. Judicial abstention in such circumstances is unjustified for the same reason that it was unjustified in the face of electoral arteriosclerosis in *Baker*: Operating alone, the political system is incapable of reestablishing an equilibrium of power, which the courts must step in to restore.

Second, in time of crisis, exclusive reliance upon political processes can result in governmental gridlock. Cutting off all funds for the Defense Department or State Department, declining to confirm a Supreme Court nominee because a President has engaged in a foolish or unconstitutional foreign-policy initiative, or commencing impeachment proceedings can hardly be seen as the constitutionally mandated manner in which the United States government must resolve internal power disputes. Thus, even Dean Choper finds judicial intervention attractive where it is necessary to "preserve our constitutional equilibrium and to avoid the unseemly conversion of a grave constitutional crisis into a street corner brawl of naked self-help that would heap scorn on both departments."[178]

Finally, an inevitable problem with the political-question doctrine is hinted at in a passage that Dean Choper quotes from *Baker v. Carr* : "[T]he political

---

tionally significant precedents. *Id.* at 297. Similarly, the court that dismissed as a political question a damages action brought in connection with the mining of Nicaragua's harbors commented, astonishingly, that "the Constitution commits to the Executive Branch the authority to make foreign policy decisions." Chaser Shipping Corp. v. United States, 649 F. Supp. 736, 738 (S.D.N.Y. 1986).

[177] Brief for The Constitutional Lawyers Committee on Undeclared War as Amicus Curiae at 76, Massachusetts v. Laird, 400 U.S. 886 (1970).

[178] J. Choper, Judicial Review and the National Political Process 298 (1980).

question doctrine, a tool for maintenance of governmental order, will not be so applied as to promote only disorder.''[179] What are the preconditions of governmental order? Political regularity surely derives, at least at the outset, from legal predictability. And predictability of procedure presupposes *knowledge* of that procedure. Thus, the application of the doctrine ineluctably promotes disorder, for judicial nondecision of a bona fide case or controversy deprives litigants as well as future actors of that knowledge. The courts decline to say *what* behavior legal procedure requires. The political-question doctrine, by denying law-respecting governmental actors knowledge of the rules they must live by, undermines predictability in public affairs and maximizes chaos.[180]

Not only is the doctrine incompatible with a public policy that favors predictability but its practical application has actually undercut that objective. A case in point is, again, *Lowry v. Reagan*.[181] In dismissing the action on political-question grounds, the district court worried that it would ''risk 'the potentiality of embarrassment [that would result] from multifarious pronouncements by various departments on one question.' ''[182] The ''volatile situation in the Persian Gulf demands, in the words of *Baker v. Carr*, a 'single-voiced statement of the Government's views. . . .' ''[183]

In fact, the dispute came before the courts precisely because the government had *failed* to speak with one voice. In the War Powers Resolution, Congress said that the President must under certain circumstances submit a certain report,[184] and the President declined to do so. ''Multifarious pronouncements'' had therefore already been made. Judicial intervention was needed to determine which branch spoke for the government—to cause the government to speak with one voice. The court's refusal to step in merely prolonged the cacophony. *Lowry* thus indicates how the political-question doctrine can in practice serve to perpetuate rather than alleviate conflicts between the political branches and impede the United States' ability to speak with a unified voice.[185]

Remedial Discretion

The district court in *Lowry* dismissed the lawsuit not only on political-question grounds but also under the doctrine of remedial discretion. Under that doc-

[179] Baker v. Carr, 369 U.S. 186, 215 (1962) *quoted in* J. Choper, Judicial Review and the National Political Process 298 (1980).

[180] Champlin & Schwartz, *The Political Question Doctrine and Allocation of the Foreign Affairs Power*, 13 Hofstra L. Rev. 215, 222–23 (1985).

[181] 676 F. Supp. 333 (D.D.C. 1987).

[182] *Id.* at 340 (citing Baker v. Carr, 369 U.S. at 217).

[183] *Id.*

[184] Resolution, § 4(a)(1).

[185] For a discussion of other instances in which the doctrine undercuts its own rationale, *see* Franck & Bob, *The Return of Humpty-Dumpty: Foreign Relations Law After the Chadha Case*, 79 Am. J. Intl. L. 912, 951 (1985).

trine, the courts will dismiss a legislator's action if that legislator could obtain relief through the enactment, repeal, or amendment of a statute.[186] In such circumstances, the plaintiffs' dispute is not really with the Executive, but is "primarily with [their] fellow legislators."[187] This was the finding of the district court in *Lowry*, a case it described as "a by-product of political disputes within Congress regarding the applicability of the War Powers Resolution to the Persian Gulf situation."[188] The court canvassed the bills that had been introduced to "compel the President to invoke"[189] the Resolution, to repeal it, and to strengthen it.[190] The "passage of legislation to enforce the Resolution . . . would pose a question ripe for review,"[191] the court said, citing Justice Powell's opinion in *Goldwater v. Carter*,[192] but none had yet been enacted; judicial review here would interject it into legislative debate.[193]

By this analysis the court revealed a misapprehension of the doctrine of remedial discretion and the case before it. The doctrine, as developed in the District of Columbia Circuit, did in fact receive its impetus during the *Goldwater* litigation.[194] But the legislative posture in that case reveals that the intended purport of the doctrine was very different. Congress in *Goldwater* was *silent* on the treaty's termination. Senator Goldwater was not suing to vindicate the will of Congress or of the Senate, which was also silent. Justice Powell, relied upon by the *Lowry* court, emphasized that congressional silence:

> Congress has taken no official action. In the present posture of this case, we do not know whether there ever will be an actual confrontation between the Legislative and Executive Branches. . . . It cannot be said that either the Senate or the House has rejected the President's claim. If the Congress chooses not to confront the President, it is not our task to do so.[195]

In *Lowry*, by contrast, Congress *chose* to confront the President by requiring him, by law, to submit a report.[196] The 110 *Lowry* plaintiffs had no dispute with their fellow legislators whether legislation should be enacted; legislation *had* been enacted, the War Powers Resolution. It had not been repealed or amended.[197] Their legal action sought its enforcement. When a law is violated,

[186] Riegle v. Federal Open Market Committee, 656 F.2d 873, 881 (D.C. Cir. 1981).

[187] *Id.*

[188] *Lowry*, at 338.

[189] *Id.*

[190] *Id.*

[191] *Id.* at 339.

[192] 444 U.S. 996 (1979) (Powell, J., concurring).

[193] *Id.*

[194] For a discussion of the doctrine's origins and scope, *see* T. Franck and M. Glennon, Foreign Relations and National Security Law 824–27 (1987).

[195] Goldwater v. Carter, 444 U.S. 979, 998 (Powell, J., concurring).

[196] *See* War Powers Resolution, § 4(a)(1).

[197] It is unclear, to put it generously, what the district court was referring to when it observed

as the War Powers Resolution was in the Persian Gulf,[198] the task of legislators is not to "enforce" the law by xeroxing it and reenacting it, as the court seemed to believe. Like any other aggrieved plaintiff who suffers injury, their task—if they wish that injury remedied—is to seek judicial relief.

Standing

An individual is required to have suffered a concrete personal injury in fact different from that suffered by the "person on the street" as a prerequisite to bringing a lawsuit. That in essence is what the courts mean when they say that a plaintiff must have "standing" to sue.[199] The district court in *Lowry* did not reach the issue of standing. Nonetheless, on appeal it was argued forcefully by both sides. The Justice Department attempted to frame the question as whether a legislator had standing to sue by virtue of "the legislators' diminished effectiveness due to defendants' unlawful conduct."[200] Although that is indeed the issue in some similar cases,[201] it was not here. For unlike cases in which the courts were compelled to decide whether a member of Congress had standing by virtue of an alleged deprivation of a constitutional entitlement of membership,[202] *Lowry* involved a statutory entitlement to information, an entitlement "on all fours" with those routinely held to confer injury in fact when violated.[203]

In resolving foreign-affairs decision-making disputes, the courts should permit members of Congress to bring an action if a colorable claim of a usurpation of constitutional power by the Executive can be advanced. In *Goldwater v. Carter*, the court of appeals found that Senator Goldwater had standing to

(ever concerned about multifarious pronouncements) that to grant the declaratory relief requested "necessarily would contradict legislative pronouncements on one side or the other of this issue." *Lowry* at 340. The court then referred to the various bills that had been introduced, but not enacted. *Id.* at note 50. By what logic does legislation *that is only introduced*—that represents the views of *one* legislator—become a "legislative pronouncement"? Under what doctrine is a court precluded from adjudicating a genuine case or controversy because some legislator has expressed a constitutionally sacrosanct opinion that cannot be contradicted—or supported? A jot of clear thinking might have revealed that the only "legislative pronouncement" on the issue was the War Powers Resolution and that judges are paid salaries to decide whether *that* sort of "legislative pronouncement" is violated.

198 *See* Chapter 3.

199 For an extended elaboration, *see* T. Franck & M. Glennon, Foreign Relations and National Security Law 799–856 (1987).

200 Brief for the Appellee, Lowry v. Reagan, Appendix A (quoting Moore v. U.S. House of Representatives, 733 F.2d 946 (D.C. Cir. 1984), *cert. denied*, 469 U.S. 1106 (1985).

201 *See id.*

202 *See, e.g.*, Kennedy v. Sampson, 511 F.2d 430 (D.C. Cir. 1974).

203 *See, e.g.*, Trafficante v. Metropolitan Life Ins. Co., 409 U.S. 205 (1972), upholding the right of two tenants to proceed against their landlord under statutory entitlements conferred by the Fair Housing Act of 1968. *See generally* L. Tribe, American Constitutional Law § 3-16 at 114–24 (1987).

challenge President Carter's termination of the treaty because if there was merit to his allegations, Carter's action would have deprived Goldwater of the opportunity to vote to prevent termination of the treaty. The President would thus have nullified the right of Senator Goldwater under the Constitution to vote to block the termination.[204] The Supreme Court has yet to tell us whether the *Goldwater* court's reasoning squares with ever-evolving standing requirements. Judge Bork argued strongly against it,[205] but his arguments are unpersuasive; "unilateral executive actions involving the waging of war . . . may encroach upon the constitutionally mandated powers of Congress and may effectively nullify a legislator's right to vote on such matters."[206]

In resolving this issue, we might again glean some insight from the approach of international law. International law distinguishes between obligations of nations toward one another and obligations toward the international community as a whole. Ordinarily, claims for violation of an international obligation may be made only by the state to whom the obligation is owed.[207] Obligations toward the international community, on the other hand, are "by their very nature . . . the concern of all States. In view of the importance of the rights involved, all States can be said to have a legal interest in their protection; they are obligations *erga omnes*."[208] The action *erga omnes* is similar to the right in Roman law of any citizen to bring an action (*actio popularis*) to protect the public interest.[209] The theory apparently was that with respect to matters of supreme public importance, every citizen had an individuated interest in ensuring that obligations owed the community by government officials not be breached.[210]

It may or may not make sense to extend standing to the public at large in connection with alleged usurpations of power by one political branch or the other; the cases denying "taxpayer standing" are not without merit.[211] Yet where *no* plaintiff would otherwise be able to challenge a fundamental governmental violation of the charter of our nation's existence, perhaps Congress is the class of plaintiffs to whom the courts should reasonably be open. When

[204] Goldwater v. Carter, 617 F.2d 697, *vacated on other grounds*, 444 U.S. 996 (1979).

[205] *See* Barnes v. Kline, 759 F.2d 21, *vacated as moot sub nom.* Burke v. Barnes, 106 S. Ct. 1258 (1986) (Bork, J., dissenting). Justice Antonin Scalia has joined in that criticism. *See* Scalia, *The Doctrine of Standing as an Essential Element of the Separation of Powers*, 17 Suffolk Univ. L. Rev. 881 (1983).

[206] Note, *The Justiciability of Congressional-Plaintiff Suits*, 82 Colum. L. Rev. 526, 548 (1982).

[207] Restatement §§ 901, 902.

[208] Case Concerning the Barcelona Traction, Light & Power Co., Ltd. (Belgium v. Spain), [1970] I.C.J. Rep. 3, 32.

[209] This was pointed out by the International Court of Justice in the earlier South West Africa Cases. In those cases, however, the International Court declined to accept this theory. [1966] I.C.J. Rep. 6, 47.

[210] *See generally* Schwebel, *The Actio Popularis and International Law*, 2 Isr. YB. H. Rts. 47 (1972).

[211] *See, e.g.*, Frothingham v. Mellon, 262 U.S. 447 (1923).

war is commenced without congressional authorization, a member of Congress surely suffers injury at least as great as that suffered by a litigant faced with the possible extinction of "the snail darter, a three-inch fish of no evident tangible value."[212] The alternative is a complete absence of any legal remedy and continued constitutional violation. "The very essence of civil liberty certainly consists in the right of any individual to claim the protection of the laws, whenever he receives an injury," Chief Justice John Marshall wrote in *Marbury v. Madison*.[213] "One of the first duties of government is to afford that protection."[214] That duty is no less when the claimant is a member of Congress and the injury is nullification of a constitutionally or statutorily required vote.

Conclusion

The Constitution, no doubt, confounds America's friends and allies from time to time, who must with good cause wonder: To whom do we listen—Congress, the President, or the courts? Our friends' task surely would be easier if our Founding Fathers *had* created the President in the image of George III,[215] if his word could not be questioned, if his act could not be challenged, if his power were not limited. In some ways, we have not one government but three. We pay a price for our system in inefficiency at home and in misunderstanding abroad.

But it is a price incurred deliberately for a benefit sought successfully.[216] No one explained the benefit of our system of divided power better than Justice Louis Brandeis:

> The doctrine of separation of powers was adopted by the Convention of 1787, not to promote efficiency but to preclude the exercise of arbitrary power. The purpose was, not to avoid friction, but, by means of the inevitable friction incident to the distribution of governmental powers among three departments, to save the people from autocracy.[217]

Arbitrary exercise of power, and the concomitant danger of autocracy, pose an ever-present danger to democratic processes. In the United States, the central safeguard against that danger is the cornerstone of the Framers' political architecture: a structured equilibrium of power that derives from setting am-

[212] L. Tribe, American Constitutional Law 117, n. 29 (1988) (referring to TVA v. Hill, 437 U.S. 153 (1978), upholding standing under the Endangered Species Act).

[213] 1 Cranch 137, 163 (U.S. 1803).

[214] *Id.*

[215] *See supra* Chapter 1, note 50 and accompanying text.

[216] That this system of division and separation of powers produces conflicts, confusion, and discordance at times is inherent, but it was deliberately so structured to assure full, vigorous and open debate on the great issues affecting the people and to provide avenues for the operation of checks on the exercise of governmental power.

Bowsher v. Synar, 106 S. Ct. 3181, 3187 (1986).

[217] Myers v. United States, 272 U.S. 52, 293 (Brandeis, J., dissenting).

bition against ambition.[218] The teaching of Justices Marshall, Jackson, and Brandeis—the jurisprudence of the Supreme Court—is that there is seldom reason to upset that balance in the realm of foreign-policy-making.

Some challenge their wisdom.[219] Under the guise of criticizing the War Powers Resolution, congressional oversight, or judicial activism, some in reality challenge our very system of separated powers. Some believe that our system of divided authority handicaps the United States in confronting totalitarian states. Our system must be changed, they argue, availing the President of the quick responses, unfettered discretion, and "less fastidious" methodology[220] open to the dictators and terrorists they oppose. They believe that the divided authority of the Constitution undermines our national interest.

[218] *See* The Federalist No. 51, at 356 (J. Madison) (Belknap Press ed. 1961) ("Ambition must be made to counteract ambition."). Lord Bryce described the Constitution as "based on the theology of Calvin and the philosophy of Hobbes . . . the work of men who believed in original sin, and were resolved to leave open for transgressors no door which they could possibly shut. . . ." 1 J. Bryce, The American Commonwealth 299 (1888).

[219] *See, e.g.*, the minority report of the Iran-Contra committees, describing Brandeis' view as a "fallacy" that "misses half the historical truth." S. Rept. 100-216 & H. Rept. 100-433, 100th Cong., 1st Sess. 458 (1987) (Iran-contra affair) (minority report). Of course, no one would argue that the Framers' experience under the Articles of Confederation left them unconcerned with efficiency; the adoption of a separate executive was one consequence of their search for it. *See* L. Fisher, President and Congress: Power and Policy 3 (1972). And in some circumstances, the separation-of-powers doctrine might actually promote efficiency, as when a foreign-policy initiative is undertaken by both branches and thus accorded broader public support. The point is simply that when the two conflict, the Framers chose liberty over efficiency.

[220] The following exchange occurred during the Iran-Contra hearings between Sen. Sam Nunn and Noel C. Koch, Principal Deputy Assistant Secretary of Defense for International Security Affairs during the Reagan Administration:

> MR. NUNN Mr. Koch you said just a minute ago that we could have solved the hostage situation rather handily, but we chose not to do so. I would certainly, and I am sure all of us would be interested, as long as it is not something that is classified, for you to tell us what the solution was and is.
>
> MR. KOCH Well, Senator, I think it is just a simple question of recognizing the way your adversaries deal with you, and being a little more creative and a little less fastidious about the way you deal with them.
>
> So, I think that would be my shorthand response. If you want a more imaginative answer, I would go pay a call on Mr. Fadallah, who is the head of Hizballah, the pro-Iranian Shi'ia faction in Beirut, and I would take him off to a nice warm dry place and I would take off something that is not lifethreatening like a finger, and wrap it in a note to Imad Mughnia need [*sic*] that says, "There is a lot more where this came from," and "I would like to see my hostages in the bar in the Commodore Hotel by Friday C.O.B., and if not, we will be sending some more of this stuff around." . . .
>
> MR. NUNN There are countries in the world that do that, are there not?
>
> MR. KOCH The Soviets get their hostages back precisely that way.
>
> MR. NUNN Something like that.

100-6 Iran-Contra Investigation: Joint Hearings Before the House Select Committee to Investigate Covert Arms Transactions with Iran and the Senate Select Committee on Secret Military Assistance to Iran and the Nicaraguan Opposition, 100th Cong., 1st Sess. 96–97 (1987).

I stood recently at the same spot in the Zeppelin stadium in Nuremberg where Hitler spoke by torchlight to columns of Nazi soldiers and frenzied crowds of supporters. As you place your hands on the cold stone and gaze out at the massive expanse, it is easy to conjure up those ghosts, to imagine the icy efficiency that must come with absolute power, to think that that efficiency must translate into invincibility.

Your imagination gets a jolt, however, when you look more closely. For you see that weeds now grow in the bleachers, bullet holes pockmark the stone, and the great copper swastika that loomed over Hitler has been blasted away by the forces of freedom. The thousand-year Reich lasted only twelve. The great monument to absolute power is now used for drag racing. And the United States recently celebrated the bicentennial of the world's oldest written constitution.

The Constitution does not undermine our national interest. It embodies it. Its constraints signify "a large part of what defines us as a nation."[221] For all its vagueness, for all its awkwardness, for all its omissions, our government under the Constitution does represent, in Lincoln's words, the world's "last, best hope."

Rather than mimic the dictatorships we have vanquished, should we not strengthen the democracy we have built?

[221] A. Chayes, The Cuban Missile Crisis: International Crises and the Role of Law xi (1987).

LOWRY V. REAGAN

[Slip Opinion]
United States Court of Appeals
For the District of Columbia Circuit

No. 87-5426 | September Term 1988
Michael E. Lowry, et al., | Civil Action No. 87-2196

Appellants

v.

Ronald W. Reagan,

Appellee

BEFORE: WALD, Chief Judge, and EDWARDS and WILLIAMS, Circuit Judges.

ORDER

Upon consideration of the parties' supplemental memoranda regarding changed conditions in the Persian Gulf, it is

ORDERED that the appeal be dismissed. Appellants' first claim, that United States Armed Forces are currently involved in present or imminent hostilities in the Persian Gulf, presents a nonjusticiable political question. The claim is in essence that hostilities remain present or imminent because the Gulf cease-fire is unstable. An assessment of the cease-fire's stability, however, would require an inquiry into the likely intentions of the Iranian and Iraqi governments. Although we express no view as to the justiciability of other claims under § 4(a)(1), we hold that an inquiry of this sort is beyond the judicial competence.

Appellants also contend that hostilities were present or imminent at some point in the past and that the President still has not submitted the required report. That claim is moot. Section 4(a)(1) of the War Powers Resolution, 50 U.S.C. § 1543(a)(1), seeks to guarantee legislators access to the information necessary for their effective co-participation in the warmaking process. Assuming, *arguendo*, that the denial of access to that information constitutes a legally cognizable injury, the injury continues only for as long as the warmaking process itself. Appellants can claim no present injury as a result of their reduced ability to participate in a process which has been completed. Appellants' assertion of continuing injury is thus logically dependent upon their ability to demonstrate that hostilities are currently present or imminent. That demonstration cannot be made. The appeal is accordingly dismissed.

The clerk is directed to withhold issuance of the mandate herein until seven days after disposition of any timely petition for rehearing. *See* D.C. Cir. Rule 15.

Per Curiam
FOR THE COURT:
/s/
By: Catherine L. Bateman
Deputy Clerk

Appendix B

THE "USE OF FORCE ACT"

A BILL

Conferring authority on the President to use force abroad, setting forth governing principles and required procedures, and for other purposes.

Be it enacted by the Senate and House of Representatives of the United States of America in Congress assembled,

SHORT TITLE

SECTION 1. This Act may be cited as the "Use of Force Act."

PURPOSE

SEC. 2. The purpose of this Act is to confer authority upon the President to use force abroad.

DEFINITIONS

SEC. 3. (a) As used in this Act—

(1) the term "use of force" means the introduction of United States Armed Forces into hostilities or situations where imminent involvement in hostilities is clearly indicated by the circumstances. Such action includes but is not limited to situations where members of the United States Armed Forces have recently been—

(A) introduced into the territory of a nation, or deployed to expand significantly the United States military presence in such territory, and are likely to incur or inflict casualties; or

(B) committed to new activities involving a substantially increased likelihood of incurring or inflicting casualties; and

(2) the term "international terrorism" means activities involving violent or dangerous acts which—

(A) violate the criminal laws of the United States, or would violate such laws if committed within the jurisdiction of the United States;

(B) are intended to intimidate or coerce the people or government of any nation; and

(C) transcend national boundaries by the means through which they are accomplished, including the locale in which their perpetrators may seek asylum.

AUTHORITY AND LIMITS

SEC. 4. (a) In the absence of a declaration of war or statutory authorization for a specific use of force, the President is authorized to use force abroad—

(1) to repel an armed attack upon the United States, its territories, or its armed forces;

(2) to respond to a foreign military threat that severely and directly jeopardizes the supreme national interests of the United States under extraordinary emergency conditions that do not permit sufficient time for Congress to consider statutory authorization;

(3) to protect the lives of citizens and nationals of the United States located abroad in situations involving a direct and imminent threat to their lives, provided they are being evacuated as rapidly as possible;

(4) to forestall an imminent act of international terrorism known to be presently directed at citizens or nationals of the United States, or to retaliate against the perpetrators of an act of international terrorism directed at such citizens or nationals;

(5) to protect, through defensive measures and with maximum emphasis on multilateral action, internationally recognized rights of innocent and free passage in the air and on the high seas; and

(6) to participate in emergency actions undertaken pursuant to the approval of the United Nations Security Council.

(b) Force may not be used for purposes of aggression, and any use of force is subject to principles of necessity and proportionality. Accordingly, force may be used only—

(1) if every effort has been made to achieve the objective set forth in subsection (a)(a)–(6) by means other than the use of force;

(2) with levels of force, in a manner, and for a duration essential to and directly connected with the achievement of such objective; or

(3) if negative diplomatic, military, economic, or humanitarian consequences are not likely to be inordinate in relation to the benefits of such objective.

CONSULTATION

SEC. 5. (a) Except in the event of an extreme national emergency, the President shall seek the advice and counsel of the Congress prior to the use of force.

(b)(1) To facilitate consultation between Congress and the President on foreign and national security policy, when Congress is in session—

(A) the Secretary of State shall meet monthly with the Committee on Foreign Relations of the Senate and the Committee on Foreign Affairs of the House of Representatives;

(B) the Secretary of Defense shall meet monthly with the Committee on Armed Services of the Senate and the Committee on Armed Services of the House of Representatives;

(C) the Director of Central Intelligence shall meet monthly with the Select Committee on Intelligence of the Senate and the Permanent Select Committee on Intelligence of the House of Representatives;

(D) the President's National Security Adviser shall meet monthly with the Speaker of the House of Representatives, the House Majority Leader the House Minority Leader, the President pro tempore of the Senate, the Senate Majority Leader, and the Senate Minority Leader; and

(E) the President shall meet at least once every three months with a Congressional Leadership Group, on which the Speaker of the House of Representatives shall serve as chairman and which shall comprise the Members referred to in paragraph (D) and the chairman and ranking minority members of the committees named in paragraphs (A), (B), and (C).

(2) Such consultation shall be carried out with the purpose of—

(A) identifying potential situations in which the use of force might be appropriate and discussing thoroughly the wisdom and lawfulness of such use; and

(B) discussing the items set forth in section 6(a) in those instances where use of force has already been undertaken.

(3) In addition, in order to facilitate consultation under unusual circumstances, the President shall meet promptly with the Congressional Leadership Group upon receipt of a special request of its chairman, who shall issue such special request pursuant to a request from a majority of the members of the Group.

(c) To ensure the integrity of the consultative process, it is the intent of each House of Congress, acting under Article I, section 5, clause 2 of the Constitution, to expel any Member who discloses significant classified information transmitted in connection with such consultation, unless one of the committees specified in this section agrees, by a vote of two-thirds of its full membership, to disclose such information.

REPORTING

SEC. 6. (a) The President shall, within forty-eight hours of commencing a use of force, submit to the Speaker of the House of Representatives and to the President pro tempore of the Senate a report in writing stating—

(1) the specific objective of such use of force and the specific clause of section 4(a) authorizing such use of force; and

(2) how such use of force complies and will comply with the provisions of section 4(b).

(b) Any written communication from the President that might reasonably be construed as constituting a report under subsection (a) of this section shall be deemed to be such a report.

(c) In any circumstances in which a report under subsection (a) of this section is not required, the President shall report promptly, fully, and regularly to Congress concerning any instance in which United States Armed Forces abroad sustain casualties, or in which such casualties are reasonably foreseeable.

CONGRESSIONAL ACTION

SEC. 7. (a) Each report transmitted under section 6(a) shall be immediately referred to the Committee on Foreign Relations of the Senate and the Committee on Foreign Affairs of the House of Representatives. If, when the report is transmitted, the Congress has adjourned sine die or has adjourned for any period in excess of three calendar days, the Speaker of the House of Representatives and the President pro tempore of the Senate, if they deem it advisable (or if petitioned by at least 30 per centum of the membership of their respective Houses) shall jointly request the President to convene Congress in order that it may consider the report and take appropriate action pursuant to this section.

(b) Within one hundred and twenty calendar days after a report is required to be submitted pursuant to section 6(a), the President shall terminate any use of force with respect to which such report was required to be submitted, unless the Congress has declared war, extended such period by specific statutory authorization, or is physically unable to meet as a result of an armed attack upon the United States.

(c) Any joint resolution shall be subject to the expedited procedures set forth in section 13 if such resolution has been introduced with the cosponsorship of 30 per centum of the membership of the House of Congress in which it is introduced, and—

(1) provides specific authorization for a use of force and states that it is intended to constitute specific statutory authorization within the meaning of this Act; or

(2) requires the President to terminate, limit, or refrain from a use of force; or

(3) finds that a use of force commenced on a specific date or that a report under section 6(a) was required.

FUNDING LIMITATIONS

SEC. 8. (a) No funds appropriated or otherwise made available under any law may be obligated or expended for any use of force inconsistent with the provisions of this Act.

(b)(1) Where the Congress, by concurrent resolution, finds that any use of force is being conducted in a manner inconsistent with the provisions of this Act, it shall thereafter not be in order in either House of Congress to consider any bill or joint resolution or any amendment thereto, or any report of a committee of conference, which authorizes or provides budget authority to carry out such use of force.

(2) Any such concurrent resolution shall be subject to the expedited procedure set forth in section 13 if such resolution has been introduced with the cosponsorship of 30 per centum of the membership of the House of Congress in which it is introduced.

(3) Any committee of either House of the Congress that reports any bill or joint resolution, and any committee of conference which submits any conference report to either such House, authorizing or providing budget authority to carry out any such use of force, shall indicate in the committee report or joint statement filed therewith, as the case may be, that such budget authority is authorized or provided in such bill, resolution, or conference report.

INTERPRETATION

SEC. 9. (a) Nothing in this Act may be construed as requiring any use of force.

(b) No authority exists for a use of force inconsistent with the provisions of this Act.

(c) Authority to use force may not be inferred—

(1) from any provision of law (whether or not in effect before the date of enactment of this Act), unless such provisions specifically authorizes use of force and states that it is intended to constitute specific statutory authorization within the meaning of this Act; or

(2) from any treaty heretofore or hereafter ratified unless such treaty is implemented by legislation specifically authorizing the use of force and stating that it is intended to constitute specific statutory authorization within the meaning of this Act.

(d) The rejection by Congress of, or the failure of Congress to enact, a measure—

(1) terminating, limiting, or prohibiting a use of force; or

(2) providing that a report was required to be submitted under section 6(a) of this Act; or

(3) otherwise indicating a belief that the President has failed to comply with this Act;

may not be construed as indicating congressional authorization or approval of, or acquiescence in, a use of force, or as a congressional finding that a use of force is being conducted in a manner consistent with this Act.

JUDICIAL REVIEW

SEC. 10. (a) Any Member of Congress may bring an action in the United States District Court for the District of Columbia for declaratory judgment and injunctive relief on the grounds that the provisions of this Act have been violated.

(b)(1) In any action in a court of the United States seeking compliance with the provisions of this Act, the court shall not decline to make a determination on the merits based upon the doctrine of political question, remedial discretion, equitable discretion, or any other finding of non-justiciability, unless such declination is required by Article III of the Constitution.

(2) Notwithstanding the number, position, or party affiliation of any plaintiffs in an action described in subsection (a) of this section, it is the intent of Congress that the courts infer congressional disapproval of any use of force inconsistent with the provisions of this Act and find that an impasse exists between Congress and the Executive which requires judicial resolution.

(c) Any court in which such an action is heard shall accord such action the highest priority and announce its judgment as speedily as the requirements of Article III of the Constitution permit.

(d) If a court finds that a report was required to be submitted under section 6(a), it shall—

(1) direct the President to submit such a report; or

(2) declare that the time period set forth in section 7(b) has commenced on the date of the court's judgment or on a previous date determined by the court with due regard to unavoidable military necessity respecting the safety of United States Armed Forces.

(e) A judgment described in subsection (c) of this section, either finding or failing to find that a report was required to be submitted, shall be directly appealable to the United States Supreme Court.

SEPARABILITY

SEC. 11. (a) If section 4(a), 5, 9 or 10 of this Act or the application thereof to any person or circumstance is held invalid, the remainder of the

Act and the application thereof to any person or circumstance shall not be affected thereby.

(b) If section 4(b), 6, 7, or 8 of this Act or the application thereof to any person or circumstance is held invalid, section 4(a) of this Act shall be deemed invalid and the application thereof to any other person or circumstance shall be null and void.

REPEALERS

SEC. 12. (a) The War Powers Resolution (50 U.S.C. 154(c); Public Law 93-148), relating to the exercise of war powers by the President under the Constitution, is repealed.

(b) Section 1013 of the Department of State Authorization Act, fiscal years 1984 and 1985 (50 U.S.C. 1546a), relating to expedited procedures for certain joint resolutions and bills, is repealed.

CONGRESSIONAL PRIORITY PROCEDURES

SEC. 13. [This section sets forth expedited procedures for resolutions introduced under section 7(c) or 8(b).]

Committee Print Number 1
September 16, 1988

GENERAL INDEX

INDEX OF CASES